WOOD PELLET SMOKER AND GRILL COOKBOOK

Over 400 Flavorful, Easy-to-Cook, and Time-Saving Recipes For Your Perfect BBQ. Smoke, Grill, Roast, and Bake Every Meal You Desire.

TABLE OF CONTENTS

INTRODUCTION 19

WHAT IS WOOD PELLET SMOKERS GRILL? 21

BENEFITS OF THE WOOD PELLET SMOKER-GRILL 23

DIFFERENCES BETWEEN SMOKING, GRILLING, AND BBQING 25

BASIC COMPONENTS OF A WOOD PELLET SMOKERS 27

USEFUL TIPS FOR GRILL WOOD PELLET SMOKER AND GRILL USERS SELECTING A SMOKER . 29

CHOOSE THE RIGHT PREFERRED WOOD PELLET 30

DIFFERENT TYPE OF WOOD PELLET SMOKER AND GRILL 32

WHICH WOOD PELLETS ARE BEST FOR SMOKING AND GRILLING? 32

FOOD-GRADE WOOD PELLETS FOR SMOKING AND GRILLING 32

NON-FOOD GRADE WOOD PELLETS FOR HEATING ONLY, NOT COOKING 35

WOOD PELLETS AND THE ENVIRONMENT 36

BEST PRACTICE TO USE IT (TIPS AND TRICKS) 37

HOW TO PICK THE BEST WOOD PELLETS 37

QUALITIES OF A GOOD BRAND OF WOOD PELLETS 38

COOKING TEMPERATURES, TIMES, AND DONENESS 39

PORK RECIPES (BREAKFAST) 40

PORK COLLAR WITH ROSEMARY MARINADE 40

SIMPLE PORK TENDERLOIN 40

SMOKED HONEY - GARLIC PORK CHOPS 41

PORK COLLAR AND ROSEMARY MARINADE 41

ROASTED HAM 42

PINEAPPLE PORK BBQ 42

BBQ SPARERIBS WITH MANDARIN GLAZE 43

SMOKED PORK SAUSAGES 44

BRAISED PORK CHILE VERDE 45

BQ PULLED PORK SANDWICHES 46

BOURBON HONEY GLAZED SMOKED PORK RIBS 46

LIME BARBECUE SMOKED PORK SHOULDER CHILI 47

CHILI SWEET SMOKED PORK TENDERLOIN 49

DELICIOUS PARMESAN ROAST PORK 49

Bacon-Wrapped Pork Tenderloin 50

Typical Nachos 51

PORK (LUNCH) 52

BBQ Breakfast Grist 52

Pig Pops (Sweet-hot Bacon on Stick) 52

Party Pulled Pork Shoulder 53

Pineapple-Pepper Pork Kebabs 54

Smoked Bacon 55

Braised Pork Carnitas 56

Pork Belly Tacos 56

Teriyaki Pork Tenderloin 57

Pork Belly Burnt Ends 57

Cajun Doubled-Smoked Ham 58

Rub-Injected Pork Shoulder 58

Smoked Spare Ribs 59

Slow Smoked Pork Belly Sliders 60

Chinese BBQ Pork 61

Bacon Grilled Cheese Sandwich 62

Apple Cider Braised Smoked BBQ Pulled Pork 63

Pigs in a Blanket 64

Smoked, Candied, and Spicy Bacon 65

Stuffed Pork Crown Roast 65

St. Louis BBQ Ribs 66

Lemon Pepper Pork Tenderloin 67

Porchetta 68

Pork Jerky 69

Grilled Carnitas 70

Stuffed Tenderloin 71

Maplewood Bourbon BBQ Ham 72

Pork Steak 73

Carolina Smoked Ribs 73

Hearty Pig Candies 74

Sauced Up Pork Spares 75

Porky Onion Soup 76

Lovely Pork Butt 76

Strawberry and Jalapeno Smoked Ribs 77

Plum Flavored Glazed Pork Belly Kebabs 79

SIMPLE WOOD PELLET SMOKED PORK RIBS 79

ROASTED PORK WITH BALSAMIC STRAWBERRY SAUCE 80

WOOD PELLET GRILL PORK CROWN ROAST 80

WET-RUBBED ST. LOUIS RIBS 81

COCOA CRUSTED PORK TENDERLOIN 81

WOOD PELLET GRILLED BACON 82

WOOD PELLET GRILLED PORK CHOPS 82

WOOD PELLET BLACKENED PORK CHOPS 83

TERIYAKI PINEAPPLE PORK TENDERLOIN SLIDERS 83

WOOD PELLET GRILLED TENDERLOIN WITH FRESH HERB SAUCE 84

WOOD PELLET GRILLED SHREDDED PORK TACOS 84

WOOD PELLET TOGARASHI PORK TENDERLOIN 85

WOOD PELLET PULLED PORK 85

LOVABLE PORK BELLY 85

COUNTY RIBS 86

WOW-PORK TENDERLOIN 87

AWESOME PORK SHOULDER 87

HERBED PRIME RIB 88

PREMIUM SAUSAGE HASH 88

EXPLOSIVE SMOKY BACON 89

BEEF RECIPES (BREAKFAST) 91

PELLET GRILL MEATLOAF 91

BBQ BRISKET 92

TRI-TIP ROAST 92

BABY BACK RIB 93

DELICIOUS SOY MARINATED STEAK 94

GRILLED STEAK AND VEGETABLE KEBABS 95

GARLIC BUTTER GRILLED STEAK 96

GRILLED COFFEE RUB BRISKET 97

GRILLED HERB STEAK 97

COCOA RUB STEAK 98

GRILLED STEAK WITH MUSHROOM CREAM SAUCE 99

BEEF TENDERLOIN 100

MUSTARD BEEF SHORT RIBS 100

MESMERIZING BEEF JERKY 101

ORIGINAL BEEF MEATBALLS 102

SMOKED UP BULGOGI 103

CREATIVE OSSO BUCO 104

AUTHENTIC INDIAN T-BONE KEBAB 105

GOURMET BEEF JERKY 106

BEEF (LUNCH) 107

THE SOUTH BARBACOA 107

SMOKED PRIME RIB 107

KOREAN BEEF RIB EYE 108

REVERSE SEARED FLANK STEAK 109

CORNED BEEF WITH CABBAGE 109

BEER BEEF 110

ITALIAN BEEF SANDWICH 111

GRILLED STEAK WITH CREAMY GREENS 111

GARLIC FILLET MIGNON 112

ROASTED PRIME RIB WITH HERBS GARLIC 112

ROSEMARY ROAST BEEF 113

PEPPERCORN STEAK WITH MUSHROOM SAUCE 114

BARBECUE STEAKS 115

BEEF CHILI 115

PAPRIKA STEAK 116

SMOKED MUSTARD BEEF RIBS 116

BRAISED BEEF SHORT RIBS 117

SMOKED PASTRAMI 117

SWEET & SPICY BEEF BRISKET 118

BRANDY BEEF TENDERLOIN 118

BEEF RUMP ROAST 119

HERBED PRIME RIB ROAST 120

SPICY CHUCK ROAST 120

BBQ SPICED FLANK STEAK 121

BEEF STUFFED BELL PEPPERS 121

BBQ MEATLOAF 122

SMOKED BEEF BRISKET IN SWEET AND SPICY RUB 123

SIMPLE SMOKED BEEF BRISKET WITH MOCHA SAUCE 124

LEMON GINGER SMOKED BEEF RIBS 125

CHOCOLATE SMOKED BEEF RIBS 125

SMOKED AND PULLED BEEF 126

SMOKED MIDNIGHT BRISKET 127

GRILLED BUTTER BASTED PORTERHOUSE STEAK 127

Cocoa Crusted Grilled Flank Steak 128

Wood Pellet Grill Prime Rib Roast 128

Smoked Longhorn Cowboy Tri-Tip 129

Wood Pellet Grill Teriyaki Beef Jerky 129

Grilled Butter Basted Rib-Eye 130

BEEF (DINNER) **131**

Smoked Beef with Smoked Garlic Mayo Dip 131

Simple Smoked Pulled Beef 131

Smoked Beef Churl Barbecue 132

Honey Glazed Smoked Beef 133

Spiced Smoked Beef with Oregano 133

BBQ Sweet Pepper Meatloaf 134

Blackened Steak 134

Prime Rib Roast 135

Thai Beef Skewers 135

Cowboy Cut Steak 136

Grilled Butter Basted Steak 137

Chili Rib Eye Steaks 137

BBQ Beef Short Ribs 138

Thai Beef Salad 138

Grilled Almond-Crusted Beef Fillet 139

Grilled Beef Eye Fillet with Herb Rubs 139

Grilled Beef Steak with Molasses and Balsamic Vinegar 140

Grilled Beef Steak with Peanut Oil and Herbs 141

Grilled Beef Steaks with Beer-Honey Sauce 141

Grilled La Rochelle Beef Steak with Curried Pineapple 142

Grilled Veal Shoulder Roast with Fennel and Thyme Rub 142

Grilled Veal with Mustard Lemony Crust 143

VEGETABLES RECIPES (BREAKFAST) **144**

Smoked Cauliflower 144

Grilled Asparagus 144

Grill Eggplants 145

Green Beans with Bacon 145

Roasted Fall Vegetables 146

Cinnamon Almonds 147

Roasted Pumpkin Seeds 147

CRISPY GARLIC POTATOES 148

STUFFED AVOCADOS 148

BACON-WRAPPED ASPARAGUS 149

BRISKET BAKED BEANS 149

GARLIC PARMESAN WEDGES 150

TWICE-BAKED SPAGHETTI SQUASH 151

SMOKED TOMATOES 152

SMOKED OLIVES 152

SPAGHETTI SQUASH WITH BROWN BUTTER AND PARMESAN 153

SMOKED JALAPENO POPPERS 154

VEGETABLES (LUNCH) **155**

BAKED HEIRLOOM TOMATO TART 155

SMOKED PICKLED GREEN BEANS 155

BAKED ASPARAGUS PANCETTA CHEESE TART 156

GEORGIA SWEET ONION BAKE 157

ROASTED OKRA 157

SWEET POTATO CHIPS 158

SOUTHERN SLAW 159

WOOD PELLET SMOKED MUSHROOMS 159

WOOD PELLET GRILLED ZUCCHINI SQUASH SPEARS 159

WHOLE ROASTED CAULIFLOWER WITH GARLIC PARMESAN BUTTER 160

WOOD PELLET COLD SMOKED CHEESE 160

WOOD PELLET GRILLED ASPARAGUS AND HONEY GLAZED CARROTS 161

WOOD PELLET GRILLED VEGETABLES 161

WOOD PELLET SMOKED ASPARAGUS 162

WOOD PELLET SMOKED ACORN SQUASH 162

VEGAN SMOKED CARROT DOGS 163

WOOD PELLET SMOKED VEGETABLES 163

WOOD PELLET GRILL SPICY SWEET POTATOES 164

VEGETABLE (DINNER) **165**

WOOD PELLET GRILLED MEXICAN STREET CORN 165

SMOKED BROCCOLI 165

SMOKED MUSHROOMS 2 165

SMOKED POTATOES 166

SMOKED BUTTERNUT SQUASH 167

SMOKE-GRILLED EGGPLANT 167

SMOKED CHERRY TOMATOES 168

SMOKED ACORN SQUASH 168

SMOKED VEGETABLES 169

SMOKED CABBAGE 169

SMOKED VEGETABLES WITH VINAIGRETTE 170

POULTRY (BREAKFAST) 171

TANDOORI CHICKEN WINGS 171

ASIAN BBQ CHICKEN 171

HOMEMADE TURKEY GRAVY 172

BACON WRAPPED TURKEY LEGS 173

SMOKE ROASTED CHICKEN 173

GRILLED ASIAN CHICKEN BURGERS 174

GRILLED SWEET CAJUN WINGS 175

THE GRILLED CHICKEN CHALLENGE 176

CHICKEN BREAST WITH LEMON 176

PELLET SMOKED CHICKEN BURGERS 177

PERFECT SMOKED CHICKEN PATTIES 177

SMOKED CHICKEN BREASTS WITH DRIED HERBS 178

GRILLED CHICKEN WITH PINEAPPLE 178

LEMON CHICKEN BREAST 179

WHOLE ORANGE CHICKEN 179

SMOKED TURKEY 180

SMOKED TURKEY PATTIES 181

APPLE SMOKED TURKEY 181

SPECIAL OCCASION'S DINNER CORNISH HEN 182

POULTRY (LUNCH) 184

CRISPY & JUICY CHICKEN 184

ULTIMATE TASTY CHICKEN 184

SOUTH-EAST-ASIAN CHICKEN DRUMSTICKS 185

GAME DAY CHICKEN DRUMSTICKS 185

GLAZED CHICKEN THIGHS 186

CAJUN CHICKEN BREASTS 187

BBQ SAUCE SMOTHERED CHICKEN BREASTS 187

BUDGET FRIENDLY CHICKEN LEGS 188

THANKSGIVING DINNER TURKEY 188

HERB ROASTED TURKEY 189

TURKEY LEGS 190

Turkey Breast 190

Apple wood-Smoked Whole Turkey 191

Savory-Sweet Turkey Legs 192

Marinated Smoked Turkey Breast 193

Maple Bourbon Turkey 193

Thanksgiving Turkey 194

Spatchcock Smoked Turkey 195

Hoisin Turkey Wings 196

Turkey Jerky 196

Smoked Whole Turkey 197

Smoked Turkey Breast 198

Whole Turkey 199

TURKEY RECIPES **201**

Herbed Turkey Breast 201

Jalapeno Injection Turkey 202

Smoked Turkey Mayo with Green Apple 203

Buttery Smoked Turkey Beer 203

Barbecue Chili Smoked Turkey Breast 204

Hot Sauce Smoked Turkey Tabasco 205

Cured Turkey Drumstick 206

Tailgate Smoked Young Turkey 207

Roast Turkey Orange 207

Smoked Chicken in Maple Flavor 208

Hot and Spicy Smoked Chicken Wings 209

Sweet Smoked Chicken in Black Tea Aroma 210

Sweet Smoked Gingery Lemon Chicken 211

POULTRY (DINNER) **212**

Hellfire Chicken Wings 212

Buffalo Chicken Thighs 212

Sweet and Sour Chicken Drumsticks 213

Smoked Whole Chicken with Honey Glaze 214

Beer-Braised Chicken Tacos with Jalapenos Relish 214

Smoked Teriyaki Chicken Wings with Sesame Dressing 216

Smoked Turkey Legs 217

Spiced Lemon Chicken 218

Slow Roasted Shawarma 218

Duck Poppers 219

BBQ Pulled Turkey Sandwiches 219

Smoked Deviled Eggs 220

Baked Garlic Parmesan Wings 221

Grilled Chicken in Wood Pellets 222

Smoked Chicken Leg Quarter in a Pellet Grill 222

Grilled Chicken Kebabs 223

Chicken Fajitas on a Wood Pellet Grill 223

Chicken Wings in Wood Pellets 224

Smoked Cornish Chicken in Wood Pellets 224

Wild Turkey Egg Rolls 225

Grilled Filet Mignon 225

FISH AND SEAFOOD RECIPES (BREAKFAST) 227

Fish Stew 227

Grilled Tilapia "Ceviche" 227

Sweet Honey Soy Smoked Salmon 228

Cranberry Lemon Smoked Mackerel 229

Citrusy Smoked Tuna Belly with Sesame Aroma 230

Savory Smoked Trout with Fennel and Black Pepper Rub 231

Garlic Salmon 232

Seared Tuna Steaks 232

Classic Smoked Trout 232

Blackened Mahi-Mahi Tacos 233

Salmon Cakes 234

Grilled Red Snapper 235

Sugar Cured Salmon 235

Cured Cold-Smoked Lox 236

FISH AND SEAFOOD (LUNCH) 238

Grilled Salmon 238

Pacific Northwest Salmon 238

Hot-Smoked Salmon 239

Cajun Catfish 239

Rogue Salmon Sandwich 240

Spring Lining Cod 240

Baja-Style Fish Tacos 241

Grilled Penang Curry Salmon 242

Lemon Garlic Smoked Salmon 243

Smoked Tilapia 243

Maple Glazed Salmon 243

Charcoal-Grilled Striped Bass 244

Greek-Style Fish with Marinated Tomatoes 245

Grilled Fish with Aromatics 246

Baked Fresh Wild Sockeye Salmon 247

Creole Wild Pacific Rockfish 248

Wood-Smoked Boned Trout 248

Spiced Salmon Kebabs 249

Grilled Onion Butter Cod 250

Grilled Cuttlefish with Spinach and Pine Nuts Salad 250

Grilled Trout in White Wine and Parsley Marinade 251

Grilled Salmon Steaks with Cilantro Yogurt Sauce 252

Southwestern Whitefish 252

Full-On Trout 253

Lemon Pepper Tuna 254

FISH AND SEAFOOD (DINNER) 255

Pineapple Maple Glaze Fish 255

Smoked Catfish Recipe 255

Cajun Smoked Shrimp 256

Candied Smoked Salmon with Orange Ginger Rub 256

Juicy Lime Smoked Tuna Belly 257

Lemon Butter Smoked Mackerel with Juniper Berries Brine 258

Smoked Crab Paprika Garlic with Lemon Butter Flavor 258

Cayenne Garlic Smoked Shrimp 259

Cinnamon Ginger Juicy Smoked Crab 260

Pellet Grilled Salmon Fillet 260

Roasted Cod with Lemon Herb Butter 261

Smoked Trout 262

Finnan Had die Recipe 262

Home Grilled Salmon 262

Smoked Fish Pie 263

Grilled Lobster Tail 264

Halibut 265

BBQ Shrimp.. 265

Oyster in Shell 266

GRILLED KING CRAB LEGS 267

CAJUN SMOKED CATFISH 268

LAMB (BREAKFAST) 269

ROSEMARY-SMOKED LAMB CHOPS 269

GREEK-STYLE ROAST LEG OF LAMB 269

LAMB CHOPS 270

CLASSIC LAMB CHOPS 271

SEARED LAMB CHOPS 271

ROASTED LEG OF LAMB 272

LAMB (LUNCH) 273

HICKORY-SMOKED LEG OF LAMB 273

SMOKED RACK OF LAMB 273

SMOKED LAMB SAUSAGE 273

PISTACHIO ROASTED LAMB 274

LAMB WRAPS 275

MOROCCAN KEBABS 276

BRAISED LAMB SHANK 276

LAMB (DINNER) 277

BRAISED LAMB TACOS 277

SMOKED RACK OF LAMB 277

ROSEMARY LAMB 278

LAMB CHOPS WITH ROSEMARY AND OLIVE OIL 279

BONELESS LEG OF LAMB 279

SMOKED LAMB SHOULDER 280

HERBY LAMB CHOPS 281

GARLIC RACK OF LAMB 282

TRADITIONAL RECIPES 283

SWEET & SPICY CHICKEN THIGHS 283

BACON WRAPPED CHICKEN BREASTS 283

GLAZED CHICKEN WINGS 284

CHICKEN CASSEROLE 285

BUTTERED TURKEY 285

GLAZED TURKEY BREAST 286

CRISPY DUCK 287

JERKED UP TILAPIA 287

Premium Salmon Nuggets 288

Creative Sablefish 289

Halibut Delight 289

Roast Rack of Lamb 290

Ultimate Lamb Burgers 290

Citrus- Smoked Trout 291

Sunday Supper Salmon with Olive Tapenade 292

Grilled Tuna 293

Grilled Swordfish 293

Lamb Kebabs 294

APPETIZERS AND SIDES 295

Grilled Carrots 295

Grilled Brussels Sprouts 295

Wood Pellet Spicy Brisket 296

Pellet Grill Funeral Potatoes 296

Smoky Caramelized Onions on the Pellet Grill 297

Hickory Smoked Green Beans 297

Smoked Corn on the Cob 298

Easy Grilled Corn 298

Seasoned Potatoes on Smoker 299

Atomic Buffalo Turds 299

Smashed Potato Casserole 300

Mushrooms Stuffed with Crab Meat 301

Bacon Wrapped with Asparagus 302

Bacon Cheddar Slider 302

Garlic Parmesan Wedge 303

Grilled Mushroom Skewers 304

Caprese Tomato Salad 305

Watermelon-Cucumber Salad 305

Fresh Creamed Corn 306

APPETIZERS AND SNACKS 307

Spinach Salad with Avocado and Orange 307

Raspberry and Blue Cheese Salad 307

Crunchy Zucchini Chips 307

Grilled Green Onions and Orzo and Sweet Peas 308

Tequila Slaw with Lime and Cilantro 308

CRANBERRY-ALMOND BROCCOLI SALAD...309

GRILLED FRENCH DIP...309

ROASTED CASHEWS...310

SMOKED JERKY..310

BACON BBQ BITES...310

SMOKED GUACAMOLE..311

JALAPENO POPPERS..311

SHRIMP COCKTAIL..312

DEVILED EGGS..312

SMOKED SUMMER SAUSAGE...313

ROASTED TOMATOES...313

ONION BACON RING..314

GRILLED WATERMELON 314

SMOKED POPCORN WITH PARMESAN HERB 314

CONCLUSION **316**

INTRODUCTION

Wood pellets are essentially the same as what you find in a log cabin. The same wood is milled into small bits to a specific size under very tight tolerances and very low dust levels, inside the bed of the grill, are a series of racks where the pellets are stored. In the top lid of a wood pellet grill is a tray of lit green lights that indicate the desired "load." That's one of the ways you control the heat and temperature of the wood pellets. Without the automatic technology that maintains pellet-firing temperature at 225 to 240 degrees, wood pellets can cook at dangerous peaks and valleys. But modern pellet grills have many safeguards against accidental overexposure. If a pellet fire started in the absence of the auto-igniter, you might damage the grease tray keeping the pellets moist and operate the pellet grill without heating the fuel.

Once you have the wood pellets loaded into the drip tray, a green light on the lid will illuminate and it's nice to see a couple of lights pointing down at the temperature. Next, flip the top half of the grill to open up the air holes into the heat chamber and you can start to care for the food. You will want to cover your food with foil. Don't ask how many bits/inches of foil to use because the manufacturer does not tell you. (We presume it is none). Just remember to keep the foil on your food as you rotate it so that you can manage the heat.

The wood pellet grills that are on the market have made wood pellet grilling more convenient. But we feel that there are enough automated controls and variable options, but we recommend using the multi-position Wood Pellet Grill. It has a larger cooking area and an adjustable temperature handle that is easy to find, even in dim light when using your smartphone. I do not assume that you can get as much heat from a portable grill as you can in a conventional gas grill or a charcoal grill. Is this because the grill is half open and without a lid? Or is this a superior heating system?

You have a pressure regulator gauge with a screwdriver in an alcove inside the grill body. Maintain pressure between 8 and 11 psi. If you have side baste trays, a crank. If not, buy some. You will love them. Use them to keep warm sides that are not in the center of the grilling surface. You will also need to readjust the pressure. More on that later. Adjust the airflow by turning the screws that fill the removable hoods.

Remember, you are not looking to uniformly sear the food. You can control the temperature of the grill, but you don't need to consistently hold the exact same temperature. Also, too hot will result in uneven cooking, not to mention you can burn the food. Therefore, you don't want to be too hot and don't try to over engage the cooking surface.

You don't need really dry wood pellets. But you should always be keeping the pellets dry. Never burn wood pellets in an enclosed space, or you can get smoke. Normally, a grill needs to be opened to burn air to cook. This air can be collected with either of the two hoods. You have the option of a "vented hood" or "vented hood/filter-wand". The "vented hood/filter-wand" takes smoke out of a small amount of the hood and filters it through a filter that you can turn on and off by a turn handle outside the hood.

You want to make sure the air goes through the hoods when you close the grill. Don't set the bar so low that the grill conditions qualify as potential smoke damage. If you have the grill on fire, there is no problem with the smoke. Usually, the temperature knob is on the "automatic" setting, and that's fine. But if you have it on the "off" or "manual" setting, make sure the knob is set to "kill" before you go to bed or otherwise leave the house. Everything should be dismissed.

Wood pellets are a special kind of fuel that can be made from all kinds of scrap wood. When you buy a bag of wood pellets, you will get more consistency than when you use lighter versus heavier wood pellets. The heavier pellets will burn hotter, and the lighter pellets will burn cooler.

WHAT IS WOOD PELLET SMOKERS GRILL?

A pellet grill is essentially a multi-functional grill which has been so designed that the compressed wood pellets end up being the real source of fuel. They are outdoor cookers and tend to combine the different striking elements of smokers, gas grills, ovens, and even charcoal. The very reason which has cemented their popularity since ages have to be the kind of quality and flavor that they tend to infuse in the food you make on them.

Not only this, by varying the kind of wood pellet you are using, but you can also bring in the variation in the actual flavor of the food as well. Often, the best chefs use a mix and match technique of wood pellets to infuse the food with their signature flavor that have people hooked to their cooking in no time.

The clinical definition of a wood pellet smoker grill is smoking, grilling, roasting, and baking barbecue using compressed hardwood sawdust such as apple, cherry, hickory, maple, mesquite, oak, and other wood pellets. It is a pit. Wood pellet smoker grills provide the flavor profile and moisture that only hardwood dishes can achieve. Depending on the manufacturer and model, the grill temperature on many models can be well over 150 ° F to 600 ° F. Gone are the days when people say they cannot bake on wood pellet smoking grills!

Wood pellet smoker grills offer the succulence, convenience, and safety not found in charcoal or gas grills. The smoke here is not as thick as other smokers common to you. Its design provides the versatility and benefits of a convection oven. A wood pellet smoker grill is safe and easy to operate.

How do they work?

The grill would run on electricity and therefore it needs to be plugged in for the sake of deriving power. The design is such that pellets have to be added to the hopper that in turn will funnel down owing to the presence of a rotating auger and a motor.

The auger aims to make sure that the pellets get pushed down to the fire pot at the pre-configured speed which is determined by the yard control panel showing the temperature. As soon as the pellets reach the fire pot, there is an ignition rod that creates a flame that in turn causes the production of smoke.

Also, a fan is present at the bottom which helps in pushing both the generated heat and smoke upwards on the grill and thereby allows for the convection style of even cooking.

This happens to be the basic mechanism of the working of a wood pellet grill. Knowing the different parts of the wood pellet grill and also the working mechanism will prepare you in a much better way to ensure that you can use the grill in the right manner.

However, before we venture further into the recipes, we are going to shift our focus on some important points about these grills. This is because the right knowledge is crucial to ensuring that you know what you are getting into.

BENEFITS OF THE WOOD PELLET SMOKER-GRILL

There are several advantages to using a wood pellet smoker-grill. Not only does it enhance the taste of your food, but it also offers several other benefits. Here are some of the biggest benefits of a wood pellet smoker-grill!

Saves Time

It is a no-brainer that anything that saves time and effort, especially when it comes to cooking, deserves a warm welcome. One of the most significant advantages of using wood pellet grills is that they save you a lot of time. You can make your smoked dishes much faster and also with much more ease and comfort. You can pre-heat them quickly, so you'll save a lot of time.

Regulates Cooking Temperature

When you use a wood fire pellet grill, you can rest assured that the heating within its chambers is even. So, your food will be cooked evenly from all sides. It also helps you control the temperature;

Hence, you get the perfect flavor in your food. Traditional grills do not offer this advantage because of their fluctuating temperature, which can be challenging to manage. Moreover, wood pellet grills provide the advantage of a heat diffuser plate on which you can place soaked hardwood chunks and wood chips. This further enhances the smoky effect of the food.

Offers Varied Cooking Options

The best thing about wood pellet smoker-grills is that they give you several options for easy cooking. They are versatile and let you easily experiment with recipes and food. You can try various smoked recipes on the grill and enjoy healthy cooking. The versatility of pellet grills is probably one of their best qualities. This ensures that you can enjoy some lip-smacking recipes in a matter of minutes. In addition, you can use pellet grills for cooking all kinds of food, from braised short ribs to chicken wings.

Offers Variety

Another significant advantage of using a wood pellet smoker-grill is that these smokers and grills come in a plethora of sizes and shapes. These grills are built and designed, keeping customers' preferences, needs, and tastes in mind. Therefore, people who are looking for convenient cooking tools can always find something for themselves in wood pellet smokers and grills. You can also choose from a wide range of flavors, such as maple, pecan, hickory, apple, and much more.

Cold Smoking

In addition to wood pellet fire grills and smokers, you can buy cold smokers from some companies. You can cook salmon and cheese dishes in these cold smokers.

Ease of Use

It is common to see many people get intimidated by the idea of using a pellet grill. However, those fears are unfounded. While a pellet grill is quite different from your standard charcoal grills or gas grills, they are surprisingly easy to use. These grills come with controls that users can set and then simply forget about. They come with several features that make the entire process of grilling a piece of cake.

These grills usually do not require any lighter fluid, and they start with a single button. Also, irrespective of the weather or the temperature outside, these grills are capable of keeping the temperature within a 10-degree range of your set temperature. This allows you to cook with zero effort like a pro. These grills are also designed to ensure that you do not overcook or over-smoke your food. Plus, they were never flare-ups. So, there is no need for you to worry about your beautiful eyebrows.

Value

While pellet smokers are slightly more expensive than standard grills, this is for a good reason. As mentioned above, these pieces of equipment offer the perfect combination of a smoker and a grill. They come with solid construction and stainless-steel components. This is precisely why they also come with a nice four-year warranty.

This means that you will not buy these grills for summer only to dispose of them come winter. In addition, fuel efficiency is another one of their advantages. They come packed with double-wall insulation, which helps them sustain their temperatures better as well as use less fuel.

So, what are you waiting for? If you like to smoke or grill your food, it is not really possible to go wrong with a good-quality pellet grill. They provide a wide range of advantages, such as their ease of use and the incredible flavor of your favorite smoked wood. Therefore, these grills are an amazing value for the money.

Keeping this in mind, let's dive right into some amazing tried-and-tested recipes using a wood pellet smoker-grill!

DIFFERENCES BETWEEN SMOKING, GRILLING, AND BBQING

There is a difference between barbecue, baking and smoking. We'll see!

Barbecue is the same as grilling. We have the same techniques that we use. While you put the meat on the fire for a while and finally cook the food.

When smoking, you must combine the two. Grill and smoke. It will generally take much longer than traditional grills and barbecues to achieve this delicious smoky flavor and texture in your meat. It will probably take you at least 2 hours for a temperature of 100-120 degrees, depending on the food you want to cook.

Note: The time and temperature will depend on the meat you are cooking. Using a meat thermometer is recommended to make sure the meat is good. This form of barbecue is also called slow and low smoking because it has to do with time and temperature.

The different types of smokers available

Charcoal Smokers / Wood Smokers

They are amazing when it comes to injecting the best smoky flavor into your meat. However, keep in mind that these smokers are a bit difficult to master, but the result is almost worth it!

Electric smoker

Electric smokers are probably the simplest. They are easy to use and designed to be exactly "Plug and Play". All you have to do is plug in the device, set the temperature, and let it be something! The smoker himself will do the rest.

You should be aware that the final smoky flavor will not be as intense as what you can get from charcoal / wood.

Gas smokers

Finally the gas smoker arrives. These have a safe temperature control mechanism and generally run on LP gas. The downside to these smokers is that you have to keep checking your smoker from time to time to make sure the gas has not run out.

Now these are included in different smoking styles. Each of them is preferred by smokers of different experiences.

The difference between smoking cold, hot and baking

Depending on the type of smoker you use, you may have the option of smoking hot or cold. With that said, let me give you a brief overview of the different types of smoking:

• Hot smoking: In this technique, the food will use both the heat from the grill and the smoke to prepare the food. This method is more suitable for objects such as chicken, lamb, breast, etc.

• Cold Smoking: In this method, you will smoke the meat at temperatures as low as 86 degrees F, making sure it does not come into direct contact with heat. It is used as a means of preserving meat and prolonging its shelf life.

• Smoking: The third type of cigarette you should smoke is smoked tobacco. This is also known as smoke baking.

BASIC COMPONENTS OF A WOOD PELLET SMOKERS

Wood pellet grills grew out of the wood pellet home heating industry that blossomed during the 1970s oil crisis. Wood pellet home heaters became increasingly popular due to the rising price of oil.

Joe Traeger, whose family operated an Oregon heating company, took the wood pellet concept to the grill and patented the first wood pellet grill smoker in 1986. His simple original design looked like a traditional offset smoker, and the electronics and thermostat features continued to develop over the years.

Thanks to that patent, Traeger was the only manufacturer in town for 20 years. Then, when the patent expired, other companies started to produce wood pellet grills. Joe sold off Traeger after the expiration of his patent, but the company that bears his name remains the big dog in the wood pellet grill world.

By 2008, there were a handful of newcomers to the industry, and the pellet story continued to grow. By 2014, there were 27 manufacturers on record. More companies are getting in on the action every year. Some new models feature stainless-steel accents, higher-heat searing, and wireless Bluetooth controls.

The inner workings of a wood pellet grill are simple yet impressive. The fuel is 100 percent hardwood with no fillers. No petroleum products are added, just the compressed hardwood pellets that resemble rabbit chow. And before you ask, no, you don't want to try to smoke rabbit chow. You would think that a little wood pellet would burn with a soft flame like a candle. Surprisingly, just a few pellets dropped into a teacup-size firepot can create a massive jet of clean heat when stoked by a thermostat-controlled fan. The sight and sound are incredible.

To the eye, a typical wood pellet grill looks straightforward. It's a barrel-shaped grill with an electric thermostat attached to a thermometer inside the cooking chamber. Hidden beneath the grate and a large drip plate is the fire pot, where the real magic happens.

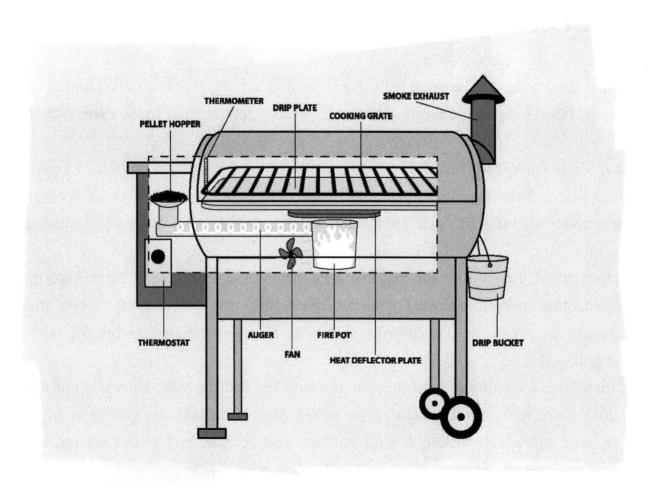

The **hopper** is a covered box that holds your pellets. Hoppers range in size to have 10 to 40 pounds of pellets and are typically positioned as a side box. Some newer models set the hopper along the entire back length of the wood pellet grill. Look for features like an easy clean-out door, a window to gauge remaining fuel, and a cover to prevent moisture. Note: Wet pellets are useless.

- The **auger** is a helical-shaped mechanism that slowly transports a small, slow, and steady flow of pellets through a tube to the firepot. The thermostat controls the flow speed.

- The **fire pot** is typically positioned in the center bottom area of the smoker. The pellets are ignited and stoked into a small but raging furnace by a small fan. Surprisingly little ash accumulates in the firepot. Ashes eventually get around the bottom of this cup, and occasional clean-out is necessary. Because the firepot takes the most abuse of the entire grill, look for ones made of durable, high-quality steel or stainless steel.

- The **heat deflector** is a heavy steel plate covering the fire pot's direct heat and dispersing the heat like a convection oven. A large drip plate, placed above the deflector plate, drains all the drippings away from any open flame, so there are no grease fires or flare-ups.

USEFUL TIPS FOR GRILL WOOD PELLET SMOKER AND GRILL USERS SELECTING A SMOKER

Electric Smokers

It requires little attention unlike other smokers like filling water bin, lighting Preferred Wood Pellet or charcoal and checking on fuel frequently. Yes, unlike traditional smoker, electric smoker just needs 2 to 4 ounce of Preferred Wood Pellet chips that turns out a delicious and flavorful smoky food. Furthermore, they maintain cooking Smoke Temperature well. On the other hand, it sleek and stylish look and small size make it appropriate if you are living in an apartment or condo. Due to their simpler functions and hassle-free cooking, the electric smoker is a good choice for beginner cooks who want to get started with smoking food.

Gas Smokers

Gas smokers or propane smoker are much like a gas grill using propane as a fuel. Therefore, Preferred Wood Pellet for cooking remains consistent and steady. Furthermore, gas smokers are as easy to use, just set the Smoke Temperature and walk away. However, frequent checks need to be done to make sure fuel does not run out. It is not a big issue, but one should keep in mind. And the best part, a gas smoker can be used when there is no electricity or when you need an oven. A gas smoker can take up to cooking Smoke Temperature to 450 degrees, making this smoker flexible to be used as an oven. Another fantastic feature of gas smoker is its portability so they can use anywhere. Just pack it and take it along with you on your camping trips or other outdoor adventures.

Charcoal Smokers

Nothing can beat the flavor charcoal gives to your food. Its best flavor just simply cannot match with any other smoker flavor. Unfortunately, setting a charcoal smoker, tuning fuel, maintaining cooking Smoke Temperature, and checking food can be a pain and you might burn the food. Not to worry, these hassles of a charcoal smoker does go away with practice and experience. Therefore, a charcoal smoker suits perfectly for serious grillers and barbecue purist who want flavors.

Pellet Smokers

Pellet smokers are making a surge due to their best feature of a pallet of maintaining a consistent Smoke Temperature. It contains an automated system to drop pallets which frees the cook to monitor fuel level. The addition of thermostat gives the user the complete control the cooking

Smoke Temperature and grilling of food under ideal condition. In addition, the smoking food uses Preferred Wood Pellet from Preferred Wood Pellet which gives food a delicious flavor. The only downside of pallet smoker is their high cost between the ranges of $100 to %600.

• <u>Choose the Right Preferred Wood Pellet</u>

Smoker Preferred Wood Pellet is an important element which you need to decide correctly to cook a delicious smoked food. The reason is that smoker chips of Preferred Wood Pellets impart different flavors on the food you are cooking in the smoker. Therefore, you should know which smoker Preferred Wood Pellet should be used to create a delicious smoked food. Here is the lowdown of smoker Preferred Wood Pellets and which food is best with them.

1- Alder: A lighter smoker Preferred Wood Pellet with natural sweetness.

Best to smoke: Any fish especially salmon, poultry, and game birds.

2- Maple: This smoker preferred Wood Pellet has a mild and sweet flavor. In addition, its sweet smoke gives the food a dark appearance. For better flavor, use it as a combination with alder, apple, or oak smoker Preferred Wood Pellets.

Best to smoke: Vegetables, cheese, and poultry.

3- Apple: A mild fruity flavor smoker Preferred Wood Pellet with natural sweetness. When mixed with oak smoker Preferred Wood Pellet, it gives a great flavor to food. Let food smoke for several hours as the smoke takes a while to permeate the food with the flavors.

Best to smoke: Poultry, beef, pork, lamb, and seafood.

4- Cherry: This smoker Preferred Wood Pellet is an all-purpose fruity flavor Preferred Wood Pellet for any type of meat. Its smoke gives the food a rich, mahogany color. Try smoking by mixing it with alder, oak, pecan, and hickory smoker Preferred Wood Pellet.

Best to smoke: Chicken, turkey, ham, pork, and beef.

5- Oak: Oak Preferred Wood Pellet gives a medium flavor to food which is stronger compared to apple Preferred Wood Pellet and cherry Preferred Wood Pellet and lighter compared to hickory. This versatile smoker Preferred Wood Pellet works well blended with hickory, apple, and cherry Preferred Wood Pellets.

Best to smoke: Sausages, brisket, and lamb.

6- Peach and Pear: Both smoker Preferred Wood Pellets are like each other. They give food a subtle light and fruity flavor with the addition of natural sweetness.

Best to smoke: Poultry, pork, and game birds.

7- Hickory: Hickory Preferred Wood Pellet infuses a strong sweet and bacon flavor into the food, especially meat cuts. Do not over smoke with this Preferred Wood Pellet as it can turn the taste of food bitter.

Best to smoke: Red meat, poultry, pork shoulder, ribs.

8- Pecan: This sweet smoker Preferred Wood Pellet lends the food a rich and nutty flavor. Use it with Mesquite Preferred Wood Pellet to balance its sweetness.

Best to smoke: Poultry, pork.

9- Walnut: This strong flavored smoker Preferred Wood Pellet is often used as a mixing Preferred Wood Pellet due to its slightly bitter flavor. Use walnut Preferred Wood Pellet with lighter smoke Preferred Wood Pellets like pecan Preferred Wood Pellet or apple Preferred Wood Pellet.

Best to smoke: Red meat and game birds.

10- Grape: Grape Preferred Wood Pellet chips give a sweet berry flavor to food. It is best to use these Preferred Wood Pellet chips with apple Preferred Wood Pellet chips.

Best to smoke: Poultry

11- Mulberry: Mulberry Preferred Wood Pellet chips is like apple Preferred Wood Pellet chips. It adds natural sweetness and gives berry finish to the food.

Best to smoke: Ham and Chicken.

12- Mesquite: Mesquite Preferred Wood Pellet chips flavor is earthy and slightly harsh and bitter. It burns fast and strongly hot. Therefore, do not use it for longer grilling.

Best to smoke: Red meat, dark meat.

DIFFERENT TYPE OF WOOD PELLET SMOKER AND GRILL

My first experience with a Pellet Smoker Grill was at my nephews' house in 2015. I saw his grill on the patio and assumed it was a gas grill. Then he showed it to me; he was pretty happy with himself for having selected a superior grill, which he used to do the outdoor cooking for his family. Pellets? What pellets? Why pellets? How does it work, and where do the pellets come from? Is it healthy? Is it safe? Is it carcinogenic? I had a lot of questions.

Now, I have all the answers, and I have joined the Pellet Smoker Grill revolution!

• **Which Wood Pellets Are Best for Smoking and Grilling?**

To comprehend things pellet, grilling entirely, then smoking, you must know what oils these inventive and ingenious barbecue machines. Manufactured wood pellets are the fuel source for pellet grills and smokers. Pellets are called "hardwood" pellets because they are created by utilizing hardwoods.

Pellet manufacturers take great care to be certain that the product is safe, reliable, and right for the intended use in all areas or research. Hardwood pellets are made from hardwoods that are ground into sawdust. Next, it is pressurized at extreme temperatures to compact and compress the pellets.

• **Food-Grade Wood Pellets for Smoking and Grilling**

During food-grade wood pellets production, hardwoods that produce only the finest flavors and aromas are carefully selected. For this reason alone, a Pellet Smoker Grill is indeed the best choice for a backyard grill.

When using your new Pellet Smoker Grill, you should know how to take care of it by always selecting the finest quality and flavor of hardwood to use to enhance the flavor of your food.

More questions may arise:

- Should you use a flavored or blended pellet?

- Which flavors go best with different types of food?

Flavored pellets, created from 100% flavored woods, contain no fillers. Here are some available varieties. The best wood pellets for smoking and grilling are:

- Mesquite

- Hickory

- Cherry

- Pecan

- Apple

As for the wood pellet types, there are three types of food-grade wood pellets for smoking and grilling:

Blended

- A blended mixture of all or a choice of the flavored pellets

- A blend of flavored and unflavored mixed together

- Example: blend hickory, maple, and cherry

Non-Flavored

- Non-flavored pellets are standard pellets and are not generally thought of as preferable due to their lack of flavor.

Flavored

- Tennessee Whisky Barrel: Sugary and misty with a fragrant tang. It is the finest blend of 199% oak, and it's flawless for all your red meats.

- Georgia Pecan: An actual slight and nutty wood that is comparable to hickory. It is a boundless versatile wood that works fine with beef, seafood, poultry, pork, vegetables, and cheese.

- Texas Mesquite: Strong aroma with a tangy and spicy flavor. It is the perfect level of bold taste to complement your Tex-Mex cuisine.

- Wisconsin Hickory: Rich with a smoky bacon-like flavor. It's highly recommended for roasts and other smoked meats.

- Pennsylvania Cherry: Somewhat sweet with an indication of the tart. It stretches your light meats, a rosy shade that is unrivaled in appearance and taste.

- New England Apple: Smoky with a mildly sweet flavor. It is highly recommended for baking and pork.

Many flavors are available in wood pellets for all types of food cooked on smoker grills. Here are some recommendations as to how to combine the flavor with your favorite meats. You may want to try to experiment, and when you find something you like, keep a small logbook and make some notes for next time.

- Beef: Georgia Pecan, Wisconsin Hickory, Texas Mesquite, Competition Blend, Tennessee Whiskey Barrel

- Poultry: Competition Blend, Pennsylvania Cherry, Texas Mesquite, Wisconsin Hickory, Georgia Pecan, New England Apple

- Pork: Texas Mesquite, New England Apple, Wisconsin Hickory, Pennsylvania Cherry, Competition Blend

- Veggies: Competition Blend, New England Apple, Wisconsin Hickory, Pennsylvania Cherry

Great quality and great flavor are things you get with today's wonderful wood pellets for the smoker grill enthusiast. You get the highest quality hardwoods, no artificial flavors or colors, no spray scents, glues, or chemicals. Only the purest ingredients are used in creating your smoker grill pellet fuels that burn hotter and are easy to use.

First, it will always be a great idea to familiarize yourself with the available manufacturers of smoker grill wood pellets and learn about each one. Check to see if they are inside or outside the USA, and if possible, look for the support or maintenance system that some manufacturers use daily. Any other considerations that may arise will probably be worth it. You will only need to do this once when you get started with your new smoker grill. Then, knowing how to order will be easy, and changing or modifying your order when you next need to supply your backyard smoker grill will be a snap.

If you have not yet purchased your new Pellet Smoker Grill, my strongest recommendation would be to go online and find the biggest and the oldest and most well-established pellet grill manufacturer and buy the grill and continue to order your high-quality pellets from them. It's a one-shop stop.

Another thing to consider when ordering and restocking your pellet stove fuel is the quality of pellets. It is important because a cheaply made pellet is just a bad idea, and here's why. Cheap pellets can ruin your food and do some serious damage to your new Pellet Smoker Grill. My best assistance on this would be to get online and find the big boys. You know what I mean. The fellas from the inception have been producing pellets the longest and know the finer points of pellet grill cuisine. They will never steer you in the wrong direction, and online ordering is easy. Most good suppliers will even help you track your usage, so you may not even have to keep placing your orders. For the things you use the most, choose automatic ordering and enjoy life.

So, don't even bother looking for sales on the pellet supply unless you find them on the high-quality brand you are already using. That would be your lucky day, and in that case, I would advise you to buy all you can afford and stock up. Once you have your pellet grill, you will not want to stop cooking on it; they are that good!

• **<u>Non-Food Grade Wood Pellets for Heating Only, Not Cooking</u>**

First-time users of Pellet Smoker Grills must be aware that there are two types of pellets available. These are "food-grade pellets" and "non-food grade pellets." Non-food grade pellets are for home heating use only and contain wood that is not meant for smoking your home-cooked meats. This type of pellet often contains pine or spruce and will ruin the taste of your food.

Food grade pellets are created purely from the carefully selected hardwood and never contain any kind of chemical binders, glue, or anything else that would be toxic or that would detract from the wonderful flavors you get when using food-grade pellets and cooking great food for your family and friends. Since food consumption is the priority, the formulation of the pellets used in your backyard smoker grill is given the same standards and practices as any other food associated product. It means that sanitation and health are always at the pinnacle of the production and packaging process for food-grade pellets.

Take great care to select only food-grade pellets when shopping for pellet replacement supply when you have exhausted your current supply or the one that came with your new stove. You must be aware that non-food grade pellets contain carcinogens, such as glues and other toxic ingredients. Shop very carefully.

It is also worth noting that heating pellets contain certain woods that are not meant for your smoker grill and may contain glues and other binder-related chemicals. These are toxic materials and must not be used to fuel a backyard smoker grill.

• **<u>Wood Pellets and the Environment</u>**

In consideration of buying your new Smoker Grill, questions might arise:

- "Is burning so much wood good for the environment?"

- "What about all the trees it would take just to cook dinner?"

- "Are wood pellets any better or more efficient than other fuel sources?"

These are all valid questions, and we have valid and sensible answers for you. Wood pellets you will use for fuel are sourced from tree farms, storm-damaged trees, or trees after their hardwood forests' lifespan transversely the country. Tree farms are consistently replacing the trees they remove to be processed as pellets. Hence, the farm is always in contained cycles of life, and every consideration is given to the environment.

- Wood pellets are pretty near to being carbon impartial. Like all the other plants on our planet, trees grip carbon dioxide after the atmosphere for the duration of their lifespan. When a hardwood tree is harvested to burn as pellets, the same amount of carbon dioxide is released into the atmosphere. As that particular tree is replaced, the cycle of life continues productively and sensitively.

- Low CO_2 production. The following is an explanation of the total cost of industrial and transport regarding the environment:

- Scorching wood pellets harvests 34g carbon dioxide per kilowatt-hour of heat formed (g/kWh)

- Compare that with 211 grams for gas and 64 grams of wood chips

• **How to Pick the Best Wood Pellets**

What makes a wood pellet smoker and grill unique is the very thing that fuels it -- wood pellets. Wood pellets are compressed sawdust, made from either pine wood, birch wood, fire wood, or crop stalks. Culinary-wise, wood pellets are used mostly as fuel for pellet smokers and grills, although they can also be used for household heating. What makes wood pellets for cooking special, though, is that they come in flavors. And speaking of flavors, here is a quick wood pellet flavor guide for you:

Apple & Cherry Pellets: These pellets possess a smoky, mild, sweet flavor. They can enhance mild meat and are usually the go-to flavor for cooking pork or poultry. Despite being able to produce great smoke, these pellets are very mild.

Alder Pellets: This type of pellet is mild and neutral, but with some sweetness in it. If you're looking for something that provides a good amount of smoke but won't overpower delicate meat like chicken and fish, this is the flavor to go to.

Hickory Pellets: Hickory pellets produce a rich, Smokey, and bacon-like flavor. These are the pellets that are widely used for barbecue. Since this type of pellet is rich and Smokey, it can tend to be overwhelming. If that is the case, consider mixing it with apple or oak pellets.

Maple Pellets: If you are looking for something that is mild and comes with a hint of sweetness, maple pellets are the best option for you. They are great to use on turkey or pork.

Mesquite Pellets: A favorite option for Texas BBQ, mesquite pellets are characterized by a strong, spicy, and tangy flavor.

Oak Pellets: Oak pellets come in between apple and hickory. They are a bit stronger than the former and a bit milder than the latter and are an excellent choice when you're cooking fish or vegetables.

Pecan Pellets: Pecan is an all-time favorite. It's very similar to Hickory, but with a touch of vanilla, nutty flavor. The perfect pellets for beef and chicken, pecan pellets are very palatable and suits all occasions.

• <u>Qualities of a Good Brand of Wood Pellets</u>

With the hundreds of different varieties and brands of wood pellets, it is often difficult to identify which brand to consider. If you are not sure what brand to opt for, it might help to try at least the top three brands you know of and compare their efficiency.

Appearance

The first factor to consider when choosing a brand of wood pellets is the appearance of the pellets. After using wood pellets for some time, you will be able to tell and judge their quality simply by how they appear. The first thing to check is the length of the pellets. Brands adhere to certain standards, so this is not a concern. Nevertheless, you need to understand that when it comes to pellet fuels, length matters, as it will affect the performance of the pellets. The dust you will find in the packaging is also another to consider. It is normal to see fines once you open the bag, but if there's an unusual number of fines, it means the pellets aren't of good quality.

Texture

The texture of the pellets is another thing. Wood pellets have a certain texture in them. If you feel that the pellets are smooth and shiny, it means they are of good quality. The same is true if the pellets do not have cracks. If the pellets are too rough with unusual racks on the surface, it means the pellets are bad. This is usually a result of incorrect pressing ratio and moisture content of the raw materials used in making the pellets.

Smell

Wood pellets are made by exposing them to high temperatures within a sealed space. During the process, the lignin contained in the biomass material is mixed with other elements, producing a smell of burnt fresh wood. If the pellets smell bad, there is a huge chance they have not been processed properly or contain impure, raw material.

Aside from the appearance, texture, and smell of the wood pellets, another way to check their quality is to see how they react with water. Place a handful of pellets in a bowl of water and allow them to settle for several minutes. If the pellets dissolve in the water and expand quickly, this means they are of good quality. On the other hand, if the pellets do not dissolve within minutes but instead expand and become hard, it means they are of bad quality.

Finally, try burning some of the pellets, as well. If the wood pellets are of excellent quality, the flame they produce will be bright and brown. If the flame they produce, on the other hand, is dark in color, it means the quality of the pellets is not good. Also, good-quality pellets produce a little ash, so if the pellets leave you with a lot of residues, it is a sign that the pellets are bad.

• <u>Cooking Temperatures, Times, and Doneness</u>

With so many recipes to try with your pellet grill, it is easy to get overwhelmed right away. One important thing to keep in mind is that lower temperatures produce smoke, while higher temperatures do not. Follow this useful guide below to know the temperature and time it requires to get the perfectly flavored meat each time.

- Beef briskets are best cooked at 250 degrees using the smoke setting for at least 4 hours by itself and covered with foil for another 4 hours.

- Pork ribs should be cooked at 275 degrees on the smoke setting for 3 hours and covered with foil for another 2-3 hours.

- Steaks require 400-450 degrees for about 10 minutes each side.

- Turkey can be cooked at 375 degrees for 20 minutes per pound of meat. For smoked turkey, the heat settings should be around 180-225 degrees for 10-12 hours or until the inside of the turkey reaches 165 degrees.

- Chicken breasts can be cooked at 400-450 degrees for 15 minutes on each side.

- A whole chicken cooks at 400-450 degrees for 1.5 hours or until the internal temperature reaches 165 degrees.

- Bacon and sausage can be cooked at 425 degrees for 5-8 minutes on each side.

- Hamburgers should be cooked at 350 degrees for at least 8 minutes for each side.

- You can smoke salmon for 1-1.5 hours and finish with a high setting for 2-3 minutes on each side.

- Shrimps cook at 400-450 degrees for 3-5 minutes on each side. If you prefer a smokier flavor, set the temperature at 225 degrees for about 30 minutes.

• Pork Collar with Rosemary Marinade

Preparation Time: 15 minutes

Cooking Time: 30 minutes

Servings: 6

Ingredients:

- 1 Pork Collar (3 - 4lb.)
- 3 tbsp. Rosemary, fresh
- 3 minced Shallots
- 2 tbsp. chopped Garlic
- ½ cup of Bourbon
- 2 tsp. Coriander, ground
- 1bottle of Apple Ale
- 1 tsp. ground Black pepper
- 2 tsp. Salt
- 3 tbsp. oil

Directions:

1. In a zip lock bag, combine the black pepper, salt, canola oil, apple ale, bourbon, coriander, garlic, shallots, and rosemary.
2. Cut the meat into slabs (2 inches) and marinate in the refrigerator overnight.
3. Preheat the grill to 450F with the lid closed. Grill the meat for 5 minutes and lower the temperature to 325F. Pour the marinade over the meat. Cook 25 minutes more.
4. Cook until the internal temperature of the meat is 160F.

5. Serve and enjoy!

Nutrition: Calories: 420 Proteins: 30g Carbohydrates: 4g Fat: 26g

• Simple Pork Tenderloin

Preparation Time: 15min

Cooking Time: 20min

Servings: 4 - 6

Ingredients:

- 2 Pork Tenderloins (12 - 15 oz. each)
- 6 tbsp. hot Sauce, Louisiana style
- 6 tbsp. melted butter
- Cajun seasoning as needed

Directions:

1. Trim the silver skin from the meat.
2. In a large bowl, combine the hot sauce and melted butter. Roll the meat in this mixture --season with Cajun seasoning.
3. Preheat the grill to 400F with the lid closed.
4. Grill the meat for 8 minutes on each side. The internal temperature should be 145F and if you want well – done, cook until 160F.

5. Let it rest for a few minutes before cutting. Serve with your favorite side dish and enjoy!

Nutrition: Calories: 150 Proteins: 20g Carbohydrates: 0 Fat: 3g

• **Smoked Honey - Garlic Pork Chops**

Preparation Time: 1 hour

Cooking Time: 1 hour and 15 minutes

Servings: 4

Ingredients:

- 1/4 cup of lemon juice freshly squeezed
- 1/4 cup honey (preferably a darker honey)
- 3 cloves garlic, minced
- 2 Tbsp. soy sauce (or tamari sauce)
- Salt and pepper to taste
- 24 ounces' center-cut pork chops boneless

Directions:

1. Combine honey, lemon juice, soy sauce, garlic, and salt and pepper in a bowl.
2. Place pork in a container and pour marinade over pork.
3. Cover and marinate in a fridge overnight.
4. Remove pork from marinade and pat dry on kitchen paper towel. (reserve marinade)

5. Start your pellet on smoke with the lid open until the fire is established (4 - 5 minutes). Increase temperature to 450°F and preheat, lid closed, for 10 - 15 minutes.
6. Arrange the pork chops on the grill racks and smoke for about one hour (depending on the thickness)
7. In the meantime, heat the remaining marinade in a small saucepan over medium heat to simmer.
8. Transfer pork chops on a serving plate, pour with the marinade and serve hot.

Nutrition: Calories: 301.5 Carbohydrates: 17g Fat: 6.5g Fiber: 0.2g Protein: 41g

• **Pork Collar and Rosemary Marinade**

Preparation Time: 15 minutes + marinate time

Cooking Time: 30 minutes

Servings: 4

Ingredients:

- 1 pork collar, 3-4 pounds
- 3 tablespoons rosemary, fresh
- 3 shallots, minced
- 2 tablespoons garlic, chopped
- ½ cup bourbon
- 2 teaspoons coriander, ground
- 1 bottle of apple ale
- 1 teaspoon ground black pepper
- 2 teaspoons salt

- 3 tablespoons oil

Directions:

1. Take a zip bag and add pepper, salt, canola oil, apple ale, bourbon, coriander, garlic, shallots, rosemary, and mix well.
2. Cut meat into slabs and add them to the marinade; let it refrigerate overnight
3. Pre-heat your smoker to 450 degrees F
4. Transfer meat to smoker and smoke for 5 minutes, lower temperature to 325 degrees F
5. Pour marinade all over and cook for 25 minutes more until the internal temperature reaches 160 degrees F
6. Serve and enjoy!

Nutrition: Calories: 420 Fats: 26g Carbohydrates: 4g Fiber: 2g

• Roasted Ham

Preparation Time: 15 minutes

Cooking Time: 2 hours 15 minutes

Servings: 4

Ingredients:

- 8-10 pounds' ham, bone-in
- 2 tablespoons mustard, Dijon
- ¼ cup horseradish
- 1 bottle BBQ Apricot Sauce

Directions:

1. Pre-heat your smoker to 325 degrees F

2. Cover a roasting pan with foil and place the ham, transfer to a smoker, and smoke for 1 hour and 30 minutes
3. Take a small pan and add sauce, mustard and horseradish, place it over medium heat and cook for a few minutes
4. Keep it on the side
5. After 1 hour 30 minutes of smoking, glaze ham and smoke for 30 minutes more until the internal temperature reaches 135 degrees F
6. Let it rest for 20 minutes, slice, and enjoy!

Nutrition: Calories: 460 Fats: 43g Carbohydrates: 10g Fiber: 1g

• Pineapple Pork BBQ

Preparation Time: 10 minutes

Cooking Time: 60 minutes

Servings: 4

Ingredients:

- 1-pound pork sirloin
- 4 cups pineapple juice
- 3 cloves garlic, minced
- 1 cup carne asada marinade
- 2 tablespoons salt
- 1 teaspoon ground black pepper

Directions:

1. Place all ingredients in a bowl and massage the pork sirloin to coat. Place inside the fridge to marinate for at least 2 hours.

2. When ready to cook, fire the Traeger Grill to 3000F. Use desired wood pellets when cooking the ribs. Close the lid and preheat for 15 minutes.

3. Place the pork sirloin on the grill grate and cook for 45 to 60 minutes. Make sure to flip the pork halfway through the cooking time.

4. At the same time, when you put the pork on the grill grate, place the marinade in a pan and place it inside the smoker. Allow the marinade to cook and reduce.

5. Baste the pork sirloin with the reduced marinade before the cooking time ends.

6. Allow resting before slicing.

Nutrition: Calories per serving: 347; Protein: 33.4 g; Carbs: 45.8 g; Fat: 4.2g Sugar: 36g

• BBQ Spareribs with Mandarin Glaze

Preparation Time: 10 minutes

Cooking Time: 60 minutes

Servings: 6

Ingredients:

- 3 large spareribs, membrane removed
- 3 tablespoons yellow mustard
- 1 tablespoon Worcestershire sauce
- 1 cup honey
- 1 ½ cup brown sugar
- 13 ounces Traeger Mandarin Glaze
- 1 teaspoon sesame oil
- 1 teaspoon soy sauce
- 1 teaspoon garlic powder

Directions:

1. Place the spareribs on a working surface and carefully remove the connective tissue membrane that covers the ribs.

2. In another bowl, mix the rest of the ingredients until well combined.

3. Massage the spice mixture onto the spareribs. Allow resting in the fridge for at least 3 hours.

4. When ready to cook, fire the Traeger Grill to 3000F.

5. Use hickory wood pellets when cooking the ribs.

6. Close the lid and preheat for 15 minutes.

7. Place the seasoned ribs on the grill grate and cover the lid.

8. Cook for 60 minutes.

9. Once cooked, allow resting before slicing.

Nutrition: Calories per serving: 1263; Protein: 36.9g; Carbs: 110.3g; Fat: 76.8g Sugar: 107g

• Smoked Pork Sausages

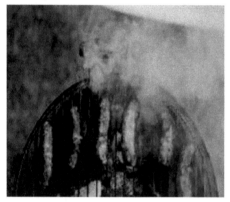

Preparation Time: 10 minutes

Cooking Time: 1 hour

Servings: 6

Ingredients:

- 3 pounds ground pork
- ½ tablespoon ground mustard
- 1 tablespoon onion powder
- 1 tablespoon garlic powder
- 1 teaspoon pink curing salt
- 1 teaspoon salt
- 1 teaspoon black pepper
- ¼ cup of ice water
- Hog casings, soaked and rinsed in cold water

Directions:

1. Mix all ingredients except for the hog casings in a bowl. Using your hands, mix until all ingredients are well-combined.

2. Using a sausage stuffer, stuff the hog casings with the pork mixture.

3. Measure 4 inches of the stuffed hog casing and twist to form into a sausage. Repeat the process until you create sausage links.

4. When ready to cook, fire the Traeger Grill to 2250F. Use apple wood pellets when cooking the ribs. Close the lid and preheat for 15 minutes.

5. Place the sausage links on the grill grate and cook for 1 hour or until the internal temperature reads at 1550F.

6. Allow resting before slicing.

Nutrition: Calories per serving: 688; Protein: 58.9g; Carbs: 2.7g; Fat: 47.3g Sugar: 0.2g

Braised Pork Chile Verde

Preparation Time: 10 minutes

Cooking Time: 40 minutes

Servings: 6

Ingredients:

- 3 pounds' pork shoulder, bone removed and cut into ½ inch cubes
- 1 tablespoon all-purpose flour
- Salt and pepper to taste
- 1-pound tomatillos, husked and washed
- 2 jalapenos, chopped
- 1 medium yellow onion, peeled and cut into chunks
- 4 cloves of garlic
- 4 tablespoons extra virgin olive oil
- 2 cup chicken stock
- 2 cans green chilies
- 1 tablespoon cumin
- 1 tablespoon oregano
- ½ lime, juiced
- ¼ cup cilantro

Directions:

1. Place the pork shoulder chunks in a bowl and toss with flour -season with salt and pepper to taste.

2. Use desired wood pellets when cooking. Place a large cast-iron skillet on the bottom rack of the grill. Close the lid and preheat for 15 minutes.

3. Place the tomatillos, jalapeno, onion, and garlic on a sheet tray lined with foil and drizzle with two tablespoons olive oil -season with salt and pepper to taste.

4. Place the remaining olive oil in the heated cast iron skillet and cook the pork shoulder. Spread the meat evenly, then close.

5. Before closing the lid, place the vegetables in the tray on the grill rack. Close the lid of the grill.

6. Cook for 20 minutes without opening the lid or stirring the pork. After 20 minutes, remove the vegetables from the grill and transfer to a blender. Pulse until smooth and pour into the pan with the pork. Stir in the chicken stock, green chilies, cumin, oregano, and lime juice -season with salt and pepper to taste. Close the grill lid and cook for another 20 minutes. Once cooked, stir in the cilantro.

Nutrition: Calories: 389; Protein: 28.5g; Carbs: 4.5g; Fat: 24.3g Sugar: 2.1g inter

• __BQ Pulled Pork Sandwiches__

Preparation Time: 10 minutes

Cooking Time: 1 hour 30 minutes

Servings: 6

Ingredients:

- 8-10lbs of bone-in pork butt roast
- 12 Kaiser Rolls
- 1 cup of yellow mustard
- Coleslaw
- 1 bottle of BBQ sauce
- 5 oz. of sugar

Directions

1. Push the temperature to 225 degrees F and set your smoker to preheat
2. Now take out the pork roast from the packaging and keep it on a cookie sheet
3. Rub it thoroughly with yellow mustard
4. Now take a bowl and mix the BBQ sauce along with sugar in it
5. Use this mix to rub the roast thoroughly and give time for the rub to seep inside and melt in the meat
6. Now place this roast in the smoker and allow it to cook for 6 hours
7. When done, remove it from the smoker and
8. then wrap it in tin foil
9. Push the temperature to 250 degrees F and cook it for a couple of hours. The internal temperature should reach 200 degrees F
10. Let the pork butt rest in the foil for an hour before pulling it out
11. Now take the Kaiser roll and cut it into half
12. Mix the pulled pork with some BBQ sauce and pile on the top of each halved roll
13. Top it with coleslaw and serve

Nutrition: Calories: 426; Protein: 65.3g; Carbs: 20.4g; Fat: 8.4g Sugar: 17.8g

• __Bourbon Honey Glazed Smoked Pork Ribs__

Preparation Time: 15 minutes

Cooking Time: 5 hours

Servings: 10

Ingredients:

- Pork Ribs (4-lbs., 1.8-kg.)
- The Marinade
- Apple juice – 1 ½ cups
- Yellow mustard – ½ cup
- The Rub
- Brown sugar – ¼ cup
- Smoked paprika – 1 tablespoon

- Onion powder – ¾ tablespoon
- Garlic powder – ¾ tablespoon
- Chili powder – 1 teaspoon
- Cayenne pepper – ¾ teaspoon
- Salt – 1 ½ teaspoon
- The Glaze
- Unsalted butter – 2 tablespoons
- Honey – ¼ cup
- Bourbon – 3 tablespoons

Directions:

1. Place apple juice and yellow mustard in a bowl, then stir until combined.
2. Apply the mixture over the pork ribs, then marinates for at least an hour.
3. In the meantime, combine brown sugar with smoked paprika, onion powder, garlic powder, chili powder, black pepper, cayenne pepper, and salt, then mix well.
4. After an hour of the marinade, sprinkle the dry spice mixture over the marinated pork ribs, then let it rest for a few minutes.
5. Plug the wood pellet smoker, then fill the hopper with the wood pellet. Turn the switch on.
6. Set the wood pellet smoker for indirect heat, then adjust the temperature to 250°F (121°C).
7. When the wood pellet smoker is ready, place the seasoned pork ribs in the wood pellet smoker and smoke for 3 hours.

8. Meanwhile, place unsalted butter in a saucepan, then melt over very low heat.
9. Once it is melted, remove it from heat, and then add honey and bourbon to the saucepan. Stir until incorporated and set aside.
10. After 3 hours of smoking, baste the honey bourbon mixture over the pork ribs and wrap it with aluminum foil.
11. Return the wrapped pork ribs to the wood pellet smoker and continue smoking for another 2 hours.
12. Once the smoked pork ribs reach 145°F (63°C), remove the smoked pork ribs from the wood pellet smoker.
13. Unwrap the smoked pork ribs and serve.

Nutrition: Calories: 313 Carbs: 5g Fat: 20g Protein: 26g

- ## **Lime Barbecue Smoked Pork Shoulder Chili**

Preparation Time: 20 minutes
Cooking Time: 6 hours 10 minutes
Servings: 8
Ingredients:
- Pork Shoulder (3.5-lb., 1.6-kg.)
- The Rub
- Brown sugar – 3 tablespoons
- Garlic powder – 1 tablespoon
- Smoked paprika -1 tablespoon

- Ground cumin – 1 tablespoon
- Salt – 1 teaspoon
- Chili powder – 1 ½ teaspoon
- Black pepper – 1 teaspoon
- The Glaze
- Red chili flakes – 1 tablespoon
- Vegetable oil – 2 tablespoons
- Minced garlic – 1 tablespoon
- Ground coriander – 1 ½ teaspoon
- Tomato ketchup – 1 ½ cups
- White sugar – ¼ cup
- Apple juice – ½ cup
- The Topping
- Fresh limes - 2

Directions:

1. Place brown sugar, garlic powder, smoked paprika, ground cumin, salt, chili powder, and black pepper in a bowl, then stir until combined.
2. Rub the spices mixture over and side by side of the pork shoulder, then let it rest for approximately an hour.
3. In the meantime, pour vegetable oil into a saucepan, then preheat over medium heat.
4. Once the oil is hot, stir in minced garlic and sauté until wilted and aromatic. Remove the saucepan from heat.
5. Stir in red chili flakes, ground coriander, and white sugar into the saucepan, then pour apple juice and tomato ketchup over the sauce. Mix well and set aside.
6. Plug the wood pellet smoker, then fill the hopper with the wood pellet. Turn the switch on.
7. Set the wood pellet smoker for indirect heat, then adjust the temperature to 250°F (121°C).
8. Place the seasoned pork shoulder in the wood pellet smoker and smoke for 3 hours. The internal temperature should be 165°F (74°C).
9. Take the pork shoulder out of the wood pellet smoker, then place it on a sheet of aluminum foil.
10. Baste the glaze over the pork shoulder, then arrange sliced limes over the pork shoulder.
11. Wrap the pork shoulder with aluminum foil, then return it to the wood pellet smoker.
12. Smoke the wrapped smoked pork shoulder for another 3 hours or until the internal temperature has reached 205°F (96°C).
13. Once it is done, remove the smoked pork shoulder from the wood pellet smoker and let it rest for approximately 15 minutes.
14. Unwrap the smoked pork shoulder and place it on a serving dish.

Nutrition: Calories: 220 Carbs: 1g Fat: 18g Protein: 16g

• Chili Sweet Smoked Pork Tenderloin

Preparation Time: 10 minutes

Cooking Time: 3 hours 30 minutes

Servings: 8

Ingredients:

- Pork Tenderloin (3-lb., 1.4-kg.)
- The Rub
- Apple juice – 1 cup
- Honey – ½ cup
- Brown sugar – ¾ cup
- Dried thyme – 2 tablespoons
- Black pepper – ½ tablespoon
- Chili powder – 1 ½ teaspoon
- Italian seasoning – ½ teaspoon
- Onion powder – 1 teaspoon

Directions:

1. Pour apple juice into a container, then stir in honey, brown sugar, dried thyme, black pepper, chili powder, Italian seasoning, and onion powder. Mix well.
2. Rub the pork tenderloin with the spice mixture, then let it rest for an hour.
3. Plug the wood pellet smoker, then fill the hopper with the wood pellet. Turn the switch on.
4. Set the wood pellet smoker for indirect heat, then adjust the temperature to 250°F (121°C).
5. When the wood pellet smoker has reached the desired temperature, place the seasoned pork tenderloin in the wood pellet smoker and smoke for 3 hours.
6. After 3 hours of smoking, increase the wood pellet smoker's temperature to 350°F (177°C) and continue smoking the pork tenderloin for another 30 minutes.
7. Once the smoked pork tenderloin's internal temperature has reached 165°F (74°C), remove it from the wood pellet smoker and transfer it to a serving dish.
8. Cut the smoked pork tenderloin into thick slices, then serve.

Nutrition: Calories: 318 Carbs: 7g Fat: 10g Protein: 8g

• Delicious Parmesan Roast Pork

Preparation Time: 10 minutes

Cooking Time: 3 hours 45 minutes

Servings: 10

Ingredients:

- 4 chopped garlic cloves.
- 2 tablespoons of olive oil.
- 1 tablespoon of minced dried basil.
- 1 tablespoon of dried and crushed oregano.
- 1 pound of boneless pork loin.
- 1 cup of bread crumbs.

- 1/4 cup of grated Parmesan cheese.

Directions:

1. Using a small mixing bowl, add in the garlic, olive oil, basil, and oregano, then mix properly to combine. Rub the mixture on the pork loin, coating all sides, then place in the large bowl. Cover the bowl with a plastic wrap, then place in the refrigerator for about two hours to overnight.

2. In another mixing bowl, add in the bread crumbs and cheese, then mix properly to combine. Dredge the pork in the cheese mixture, then set aside. Preheat a Wood Pellet Smoker and Grill to 225 degrees F, place the pork on the grill, cover the lid and smoke the pork for about three to four hours until an inserted thermometer reads 155 degrees F.

3. Wrap the pork in aluminum foil and let stand for about ten minutes. Slice and serve.

Nutrition: Calories 250 Fat 10g Carbohydrates 3g Protein 34g

- ## **Bacon-Wrapped Pork Tenderloin**

Preparation Time: 15 minutes

Cooking Time: 40 minutes

Servings: 4

Ingredients:

- 1 pork tenderloin.
- 4 strips of bacon.

- Rub:
- 8 tablespoons of brown sugar.
- 3 tablespoons of kosher salt to taste.
- 1 tablespoon of chili powder.
- 1 teaspoon of black pepper to taste.
- 1 teaspoon of onion powder.
- 1 teaspoon of garlic powder.

Directions:

1. Using a small mixing bowl, add sugar, chili powder, onion powder, garlic powder, salt, and pepper to taste, mix properly to combine, and set aside. Use a sharp knife to trim off fats present on the pork, then coat with 1/4 of the prepared rub. Make sure you coat all sides.

2. Roll each pork tenderloin with a piece of bacon, lay the meat on a cutting board, then pound with a meat mallet to give an even thickness, secure the ends of the bacon with toothpicks to hold still. Coat the meat again with just a little more of the rub spice, then set aside.

3. Preheat a Wood Pellet Smoker and Grill to 350 degrees F, place the pork tenderloin on the grill, and grill for about fifteen minutes. Increase the temperature of the grill to 400 degrees F and cook for another fifteen minutes until it is cooked through and reads an internal temperature of 145 degrees F.

4. Once cooked, let the pork rest for a few minutes, slice, and serve.

Nutrition: Calories 236 Fat 8g Carbohydrates 10g Protein 29g

• **Typical Nachos**

Preparation Time: 15 minutes

Cooking Time: 10 minutes

Servings: 4

Ingredients:

- 2 cups leftover smoked pulled pork
- 1 small sweet onion, diced
- 1 medium tomato, diced
- 1 jalapeño pepper, seeded and diced
- 1 garlic clove, minced
- 1 teaspoon salt
- 1 teaspoon freshly ground black pepper
- 1 bag tortilla chips
- 1 cup shredded Cheddar cheese
- ½ cup Bill's Best BBQ Sauce, divided
- ½ cup shredded jalapeño Monterey Jack cheese
- Juice of ½ lime
- 1 avocado, halved, pitted, and sliced
- 2 tablespoons sour cream
- 1 tablespoon chopped fresh cilantro

Directions:

1. Supply your smoker with wood pellets and follow the manufacturer's specific start-up procedure. Preheat, with the lid, closed, to 375°F.

2. Heat the pulled pork in the microwave.

3. In a medium bowl, combine the onion, tomato, jalapeño, garlic, salt, and pepper, and set aside.

4. Arrange half of the tortilla chips in a large cast-iron skillet. Spread half of the warmed pork on top and cover with the Cheddar cheese. Top with half of the onion-jalapeño mixture, then drizzle with ¼ cup of barbecue sauce

5. Layer on the remaining tortilla chips, then the remaining pork and the Monterey Jack cheese. Top with the remaining onion-jalapeño mixture and drizzle with the remaining ¼ cup of barbecue sauce.

6. Place the skillet on the grill, close the lid, and smoke for about 10 minutes, or until the cheese is melted and bubbly. (Watch to make sure your chips don't burn!)

7. Squeeze the lime juice over the nachos, top with the avocado slices and sour cream, and garnish with the cilantro before serving hot.

Nutrition: Calories per serving: 688; Protein: 58.9g; Carbs: 2.7g; Fat: 47.3g Sugar: 0.2g

• BBQ Breakfast Grist

Preparation Time: 20 minutes

Cooking Time: 30 to 40 minutes

Servings: 8

Ingredients:

- 1 cup of water
- 1 cup quick-cooking grits
- 3 tablespoons unsalted butter
- 2 tablespoons minced garlic
- 1 medium onion, chopped
- 1 jalapeño pepper, stemmed, seeded, and chopped
- 1 teaspoon cayenne pepper
- 2 teaspoons red pepper flakes
- 1 tablespoon hot sauce
- 1 cup shredded Monterey Jack cheese
- 1 cup sour cream
- Salt
- Freshly ground black pepper
- 2 eggs, beaten
- ⅓ cup half-and-half
- 3 cups leftover pulled pork (preferably smoked)

Directions:

1. Supply your smoker with wood pellets and follow the manufacturer's specific start-up procedure. Preheat, with the lid, closed, to 350°F.
2. On your kitchen stovetop, in a large saucepan over high heat, bring the chicken stock and water to a boil.
3. Add the grits and reduce the heat to low, then stir in the butter, garlic, onion, jalapeño, cayenne, red pepper flakes, hot sauce, cheese, and sour cream. Season with salt and pepper, then cook for about 5 minutes.
4. Temper the beaten eggs and incorporate them into the grits. Remove the saucepan from the heat and stir in the half-and-half and pulled pork.
5. Pour the grits into a greased grill-safe 9-by-13-inch casserole dish or aluminum pan.
6. Transfer to the grill, close the lid, and bake for 30 to 40 minutes, covering with aluminum foil toward the end of cooking if the grits start to get too brown on top.

Nutrition: Calories per serving: 1263; Protein: 36.9g; Carbs: 110.3g; Fat: 76.8g Sugar: 107g

• Pig Pops (Sweet-hot Bacon on Stick)

Preparation Time: 15 minutes

Cooking Time: 25 to 30 minutes

Servings: 24

Ingredients:

- Nonstick cooking spray, oil, or butter, for greasing
- 2 pounds thick-cut bacon (24 slices)

- 24 metal skewers
- 1 cup packed light brown sugar
- 2 to 3 teaspoons cayenne pepper
- ½ cup maple syrup, divided

Directions:

1. Supply your smoker with wood pellets and follow the manufacturer's specific start-up procedure. Preheat, with the lid, closed, to 350°F.

2. Coat a disposable aluminum foil baking sheet with cooking spray, oil, or butter.

3. Thread each bacon slice onto a metal skewer and place on the prepared baking sheet.

4. In a medium bowl, stir together the brown sugar and cayenne.

5. Baste the top sides of the bacon with ¼ cup of maple syrup.

6. Sprinkle half of the brown sugar mixture over the bacon

7. Place the baking sheet on the grill, close the lid, and smoke for 15 to 30 minutes.

8. Using tongs, flip the bacon skewers. Baste with the remaining ¼ cup of maple syrup and top with the remaining brown sugar mixture.

9. Continue smoking with the lid closed for 10 to 15 minutes, or until crispy. You can eyeball the bacon and smoke to your desired doneness, but the actual ideal internal temperature for bacon is 155°F (if you want to try to get a thermometer into it—ha!).

10. Using tongs, carefully remove the bacon skewers from the grill. Let cool completely before handling.

Nutrition: Calories: 318 Carbs: 7g Fat: 10g Protein: 8g

- ## **Party Pulled Pork Shoulder**

Preparation Time: 30 minutes

Cooking Time: 8 to 9 minutes

Servings: 10

Ingredients:

- 1 (5-pound) Boston butt (pork shoulder)
- ¼ cup prepared table mustard
- ½ cup Our House Dry Rub or your favorite rub, divided
- 2 cups apple juice
- ½ cup of salt

Directions:

1. Slather the meat with the mustard and coat with ¼ cup of the dry rub

2. In a spray bottle, mix the apple juice and salt and shake until the salt is dissolved

3. Supply your smoker with wood pellets and follow the manufacturer's specific start-up procedure. Preheat, with the lid, closed, to 225°F.

4. Place the pork fat-side up in an aluminum pan, transfer to the grill, close the lid, and smoke for 8 to 9 hours, spritzing well all over with the

salted apple juice every hour, until a meat thermometer inserted in the thickest part of the meat reads 205°F. Cover the pork loosely with aluminum foil toward the end of cooking, if necessary, to keep the top from blackening.

5. Drain the liquid from the pan, cover, and allow the meat to cool for a few minutes before using two forks to shred it.

6. Sprinkle the remaining rub over the meat and serve with barbecue sauce.

Nutrition: Calories: 426; Protein: 65.3g; Carbs: 20.4g; Fat: 8.4g Sugar: 17.8g

- ## Pineapple-Pepper Pork Kebabs

Preparation Time: 20 minutes

Cooking Time: 10 to 12 minutes

Servings: 6

Ingredients:

- 1 (20-ounce) bottle hoisin sauce
- ½ cup Sriracha
- ¼ cup honey
- ¼ cup apple cider vinegar
- 2 tablespoons canola oil
- 2 teaspoons minced garlic
- 2 teaspoons onion powder
- 1 teaspoon ground ginger
- 1 teaspoon salt
- 1 teaspoon freshly ground black pepper

- 2 pounds thick-cut pork chops or pork loin, cut into 2-inch cubes
- 10 ounces' fresh pineapple, cut into chunks
- 1 red onion, cut into wedges
- 1 bag mini sweet peppers, tops removed and seeded
- 12 metal or wooden skewers (soaked in water for 30 minutes if wooden)

Directions:

1. In a small bowl, stir together the hoisin, Sriracha, honey, vinegar, oil, minced garlic, onion powder, ginger, salt, and black pepper to create the marinade. Reserve ¼ cup for basting.

2. Toss the pork cubes, pineapple chunks, onion wedges, and mini peppers in the remaining marinade. Cover and refrigerate for at least 1 hour or up to 4 hours.

3. Supply your smoker with wood pellets and follow the manufacturer's specific start-up procedure. Preheat, with the lid, closed, to 450°F.

4. Remove the pork, pineapple, and veggies from the marinade; do not rinse. Discard the marinade.

5. Use the double-skewer technique to assemble the kebabs (see Tip below). Thread each of 6 skewers with pork, a piece of pineapple, a piece of onion, and sweet mini pepper, making sure that the skewer goes through the left

side of the ingredients. Repeat the threading on each skewer two more times. Double-skewer the kebabs by sticking another 6 skewers through the right side of the ingredients.

6. Place the kebabs directly on the grill, close the lid, and smoke for 10 to 12 minutes, turning once. They are done when a meat thermometer inserted in the pork reads 160°F.

Nutrition: Calories per serving: 347; Protein: 33.4 g; Carbs: 45.8 g; Fat: 4.2g Sugar: 36g

• **Smoked Bacon**

Preparation Time: 20 minutes

Cooking Time: 3 hours

Servings: 12

Ingredients:

- Pork belly, fat trimmed – 2 pounds
- Salt – ½ cup
- Brown sugar – ½ cup
- Ground black pepper – 1 tablespoon

Directions:

1. Before preheating the grill, cure the pork and for this, stir together all of the ingredients for it and then rub it well on the pork belly.

2. Place pork belly into a large plastic bag, seal it, and let it rest for 8 days in the refrigerator.

3. Then remove pork belly from the refrigerator, rinse well and pat dry.

4. When the grill has preheated, place the pork belly on the grilling rack and let smoke for 3 hours or until the control panel shows the internal temperature of 150 degrees F, turning halfway.

5. Check the fire after one hour of smoking and add more wood pallets if required.

6. When done, remove pork from the grill, wrap it in plastic wrap, and rest for 1 hour in the freezer until pork is firm and nearly frozen.

7. When ready to eat, cut pork into slices and then serve.

Nutrition: Calories per serving: 688; Protein: 58.9g; Carbs: 2.7g; Fat: 47.3g Sugar: 0.2g

• Braised Pork Carnitas

Preparation Time: 20 minutes

Cooking Time: 3 hours and 30 minutes

Servings: 6

Ingredients:

- Pork shoulder, boneless, fat trimmed, marbled – 4 pounds
- Beer – 12 ounces
- Salt – 2 teaspoons
- Ground cumin – ½ teaspoon
- Vegetable shortening – 2 tablespoons

Directions:

1. Meanwhile, cut pork into 2-inch pieces and then place them in a Dutch oven.
2. Add salt and cumin, pour in beer, and then pour in water until pork pieces are covered.
3. Place the pot over medium-high heat and then bring the mixture to a boil.
4. When the grill has preheated, place the pot on the grilling rack and let smoke for 3 hours or until pork pieces have turned tender.
5. Check the fire after one hour of smoking and add more wood pallets if required.
6. When done, remove the pot from the grill, drain the cooking liquid, and break it into bite-size pieces using two forks.
7. Add shortening into the pot, return it onto the grilling rack, switch temperature of the grill to 400 degrees F, and continue cooking for 20 minutes until pork has turned nicely brown, stirring frequently.
8. When done, divide pork evenly among tortillas, add servings as desired, and then serve.

• Pork Belly Tacos

Preparation Time: 20 minutes

Cooking Time: 2 hours and 30 minutes

Servings: 6

Ingredients:

- Pork belly, scored, deskinned – 4 pounds

- Salt – 4 tablespoons
- Ground black pepper – ½ tablespoon
- Brown sugar – 4 tablespoons

Directions:

1. In the meantime, prepare the pork and for this, stir together salt, black pepper, and sugar and then rub this mixture generously on all sides until coated.
2. When the grill has preheated, place pork on a roasting pan, place on a grilling rack, and let smoke for 30 minutes.
3. Then switch the temperature of the grill to 250 degrees F and continue smoking the pork for 2 hours until tender.
4. Check the fire after one hour of smoking and add more wood pallets if required.
5. When done, remove pork from the grill and let it rest for 30 minutes.
6. Then cut pork into slices, divide evenly among tortillas, add cilantro and then serve.

Nutrition: Calories: 230;Total Fat: 8 g; Saturated Fat: 1.5 g; Protein: 13 g; Carbs: 26 g; Fiber: 4 g; Sugar: 2 g

• Teriyaki Pork Tenderloin

Preparation Time: 30 minutes

Cooking Time: 1 to 2 hours

Servings: 4 to 6

Ingredients:

- 2 (1-pound) pork tenderloins
- 1 batch Easy Teriyaki Marinade
- Smoked salt

Directions:

1. In a large zip-top bag, combine the tenderloins and marinade. Seal the bag, turn to coat, and refrigerate the pork for at least 30 minutes—I recommend up to overnight.
2. Supply your smoker with wood pellets and follow the manufacturer's specific start-up procedure. Preheat the grill, with the lid closed, to 180°F
3. Remove the tenderloins from the marinade and season them with smoked salt.
4. Place the tenderloins directly on the grill grate and smoke for 1 hour
5. Increase the grill's temperature to 300°F and continue to cook until the pork's internal temperature reaches 145°F
6. Remove the tenderloins from the grill and let them rest for 5 to 10 minutes before thinly slicing and serving.

Nutrition: Calories: 150 Fat: 4g Saturated Fat: 2g

• Pork Belly Burnt Ends

Preparation Time: 30 minute

Cooking Time: 6 hours

Servings: 8 to 10

Ingredients:

- 1 (3-pound) skinless pork belly (if not already skinned, use a sharp boning knife to remove the skin from the belly), cut into 1½- to 2-inch cube
- 1 batch Sweet Brown Sugar Rub
- ½ cup honey
- 1 cup Bill's Best BBQ Sauce
- 2 tablespoons light brown sugar

Directions:

1. Supply your smoker with wood pellets and follow the manufacturer's specific start-up procedure. Preheat the grill, with the lid closed, to 250°F.
2. Generously season the pork belly cubes with the rub. Using your hands, work the rub into the meat
3. Place the pork cubes directly on the grill grate and smoke until their internal temperature reaches 195°F.
4. Transfer the cubes from the grill to an aluminum pan. Add the honey, barbecue sauce, and brown sugar. Stir to combine and coat the pork.
5. Place the pan in the grill and smoke the pork for 1 hour, uncovered. Remove the pork from the grill and serve immediately.

Nutrition: Calories 1301 Fat: 124g Saturated Fat: 46g

Cajun Doubled-Smoked Ham

Preparation Time: 20 minutes

Cooking Time: 4 to 5 hours

Servings: 10 to 12

Ingredients:

- 1 (5- or 6-pound) bone-in smoked ham
- 1 batch Cajun Rub
- 3 tablespoons honey

Directions:

1. Supply your smoker with wood pellets and follow the manufacturer's specific start-up procedure. Preheat the grill, with the lid closed, to 225°F.
2. Generously season the ham with the rub and place it either in a pan or directly on the grill grate. Smoke it for 1 hour.
3. Drizzle the honey over the ham and continue to smoke it until the ham's internal temperature reaches 145°F.
4. Remove the ham from the grill and let it rest for 5 to 10 minutes before thinly slicing and serving.

Nutrition: Calories: 60 Saturated Fat: .5g Cholesterol 25mg Carbs 2g

Rub-Injected Pork Shoulder

Preparation Time: 15 minute

Cooking Time: 16 to 20 hours

Servings: 8 to 12

Ingredients:

- 1 (6- to 8-pound) bone-in pork shoulder
- 2 cups Tea Injectable made with Not-Just-for-Pork Rub
- 2 tablespoons yellow mustard

- 1 batch Not-Just-for-Pork Rub

Directions:

1. Supply your smoker with wood pellets and follow the manufacturer's specific start-up procedure. Preheat the grill, with the lid closed, to 225°F.

2. Inject the pork shoulder throughout with the tea injectable.

3. Coat the pork shoulder all over with mustard and season it with the rub. Using your hands, work the rub into the meat.

4. Place the shoulder directly on the grill grate and smoke until its internal temperature reaches 160°F and a dark bark has formed on the exterior.

5. Pull the shoulder from the grill and wrap it completely in aluminum foil or butcher paper.

6. Increase the grill's temperature to 350°F.

7. Return the pork shoulder to the grill and cook until its internal temperature reaches 195°F.

8. Pull the shoulder from the grill and place it in a cooler. Cover the cooler and let the pork rest for 1 or 2 hours.

9. Remove the pork shoulder from the cooler and unwrap it. Remove the shoulder bone and pull the pork apart using just your fingers. Serve immediately.

Nutrition: Calories per serving: 688; Protein: 58.9g; Carbs: 2.7g; Fat: 47.3g

- ## **Smoked Spare Ribs**

Preparation Time: 25 minutes

Cooking Time: 4 to 6 hours

Servings: 4 to 8

Ingredients:

- 2 (2- or 3-pound) racks spare ribs
- 2 tablespoons yellow mustard
- 1 batch Sweet Brown Sugar Rub
- ¼ cup Bill's Best BBQ Sauce

Directions:

1. Supply your smoker with wood pellets and follow the manufacturer's specific start-up procedure. Preheat the grill, with the lid closed, to 225°F.

2. Remove the membrane from the backside of the ribs. This can be done by cutting just through the membrane in an X pattern and working a paper towel between the membrane and the ribs to pull it off.

3. Coat the ribs on both sides with mustard and season with the rub. Using your hands, work the rub into the meat.

4. Place the ribs directly on the grill grate and smoke until their internal temperature reaches between 190°F and 200°F.

5. Baste both sides of the ribs with barbecue sauce.

6. Increase the grill's temperature to 300°F and continue to cook the ribs for 15 minutes more.

7. Remove the racks from the grill, cut them into individual ribs, and serve immediately.

Nutrition: Calories:277 Fat: 23g Protein: 16g

• Slow Smoked Pork Belly Sliders

Preparation Time: 20 minutes

Cooking Time: 4 hours

Servings: 8 to 10

Ingredients:

- 4-5 lbs. of pork belly, cut into 1-inch chunks
- 1 – 2 cups cabbage slaw
- 12 brioche slider
- 2 cups of cherry cola
- 1 tsp of coriander
- ½ cup of dark brown sugar
- 1 tsp of onion powder
- 1 cup of ketchup
- 1 tsp of liquid smoke
- 1 tsp of garlic powder
- ½ cup of molasses
- 1 tbsp. of Worcestershire sauce
- 1 tsp of ground ginger
- Sweet heat rub & grill
- Salt and pepper
- 1 tsp of smoked paprika

Directions:

For the BBQ sauce

1. Take a saucepan and add ketchup along with molasses, liquid smoke, dark brown sugar, onion powder, coriander, ground ginger, cherry cola, garlic powder, Worcestershire sauce, smoked paprika, and salt-pepper

2. Cook it on medium heat till everything seem to have combined well and begins to bubble

3. Reduce the heat to slow and let the sauce thicken till it simmers properly and keep aside.

For the main course

1. Preheat the grill to 225 degrees F

2. Now cut the surface of the pork belly using a sharp knife and make ¼ inch deep marks

3. Apply sweet heat rub generously on all parts of the pork belly, and then let it sit at room temperature for 20 minutes

4. Place it on the grill and smoke it for nearly 4 hours

5. In between, brush it with BBQ sauce every 30 minutes

6. Remove it from the smoker and cut into small bite-sized portions

7. Place it on the brioche buns and top it with BBQ sauce and coleslaw

8. Serve

Nutrition: Calories: 310 Fats: 26g Protein: 17g

• **Chinese BBQ Pork**

Preparation Time: 10 minutes

Cooking Time: 20 minutes

Servings: 6

Ingredients:

- Pork & Marinade
- 2 Pork Tenderloins, Silver Skin Removed
- 1/4 Cup Hoisin Sauce
- 1/4 Cup Honey
- 1 1/2 Tbsp. Brown Sugar
- 3 Tbsp. Soy Sauce
- 1 Tbsp. Asian Sesame Oil
- 1 Tbsp. Oyster Sauce, Optional
- 1 Tsp Chinese Five Spice
- 1 Garlic Clove, Minced
- 2 Tsp Red Food Coloring, Optional
- Five Spice Dipping Sauce
- 1/4 Cup Ketchup
- 3 Tbsp. Brown Sugar
- 1 Tsp Yellow Mustard
- 1/4 Tsp Chinese Five Spice

Directions:

1. In a medium bowl, whisk together marinade thoroughly, making sure brown sugar is dissolved. Add pork and marinade to a glass pan or resealable plastic bag and marinate for at least 8 hours or overnight, occasionally turning to ensure all pork sides are well coated.

2. When ready to cook, set the temperature to 225°F and preheat, lid closed for 15 minutes.

3. Remove pork from marinade and boil marinade in a saucepan over medium-high heat on the stovetop for 3 minutes to use for basting pork. Cool slightly, then whisk in 2 additional Tablespoons of honey.

4. Arrange the tenderloins on the grill grate and smoke pork until the internal temperature reaches 145°F.

5. Baste pork with reserved marinade halfway through cooking. Remove pork from grill and, if desired, increase the temperature to High and return pork to grill for a few minutes per side to slight char and set the sauce. Alternatively, you can broil in the oven, just a couple of minutes per side.

6. For the 5 Spice Sauce: In a small saucepan over low heat, mix ketchup, brown sugar, mustard, and five-spice until sugar is dissolved and sauce is smooth. Let cool, and serve chilled or at room temperature.

7. Serve pork immediately with Jasmine rice, or cool and refrigerate for future use as an appetizer, served with Five Spice dipping sauce and toasted sesame seeds. Enjoy!

8. In a medium bowl, whisk together marinade thoroughly, making sure brown sugar is dissolved. Add pork and marinade to a glass pan or resealable plastic bag and marinate for at least 8 hours or overnight, occasionally turning to ensure all sides of pork are well coated.

9. When ready to cook, set the temperature to 225°F and preheat, lid closed for 15 minutes.

10. Remove pork from marinade and boil marinade in a saucepan over medium-high heat on the stovetop for 3 minutes to use for basting pork. Cool slightly, then whisk in 2 additional Tablespoons of honey.

11. Arrange the tenderloins on the grill grate and smoke pork until the internal temperature reaches 145°F.

12. Baste pork with reserved marinade halfway through cooking. Remove pork from grill and, if desired, increase the temperature to High and return pork to grill for a few minutes per side to slight char and set the sauce. Alternatively, you can broil in the oven, just a couple of minutes per side.

13. For the 5 Spice Sauce: In a small saucepan over low heat, mix ketchup, brown sugar, mustard, and five-spice until sugar is dissolved and sauce is smooth. Let cool, and serve chilled or at room temperature.

14. Serve pork immediately with Jasmine rice, or cool and refrigerate for future use as an appetizer, served with Five Spice dipping sauce and toasted sesame seeds. Enjoy!

Nutrition: Calories: 324 Total Fat: 11.6g Cholesterol: 6mg Sodium: 1029mg

- ## **Bacon Grilled Cheese Sandwich**

Preparation Time: 15 minutes
Cooking Time: 5 minutes
Servings: 4
Ingredients:

- 1 Lb. Applewood Smoked Bacon Slices, Cooked
- 8 Slices Texas Toast
- 16 Slices Cheddar Cheese
- Mayonnaise

- Butter

Directions:

1. When ready to cook, set the temperature to 350°F and preheat, lid closed for 15 minutes.

2. Spread a little bit of mayonnaise on each piece of bread, place 1 piece of cheddar on a slice then top with a couple of slices of bacon. Add another slice of cheese, then top with the other piece of bread. Spread softened butter on the exterior of the top piece of bread.

3. When the grill is hot, place the grilled cheese directly on a cleaned, oiled grill grate buttered side down. Then spread softened butter on the exterior of the top slice.

4. Cook the grilled cheese on the first side for 5-7 minutes until grill marks develop and the cheese has begun to melt. Flip the sandwich and repeat on the other side.

5. Remove from the grill when the cheese is melted, and the exterior is lightly toasted. Enjoy!

Nutrition: Calories: 500 Carbs: 30g Fat: 29g Protein: 28g

• **Apple Cider Braised Smoked BBQ Pulled Pork**

Preparation Time: 20 minutes

Cooking Time: 6 to 7 hours

Servings: 4

Ingredients:

- 7–9 lb. bone-in pork butt/shoulder roast
- RUB
- 4 tablespoons brown sugar
- 1 tablespoon garlic powder
- 1 tablespoon onion powder
- 1 tablespoon kosher salt
- 1/2 tablespoon pepper
- 1.5 tablespoons smoked paprika
- 2 teaspoons dry mustard
- 1 tablespoon coriander
- 1 tablespoon chili powder
- SPRAY
- 1/2 cup apple cider
- 1/2 cup apple cider vinegar
- BRAISING
- 2 cups apple cider
- 3–4 sweet, crisp red apples, peeled and sliced
- 2 onions, sliced
- SAUCE
- 1 cup ketchup
- 1/2 cup apple jelly
- 1/4 cup apple cider
- 1 tablespoon apple cider vinegar
- 1 teaspoon liquid smoke
- 1/2 tablespoon Worcestershire sauce
- 1 teaspoon chili powder
- 1/2 teaspoon onion powder
- 1 cup pan juices from the roast (fat separated)

Directions:

1. Pat roast dry. Combine all rub ingredients and a pat on all sides of the roast, rubbing in well. Cover roast and let sit overnight in the fridge.

2. When ready to cook, preheat smoker to 225 degrees and smoke roast directly on the grill for 5 hours. While cooking, combine spray ingredients in a clean spray bottle and spritz roast all over once every hour.

3. While roast is smoking, combine all sauce ingredients and whisk them together in a pan. Set aside until pan juices are ready.

4. After smoking, transfer your roast to either your slow cooker (if it fits, remember you have more stuff going in there!) or a roasting pan or disposable roasting pan (if you'll continue cooking on the smoker.)

5. Place apples, onions, and 2 cups apple cider around the roast in the roasting pan. Cover with a lid or tightly with foil. Cook in the slow cooker on high for 6-7 hours (or low for more like 8-10 if you want/need to drag it out, overnight, for example.) If you are cooking in the oven, set the temperature to 275 degrees. In the smoker, you can increase the temperature to 275 as well. Cook until internal temperature reaches 200-210 degrees, usually about 6-7 hours.

6. Let pork rest, covered for at least 15 minutes (longer is just fine) before discarding bones, separating fat, etc.

7. Pour pan juices into a fat separator. Pour 1 cup of juices into your BBQ sauce and bring to a simmer. Simmer for about 15 minutes until slightly thickened.

8. Pour a little of the remaining juices over shredded pork. Use a slotted spoon to grab the onions and apples and mix them in with the pork. Serve alone or on rolls or over rice. Freezes great! Excellent on nachos, pizzas, and more.

Nutrition: Calories: 426; Protein: 65.3g; Carbs: 20.4g; Fat: 8.4g Sugar: 17.8g

• Pigs in a Blanket

Preparation Time: 10 minutes
Cooking Time: 45 minutes
Servings: 4
Ingredients:

- Pork sausages - 1 pack
- Biscuit dough - 1 pack

Directions:

1. Preheat your wood pellet grill to 350 degrees.

2. Cut the sausages and the dough into thirds.

3. Wrap the dough around the sausages. Place them on a baking sheet.

4. Grill with a closed lid for 20-25 minutes or until they look cooked.

5. Take them out when they are golden brown.

6. Serve with a dip of your choice.

Nutrition: Protein: 9 g Fat: 22 g Sodium: 732 mg Cholesterol: 44 mg

• Smoked, Candied, and Spicy Bacon

Preparation Time: 10 minutes

Cooking Time: 45 minutes

Servings: 4

Ingredients:

- Center-cut bacon - 1 lb.
- Brown sugar - ½ cup
- Maple syrup - ½ cup
- Hot sauce - 1 tablespoon
- Pepper - ½ tablespoon

Directions:

1. Mix the maple syrup, brown sugar, hot sauce, and pepper in a bowl.

2. Preheat your wood pellet grill to 300 degrees.

3. Line a baking sheet and place the bacon slices on it.

4. Generously spread the brown sugar mix on both sides of the bacon slices.

5. Place the pan on the wood pellet grill for 20 minutes. Flip the bacon pieces.

6. Leave them for another 15 minutes until the bacon looks cooked, and the sugar is melted.

7. Remove from the grill and let it stay for 10-15 minutes.

8. Voila! Your bacon candy is ready!

Nutrition: Carbohydrates: 37 g Protein: 9 g Sodium: 565 mg Cholesterol: 49 mg

• Stuffed Pork Crown Roast

Preparation Time: 10 minutes

Cooking Time: 3 hours 5 minutes

Servings: 4

Ingredients:

- 12-14 ribs or 1 Snake River Pork Crown Roast
- Apple cider vinegar - 2 tablespoon
- Apple juice - 1 cup
- Dijon mustard - 2 tablespoon
- Salt - 1 teaspoon
- Brown sugar - 1 tablespoon
- Freshly chopped thyme or rosemary - 2 tablespoon
- Cloves of minced garlic - 2
- Olive oil - ½ cup
- Coarsely ground pepper - 1 teaspoon
- Your favorite stuffing - 8 cups

Directions:

1. Set the pork properly in a shallow roasting pan on a flat rack. Cover both ends of the bone with a piece of foil.

2. To make the marinade, boil the apple cider or apple juice on high heat until about half its quantity. Remove the content from the heat and whisk in the mustard, vinegar, thyme, garlic,

brown sugar, pepper, and salt. Once all that is properly blended, whisk in the oil slowly.

3. Use a pastry brush to apply the marinade to the roast. Ensure that you coat all the surfaces evenly. Cover it on all sides using plastic wrap. Allow it to sit for about 60 minutes until the meat has reached room temperature.

4. At this time, feel free to brush the marinade on the roast again. Cover it and return it to the refrigerator until it is time to cook it. When you are ready to cook it, allow the meat to reach room temperature, then put it on the pellet grill. Ensure that the grill is preheated for about 15 minutes before you do.

5. Roast the meat for 30 minutes, then reduce the temperature of the grill. Fill the crown loosely with the stuffing and mound it at the top. Cover the stuffing properly with foil. You can also bake the stuffing separately alongside the roast in a pan.

6. Roast the pork thoroughly for 90 more minutes. Get rid of the foil and continue to roast the stuffing for 30-90 minutes until the pork reaches an internal temperature of 150 degrees Fahrenheit. Ensure that you do not touch the bone of the meat with the temperature probe or get a false reading.

7. Remove the roast from the grill. Allow it to rest for around 15 minutes so that the meat soaks in all the juices. Remove the foil covering the bones. Leave the butcher's string on until you are ready to carve it. Now, transfer it to a warm platter, carve between the bones, and enjoy!

Nutrition: Carbohydrates: 37 g Protein: 9 g Sodium: 565 mg Cholesterol: 49 mg

• St. Louis BBQ Ribs

Preparation Time: 10 minutes

Cooking Time: 4 hours 5 minutes

Servings: 4

Ingredients:

- Traeger pork as well as a poultry rub - 6 oz.
- St. Louis bone in the form of pork ribs - 2 racks
- Traeger Heat and Sweet BBQ sauce - 1 bottle
- Apple juice - 8 oz.

Directions:

1. Trim the ribs and peel off their membranes from the back.

2. Apply an even coat of the poultry rub on the front and back of the ribs. Let the coat sit for at least 20 minutes. If you wish to refrigerate it, you can do so for up to 4 hours.

3. Once you are ready to cook it, preheat the pellet grill for around 15 minutes. Place the ribs on the grill grate, bone side down. Put the apple juice in an easy spray bottle and then spray it evenly on the ribs.

4. Smoke the meat for 1 hour.

5. Remove the ribs from the pellet grill and wrap them securely in aluminum foil. Ensure that there is an opening in the wrapping at one end. Pour the remaining 6 oz. of apple juice into the foil. Wrap it tightly.

6. Place the ribs on the grill again, meat side down. Smoke the meat for another 3 hours.

7. Once the ribs are done and cooked evenly, get rid of the foil. Gently brush a layer of the sauce on both sides of the ribs. Put them back on the grill to cook for another 10 minutes to ensure that the sauce is set properly.

8. Once the sauce sets, take the ribs off the pellet grill and let them rest for at least 10 minutes so that they can soak in all the juices.

9. Slice the ribs to serve and enjoy!

Nutrition: Carbohydrates: 37 g Protein: 9 g Sodium: 565 mg Cholesterol: 49 mg

• **Lemon Pepper Pork Tenderloin**

Preparation Time: 20 minutes

Cooking Time: 20 minutes

Servings: 6

Ingredients:

- 2 pounds' pork tenderloin, Fat: trimmed
- For the Marinade:
- ½ teaspoon minced garlic
- 2 lemons, zested
- 1 teaspoon minced parsley
- 1/2 teaspoon salt
- 1/4 teaspoon ground black pepper
- 1 teaspoon lemon juice
- 2 tablespoons olive oil

Directions:

1. Prepare the marinade and for this, take a small bowl, place all of its ingredients in it and whisk until combined.

2. Take a large plastic bag, pour marinade in it, add pork tenderloin, seal the bag, turn it upside down to coat the pork, and let it marinate for a minimum of 2 hours in the refrigerator.

3. When ready to cook, switch on the Traeger grill, fill the grill hopper with apple-flavored wood pellets, power the grill on by using the control panel, select 'smoke' on the temperature dial, or set the temperature to 375 degrees F and let it preheat for a minimum of 15 minutes.

4. When the grill has preheated, open the lid, place pork tenderloin on the grill grate, shut the grill, and smoke for 20 minutes until the internal temperature reaches 145 degrees F, turning pork halfway.

5. When done, transfer pork to a cutting board, let it rest for 10 minutes, then cut it into slices and serve.

Nutrition: Calories: 288.5 Cal Fat: 16.6 g Carbs: 6.2 gProtein: 26.4 g Fiber: 1.2 g

- ## Porchetta

Preparation Time: 30 minutes

Cook time: 3 hours

Servings: 12

Ingredients:

- 6 pounds' skin-on pork belly
- 4 pounds' center-cut pork loin
- 4 tbsp. olive oil

- 1 cup apple juice
- 2 garlic cloves (minced)
- 1 onion (diced)
- 1 ¼ cups grated pecorino Romano cheese
- 1 tsp ground black pepper
- 2 tsp kosher salt - 3 tbsp. fennel seeds
- 1 tbsp. freshly chopped rosemary
- 1 tbsp. freshly chopped sage
- 1 tbsp. freshly chopped thyme
- 1 tbsp. grated lemon zest

Rub:

- 1 tbsp. chili powder - 2 tsp grilling seasoning
- 1 tsp salt or to taste
- ½ tsp cayenne
- 1 tsp oregano - 1 tsp paprika
- 1 tsp mustard powder

Directions:

1. Butterfly the pork loin and place it in the middle of two plastic wraps. On a flat surface, pound the pork evenly until it is ½ inch thick.

2. Combine all the rub ingredients in a small mixing bowl.

3. Place the butterflied pork on a flat surface, cut side up. Season the cut side generously with 1/3 of the rub.

4. Heat 1 tbsp. olive oil in a frying pan over medium to high heat. Add the onion, garlic, and fennel seed. Sauté until the veggies are tender.

5. Stir the black pepper, 1 tsp kosher salt, rosemary, sage, thyme, and lemon zest. Cook for 1 minute and stir in the cheese.

6. Put the sautéed ingredients on the flat pork and spread evenly. Roll up the pork like you are rolling a burrito.

7. Brush the rolled pork loin with 1 tbsp. oil and season with the remaining rub. The loin with butcher's string at the 1-inch interval.

8. Roll the pork belly around the pork, skin side out. Brush the pork belly with the remaining oil and season with 1 tsp salt.

9. Set a rack into a roasting pan and place the Porchetta on the rack. Pour the wine into the bottom of the roasting pan.

10. Start your grill on smoke mode, leaving the lid opened for 5 minutes until the fire starts.

11. Close the lid and preheat the grill to 325°F, using maple or apple hardwood pellets.

12. Place the roasting pan on the grill and roast Porchetta for about 3 hours or until the Porchetta's internal temperature reaches 155°F.

13. Remove the Porchetta from heat and let it rest for a few minutes to cool.

14. Remove the butcher's string. Slice Porchetta into sizes and serve.

Nutrition: Calories: 611 Fat: 22.7g Cholesterol: 252mg Carbohydrate: 6.6g Protein: 89.4g

- ## Pork Jerky

Preparation Time: 15 minutes
Cook time: 2 hours 30 minutes
Servings: 12
Ingredients:
- 4 pounds' boneless center-cut pork (trimmed of excess fat and sliced into ¼ inch thick slices)

Marinade:
- 1/3 cup soy sauce
- 1 cup pineapple juice
- 1 tbsp. rice wine vinegar
- 2 tsp black pepper

- 1 tsp red pepper flakes
- 5 tbsp. brown sugar
- 1 tsp paprika
- 1 tsp onion powder
- 1 tsp garlic powder
- 2 tsp salt or to taste

Directions:

1. Combine and mix all the marinade ingredients in a mixing bowl.
2. Put the sliced pork in a gallon-sized zip-lock bag and pour the marinade into the bag. Massage the marinade into the pork. Seal the bag and refrigerate for 8 hours.
3. Activate the pellet grill smoker setting and leave the lip open for 5 minutes until the fire starts.
4. Close the lid and preheat your pellet grill to 180°F, using a hickory pellet.
5. Remove the pork slices from the marinade and pat them dry with a paper towel.
6. Arrange the pork slices on the grill in a single layer. Smoke the pork for about 2 ½ hours, often turning after the first 1 hour of smoking. The jerky should be dark and dry when it is done.
7. Remove the jerky from the grill and let it sit for about 1 hour to cool.
8. Serve immediately or store in airtight containers and refrigerate for future use.

Nutrition: Calories: 260 Fat: 11.4g Cholesterol: 80mg Carbohydrate: 8.6g Protein: 28.1g

- ## **Grilled Carnitas**

Preparation Time: 20 minutes

Cook time: 10 hours

Servings: 12

Ingredients:

- 1 tsp paprika
- 1 tsp oregano
- 1 tsp cayenne pepper
- 2 tsp brown sugar
- 1 tsp mint
- 1 tbsp. onion powder
- 1 tsp cumin
- 1 tsp chili powder
- 2 tbsp. salt
- 1 tsp garlic powder
- 1 tsp Italian seasoning
- 2 tbsp. Olive oil.
- 5 pounds' pork shoulder roast

Directions:

1. Trim the pork of any excess fat.
2. To make a rub, combine the paprika, oregano, cayenne, sugar, mint, onion

powder, garlic powder, cumin, chili, salt, and Italian seasoning in a small mixing bowl.

3. Rub all sides of the pork with the rub.

4. Start your grill for smoking, leaving the lid open until the fire starts.

5. Close the lid and preheat the grill to 325°F with the lid closed for 15 minutes.

6. Place the pork in a foil pan and place the pan on the grill—Cook for about 2 hours.

7. After 2 hours, increase the heat to 325°F and smoke pork for an additional 8 hours or until the pork's internal temperature reaches 190°F.

8. Remove pork from it and let it sit until it is cook and easy to handle.

9. Shred the pork with two forks.

10. Place a cast-iron skillet on the grill grate and add the olive oil.

11. Add the pork and sear until the pork is brown and crispy.

12. Remove pork from heat and let it rest for a few minutes. Serve!

Nutrition: Calories: 514 Fat: 41.1g Cholesterol: 134mg Carbohydrate: 1.6g Protein: 32g

- ## **Stuffed Tenderloin**

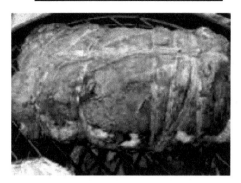

Preparation Time: 15 minutes

Cook time: 3 hours

Servings: 8

Ingredients:

- 1 pork tenderloin
- 12 slices of bacon
- ¼ cup cheddar cheese
- ¼ cup mozzarella cheese
- 1 small onion (finely chopped)
- 1 carrot (finely chopped)

Rub:

- ½ tsp granulated garlic (not garlic powder)
- ½ tsp cayenne pepper
- 1 tsp paprika
- ½ tsp ground pepper
- 1 tsp chili
- ½ tsp onion powder
- ¼ tsp cumin
- 1 tsp salt

Directions:

1. Butterfly the pork tenderloin and place between 2 plastic wraps. Pound the tenderloin evenly with a mallet until it is ½ inch thick.

2. Place the cheddar, mozzarella, onion, and carrot on one end of the flat pork. Roll up the pork like a burrito.

3. Combine all the ingredients for the rub in a mixing bowl. Rub the seasoning mixture all over the pork.

4. Wrap the pork with bacon slices.

5. Preheat the grill to 275°F for 10-15 minutes. Use apple, hickory, or mesquite hardwood pellets.

6. Place the pork on the grill and smoke for 3 hours, or until the pork's internal temperature reaches 165°F and the bacon wrap is crispy.

7. Remove the pork from heat and let it rest for about 10 minutes.

8. Cut into sizes and serve.

Nutrition: Calories: 241 Fat: 14.8g Cholesterol: 66mg Carbohydrate: 2.7g Protein: 22.9g

• <u>Maplewood Bourbon BBQ Ham</u>

Preparation Time: 15 minutes

Cook time: 2 hours 30 minutes

Servings: 8

Ingredients:

- 1 large ham
- 1/2 cup brown sugar
- 3 tbsp. bourbon
- 2 tbsp. lemon
- 2 tbsp. Dijon mustard
- ¼ cup apple juice
- ¼ cup maple syrup
- 1 tsp salt
- 1 tsp freshly ground garlic
- 1 tsp ground black pepper

Directions:

1. Start your grill on a smoke setting, leaving for 5 minutes, until the fire starts.

2. Close the lid and preheat the grill to 325°F.

3. Place the ham on a smoker rack and place the rack on the grill. Smoke for 2 hours or until the internal temperature of the ham reaches 125°F.

4. Combine the sugar, bourbon, lemon, mustard, apple juice, salt, pepper, and maple in a saucepan over medium to high heat.

5. Bring mixture to a boil, reduce the heat and simmer until the sauce thickens.

6. Glaze the ham with maple mixture.

7. Increase the grill temperature to 375°F and continue cooking until the internal temperature of the ham reaches 140°F.

8. Remove the glazed ham from the grill and let it rest for about 15 minutes.

9. Cut ham into small sizes and serve.

Nutrition: Calories: 163 Fat: 4.6g Cholesterol: 29mg Carbohydrate: 19g Protein: 8.7g

• **Pork Steak**

Preparation Time: 10 minutes

Cooking Time: 20 minutes

Servings: 4

Ingredients:

For the Brine:

- 2-inch piece of orange peel
- 2 sprigs of thyme
- 4 tablespoons salt
- 4 black peppercorns
- 1 sprig of rosemary
- 2 tablespoons brown sugar
- 2 bay leaves
- 10 cups water

For Pork Steaks:

- 4 pork steaks, fat trimmed
- Game rub as needed

Directions:

1. Prepare the brine and for this, take a large container, place all of its ingredients in it and stir until sugar has dissolved.

2. Place steaks in it, add some weights to keep steak submerge into the brine, and let soak for 24 hours in the refrigerator.

3. Fill the grill hopper with hickory flavored wood pellets, power the grill on by using the control panel, select 'smoke' on the temperature dial, or set the temperature to 225°F and let it preheat for a minimum of 15 minutes.

4. Remove steaks from the brine, rinse well, and pat dry with paper towels and then season well with game rub until coated.

5. When the grill has preheated, open the lid, place steaks on the grill grate, shut the grill, and smoke for 10 minutes per side until the internal temperature reaches 140°F.

6. Transfer steaks to a cutting board, rest for 10 minutes, and then cut into slices and serve.

Nutrition: Calories: 260 Fat: 21g Carbs: 1g Protein: 17g

• **Carolina Smoked Ribs**

Preparation Time: 30 minutes

Cooking Time: 4 hours 30 minutes

Serving: 10

Ingredients:

- 1/2 a cup of brown sugar
- 1/3 cup of fresh lemon juice
- ¼ cup of white vinegar

- 1/4 cup of apple cider vinegar
- 1 tablespoon of Worcestershire sauce
- ¼ cup of molasses
- 2 cups of prepared mustard
- 2 teaspoons of garlic, minced
- 2 teaspoons of salt
- 1 teaspoon of ground black pepper
- 1 teaspoon of crushed red pepper flakes
- ½ a teaspoon of white pepper
- ¼ teaspoon of cayenne pepper
- 2 racks of pork spare ribs
- ½ a cup of barbeque seasoning

Directions:

1. Take a medium-sized bowl and whisk in brown sugar, white vinegar, lemon juice, mustard, Worcestershire sauce, mustard, molasses
2. Mix well and season the mixture with granulated garlic, pepper, salt, red pepper flakes, white pepper flakes, cayenne pepper
3. Take your drip pan and add water; cover with aluminum foil. Pre-heat your smoker to 225 degrees F
4. Use water fill water pan halfway through and place it over drip pan. Add wood chips to the side tray
5. Rub the ribs with your prepared seasoning and transfer to your smoker
6. Cover the meat with aluminum foil and smoke for 4 hours, making sure to add chips after every 60 minutes
7. After the first 3 and a ½ hours, make sure to uncover the meat and baste it generously with the prepared mustard sauce
8. Take the meat out and serve with remaining sauce
9. Enjoy!

Nutrition: Calories: 750 Fat: 50g Carbohydrates: 24g Fiber: 2.2g

• **Hearty Pig Candies**

Preparation Time: 20 minutes

Cooking Time: 2 hours

Servings: 10

Ingredients:

- Nonstick cooking spray
- 2 pound of bacon slices
- 1 cup of firmly packed brown sugar
- 2-3 teaspoon of cayenne pepper
- ½ a cup of maple syrup

Directions:

1. Take your drip pan and add water; cover with aluminum foil. Pre-heat your smoker to 225 degrees F
2. Use water fill water pan halfway through and place it over drip pan. Add wood chips to the side tray
3. Remove the grill rack from your smoker and cover with aluminum foil; spray the foils with cooking spay

4. Lay the bacon in a single layer, making sure to leave a bit of space in between

5. Take a small bowl and add brown sugar, cayenne, and mix

6. Baste the bacon with ¼ cup of maple syrup

7. Sprinkle half of the rub on top of the bacon

8. Transfer the rack to the smoker alongside the bacon and smoke for 1 hour

9. Flip the bacon and baste with another ¼ cup of maple syrup, sprinkle more rub, and a smoker for 1 hour more

10. Once the bacon is brown and firm, it's ready to be served!

Nutrition: Calories: 152 Fats: 10g Carbs: 13g Fiber: 2g

• Sauced Up Pork Spares

Preparation Time: 5 hours

Cooking Time: 4 hours

Serving: 6

Ingredients:

- 6 pound of pork spareribs

For Dry Rub

- ½ a cup of packed brown sugar
- 2 tablespoons of chili powder
- 1 tablespoon of paprika
- 1 tablespoon of freshly ground black pepper
- 2 tablespoons of garlic powder
- 2 teaspoons of onion powder
- 2 teaspoons of kosher salt
- 2 teaspoons of ground cumin
- 1 teaspoon of ground cinnamon
- 1 teaspoon of jalapeno seasoning salt
- 1 teaspoon of Cayenne pepper

For Mop Sauce

- 1 cup of apple cider
- ¾ cup of apple cider vinegar
- 1 tablespoon of onion powder
- 1 tablespoon of garlic powder
- 2 tablespoon of lemon juice
- 1 jalapeno pepper, chopped
- 3 tablespoon of hot pepper sauce
- Kosher salt as needed
- Black pepper as needed
- 2 cups of soaked wood chips

Directions:

1. Take a medium-sized bowl and add brown sugar, chili powder, 2 tablespoons of garlic powder, 2 teaspoons of onion powder, cumin, cinnamon, kosher salt, cayenne pepper, jalapeno seasoning

2. Mix well and rub the mixture over the pork spare ribs

3. Allow it to refrigerate for 4 hours

4. Take your drip pan and add water; cover with aluminum foil. Pre-heat your smoker to 225 degrees F

5. Use water fill water pan halfway through and place it over drip pan. Add wood chips to the side tray

6. Take a medium bowl and stir in apple cider, apple cider vinegar, 1 tablespoon of onion powder, jalapeno, 1 tablespoon of garlic powder, salt, pepper, and lemon juice

7. Add a handful of soaked wood chips and transfer the ribs to your smoker middle rack

8. Smoke for 3-4 hours, making sure to keep adding chips after every hour

9. Take the meat out and serve!

Nutrition: Calories: 1591 Fats: 120g Carbs: 44g Fiber: 3g

• Porky Onion Soup

Preparation Time: 2 hours

Cooking Time: 4 hours 30 minutes

Serving: 6

Ingredients:

- 1 full rack of pork spare ribs
- 2 packs onion soup mix of your choice
- BBQ Pork Rub
- 4 cups of water

Directions:

1. Remove the white membrane of the pork meat and trim off any excess fat

2. Take your drip pan and add water; cover with aluminum foil. Pre-heat your smoker to 225 degrees F

3. Use water fill water pan halfway through and place it over drip pan. Add wood chips to the side tray

4. Prepare your rub mixture by mixing salt, garlic powder, pepper, and paprika in a bowl

5. Rub the rib with the mixture

6. Transfer to the smoker and smoker for 2 hours

7. Blend 2 packs of onion soup with 4 cups of water

8. Once smoking is complete, take a heavy aluminum foil and transfer the meat to the foil, pour the soup mix all over

9. Seal the ribs

10. Smoke for another 1 and a ½ hours

11. Gently open the foil and turn the rib, seal it up and smoke for 1 hour more

12. Slice and serve!

Nutrition: Calories: 461 Fats: 22g Carbs: 17g Fiber: 4g

• Lovely Pork Butt

Preparation Time: 2 hours + 4 hours soak time

Cooking Time: 20 minutes

Servings: 18

Ingredients:

- 7 pounds' fresh pork butt roast
- 2 tablespoons ground Mexico Chile Powder
- 4 tablespoons brown sugar, packed

Directions:

1. Start by soaking up your Pork Butt in a finely prepared brine (salt) solution

for 4 hours at least and overnight at max

2. Make sure to cover the Butt up before placing it in your fridge

3. Take your drip pan and add water; cover with aluminum foil. Pre-heat your smoker to 225 degrees F

4. Use water fill water pan halfway through and place it over drip pan. Add wood chips to the side tray

5. Take a small-sized bowl and toss in the chili powder, brown sugar alongside any other seasoning which you may fancy

6. Rub the butt with your prepared mixture finely

7. Finely take a roasting rack and place it in a drip pan

8. Lay your butt on top of the rack

9. Smoke the butt for about 6-18 hours (Keep in mind that the pork will be done once the temperature of its internals reaches 100-degree Fahrenheit)

10. Serve hot

Nutrition: Calories: 326 Fats: 21g Carbs:4g Fiber: 0.5g

- ## **Strawberry and Jalapeno Smoked Ribs**

Preparation Time: 15 minutes

Cooking Time: 90 minutes

Serving: 8

Ingredients:

- 3 tablespoons of Kosher Salt
- 2 tablespoons of Ground Cumin
- 1 tablespoon of Dried Oregano
- 1 tablespoon of garlic, minced
- 2 teaspoons of chili powder
- 1 teaspoon of ground black pepper
- 1 teaspoon of celery seed
- 1 teaspoon of dried thyme
- 1 rack of spareribs
- 2 slabs of baby back pork ribs
- 1 cup of apple juice
- 2 jalapeno peppers. cut half in lengthwise and deseeded
- ½ a mug of beer
- ½ onion, chopped
- ¼ cup of sugar-free strawberry
- 3 tablespoon of BBQ sauce
- 1 tablespoon of olive oil
- 2 cloves of garlic
- Sea salt as needed
- Ground pepper as needed

Directions:

1. Take a bowl first and blend in your salt, oregano, cumin, minced garlic, 1 teaspoon of ground black pepper, chili powder, ground thyme, and celery seed ad toss them in a food processor

2. Place your baby back rib slabs and spare rib rack on sheets of aluminum foil and rub the spice mix all over their body

3. Fold up the foil around each of them

4. Divide and pour the apple juice amongst the foil packets and foil the edges together to seal them up

5. Let them marinate for about 8 hours or overnight

6. Prepare your oven rack and place it about 6 inches away from the heat source, and pre-heat your ove3n's broiler

7. Line up a baking sheet with the aluminum foil and place your jalapeno pepper on top of it, with the cut upsides down

8. Cook Jalapeno peppers for 8 minutes under the broiler until the skin is blackened

9. Toss them and seal it up using a plastic wrap

10. Let the peppers steam off for 20 minutes

11. Remove them and discard the skin

12. Blend the jalapeno peppers, onion, beer, strawberry preserve, olive oil, BBQ sauce, sea salt, and just a pinch of ground black pepper altogether in a blender until the sauce is fully smoothened out

13. Transfer the sauce to a container and let cover it up with a lid; let it chill for 8 hours or overnight

14. Take your drip pan and add water; cover with aluminum foil. Pre-heat your smoker to 225 degrees F

15. Use water fill water pan halfway through and place it over drip pan. Add wood chips to the side tray

16. Smoke for 60 minutes

17. Increase the temp to 225 degrees Fahrenheit or 110 degrees Celsius and keep cooking for another 2-3 hours

18. Preheat your smoker to a temperature of 250 degrees Fahrenheit or 120 degrees Celsius

19. Unwrap your cooked ribs and toss away the apple juice

20. Place them on top of your smoker

21. Cook on your smoker until the surface of your meat is finely dried up; it should take about 5-10 minutes

22. After which, continue cooking, making sure to brush it up with the sauce after every 15 minutes

23. Turn it around after 30 minutes

24. Repeat and cook for 1 hour

25. Serve hot when tender

Nutrition: Fats: 41.2g Carbs: 8.2g Fiber: 0.7g

Plum Flavored Glazed Pork Belly Kebabs

Preparation Time: 10-15 minutes
Cooking Time: 4 hours 30 minutes
Serving: 4
Ingredients:

- 1-pound pork belly
- ½ cup Asia plum sauce
- 2 teaspoons Asian chili paste
- 1 tablespoon soy sauce
- 2 garlic clove, minced
- Salt to taste
- Pepper to taste
- 8 skewers

Directions:

1. Cut pork belly into cubes of 1-inch thickness, thread onto skewers, and season with salt and pepper
2. Make plum glaze by taking a medium-sized bowl and adding Asian plum sauce, chili paste, soy sauce, garlic, and mix
3. Take your drip pan and add water; cover with aluminum foil. Pre-heat your smoker to 250 degrees F
4. Use water fill water pan halfway through and place it over drip pan. Add wood chips to the side tray
5. Place kebab threaded skewers on the grid and cook for 3-4 hours' minutes, making sure to turn occasionally
6. Make sure to baste for just 10 minutes before cooking completes; make sure not to burn it
7. Once turn, remove from grill and serve
8. Enjoy!

Nutrition: Calories: 135 Fat: 9g Carbohydrates: 5g Protein: 17g

Simple Wood Pellet Smoked Pork Ribs

Preparation Time: 15 Minutes
Cooking Time: 5 Hours
Servings: 7
Ingredients:

- Three rack baby back ribs
- 3/4 cup pork and poultry rub
- 3/4 cup Que BBQ Sauce

Directions:

1. Peel the membrane from the backside of the ribs and trim any fat.
2. Season the pork generously with the rub.
3. Set the wood pellet grill to 180°F and preheat for 15 minutes with the lid closed.
4. Place the pork ribs on the grill and smoke them for 5 hours.
5. Remove it from the grill and wrap them in a foil with the BBQ sauce.
6. Place back the pork and increase the temperature to 350°F—Cook for 45 more minutes.

7. Remove the pork from the grill and let it rest for 20 minutes before serving. Enjoy.

Nutrition: Calories 762 Total Fat 57g Saturated Fat 17g Total Carbs 23g Net Carbs 22.7g Protein 39g Sugar 18g Fiber 0.5g Sodium: 737mg Potassium 618mg

• Roasted Pork with Balsamic Strawberry Sauce

Preparation Time: 15 Minutes
Cooking Time: 35 Minutes
Servings: 3
Ingredients:

- 2 lb. pork tenderloin
- Salt and pepper to taste
- 2 tbsp. rosemary, dried
- 2 tbsp. olive oil
- 12 strawberries, fresh
- 1 cup balsamic vinegar
- 4 tbsp. sugar

Directions:

1. Set the wood pellet grill to 350°F and preheat for 15 minutes with a closed lid.
2. Meanwhile, rinse the pork and pat it dry—season with salt, pepper, and rosemary.
3. In an oven skillet, heat oil until smoking. Add the pork and sear on all sides until golden brown.
4. Set the skillet in the grill and cook for 20 minutes or until the meat is no longer pink and the internal temperature is 150°F.
5. Remove the pork from the grill and let rest for 10 minutes.
6. Add berries to the skillet and sear over the stovetop for a minute. Remove the strawberries from the skillet.
7. Add vinegar in the same skillet and scrape any browned bits from the skillet bottom. Bring it to boil, then reduce heat to low. Stir in sugar and cook until it has reduced by half.
8. Slice the meat and place the strawberries on top, then drizzle vinegar sauce. Enjoy.

Nutrition: Calories 244 Total Fat 9g Saturated Fat 3g Total Carbs 15g Net Carbs 13g Protein 25g Sugar 12g Fiber 2g Sodium: 159mg

• Wood Pellet Grill Pork Crown Roast

Preparation Time: 5 Minutes
Cooking Time: 60 Minutes
Servings: 5
Ingredients:

- 13 ribs pork
- 1/4 cup favorite rub
- 1 cup apple juice
- 1 cup Apricot BBQ sauce

Directions:

1. Set the wood pellet temperature to 375°F to preheat for 15 minutes with the lid closed.
2. Meanwhile, season the pork with the rub, then let sit for 30 minutes.
3. Wrap the tips of each crown roast with foil to prevent the burns from turning black.
4. Place the meat on the grill grate and cook for 90 minutes. Spray apple juice every 30 minutes.
5. When the meat has reached an internal temperature of 125°F, remove the foils.
6. Spray the roast with apple juice again and let cook until the internal temperature has reached 135°F.
7. In the latter 10 minutes of cooking, baste the roast with BBQ sauce.
8. Remove from the grill and wrap with foil. Let rest for 15 minutes before serving. Enjoy.

Nutrition: Calories 240 Total fat 16g Saturated fat 6g Protein 23g Sodium: 50mg

• **Wet-Rubbed St. Louis Ribs**

Preparation Time: 15 Minutes

Cooking Time: 4 Hours

Servings: 3

Ingredients:

- 1/2 cup brown sugar
- 1 tbsp. cumin, ground
- 1 tbsp. Ancho Chile powder
- 1 tbsp. smoked paprika

- 1 tbsp. garlic salt
- 3 tbsp. balsamic vinegar
- 1 Rack St. Louis style ribs
- 2 cup apple juice

Directions:

1. Add all the ingredients except ribs in a mixing bowl and mix until well mixed. Place the rub on both sides of the ribs and let sit for 10 minutes.
2. Set the wood pellet temperature to 180°F and preheat for 15 minutes. Smoke the ribs for 2 hours.
3. Increase the temperature to 250°F and wrap the ribs and apple juice with foil or tinfoil.
4. Place back the pork and cook for an additional 2 hours.
5. Remove from the grill and let rest for 5 minutes before serving. Enjoy.

Nutrition: Calories 210 Total fat 13g Saturated fat 4g Total Carbs 0g Net Carbs 0g Protein 24g Sodium: 85mg

• **Cocoa Crusted Pork Tenderloin**

Preparation Time: 30 Minutes

Cooking Time: 25 Minutes

Servings: 5

Ingredients:

- One pork tenderloin
- 1/2 tbsp. fennel, ground
- 2 tbsp. cocoa powder, unsweetened
- 1 tbsp. smoked paprika

- 1/2 tbsp. kosher salt
- 1/2 tbsp. black pepper
- 1 tbsp. extra virgin olive oil
- Three green onion

Directions:

1. Remove the silver skin and the connective tissues from the pork loin.
2. Combine the rest of the ingredients in a mixing bowl, then rub the mixture on the pork. Refrigerate for 30 minutes.
3. Preheat the wood pellet grill for 15 minutes with the lid closed.
4. Sear all sides of the loin at the front of the grill, then reduce the temperature to 350°F and move the pork to the center grill.
5. Cook for 15 more minutes or until the internal temperature is 145°F.
6. Remove from grill and let rest for 10 minutes before slicing. Enjoy

Nutrition: Calories 264 Total fat 13.1g Saturated fat 6g Total Carbs 4.6g Net Carbs 1.2g Protein 33g Sugar 0g Fiber 3.4g Sodium: 66mg

• **Wood Pellet Grilled Bacon**

Preparation Time: 30 Minutes

Cooking Time: 25 Minutes

Servings: 6

Ingredients:

- 1 lb. bacon, thickly cut

Directions:

1. Preheat your wood pellet grill to 375°F.
2. Line a baking sheet with parchment paper, then place the bacon on it in a single layer.
3. Close the lid and bake for 20 minutes. Flip over, close the top, and bake for an additional 5 minutes.
4. Serve with the favorite side and enjoy it.

Nutrition: Calories 315 Total fat 14g Saturated fat 10g Protein 9g Sodium: 500mg

• **Wood Pellet Grilled Pork Chops**

Preparation Time: 20 Minutes

Cooking Time: 10 Minutes

Servings: 6

Ingredients:

- Six pork chops, thickly cut
- BBQ rub

Directions:

1. Preheat the wood pellet to 450°F.
2. Season the pork chops generously with the BBQ rub. Place the pork chops on the grill and cook for 6 minutes or until the internal temperature reaches 145°F.
3. Remove from the grill and let sit for 10 minutes before serving.
4. Enjoy.

Nutrition: Calories 264 Total fat 13g Saturated fat 6g Total Carbs 4g Net Carbs 1g Protein 33g Fiber 3g Sodium: 66mg

Wood Pellet Blackened Pork Chops

Preparation Time: 5 Minutes

Cooking Time: 20 Minutes

Servings: 6

Ingredients:

- Six pork chops
- 1/4 cup blackening seasoning
- Salt and pepper to taste

Directions:

1. Preheat your grill to 375°F.
2. Meanwhile, generously season the pork chops with the blackening seasoning, salt, and pepper.
3. Place the pork chops on the grill and close the lid.
4. Let grill for 8 minutes, then flip the chops. Cook until the internal temperature reaches 142°F.
5. Remove the chops from the grill and let rest for 10 minutes before slicing.
6. Serve and enjoy.

Nutrition: Calories 333 Total fat 18g Saturated fat 6g Total Carbs 1g Protein 40g, Fiber 1g Sodium: 3175mg

Teriyaki Pineapple Pork Tenderloin Sliders

Preparation Time: 20 Minutes

Cooking Time: 20 Minutes

Servings: 6

Ingredients:

- 1-1/2 lb. pork tenderloin
- One can pineapple ring
- One package king's Hawaiian rolls
- 8 oz. teriyaki sauce
- 1-1/2 tbsp. salt
- 1 tbsp. onion powder
- 1 tbsp. paprika
- 1/2 tbsp. garlic powder
- 1/2 tbsp. cayenne pepper

Directions:

1. Add all the fixings for the rub in a mixing bowl and mix until well mixed. Generously rub the pork loin with the mixture.
2. Heat the pellet to 325°F. Place the meat on a grill and cook while you turn it every 4 minutes.
3. Cook until the internal temperature reaches 145°F. remove from the grill and let it rest for 5 minutes.
4. Meanwhile, open the pineapple can and place the pineapple rings on the grill. Flip the rings when they have a dark brown color.
5. At the same time, half the rolls and place them on the grill and grill them until toasty browned.
6. Assemble the slider by putting the bottom roll first, followed by the pork tenderloin, pineapple ring, a drizzle of sauce, and top with the other roll half. Serve and enjoy.

Nutrition: Calories 243 Total fat 5g Saturated fat 2g Total Carbs 4g Net Carbs

15g Protein 33g Sugar 10g, Fiber 1g Sodium: 2447mg

Wood Pellet Grilled Tenderloin with Fresh Herb Sauce

Preparation Time: 10 Minutes

Cooking Time: 15 Minutes

Servings: 4

Ingredients:

- One pork tenderloin, silver skin removed and dried
- BBQ seasoning
- One handful basil, fresh
- 1/4 tbsp. garlic powder
- 1/3 cup olive oil
- 1/2 tbsp. kosher salt

Directions:

1. Preheat the wood pellet grill to medium heat.
2. Coat the pork with BBQ seasoning, then cook on semi-direct heat of the grill. Turn the pork regularly to ensure even cooking.
3. Cook until the internal temperature is 145°F. Remove from the grill and let it rest for 10 minutes.
4. Meanwhile, make the herb sauce by pulsing all the sauce ingredients in a food processor—pulse for a few times or until well chopped.
5. Slice the pork diagonally and spoon the sauce on top. Serve and enjoy.

Nutrition: Calories 300 Total fat 22g Saturated fat 4g Total Carbs 13g Net Carbs 12g Protein 14g Sugar 10g Fiber 1g Sodium: 791mg

Wood Pellet Grilled Shredded Pork Tacos

Preparation Time: 15 Minutes

Cooking Time: 7 Hours

Servings: 8

Ingredients:

- 5 lb. pork shoulder, bone-in
- 3 tbsp. brown sugar
- 1 tbsp. salt
- 1 tbsp. garlic powder
- 1 tbsp. paprika
- 1 tbsp. onion powder
- 1/4 tbsp. cumin
- 1 tbsp. cayenne pepper

Directions:

1. Mix all the dry rub ingredients and rub on the pork shoulder.
2. Preheat the grill to 275°F and cook the pork directly for 6 hours or until the internal temperature has reached 145°F.
3. If you want to fall off the bone tender pork, then cook until the internal temperature is 190°F.
4. Let rest for 10 minutes before serving. Enjoy

Nutrition: Calories 566 Total fat 41g Saturated fat 15g Total Carbs 4g Net Carbs

4g Protein 44g Sugar 3g Fiber 0g Sodium: 659mg

Wood Pellet Togarashi Pork Tenderloin

Preparation Time: 5 Minutes

Cooking Time: 25 Minutes

Servings: 6

Ingredients:

- 1 Pork tenderloin
- 1/2tbsp kosher salt
- 1/4 cup Togarashi seasoning

Directions:

1. Cut any excess silver skin from the pork and sprinkle with salt to taste. Rub generously with the togarashi seasoning
2. Place in a preheated oven at 400°F for 25 minutes or until the internal temperature reaches 145°F.
3. Remove from the grill and let rest for 10 minutes before slicing and serving.
4. Enjoy.

Nutrition: Calories 390 Total fat 13g Saturated fat 6g Total Carbs 4g Net Carbs 1g Protein 33g Sugar 0g Fiber 3g Sodium: 66mg

Wood Pellet Pulled Pork

Preparation Time: 15 Minutes

Cooking Time: 12 Hours

Servings: 12

Ingredients:

- 8 lb. pork shoulder roast, bone-in
- BBQ rub
- 3 cups apple cider, dry hard

Directions:

1. Fire up the wood pellet grill and set it to smoke.
2. Meanwhile, rub the pork with BBQ rub on all sides, then place it on the grill grates. Cook for 5 hours, flipping it every 1 hour.
3. Increase the heat to 225°F and continue cooking for 3 hours directly on the grate.
4. Transfer the pork to a foil pan and place the apple cider at the bottom of the pan.
5. Cook until the internal temperature reaches 200°F then remove it from the grill. Wrap the pork loosely with foil, then let it rest for 1 hour.
6. Remove the fat layer and use forks to shred it.
7. Serve and enjoy.

Nutrition: Calories 912 Total fat 65g Saturated fat 24g Total Carbs 7g Net Carbs 7g Protein 70g Sugar 6g Fiber 0g Sodium: 208mg

Lovable Pork Belly

Preparation Time: 15 Minutes

Cooking Time: 4 Hours and 30 Minutes

Servings: 4

Ingredients:

- 5 pounds of pork belly
- 1 cup dry rub

- Three tablespoons olive oil

For Sauce

- Two tablespoons honey
- Three tablespoons butter
- 1 cup BBQ sauce

Directions:

1. Take your drip pan and add water. Cover with aluminum foil.
2. Pre-heat your smoker to 250 degrees F
3. Add pork cubes, dry rub, olive oil into a bowl and mix well
4. Use water fill water pan halfway through and place it over drip pan.
5. Add wood chips to the side tray
6. Transfer pork cubes to your smoker and smoke for 3 hours (covered)
7. Remove pork cubes from the smoker and transfer to foil pan, add honey, butter, BBQ sauce, and stir
8. Cover the pan with foil and move back to a smoker, smoke for 90 minutes more
9. Remove foil and smoke for 15 minutes more until the sauce thickens
10. Serve and enjoy!

Nutrition: Calories: 1164 Fat: 68g Carbohydrates: 12g Protein: 104g

• **County Ribs**

Preparation Time: 15 Minutes

Cooking Time: 3 Hours

Servings: 4

Ingredients:

- 4 pounds country-style ribs
- Pork rub to taste
- 2 cups apple juice
- ½ stick butter, melted
- 18 ounces BBQ sauce

Directions:

1. Take your drip pan and add water. Cover with aluminum foil.
2. Pre-heat your smoker to 275 degrees F
3. Season country style ribs from all sides
4. Use water fill water pan halfway through and place it over drip pan.
5. Add wood chips to the side tray.
6. Transfer the ribs to your smoker and smoke for 1 hour and 15 minutes until the internal temperature reaches 160 degrees F
7. Take foil pan and mix melted butter, apple juice, 15 ounces BBQ sauce and put ribs back in the pan, cover with foil
8. Transfer back to smoker and smoke for 1 hour 15 minutes more until the internal temperature reaches 195 degrees F
9. Take ribs out from liquid and place them on racks, glaze ribs with more BBQ sauce, and smoke for 10 minutes more
10. Take them out and let them rest for 10 minutes, serve and enjoy!

Nutrition: Calories: 251 Fat: 25g Carbohydrates: 35g Protein: 76g

• <u>Wow-Pork Tenderloin</u>

Preparation Time: 15 Minutes

Cooking Time: 3 Hours

Servings: 4

Ingredients:

- One pork tenderloin
- ¼ cup BBQ sauce
- Three tablespoons dry rub

Directions:

1. Take your drip pan and add water. Cover with aluminum foil.
2. Pre-heat your smoker to 225 degrees F
3. Rub the spice blend all finished the pork tenderloin
4. Use water fill water pan halfway through and place it over drip pan.
5. Add wood chips to the side tray
6. Transfer pork meat to your smoker and smoke for 3 hours until the internal temperature reaches 145 degrees F
7. Brush the BBQ sauce over pork and let it rest
8. Serve and enjoy!

Nutrition: Calories: 405 Fat: 9g Carbohydrates: 15g Protein: 59g

• <u>Awesome Pork Shoulder</u>

Preparation Time: 15 Minutes + 24 Hours

Cooking Time: 12 Hours

Servings: 4

Ingredients:

- 8 pounds of pork shoulder

For Rub

- One teaspoon dry mustard
- One teaspoon black pepper
- One teaspoon cumin
- One teaspoon oregano
- One teaspoon cayenne pepper
- 1/3 cup salt
- ¼ cup garlic powder
- ½ cup paprika
- 1/3 cup brown sugar
- 2/3 cup sugar

Directions:

1. Bring your pork under salted water for 18 hours
2. Pull the pork out from the brine and let it sit for 1 hour
3. Rub mustard all over the pork
4. Take a bowl and mix all rub ingredients. Rub mixture all over the meat
5. Wrap meat and leave it overnight
6. Take your drip pan and add water. Cover with aluminum foil. Pre-heat your smoker to 250 degrees F
7. Use water fill water pan halfway through and place it over drip pan. Add wood chips to the side tray.
8. Transfer meat to smoker and smoke for 6 hours

9. Take the pork out and wrap in foil, smoke for 6 hours more at 195 degrees F
10. Shred and serve
11. Enjoy!

Nutrition: Calories: 965 Fat: 65g Carbohydrates: 19g Protein: 71g

• Herbed Prime Rib

Preparation Time: 15 Minutes
Cooking Time: 4 Hours
Servings: 4
Ingredients:

- 5 pounds prime rib
- Two tablespoons black pepper
- ¼ cup olive oil
- Two tablespoons salt

Herb Paste

- ¼ cup olive oil
- One tablespoon fresh sage
- One tablespoon fresh thyme
- One tablespoon fresh rosemary
- Three garlic cloves

Directions:

1. Take a blender and add herbs, blend until thoroughly combined
2. Take your drip pan and add water. Cover with aluminum foil.
3. Pre-heat your smoker to 225 degrees F
4. Use water fill water pan halfway through and place it over drip pan.
5. Add wood chips to the side tray

6. Coat rib with olive oil and season it well with salt and pepper
7. Transfer seasoned rib to your smoker and smoke for 4 hours
8. Remove rib from the smoker and keep it on the side. Let it cool for 30 minutes
9. Cut into slices and serve
10. Enjoy!

Nutrition: Calories: 936 Fat: 81g Carbohydrates: 2g Protein: 46g

• Premium Sausage Hash

Preparation Time: 30 Minutes
Cooking Time: 45 Minutes
Servings: 4
Ingredients:

- Nonstick cooking spray
- Two finely minced garlic cloves
- One teaspoon basil, dried
- One teaspoon oregano, dried
- One teaspoon onion powder
- One teaspoon of salt
- 4-6 cooked smoker Italian Sausage (Sliced)
- One large-sized bell pepper, diced
- One large onion, diced
- Three potatoes, cut into 1-inch cubes
- Three tablespoons of olive oil
- French bread for serving

Directions:

1. Pre-heat your smoker to 225 degrees Fahrenheit using your desired wood chips
2. Cover the smoker grill rack with foil and coat with cooking spray
3. Take a small bowl and add garlic, oregano, basil, onion powder, and season the mix with salt and pepper
4. Take a large bowl and add sausage slices, bell pepper, potatoes, onion, olive oil, and spice mix
5. Mix well and spread the mixture on your foil-covered rack
6. Place the rack in your smoker and smoke for 45 minutes
7. Serve with your French bread
8. Enjoy!

Nutrition: Calories: 193 Fats: 10g Carbs: 15g Fiber: 2g

• **Explosive Smoky Bacon**

Preparation Time: 20 Minutes

Cooking Time: 2 Hours and 10 Minutes

Servings: 10

Ingredients:

- 1 pound thick-cut bacon
- One tablespoon BBQ spice rub
- 2 pounds bulk pork sausage
- 1 cup cheddar cheese, shredded
- Four garlic cloves, minced
- 18 ounces BBQ sauce

Directions:

1. Take your drip pan and add water; cover with aluminum foil.
2. Pre-heat your smoker to 225 degrees F
3. Use water fill water pan halfway through and place it over drip pan.
4. Add wood chips to the side tray
5. Reserve about ½ a pound of your bacon for cooking later on
6. Lay 2 strips of your remaining bacon on a clean surface in an X formation
7. Alternate the horizontal and vertical bacon strips by waving them tightly in an over and under to create a lattice-like pattern
8. Sprinkle one teaspoon of BBQ rub over the woven bacon
9. Arrange ½ a pound of your bacon in a large-sized skillet and cook them for 10 minutes over medium-high heat
10. Drain the cooked slices on a kitchen towel and crumble them
11. Place your sausages in a large-sized re-sealable bag
12. While the sausages are still in the bag, roll them out to a square that has the same sized as the woven bacon
13. Cut off the bag from the sausage and arrange them sausage over the woven bacon
14. Toss away the bag
15. Sprinkle some crumbled bacon, green onions, cheddar cheese, and garlic over the rolled sausages

16. Pour about ¾ bottle of your BBQ sauce over the sausage and season with some more BBQ rub
17. Roll up the woven bacon tightly all around the sausage, forming a loaf
18. Cook the bacon-sausage loaf in your smoker for about one and a ½ hour
19. Brush up the woven bacon with remaining BBQ sauce and keep smoking for about 30 minutes until the center of the loaf is no longer pink
20. Use an instant thermometer to check if the internal temperature is at least 165 degrees Fahrenheit
21. If yes, then take it out and let it rest for 30 minutes
22. Slice and serve!

Nutrition: Calories: 507 Fats: 36g Carbs: 20g Fiber: 2g

• Pellet Grill Meatloaf

Preparation Time: 30 minutes

Cooking Time: 6 Hours

Servings: 8

Ingredients:

- 1 cup breadcrumbs
- 2 pounds ground beef
- ¼ pound ground sausage
- 2 large eggs (beaten)
- 2 garlic cloves (grated)
- ½ teaspoon ground black pepper
- ¼ teaspoon red pepper flakes
- ½ teaspoon salt or to taste
- 1 teaspoon dried parsley
- 1 green onion (chopped)
- 1 teaspoon paprika
- ½ teaspoon Italian seasoning
- 1 small onion (chopped)
- 1 cup milk
- 1 cup BBQ sauce
- ½ cup apple juice

Directions:

1. Preheat the grill to 225°F with the lid closed for 15 minutes, using apple pellet
2. In a large mixing bowl, combine the egg, milk, parsley, onion, green onion, paprika, Italian seasoning, breadcrumbs, ground beef, ground sausage, salt, pepper flakes, black pepper, and garlic. Mix thoroughly until the ingredients are well combined.
3. Form the mixture into a loaf, wrap the loaf loosely in tin foil and use a knife to poke some holes in the foil. The holes will allow the smoke flavor to enter the loaf.
4. Place the wrapped loaf on the grill grate and grill for 1 hour 30 minutes.
5. Meanwhile, combine the BBQ sauce and apple juice in a mixing bowl.
6. Tear off the top half of the tin foil to apply the glaze. Apply the glaze over the meatloaf. Continue grilling until the internal temperature of the meatloaf is 160°F.
7. Remove the meatloaf from the grill and let it sit for a few minutes to cool.
8. Cut and serve.

Nutrition: Carbohydrates: 22 g Protein: 28 g Fat: 6 g Sodium: 1213 mg Cholesterol: 81 mg

• **BBQ Brisket**

Preparation Time: 30 minutes

Cooking Time: 6 Hours

Servings: 8

Ingredients:

- 1 (12-14) packer beef brisket
- 1 teaspoon cayenne pepper
- 1 teaspoon cumin
- 2 tablespoons paprika
- 1 tablespoon smoked paprika
- 1 tablespoon onion powder
- 1 /2 tablespoon maple sugar
- 2 teaspoons ground black pepper
- 2 teaspoons kosher salt

Directions:

1. Combine all the ingredients except the brisket in a mixing bowl.
2. Season all sides of the brisket with the seasoning mixture as needed and wrap it in a plastic wrap. Refrigerate for 12 hours or more.
3. Unwrap the brisket and let it sit for about 2 hours or until the brisket is at room temperature.
4. Preheat the pellet grill to 225°F with lid close, using mesquite or oak wood pellet.
5. Place the brisket on the grill grate and grill for about 6 hours. Remove the brisket from the grill and wrap with foil.
6. Return brisket to the grill and cook for about 4 hours or until the brisket's temperature reaches 204°F.
7. Remove the brisket from the grill and let it sit for about 40 minutes to cool.
8. Unwrap the brisket and cut it into slices.

Nutrition: Carbohydrates: 22 g Protein: 28 g Fat: 6 g Sodium: 1213 mg Cholesterol: 81 mg

• **Tri-tip Roast**

Preparation Time: 30 minutes

Cooking Time: 50 minutes

Servings: 8

Ingredients:

- 2 pounds tri-tip roast (silver skin and the fat cap removed)
- 1 teaspoon salt
- 1 teaspoon ground black pepper

- ½ teaspoon paprika
- 1 teaspoon fresh rosemary
- 1 teaspoon garlic powder
- 1 tablespoon olive oil

Directions:

1. Combine salt, pepper, garlic, paprika, and rosemary.
2. Brush the tri-tip generously with olive oil. Season the roast with seasoning mixture generously.
3. Preheat the grill smoker 225°F with the lid closed for 15 minutes, using hickory, mesquite, or oak wood pellet.
4. Place the tri-tip roast on the grill grate directly and cook for about 1 hour or until the tri tip's temperature reaches 135°F.
5. Remove the tri-tip from the grill and wrap it with heavy-duty foil. Set aside in a cooler.
6. Adjust the grill temperature to high and preheat with lid closed for 15 minutes.
7. Remove the tri-tip from the foil, place it on the grill, cook for 8 minutes, and turn the tri-tip after the first 4 minutes.
8. Remove the tri-tip from the grill and let it rest for a few minutes to cool.
9. Cut them into slices against the grain and serve.

Nutrition: Carbohydrates: 22 g Protein: 28 g Fat: 6 g Sodium: 13 mg Cholesterol: 81 mg

- **Baby Back Rib**

Preparation Time: 30 minutes
Cooking Time: 5 hours
Servings: 8
Ingredients:

- ½ cup BBQ sauce
- 1 rack baby back ribs
- 1 cup apple cider
- 1 tablespoon Worcestershire sauce
- 1 teaspoon paprika
- ½ cup packed dark brown sugar
- 2 tablespoons yellow mustard
- 2 tablespoon honey
- 2 tablespoon BBQ rub

Directions:

1. Remove the membrane on the back of the rib with a butter knife.
2. Combine the mustard, paprika, ½ cup apple cider, and Worcestershire sauce.
3. Rub the mixture over the rib and season the rib with BBQ rub.
4. Start your grill on the smoke setting and leave the lid opened until the fire starts.

5. Close the lid and preheat the grill to 180°F using a hickory wood pellet.

6. Place the rib on the grill, smoke side up --smoke for 3 hours.

7. Remove the ribs from the grill.

8. Tear off two large pieces of heavy-duty aluminum foil and place one on a large working surface. Place the rib on the foil, rib side up.

9. Sprinkle the sugar over the rib. Top it with honey and the remaining apple cider.

10. Place the other piece of foil over the rib and crimp the aluminum foil pieces' edges together to form an airtight seal.

11. Place the sealed rib on the grill and cook for 2 hours.

12. After the cooking cycle, gently remove the foil from the rib and discard it.

13. Brush all sides of the baby back rib with the BBQ sauce.

14. Return the rib to the grill grate directly and cook for an additional 30 minutes or until the sauce coating is firm and thick.

15. Remove the rib from the grill and let it cool for a few minutes.

16. Cut into sizes and serve.

Nutrition: Carbohydrates: 22 g Protein: 28 g Fat: 6 g Sodium: 13 mg Cholesterol: 81 mg

• **Delicious Soy Marinated Steak**

Preparation Time: 20 minutes

Cooking Time: 55 minutes

Servings: 4

Ingredients:

- 1/2 chopped onion
- 3 chopped cloves of garlic
- 1/4 cup of olive oil
- 1/4 cup of balsamic vinegar
- 1/4 cup of soy sauce
- 1 tablespoon of Dijon mustard
- 1 tablespoon of rosemary
- 1 teaspoon of salt to taste
- 1/2 teaspoon of ground black pepper to taste
- 1 1/2 pounds of flank steak

Directions:

1. Using a large mixing bowl, add all the ingredients on the list aside from the steak, then mix properly to combine.

2. Place the steak in a Ziploc bag, pour in the prepared marinade then shake properly to coat.

3. Place the bag in the refrigerator and let the steak marinate for about thirty minutes to two full days.

4. Preheat the Wood Pellet Smoker and Grill to 350-400°F, remove the steak from its marinade, then set the marinade aside for blasting.

5. Place the steak on the preheated grill, then grill for about six to eight minutes until the beef is heated through.

6. Flip the steak over and cook for an additional six minutes until an inserted thermometer reads 150°F.

7. Place the steak on a cutting board and let rest for about five minutes. Slice and serve.

Nutrition: Calories: 300 Fat: 20g Carbs: 8g Protein: 22g

• **Grilled Steak and Vegetable Kebabs**

Preparation Time: 15 minutes

Cooking Time: 20 minutes

Servings: 5

Ingredients:

Marinade

- 1/4 cup of olive oil
- 1/4 cup of soy sauce
- 1 1/2 tablespoons of fresh lemon juice
- 1 1/2 tablespoons of red wine vinegar
- 2 1/2 tablespoons of Worcestershire sauce
- 1 tablespoon of honey
- 2 teaspoons of Dijon mustard
- 1 tablespoon of garlic
- 1 teaspoon of freshly ground black pepper to taste

Kebabs

- 1 3/4 lbs. of sirloin steak
- 1 sliced zucchini.
- 3 sliced bell peppers
- 1 large and sliced red onion
- 1 tablespoon of olive oil
- Salt and freshly ground black pepper to taste
- 1/2 teaspoon of garlic powder

Directions:

1. Using a large mixing bowl, add in the oil, soy sauce, lemon juice, red wine vinegar, Worcestershire sauce, Dijon, honey, garlic, and pepper to taste, then mix properly to combine.

2. Use a sharp knife, cut the steak into smaller pieces or cubes, and then add to a resealable bag.

3. Pour the marinade into the bag with steak, then shake to coat. Let the steak marinate for about three to six hours in the refrigerator.

4. Preheat the Wood Pellet Smoker and Grill to 425°F, place the veggies into a mixing bowl, add in oil, garlic powder, salt, and pepper to taste, then mix to combine.

5. Thread the veggies and steak alternately unto skewers, place the skewers on the preheated grill, and grill for about eight to nine minutes until it is cooked through.

6. Make sure you turn the kebabs occasionally as you cook. Serve.

Nutrition: Calories: 350 Fat: 14g Carbs: 18g Protein: 34g

• **Garlic Butter Grilled Steak**

Preparation Time: 15 minutes

Cooking Time: 25 minutes

Servings: 4

Ingredients:

- 3 tablespoons of unsalted butter
- 4 cloves of garlic
- 1 tablespoon of chopped parsley
- 1 tablespoon of olive oil
- 4 strip steaks
- Salt and pepper to taste

Directions:

1. Using a large mixing bowl, add in the butter, garlic, and parsley, then mix properly to combine, set aside in the refrigerator.

2. Preheat a Wood Pellet Smoker and Grill to 400° F, use paper towels to pat the steak dry, rub oil on all sides, then season with some sprinkles of salt and pepper to taste.

3. Place the seasoned steak on the preheated grill and grill for about four to five minutes.

4. Flip the steak over and grill for an additional four to five minutes until it becomes brown and cooked as desired.

5. Rub the steak with the butter mixture, heat on the grill for a few minutes, slice and serve.

Nutrition: Calories: 543 Fat: 25g Carbs: 1g Protein: 64g

• <u>Grilled Coffee Rub Brisket</u>

Preparation Time: 30 minutes

Cooking Time: 15 hours

Servings: 4

Ingredients:

- 1 (14 pounds) whole brisket
- Coffee Rub
- 2 tablespoons of coarse salt to taste
- 2 tablespoons of instant coffee
- 2 tablespoons of garlic powder
- 2 tablespoons of smoked paprika
- 1 tablespoon of pepper to taste
- 1 tablespoon of crushed coriander
- 1 tablespoon of onion powder
- 1 teaspoon of chili powder
- 1/2 teaspoon of cayenne

Directions:

1. Using a large mixing bowl, add in the instant coffee, garlic powder, paprika, coriander, onion powder, chili powder, cayenne, salt, and pepper to taste then mix properly to combine.
2. Rub the brisket with the prepared rub, coating all sides then set aside.
3. Preheat a Wood Pellet Smoker and Grill to 225°F, add in the seasoned brisket, cover the smoker, and smoke for about eight hours until a thermometer reads 165°For the briskets.
4. Place the brisket in an aluminum foil then wrap up. Place the foil-wrapped brisket on the wood Pellet smoker and cook for another five to eight hours until the meat reaches an internal temperature of 225°F.
5. Once cooked, let the brisket rest on the cutting board for about one hour, slice against the grain then serve.

Nutrition: Calories: 420 Fat: 11g Cholesterol: 100mg Carbs: 15g

• <u>Grilled Herb Steak</u>

Preparation Time: 15 minutes

Cooking Time: 20 minutes

Servings: 4

Ingredients:

- 1 tablespoon of peppercorns
- 1 teaspoon of fennel seeds
- 3 large and minced cloves of garlic
- 2 teaspoons of kosher salt to taste
- 1 tablespoon of chopped rosemary
- 1 tablespoon of chopped thyme
- 2 teaspoons of black pepper to taste
- 2 teaspoons of olive oil
- 1 pound of flank steak

Directions:

1. Using a grinder or a food processor, add in the peppercorns and the fennel seeds then blend until completely crushed then add to a mixing bowl.

2. Add in the garlic, rosemary, thyme, salt, and pepper to taste then mix properly to combine, set aside.

3. Rub the steak with oil, coating all sides then coat with half of the peppercorn mixture. Make sure the steak is coated all round.

4. Place the steak in a Ziploc plastic bag then let marinate in the refrigerator for about 2 to 8 minutes.

5. Preheat a Wood Pellet Smoker and Grill to 450°F, place the coated steak on the grill and cook for about five to six minutes.

6. Flip the steak over and cook for another five to six minutes until cooked through.

7. Once cooked, let the steak cool for a few minutes, slice, and serve.

Nutrition: Calories: 440 Fat: 25g Cholesterol: 90mg Carbs: 20g Protein: 35g

- ## Cocoa Rub Steak

Preparation Time: 20 minutes

Cooking Time: 40 minutes

Servings: 4

Ingredients:

- 4 ribeye steaks
- 2 tablespoons of unsweetened cocoa powder
- 1 tablespoon of dark brown sugar
- 1 tablespoon of smoked paprika
- 1 teaspoon of sea salt to taste
- 1 teaspoon of black pepper
- 1/2 teaspoon of garlic powder
- 1/2 teaspoon of onion powder

Directions:

1. Using a large mixing bowl, add in the cocoa powder, brown sugar, paprika, garlic powder, onion powder, and salt to taste, then mix properly to combine

2. Rub the steak with about two tablespoons of the spice mixture, coating all sides, then let rest for a few minutes.

3. Preheat the Wood Pellet Smoker and Grill to 450°F, place the steak on the grill, and grill for a few minutes on both sides until it is cooked as desired.

4. Once cooked, cover the steak in foil and let rest for a few minutes serve and enjoy.

Nutrition: Calories: 480 Fat: 30g Carbs: 4g Protein: 40g

• **Grilled Steak with Mushroom Cream Sauce**

Preparation Time: 25 minutes

Cooking Time: 1 hour and 30 minutes

Servings: 6

Ingredients:

- 1/2 cup of Dijon mustard
- 2 minced cloves of garlic
- 2 tablespoons of bourbon
- 1 tablespoon of Worcestershire sauce
- 4 beefsteak tenderloin
- 1 tablespoon of peppercorns
- Others
- 1 tablespoon of extra-virgin olive oil
- 1 small and diced onion
- 1 minced clove of garlic
- 1/2 cup of white wine
- 1/2 cup of chicken stock
- 16 ounces of sliced mushrooms
- 1/2 cup of heavy cream
- Salt and pepper to taste

Directions:

1. Using a small mixing bowl, add in the mustard, garlic, bourbon, and Worcestershire sauce,, then mix properly to combine

2. Place the steak in a Ziploc back, pour in the mustard mixture, then shake properly to coat. Let the steak sit for about sixty minutes.

3. Using a small mixing bowl, add in the peppercorns, salt, and pepper to taste, then mix to combine.

4. Remove the steak from the Ziploc bag, season the steak with the peppercorn mixture, and, and then use clean handstribute the seasoning.

5. Preheat the Wood Pellet Smoker and grill to 180°F, then close the lid for fifteen minutes.

6. Add the seasoned steak to the grill and smoke for about sixty minutes. Take the steak out of the grill, increase the temperature of the grill to 350 degrees, and grill for 20 to 30 minutes until it attains an internal temperature of 130°F.

7. To make the sauce, place a pan on the griddle, add oil and onions, and then cook for a few minutes.

8. Cook the garlic for one minute. Add in the mushrooms and cook for a few more minutes.

9. Add in the stock, wine, salt, and pepper to taste, stir to combine, then bring to a simmer. Simmer the sauce for 5 to 7 minutes, then add in the heavy cream.

10. Stir to combine, then serve the steak with the sauce, enjoy.

Nutrition: Calories: 470 Fat: 25g Carbs: 10g Protein: 50g

• Beef Tenderloin

Preparation Time: 10 minutes

Cooking Time: 1 hour 20 minutes

Servings: 12

Ingredients:

- 1 (5-pound) beef tenderloin, trimmed
- Kosher salt, as required
- ¼ cup olive oil
- Freshly ground black pepper, as required

Directions:

1. With kitchen strings, tie the tenderloin at 7-8 places.

2. Season tenderloin with kosher salt generously.

3. With a plastic wrap, cover the tenderloin and keep aside at room temperature for about 1 hour.

4. Preheat the Z Grills Wood Pellet Grill & Smoker on grill setting to 225-250°F.

5. Coat tenderloin with oil evenly and season with black pepper.

6. Arrange tenderloin onto the grill and cook for about 55-65 minutes.

7. Place cooking grate directly over hot coals and sear tenderloin for about 2 minutes per side.

8. Remove the tenderloin from the grill and place onto a cutting board for about 10-15 minutes before serving.

9. With a sharp knife, cut the tenderloin into desired-sized slices and serve.

Nutrition: Calories: 425 Fat: 21g Cholesterol: 170mg Protein: 55g

• Mustard Beef Short Ribs

Preparation Time: 15 minutes

Cooking Time: 3 hours

Servings: 6

Ingredients:

For Mustard Sauce:

- 1 cup prepared yellow mustard
- 1/4 cup red wine vinegar
- 1/4 cup dill pickle juice
- 2 tablespoons soy sauce
- 2 tablespoons Worcestershire sauce
- 1 teaspoon ground ginger
- 1 teaspoon granulated garlic

For Spice Rub:

- 2 tablespoons salt
- 2 tablespoons freshly ground black pepper
- 1 tablespoon white cane sugar
- 1 tablespoon granulated garlic

For Ribs:

- 6 (14-ounce) (4-5-inch long) beef short ribs

Directions:

1. Preheat the Z Grills Wood Pellet Grill & Smoker on smoke setting to 230-250°F, using charcoal.
2. In a bowl, mix all ingredients.
3. Coat the ribs with sauce generously and then sprinkle with spice rub evenly.
4. Place the ribs onto the grill over indirect heat, bone side down. Cook for about 1-1½ hours.
5. Flip the side and cook for about 45 minutes. Repeat.
6. Remove the ribs from the grill and place onto a cutting board for about 10 minutes before serving.
7. With a sharp knife, cut the ribs into equal-sized individual pieces and serve.

Nutrition: Calories: 867 Fat: 37g Cholesterol: 361 mg Carbs: 7 g Protein: 117g

- ## **Mesmerizing Beef Jerky**

Preparation Time: 15 minutes

Cooking Time: 12 hours 15 minutes

Servings: 12

Ingredients:

- 2 cups of teriyaki sauce
- 1 cup of soy sauce
- 1 cup of brown sugar
- 1 dash of Worcestershire sauce
- ¼ pound fresh pineapple, peeled and sliced
- 2 cloves of garlic
- 2 pound of ground beef cut up into ½ inch thick strips

Directions:

1. Take a large-sized bowl and add teriyaki sauce, brown sugar, soy sauce, and Worcestershire sauce
2. Add garlic and pineapple to a food processor and process until smooth
3. Pour the pineapple mixture into the sauce mix and stir; transfer the whole mix to a resealable bag. Transfer the beef to the bag as well and coat it

thoroughly, squeeze out as much air as possible, and zip the bag

4. Store in your fridge and allow it to marinate for 6-8 hours
5. Take your drip pan and add water; cover with aluminum foil. Preheat your Smoker to 225 degrees F
6. Use water fill water pan halfway through and place it over drip pan. Add wood chips to the side tray
7. Drain the beet from the marinade and transfer to your Smoker
8. Smoke for 6-8 hours until the jerky is chewy but not crispy. Serve and enjoy!

Nutrition: Calories: 207 Fats: 4.3g Carbs: 28g Fiber: 0.4g

• **Original Beef Meatballs**

Preparation Time: 30 minutes

Cooking Time: 2 hours

Servings: 10

Ingredients:

- 1 pound of ground beef
- ½ a pound of ground bacon
- 1 pound of pork
- 3 ounce of asiago cheese, grated
- ½ of red bell pepper, chopped
- ¼ of a large yellow onion, chopped
- 3 garlic cloves
- 1/3 cup of breadcrumbs
- 2 whole eggs
- 1/2 a cup of rub

- BBQ Sauce of your favorite brand
- For rub
- 2 teaspoons of salt
- 1 teaspoon of basil
- 1 teaspoon of sage
- 1 teaspoon of oregano
- ½ a teaspoon of thyme
- 1 and a ½ teaspoon of garlic powder
- 1 teaspoon of dill
- 1 teaspoon of marjoram
- 1 teaspoon of cornstarch
- 1 teaspoon of pepper
- 1 teaspoon of dried parsley flakes
- 1 teaspoon of rosemary
- ½ a teaspoon of ground cinnamon
- ½ a teaspoon of ground nutmeg

Directions:

1. For making the rub, add all of the listed (rub) ingredients into a blender and blend them well to a fine powder
2. Clear up your blender and add your roughly chopped onion, bell pepper, and garlic to your food processor
3. Pulse it well until it is nicely pureed
4. Add all of the ingredients into a bowl of a stand mixer
5. Using a paddle attachment, mix everything for about 1 minute at medium settings
6. Once the mixture is nicely tacky, it is ready

7. Take your drip pan and add water; cover with aluminum foil. Preheat your Smoker to 225 degrees F
8. Use water fill water pan halfway through and place it over drip pan. Add wood chips to the side tray
9. Using the meat mixture, form them into as many balls as possible
10. Use Frogrmats if possible and place them on top of the grate
11. Place your meatballs and smoke them for about 1 or 1 and a half hour until the internal temperature reaches 165 degrees Fahrenheit. Once done, transfer them to a pan and toss them in the BBQ sauce
12. Serve!

Nutrition: Calories: 139 Fats: 12g Carbs: 5g Fiber: 0g

• <u>Smoked Up Bulgogi</u>

Preparation Time: 15 minutes
Cooking Time: 16 hours + 30 minutes
Serving: 8-10
Ingredients:

- 5 pound of Chuck Roast
- Everyday yellow mustard
- Foil pan

For Rub

- 1 tablespoon of salt
- 2 teaspoons of black pepper
- 1 teaspoon of cayenne pepper
- 1 teaspoon of oregano
- ½ a teaspoon of chili powder

- 2 teaspoons of garlic powder

For Bulgogi

- 2 pound (or more) of shaved chuck roast beef
- 4 cloves of garlic
- 1 inch of ginger
- 1 teaspoon of chili flakes
- 3 tablespoon of Korean hot sauce
- 4 tablespoon of red wine vinegar
- 6 tablespoon of soy sauce
- 6 tablespoon of sesame oil

Vegetables

- 1 green pepper
- 1 medium-sized onion
- 2 carrots
- Oil as needed

Directions:

1. Rinse meat thoroughly under cold water
2. Apply a nice coating of yellow mustard over the meat
3. Take a small bowl and mix all the ingredients listed under the rub
4. Sprinkle/massage the rub all over the sides of your meat
5. Take your drip pan and add water; cover with aluminum foil. Preheat your Smoker to 235 degrees F
6. Use water fill water pan halfway through and place it over drip pan. Add wood chips to the side tray
7. Gently place your meat onto the smoker grate

8. Smoke them for about 8-12 hours until the thickest part of the beef gives an internal temperature of 195 degrees Fahrenheit

9. Once the temperature is reached, wrap it up and let it rest for about 1 hour

10. It is now ready to be used for the Bulgogi

11. Slice up about 2-3 pound of meat off your chuck roast

12. Take a food processor and add garlic and ginger; process them until a fine paste forms

13. Take a bowl and add pepper flakes, garlic/ginger paste, brown sugar, Korean hot sauce, rice wine vinegar, sesame oil, and soy sauce

14. Mix them well to prepare the marinade

15. Take a hot pan and add the beef slices alongside the marinade and simmer them until fully cooked

16. Take another pan and add butter

17. Add the vegetables and stir fry them to brown them

18. If you are serving in a burger bun, then take your bread and place a layer of cheese

19. Add the meat followed by the vegetables, according to your preference

20. Let it rest for about 2 minutes and serve!

Nutrition: Calories: 948 Fats: 54g Carbs: 41g Fiber: 6g

• __Creative Osso Buco__

Preparation Time: 15 minutes

Cooking Time: 7 hours

Servings: 4

Ingredients:

- 2 large-sized beef shanks
- Kosher salt as needed
- Pepper as needed
- Garlic powder as needed
- Onion powder as needed
- Ground thyme as needed
- 1 tablespoon of vegetable oil
- ½ a cup onion, chopped
- 2 celery stalks, chopped
- 2 carrots, peeled and chopped
- 3 garlic cloves, minced
- 1 cup of dry red wine
- 1 cup of beef broth
- 1/3 cup Kalamata olives, chopped
- 2 cups tomato, chopped
- 1 – 6 ounce can of tomato paste
- 1 teaspoon of kosher salt

- 1 teaspoon of course ground black pepper
- 1 bay leaf

Directions:

1. Take your drip pan and add water; cover with aluminum foil. Preheat your Smoker to 275 degrees F
2. Use water fill water pan halfway through and place it over drip pan. Add wood chips to the side tray
3. Season your beef shanks properly by rubbing them with salt, garlic powder, onion powder, and thyme on both sides
4. Place your prepared shanks on your smoker grate
5. Smoke them for 4 hours
6. Take a large-sized a cast iron pot and place it over medium heat on a stove
7. Add celery, onions, carrots, and garlic and Sauté them for until properly softened
8. Add the rest of the ingredients and mix them well
9. Add your prepared shanks into the pot and place the pot over your Smoker
10. Smoke for 3 hours more at 275-degree Fahrenheit
11. Once done, take it out and serve with some polenta or pasta!

Nutrition: Calories: 490 Fats: 19g Carbs: 8g Fiber: 1g

- ## **Authentic Indian T-Bone Kebab**

Preparation Time: 20 minutes +4-8 hours marinating time
Cooking Time: 45-60 minutes
Servings: 8
Ingredients:

- 1-pound beef tenderloin, cut into 1-inch cubes
- 2 pounds strip steak, cut into 1-inch cubes
- 1 large onion, cubed
- 1 bell pepper, cubed
- 1 zucchini, cubed
- ¼ cup olive oil
- ½ cup steak seasoning

Directions:

1. Take a large bowl and add tenderloin, strip steak, onion, zucchini, bell pepper, tomatoes and mix well with olive oil
2. Season with steak seasoning and stir until the meat has been coated well
3. Cover the meat and allow it to refrigerate for 4-8 hours
4. Take your drip pan and add water; cover with aluminum foil. Preheat your Smoker to 225 degrees F
5. Use water fill water pan halfway through and place it over drip pan. Add wood chips to the side tray

6. Make the kebabs by skewering meat and veggies alternatively

7. Make sure to begin with meat and end with meat

8. Transfer the skewers to your smoker rack and smoke for 45 minutes

9. Remove once the internal temperature reaches 135 degrees Fahrenheit (for a RARE finish). Serve and enjoy!

Nutrition: Calories: 559 Fats: 5g Carbs: 57g Fiber: 1g

• **Gourmet Beef Jerky**

Preparation Time: 8-10 hours

Cooking Time: 6-8 hours

Servings: 6

Ingredients:

- 2 cups of soy sauce
- 1 cup of Worcestershire sauce
- 1 cup of cranberry grape juice
- 1 cup of teriyaki sauce
- 1 tablespoon of hot pepper sauce
- 2 tablespoon of steak sauce
- 1 cup of light brown sugar
- ½ a teaspoon of ground black pepper
- 2 pound of flank steak, cut up into ¼ inch slices

Directions:

1. Take a bowl and whisk in soy sauce, cranberry grape juice, teriyaki sauce, Worcestershire sauce, steak sauce, brown sugar, hot sauce, and black pepper

2. Mix well and pour the mixture into a resealable bag

3. Add flank steak to the bag and coat with the marinade

4. Squeeze as much air as possible and seal. Allow it to refrigerate for 8-10 hours

5. Remove the steak from the marinade and wipe any excess

6. Take your drip pan and add water, cover with aluminum foil. Preheat your Smoker to 225 degrees F

7. Use water fill water pan halfway through and place it over drip pan. Add wood chips to the side tray and transfer the steak to your middle rack of the Smoker and Smoker for 6-8 hours, making sure to keep adding more chips after every 1 hour. Serve and enjoy!

Nutrition: Calories: 371 Fats: 10g Carbs: 39g Fiber: 1g

• The South Barbacoa

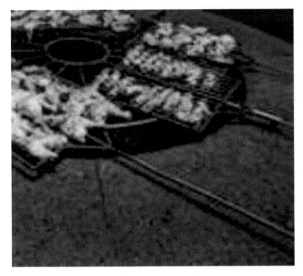

Preparation Time: 15 minutes

Cooking Time: 3 hours

Servings: 10

Ingredients:

- 1 and ½ teaspoon pepper
- 1 tablespoon dried oregano
- 1 and ½ teaspoon cayenne pepper
- 1 and ½ teaspoon chili powder
- 1 and ½ teaspoon garlic powder
- 1 teaspoon ground cumin
- 1 teaspoon salt
- 3 pounds' boneless beef chuck roast

Directions:

1. Add dampened hickory wood to your smoker and preheat to 200 degrees Fahrenheit
2. Take a small bowl and add oregano, cayenne pepper, black pepper, garlic powder, chili powder, cumin, salt, and seasoned salt
3. Mix well
4. Dip the chuck roast into your mixing bowl and rub the spice mix all over
5. Transfer the meat to your smoker and smoker for one and a ½ hours
6. Make sure to turn the meat after every 30 minutes; if you see less smoke formation, add more Pellets after every 30 minutes as well
7. Once the beef shows a dark red color with darkened edges, transfer the meat to a roasting pan and seal it tightly with an aluminum foil
8. Preheat your oven to 325 degrees Fahrenheit
9. Transfer the meat to your oven and bake for one and a ½ hours more
10. Shred the meat using two forks and serve!

Nutrition Calories: 559 Fats: 5g Carbs: 57g Fiber: 1g

• Smoked Prime Rib

Preparation Time: 25 minutes

Cooking Time: 4 hours

Servings: 12

Ingredients:

- 1 whole (8 pounds) prime rib roast
- 2 onions, thickly sliced
- Smoked teriyaki marinade
- Salt as needed
- Fresh ground pepper as needed

Directions:

1. Take a large container and add meat and marinade
2. Combine onion slices and pour cover well
3. Marinade for 2 hours
4. Turn the meat over, then cover it, refrigerate for 2 hours more Preheat your smoker to 225 degrees Fahrenheit using oak wood. Remove the roast and onions from the container and discard the marinade
5. Skewer the onion slices making "onion lollipops" Season the rib with pepper and salt, and transfer the meat and skewered onion to your smoker rack Smoke for 4-6 hours
6. Remove the meat when the internal temperature reaches 135 degrees Fahrenheit
7. Allow it to rest for 15 minutes and serve!

Nutrition Calories: 503 Fats: 36g Carbs: 0g Fiber: 0.5g

- ## Korean Beef Rib Eye

Preparation Time: 10 minutes

Cooking Time: 15 minutes

Servings: 6

Ingredients:

- ½ cup of soy sauce
- ¼ cup scallions, chopped
- 2 tablespoons garlic, minced
- 2 tablespoons Korean chili paste
- 1 tablespoon honey
- 2 teaspoons ground ginger
- 2 teaspoons onion powder
- 2 boneless rib-eye steaks, 8-12 ounces
- Smoked coleslaw
- 12 flour tortillas

Directions:

1. Preheat your smoker to 200 degrees Fahrenheit with peach or pearwood
2. Take a small bowl and whisk in soy sauce, garlic, scallion, honey, ginger, onion powder, and mix to make the paste
3. Spread the paste on both sides of the steak

4. Transfer the steak to your smoker and smoke for 15 minutes per pound

5. Remove the steak when the internal temperature reaches 115 degrees Fahrenheit

6. Cut the steak into strips and serve with coleslaw wrapped in tortillas

7. Enjoy!

Nutrition Calories: 240 Fats: 11g Carbs: 8g Fiber: 1g

• <u>Reverse Seared Flank Steak</u>

Preparation Time: 10 minutes

Cooking Time: 20 minutes

Servings: 2

Ingredients:

- 3 lb. flank steaks
- 1 tbsp. salt
- 1/2 tbsp. onion powder
- 1/4 tbsp. garlic powder
- 1/2 black pepper, coarsely ground

Directions:

1. Preheat the Traeger to 2250F.

2. All the ingredients in a bowl and mix well.

3. Add the steaks and rub them generously with the rub mixture.

4. Place the steak on the grill and close the lid. Let cook until its internal temperature is 100F under your desired temperature. 1150F for rare, 1250F for the medium rear, and 1350F for medium.

5. Wrap the steak with foil and raise the grill temperature to high.

6. Place back the steak and grill for 3 minutes on each side.

7. Pat with butter and serve when hot.

Nutrition: Calories 112, Total fat 5g, Saturated fat 2g, Total carbs 1g, Net carbs 1g Protein 16g, Sodium 737mg

• <u>Corned Beef with Cabbage</u>

Preparation Time: 20 minutes

Cooking Time: 5 hours

Servings: 6 - 8

Ingredients:

- 1 Cabbage head, chopped into wedges
- 1 lb. Potatoes
- 2 cups halved Carrots
- 2 tbsp. Dill, chopped
- ¼ tsp. of Garlic salt
- ½ cup unsalted butter
- 1 can Beer (12 oz.)
- 4 cups Chicken Stock
- 3 - 5 lbs. (1 piece) Beef Brisket, corned

Directions:

1. Preheat the grill to reach 180F.

2. Rinse the meat and use paper towels to pat dry and place on the grate. Smoke for 2 hours.

3. Increase the temperature, 325F with the lid closed.

4. Transfer the brisket to a pan for roasting. Sprinkle with seasoning. Pour the beer and stock in the pan.

5. Cover with foil tightly and let it cook for 2 ½ hours.

6. Remove the foil and add the potatoes and carrots. Season with garlic salt and add butter slices.

7. Cover with foil again. Cook 20 minutes. Add the cabbage, recover, and cook for an additional 20 minutes.

8. Serve garnished with chopped dill and enjoy.

Nutrition: Calories: 180 Proteins: 9g Carbohydrates: 19g Fat: 8g

• __Beer Beef__

Preparation Time: 15 minutes

Cooking Time: 7 hours

Servings: 8 - 12

Ingredients:

- 1 Beef Brisket 9 - 12 lbs. the fat outside trimmed
- 5 garlic cloves, smashed
- 1 Onion, sliced
- 5 tbsp. of Pickling Spice
- 1 tbsp. of curing salt for each lb. of meat
- ½ cup of Brown sugar
- 1 ½ cups Salt
- 3x12 oz. Dark beer
- 3 quarts Water, cold
- Rib seasoning

Directions:

1. In a stockpot, combine the curing salt, brown sugar, salt, beer, and water. Stir until well dissolved and add the garlic, onion, and pickling spice -- place in the fridge.

2. Add the meat to the brine but make sure that it is submerged completely. Brine for 2 - 4 days. Stir once every day and rinse the brisket under cold water. Sprinkle with rib seasoning.

3. Preheat the grill to 250F.

4. Cook the brisket for 4 to 5 hours. The inside temperature should be 160F.

5. Wrap the meat in a foil (double layer) and add water (1 ½ cup). Place it back on the grill and let it cook for 3 to 4 hours until it reaches 204F internal temperature.

6. Set aside and let it sit for 30 min. Crave into thin pieces and serve. Enjoy!

Nutrition: Calories: 320 Proteins: 38g Carbohydrates: 14g Fat: 12g

• Italian Beef Sandwich

Preparation and Cooking Time: 3 hours and 20 minutes

Serving Size: 8

Ingredients:

- 4 lb. beef roast
- Dry steak rub
- Salt and pepper to taste
- 4 cloves garlic, minced
- 6 cups beef broth
- 8 hoagie rolls, sliced
- 6 slices Swiss cheese
- 1 cup pickled vegetables, chopped

Directions:

1. Preheat your wood pellet grill to 450 degrees F. Close the lid for 15 minutes and sprinkle all-beef roast sides with steak rub, salt, and pepper.
2. Make several slits on the roast and insert the garlic cloves in the slits and grill the roast for 30 minutes.
3. Turn and grill for another 30 minutes and transfer the roast to a Dutch oven.
4. Pour in the broth and cover with foil and place it back on the grill. Reduce temperature to 300 degrees F.
5. Cook for 4 hours, shred the roast, and put the shredded meat back in the Dutch oven.
6. Stir with the cooking liquid.
7. Add the shredded meat and cheese slices to the hoagie rolls and put on the grill for 10 minutes.
8. Sprinkle with the pickled vegetables and serve.

Nutrients: Calories 754 Fat 24 g Saturated Fat 10.4 g Carbohydrate 46.6 g Dietary Fiber 7 g Protein 88.2 g Cholesterol 222 mg Sugars 4.8 g Sodium 1278 mg Potassium 1091 mg

• Grilled Steak with Creamy Greens

Preparation and Cooking Time: 45 minutes

Serving Size: 6

Ingredients:

- 2 porterhouse steaks
- Salt and pepper to taste
- 2 tablespoons butter
- 1 shallot, chopped
- 2 cloves garlic, minced
- 1 cup heavy cream
- Pinch ground nutmeg
- 4 tablespoons butter
- 3 lb. mixed salad greens

Directions:

1. Sprinkle both sides of the steak with salt and pepper.
2. Preheat your wood pellet grill to 225 degrees F for 15 minutes, and add the steaks for 45 minutes.

3. Take the steaks out of the grill and increase the temperature to 500 degrees F.
4. Close the lid for 15 minutes. Put the steaks back to the grill.
5. Cook for 5 minutes per side.
6. Take the steaks out of the grill and let rest for 5 minutes.
7. Add the butter to a pan over medium heat and cook the shallots and garlic for 5 minutes, stirring often.
8. Stir in the cream and reduce heat and simmer for 10 minutes.
9. Season with the salt and nutmeg and transfer to a food processor.
10. Pulse until smooth and add the remaining butter to the pan.
11. Stir in the greens and cook for 5 minutes.
12. Pour in the cream mixture and simmer for 5 minutes.
13. Serve the steaks with the creamy greens.

Nutrients per Serving: Calories 555 Fat 35.5 g Saturated Fat 18.6 g Cholesterol 157 mg Sodium 266 mg Carbohydrate 8.5 g Dietary Fiber 0 g Sugars 0.1 g Protein 49.7 g Potassium 930 mg

• Garlic Fillet Mignon

Preparation and Cooking Time: 30 minutes

Serving Size: 4

Ingredients:

- 4 filet mignon steaks
- 1 teaspoon garlic salt
- Salt and pepper to taste
- 1 tablespoon Dijon mustard
- 1 cup Parmesan cheese
- 2 cloves garlic, minced

Directions:

1. Preheat your wood pellet grill to high and close the lid for 15 minutes.
2. Sprinkle both sides of steaks with the garlic salt, salt, and pepper and add them to the grill.
3. Grill for 5 minutes per side and spread the steaks with the mustard.
4. Sprinkle with the Parmesan cheese and minced garlic and grill for another 2 minutes.
5. Let rest for at least 5 minutes before serving.

Nutrients per Serving: Calories 552 Fat 25.7 g Saturated Fat 10 g Carbohydrate 1.5 g Dietary Fiber 0.2 g Protein 74.6 g Cholesterol 221 mg Sugars 0.2 g Sodium 272 mg Potassium 20 mg

• Roasted Prime Rib with Herbs Garlic

Preparation and Cooking Time: 5 hours and 40 minutes

Serving Size: 8

Ingredients:

- 6 lb. prime rib roast (boneless)
- 2 tablespoons red wine vinegar

- 5 cloves garlic, chopped
- 1 tablespoon rosemary, chopped
- ½ cup parsley, chopped
- ½ cup olive oil
- Prime rib rub
- 4 cups beef stock, divided
- Salt and pepper to taste

Directions:

1. Tie the rib roast with butcher's wine and add the red wine vinegar, garlic, rosemary, and parsley to a food processor.
2. Stir in the olive oil and pulse for a few more seconds, until fully blended.
3. Add the rib roast to a large plastic bag and pour the vinegar mixture into the bag.
4. Turn to coat evenly and marinate in the refrigerator for 2 hours.
5. After 2 hours, take the rib roast out of the refrigerator and season the rib roast with the prime rib rub.
6. Place the rib roast in a roasting pan and pour the beef broth into the pan.
7. Preheat your wood pellet grill to 400 degrees F and close the lid for 15 minutes.
8. Place the pan over the grill and cook for 30 minutes.
9. Reduce temperature to 225 degrees F and cook for 3 hours.

Nutrients: Calories 523 Fat 43 g Saturated Fat 14 g Carbohydrate 3.2 g Dietary Fiber 0.3 g Protein 29.6 g Cholesterol 100 mg Sugars 0.1 g Sodium 1334 mg Potassium 100 mg

• <u>Rosemary Roast Beef</u>

Preparation and Cooking Time: 1 hour and 40 minutes

Serving Size: 8

Ingredients:

- 8 lb. rib-eye roast, sliced into 2
- 4 tablespoons olive oil, divided
- ½ cup garlic, minced
- 3 sprigs rosemary, chopped
- 3 sprigs thyme, chopped
- 4 tablespoons peppercorns, crushed
- ½ cup smoked salt

Directions:

1. Set your wood pellet grill to smoke and reheat for 10 minutes with the lid open.
2. Set grill to high and add 3 tablespoons olive oil to a roasting pan.
3. Place it on the grill, add the roast to the pan, and sear on both sides until golden.
4. Transfer to a plate and let cool. In a bowl, combine the garlic, rosemary, thyme, peppercorns, smoked salt, and remaining olive oil and rub the roast with this mixture.
5. Cook the roast on the grill for 30 minutes on high, reduce heat to 300

degrees F and cook for another 40 minutes.

6. Let rest for 15 to 20 minutes before slicing and serving.

Nutrients: Calories 638 Fat 35.3 g Saturated Fat 12 g Carbohydrate 3.3 g Dietary Fiber 0.5 g Protein 72.5 g Cholesterol 203 mg Sugars 0.1 g Sodium 3497 mg Potassium 1354 mg

• **Peppercorn Steak with Mushroom Sauce**

Preparation and Cooking Time: 3 hours and 30 minutes

Serving Size: 4

Ingredients:

- 2 cloves garlic, minced
- ½ cup Dijon mustard
- 1 tablespoon Worcestershire sauce
- 2 tablespoons bourbon
- 4 beef tenderloin steaks
- Salt to taste
- 1 tablespoon tri-color peppercorns
- 1 tablespoon olive oil
- 1 onion, diced
- 1 clove garlic, minced
- ½ cup chicken broth
- ½ cup white wine
- 16 oz. Cremini mushrooms, sliced
- ½ cup heavy cream
- Salt and pepper to taste

Directions:

1. Combine the garlic, mustard, Worcestershire sauce, and bourbon in a bowl and place the steaks on top of foil sheets.

2. Spread both sides with the mustard mixture and wrap with the foil.

3. Marinate at room temperature for 1 hour, unwrap the foil and sprinkle both sides of the steaks with the salt and peppercorns.

4. Preheat your wood pellet grill to 180 degrees F and close the lid for 15 minutes.

5. Grill the steaks for 1 hour and transfer the steaks to a plate.

6. Increase temperature to high and close the lid for another 15 minutes.

7. Put the steaks back to the grill and cook for another 30 minutes.

8. Add the olive oil to a pan over medium heat and cook the onions and garlic for 2 minutes.

9. Add the mushrooms and pour in the broth and wine. Let it simmer for 5 minutes.

10. Reduce heat to low and pour in the cream.

11. Season with salt and pepper and let the steak rest for 10 minutes before slicing.

12. 25. Pour the sauce over the steak slices and serve.

Nutrients: Calories 986 Fat 37.1 g Saturated Fat 14.1 g Carbohydrate 11.5 g Dietary Fiber 2.3 g Protein 134.6 g Cholesterol 401 mg Sugars 4.5 g Sodium 826 mg Potassium 2378 mg

• Barbecue Steaks

Preparation and Cooking Time: 3 hours

Serving Size: 4

Ingredients:

- 32 oz. tomahawk rib-eye
- ¼ cup dry barbecue rub
- Salt to taste
- 3 tablespoons butter

Directions:

1. Rub the steaks with the salt and let sit at room temperature for 1 hour.
2. Close the lid for 15 minutes and sprinkle both sides of the steak with the dry barbecue rub.
3. Let sit for 15 minutes and add the steaks to the grill.
4. Cook for 45 minutes and let rest for 10 minutes.
5. Put a cast-iron pan on the grill and increase temperate to 500 degrees F.
6. Once the pan is very hot, sear the steak on the pan for 1 minute per side and transfer it to a plate.
7. Top with the butter and let rest for 10 minutes before serving.

Nutrients: Calories 551 Fat 20 g Saturated Fat 9.4 g Cholesterol 227 mg Sugars 4.1 g Carbohydrate 5.7 g Dietary Fiber 0.1 g Protein 82 g Sodium 377 mg Potassium 793 mg

• Beef Chili

Preparation and Cooking Time: 2 hours and 15 minutes

Serving Size: 8

Ingredients:

- 1 lb. lean ground beef
- 1 lb. ground chorizo
- 2 tablespoons butter
- 1 onion, chopped
- 1 red bell pepper, chopped
- 1 green bell pepper, chopped
- 2 cloves garlic, minced
- 15 oz. canned tomato sauce
- 2 tablespoons tomato paste
- 15 oz. canned stewed tomatoes
- 30 oz. canned ranch-style beans
- 3 tablespoons cumin
- 2 bay leaves
- 3 tablespoons chili powder
- 3 tablespoons Mexican oregano
- Salt to taste

Directions:

1. Preheat your wood pellet grill to 350 degrees F and close the lid for 15 minutes.
2. In a Dutch oven over medium heat, cook the ground beef and chorizo until browned and drain the fat.

3. Add the butter and cook onion and bell peppers for 10 minutes, stir in the garlic and cook for 2 minutes.

4. Pour in the tomato sauce, tomato paste, stewed tomatoes, and beans and bring to a boil.

5. Add the cumin, bay leaves, chili powder, oregano, and salt and reduce heat and simmer for 10 minutes.

6. Transfer the Dutch oven to the grill and cook for 1 hour.

Nutrients: Calories 406 Fat 15 g Saturated Fat 6 g Carbohydrate 13.2 g Dietary Fiber 4.3 g Protein 54.4 g

Cholesterol 160 mg Sugars 6.6 g Sodium 471 mg Potassium 1231mg

• Paprika Steak

Preparation and Cooking Time: 1 hour and 40 minutes

Serving Size: 4

Ingredients:

- ½ tablespoon onion powder
- 1 tablespoon paprika
- Salt and pepper to taste
- ½ tablespoon garlic powder
- 1 teaspoon ground mustard
- ½ tablespoon brown sugar
- ¼ teaspoon cayenne pepper
- 2 tomahawk steaks

Directions:

1. Combine the paprika, garlic powder, mustard, brown sugar, onion powder, cayenne pepper, salt, and pepper in a bowl and sprinkle both sides of the steaks with this mixture.

2. Preheat your wood pellet grill to 225 degrees F and close the lid for 15 minutes.

3. Grill the steaks for 1 hour and increase the temperature to 450 degrees F.

4. Cook the steaks for 10 minutes per side.

5. Let steaks rest for 5 to 10 minutes before serving.

Nutrients: Calories 862 Fat 38.5 g Saturated Fat 14.3 g Carbohydrate 3.9 g Dietary Fiber 1 g Protein 117 g

Cholesterol 225 mg Sugars 1.9 g Sodium 303 mg Potassium 1460 mg

• Smoked Mustard Beef Ribs

Preparation Time: 25 minutes

Cooking Time: 4 to 6 hours

Servings: 4 to 8

Ingredients:

- 2 (2- or 3-pound / 907- or 1360-g) racks beef ribs
- 2 tablespoons yellow mustard
- 1 batch sweet and spicy cinnamon rub

Directions:

1. Preheat the grill, with the lid closed, to 225°F (107°C).

2. Remove the membrane from the backside of the ribs. This can be done by cutting just through the membrane in an X pattern and working a paper

towel between the membrane and the ribs to pull it off.

3. Coat the ribs all over with mustard and season them with the rub. Using your hands, work the rub into the meat.

4. Place the ribs directly on the grill grate and smoke until their internal temperature reaches between 190°F (88°C) and 200°F (93°C).

5. Remove the racks from the grill and cut them into individual ribs. Serve immediately.

Nutrition: Calories: 503 Fats: 36g Carbs: 0g Fiber: 0.5g

• **Braised Beef Short Ribs**

Preparation Time: 25 minutes

Cooking Time: 4 hours

Servings: 2 to 4

Ingredients:

- 4 beef short ribs
- Salt, to taste
- Freshly ground black pepper, to taste
- ½ cup beef broth

Directions:

1. Preheat the grill, with the lid closed, to 180°F (82°C).

2. Season the ribs on both sides with salt and pepper.

3. Place the ribs directly on the grill grate and smoke for 3 hours.

4. Pull the ribs from the grill and place them on enough aluminum foil to wrap them completely.

5. Increase the grill's temperature to 375°F (191°C).

6. Fold in three sides of the foil around the ribs and add the beef broth. Fold in the last side, completely enclosing the ribs and liquid. Return the wrapped ribs to the grill and cook for 45 minutes more. Remove the short ribs from the grill, unwrap them, and serve immediately.

Nutrition: Carbohydrates: 22 g Protein: 28 g Fat: 6 g Sodium: 13 mg Cholesterol: 81 mg

• **Smoked Pastrami**

Preparation Time: 15 minutes

Cooking Time: 12 to 16 hours

Servings: 6 to 8

Ingredients:

- 1 (8-pound / 3.6-kg) corned beef brisket
- 2 tablespoons yellow mustard
- 1 batch Espresso Brisket Rub
- Worcestershire Mop and Spritz, for spritzing

Directions:

1. Preheat the grill, with the lid closed, to 225°F (107°C).

2. Coat the brisket all over with mustard and season it with the rub. Using your hands, work the rub into the meat. Pour the mop into a spray bottle.

3. Place the brisket directly on the grill grate and smoke until its internal temperature reaches 195°F (91°C), spritzing it every hour with the mop.

4. Pull the corned beef brisket from the grill and wrap it completely in aluminum foil or butcher paper. Place the wrapped brisket in a cooler, cover the cooler, and let it rest for 1 or 2 hours.

5. Remove the corned beef from the cooler and unwrap it. Slice the corned beef and serve.

Nutrition Calories: 503 Fats: 36g Carbs: 0g Fiber: 0.5g

• Sweet & Spicy Beef Brisket

Preparation Time: 10 minutes

Cooking Time: 7 hours

Servings: 10

Ingredients:

- 1 cup paprika
- ¾ cup sugar
- 3 tablespoons garlic salt
- 3 tablespoons onion powder
- 1 tablespoon celery salt
- 1 tablespoon lemon pepper
- 1 tablespoon ground black pepper
- 1 teaspoon cayenne pepper
- 1 teaspoon mustard powder
- ½ teaspoon dried thyme, crushed
- 1 (5-6-pound) beef brisket, trimmed

Directions:

1. In a bowl, place all ingredients except for beef brisket and mix well.

2. Rub the brisket with spice mixture generously.

3. With a plastic wrap, cover the brisket and refrigerate overnight.

4. Preheat the Z Grills Wood Pellet Grill & Smoker on grill setting to 250 degrees F.

5. Place the brisket onto grill over indirect heat and cook for about 3-3½ hours.

6. Flip and cook for about 3-3½ hours more.

7. Remove the brisket from grill and place onto a cutting board for about 10-15 minutes before slicing.

8. With a sharp knife, cut the brisket in desired sized slices and serve.

Nutrition: Calories 536 Total Fat 15.6 g Saturated Fat 5.6 g Cholesterol 203 mg Sodium 158 mg Total Carbs 24.8 g Fiber 4.5 g Sugar 17.4 g Protein 71.1 g

• Brandy Beef Tenderloin

Preparation Time: 15 minutes

Cooking Time: 2 hours 2 minutes

Servings: 6

Ingredients:

For Brandy Butter:

- ½ cup butter
- 1 ounce brandy

For Brandy Sauce:

- 2 ounces brandy

- 8 garlic cloves, minced
- ¼ cup mixed fresh herbs (parsley, rosemary and thyme), chopped
- 2 teaspoons honey
- 2 teaspoons hot English mustard

For Tenderloin:

- 1 (2-pound) center-cut beef tenderloin
- Salt and cracked black peppercorns, as required

Directions:

1. Preheat the Z Grills Wood Pellet Grill & Smoker on grill setting to 230 degrees F.
2. For brandy butter: in a pan, melt butter over medium-low heat.
3. Stir in brandy and remove from heat.
4. Set aside, covered to keep warm.
5. For brandy sauce: in a bowl, add all ingredients and mix until well combined.
6. Season the tenderloin with salt and black peppercorns generously.
7. Coat tenderloin with brandy sauce evenly.
8. With a baster-injector, inject tenderloin with brandy butter.
9. Place the tenderloin onto the grill and cook for about ½-2 hours, injecting with brandy butter occasionally.
10. Remove the tenderloin from grill and place onto a cutting board for about 10-15 minutes before serving.
11. With a sharp knife, cut the tenderloin into desired-sized slices and serve.

Nutrition: Calories 496 Total Fat 29.3 g Saturated Fat 15 g Cholesterol 180 mg Sodium 240 mg Total Carbs 4.4 g Fiber 0.7 g Sugar 2 g Protein 44.4 g

• **Beef Rump Roast**

Preparation Time: 10 minutes
Cooking Time: 6 hours
Servings: 8
Ingredients:

- 1 teaspoon smoked paprika
- 1 teaspoon cayenne pepper
- 1 teaspoon onion powder
- 1 teaspoon garlic powder
- Salt and ground black pepper, as required
- 3 pounds beef rump roast
- ¼ cup Worcestershire sauce

Directions:

1. Preheat the Z Grills Wood Pellet Grill & Smoker on smoke setting to 200 degrees F, using charcoal.
2. In a bowl, mix together all spices.
3. Coat the rump roast with Worcestershire sauce evenly and then, rub with spice mixture generously.
4. Place the rump roast onto the grill and cook for about 5-6 hours.
5. Remove the roast from the grill and place onto a cutting board for about 10-15 minutes before serving.

6. With a sharp knife, cut the roast into desired-sized slices and serve.

Nutrition: Calories 252 Total Fat 9.1 g Saturated Fat 3 g Cholesterol 113 mg Sodium 200 mg Total Carbs 2.3 g Fiber 0.2 g Sugar 1.8 g Protein 37.8 g

• Herbed Prime Rib Roast

Preparation Time: 10 minutes
Cooking Time: 3 hours 50 minutes
Servings: 10
Ingredients:

- 1 (5-pound) prime rib roast
- Salt, as required
- 5 tablespoons olive oil
- 2 teaspoons dried thyme, crushed
- 2 teaspoons dried rosemary, crushed
- 2 teaspoons garlic powder
- 1 teaspoon onion powder
- 1 teaspoon paprika
- ½ teaspoon cayenne pepper
- Ground black pepper, as required

Directions:

1. Season the roast with salt generously.
2. With a plastic wrap, cover the roast and refrigerate for about 24 hours.
3. In a bowl, mix together remaining ingredients and set aside for about 1 hour.
4. Rub the roast with oil mixture from both sides evenly.
5. Arrange the roast in a large baking sheet and refrigerate for about 6-12 hours.

6. Preheat the Z Grills Wood Pellet Grill & Smoker on smoke setting to 225-230 degrees F, using pecan wood chips.
7. Place the roast onto the grill and cook for about 3-3½ hours.
8. Meanwhile, preheat the oven to 500 degrees F.
9. Remove the roast from grill and place onto a large baking sheet.
10. Place the baking sheet in oven and roast for about 15-20 minutes.
11. Remove the roast from oven and place onto a cutting board for about 10-15 minutes before serving.
12. With a sharp knife, cut the roast into desired-sized slices and serve.

Nutrition: Calories 605 Total Fat 47.6 g Saturated Fat 17.2 g Cholesterol 135 mg Sodium 1285 mg Total Carbs 3.8 g Fiber 0.3 g Sugar0.3 g Protein 38 g

• Spicy Chuck Roast

Preparation Time: 10 minutes
Cooking Time: 4½ hours
Servings: 8
Ingredients:

- 2 tablespoons onion powder
- 2 tablespoons garlic powder
- 1 tablespoon red chili powder
- 1 tablespoon cayenne pepper
- Salt and ground black pepper, as required
- 1 (3 pound) beef chuck roast

- 16 fluid ounces warm beef broth

Directions:

1. Preheat the Z Grills Wood Pellet Grill & Smoker on grill setting to 250 degrees F.
2. In a bowl, mix together spices, salt and black pepper.
3. Rub the chuck roast with spice mixture evenly.
4. Place the rump roast onto the grill and cook for about 1½ hours per side.
5. Now, arrange chuck roast in a steaming pan with beef broth.
6. With a piece of foil, cover the pan and cook for about 2-3 hours.
7. Remove the chuck roast from grill and place onto a cutting board for about 20 minutes before slicing.
8. With a sharp knife, cut the chuck roast into desired-sized slices and serve.

Nutrition: Calories 645 Total Fat 48 g Saturated Fat 19 g Cholesterol 175 mg Sodium 329 mg Total Carbs 4.2 g Fiber 1 g Sugar 1.4 g Protein 46.4 g

• BBQ Spiced Flank Steak

Preparation Time: 15 minutes

Cooking Time: 30 minutes

Servings: 6

Ingredients:

- 1 (2-pound) beef flank steak
- 2 tablespoons olive oil
- ¼ cup BBQ rub

- 3 tablespoons blue cheese, crumbled
- 2 tablespoons butter, softened
- 1 teaspoon fresh chives, minced

Directions:

1. Preheat the Z Grills Wood Pellet Grill & Smoker on grill setting to 225 degrees F.
2. Coat the steak with oil evenly and season with BBQ rub.
3. Place the steak onto the grill and cook for about 10-15 minutes per side.
4. Remove the steak from grill and place onto a cutting board for about 10 minutes before slicing.
5. Meanwhile, in a bowl, add blue cheese, butter and chives and mix well.
6. With a sharp knife, cut the steak into thin strips across the grain.
7. Top with cheese mixture and serve.

Nutrition: Calories 370 Total Fat 19.1 g Saturated Fat 7.5 g Cholesterol 148 mg Sodium 1666 mg Total Carbs 0.1 g Fiber 0 g Sugar 0 g Protein 46.8 g

• **Beef Stuffed Bell Peppers**

Preparation Time: 20 minutes

Cooking Time: 1 hour

Servings: 6

Ingredients:

- 6 large bell peppers
- 1 pound ground beef
- 1 small onion, chopped
- 2 garlic cloves, minced

- 2 cups cooked rice
- 1 cup frozen corn, thawed
- 1 cup cooked black beans
- 2/3 cup salsa
- 2 tablespoons Cajun rub
- 1½ cups Monterey Jack cheese, grated

Directions:

1. Cut each bell pepper in half lengthwise through the stem.
2. Carefully, remove the seeds and ribs.
3. For stuffing: heat a large frying pan and cook the beef for about 6-7 minutes or until browned completely.
4. Add onion and garlic and cook for about 2-3 minutes.
5. Stir in remaining ingredients except cheese and cook for about 5 minutes.
6. Remove from the heat and set aside to cool slightly.
7. Preheat the Z Grills Wood Pellet Grill & Smoker on grill setting to 350 degrees F.
8. Stuff each bell pepper half with stuffing mixture evenly.
9. Arrange the peppers onto grill, stuffing side up and cook for about 40 minutes.
10. Sprinkle each bell pepper half with cheese and cook for about 5 minutes more.
11. Remove the bell peppers from grill and serve hot.

Nutrition: Calories 675 Total Fat 14.8 g Saturated Fat 7.5 g Cholesterol 93 mg Sodium 1167 mg Total Carbs 90.7 g Fiber 8.7 g Sugar 9.1 g Protein 43.9 g

- ## **BBQ Meatloaf**

Preparation Time: 20 minutes

Cooking Time: 2½ hours

Servings: 8

Ingredients:

For Meatloaf:

- 3 pounds ground beef
- 3 eggs
- ½ cup panko breadcrumbs
- 1 (10-ounce) can diced tomatoes with green chile peppers
- 1 large white onion, chopped
- 2 hot banana peppers, chopped
- 2 tablespoons seasoned salt
- 2 teaspoons liquid smoke flavoring
- 2 teaspoons smoked paprika
- 1 teaspoons onion salt
- 1 teaspoons garlic salt
- Salt and ground black pepper, as required

For Sauce:

- ½ cup ketchup
- ¼ cup tomato-based chile sauce
- ¼ cup white sugar
- 2 teaspoons Worcestershire sauce
- 2 teaspoons hot pepper sauce
- 1 teaspoon red pepper flakes, crushed
- 1 teaspoon red chili pepper

- Salt and ground black pepper, as required

Directions:

1. Preheat the Z Grills Wood Pellet Grill & Smoker on smoke setting to 225 degrees F, using charcoal.
2. Grease a loaf pan.
3. For meatloaf: in a bowl, add all ingredients and with your hands, mix until well combined.
4. Place the mixture into prepared loaf pan evenly.
5. Place the pan onto the grill and cook for about 2 hours.
6. For sauce: in a bowl, add all ingredients and beat until well combined.
7. Remove the pan from grill and drain excess grease from meatloaf.
8. Place sauce over meatloaf evenly and place the pan onto the grill.
9. Cook for about 30 minutes.
10. Remove the meatloaf from grill and set aside for about 10 minutes before serving.
11. Carefully, invert the meatloaf onto a platter.
12. Cut the meatloaf into desired-sized slices and serve.

Nutrition: Calories 423 Total Fat 13 g Saturated Fat 4.7 g Cholesterol 213 mg Sodium 1879 mg Total Carbs 15.7 g Fiber 1.5 g Sugar 12.3 g Protein 54.9 g

• Smoked Beef Brisket in Sweet and Spicy Rub

Preparation Time: 15 minutes

Cooking Time: 1 hour

Servings: 10

Ingredients:

- Beef Brisket (6-lbs., 2.7-kgs)
- 1 cup paprika
- ½ cup salt
- 1 cup brown sugar
- ½ cup cumin
- ½ cup pepper
- ½ cup chili powder ¼ cup cayenne pepper

Directions:

1. Combine paprika, salt, brown sugar, cumin, pepper, chili powder, and cayenne pepper in a bowl then stir until incorporated.
2. Rub the beef brisket with the spice mixture then marinate overnight. Store in the refrigerator to keep it fresh.
3. Remove the beef brisket from the refrigerator then thaw until it reaches room temperature.
4. Preheat the smoker to 250°F (121°C) with charcoal and hickory chips—using indirect heat. Don't forget to soak the wood chips before using.
5. When the smoker has reached the desired temperature, wrap the beef

brisket with aluminum foil then place it in the smoker.

6. Smoke the wrapped beef brisket for 8 hours. Check the temperature every hour then adds more charcoal and hickory chips if it is necessary.

7. Once the smoked beef brisket is ready, remove from the smoker then let it sit for a few minutes until warm.

8. Unwrap the smoked beef brisket then place on a flat surface.

9. Cut the smoked beef brisket into thick slices then place on a serving dish.

10. Serve and enjoy.

Nutrition: Calories: 180 Carbs: 3g Fat: 3g Protein: 35g

• **Simple Smoked Beef Brisket with Mocha Sauce**

Preparation Time: 15 minutes

Cooking Time: 1 hour

Servings: 10

Ingredients:

- 5 pounds beef brisket
- 1 ½ tablespoons garlic powder
- 1 ½ tablespoons onion powder
- 4 tablespoons salt
- 4 tablespoons pepper
- 2 ½ tablespoons olive oil
- 1 cup chopped onion
- 2 teaspoons salt
- ¼ cup chopped chocolate dark
- ¼ cup sugar –

- ½ cup beer –
- 2 shots espresso

Directions:

1. Rub the beef brisket with garlic powder, onion powder, salt, and black pepper.

2. Wrap the seasoned beef brisket with a sheet of plastic wrap then store in the refrigerator overnight.

3. In the morning, remove the beef brisket from the refrigerator and thaw for about an hour.

4. Preheat the smoker to 250°F (121°C) with charcoal and hickory chips— using indirect heat. Place the beef brisket in the smoker and smoke for 8 hours.

5. Keep the temperature remain at 250°F (121°C) and add some more charcoal and hickory chips if it is necessary.

6. Meanwhile, preheat a saucepan over medium heat then pour olive oil into the saucepan.

7. Once the oil is hot, stir in chopped onion then sauté until wilted and aromatic.

8. Reduce the heat to low then add the remaining sauce ingredients to the saucepan. Mix well then bring to a simmer.

9. Remove the sauce from heat then set aside.

10. When the smoked beef brisket is ready, or the internal temperature has reached 190°F (88°C), remove from the smoker then transfer to a serving dish.

11. Drizzle the mocha sauce over the smoked beef brisket then serve.

12. Enjoy warm.

Nutrition: Calories: 210 Carbs: 1g Fat: 13g Protein: 19g

- ## <u>Lemon Ginger Smoked Beef Ribs</u>

Preparation Time: 10 minutes

Cooking Time: 10 hours

Servings: 10

Ingredients:

- 6 pounds beef ribs
- 3 tablespoons paprika
- ¼ cup brown sugar
- 1 ½ tablespoons dry mustard
- 1 ½ tablespoons ginger
- 1 tablespoon onion powder
- 1 ½ tablespoons salt
- 1 tablespoon pepper
- 3 tablespoons lemon juice

Directions:

1. Combine paprika with brown sugar, dry mustard, onion powder, salt, and pepper then mix well.

2. Rub the beef ribs with the spice mixture then place on a sheet of aluminum foil.

3. Splash lemon juice over the beef ribs then sprinkle ginger on top.

4. Wrap the seasoned beef ribs with the aluminum foil then set aside.

5. Preheat the smoker to 250°F (121°C) with charcoal and hickory chips—don't forget to soak the wood chips before using.

6. Place the wrapped beef ribs in the smoker and smoke for 10 hours.

7. Check the temperature remain at 250°F (121°C) and add some more charcoal and hickory chips if it is necessary.

8. Once the smoked beef ribs are done, remove from the smoker.

9. Unwrap the smoked beef ribs then place on a serving dish.

10. Serve and enjoy.

Nutrition: Calories: 415 Fat: 35g Protein: 25g

- ## <u>Chocolate Smoked Beef Ribs</u>

Preparation Time: 15 minutes

Cooking Time: 19 hours

Servings: 10

Ingredients:

- 6 pounds beef ribs
- 1 ¼ cups cocoa powder
- ¾ cup chili powder
- ¾ cup sugar
- ¾ cup salt

- ¼ cup black pepper
- ¼ cup cumin

Directions:

1. Place the cocoa powder in a bowl then add chili powder, sugar, salt, black pepper, and cumin in the bowl. Mix well.
2. Rub the beef ribs with the cocoa powder mixture then cover with plastic wrap.
3. Marinate the beef ribs overnight and store in the refrigerator to keep it fresh.
4. In the morning, remove the beef ribs from the refrigerator and thaw for about an hour.
5. Preheat the smoker to 250°F (121°C) with charcoal and hickory chips—using indirect heat. Place the beef ribs in the smoker and smoke for 10 hours.
6. Keep the temperature remain at 250°F (121°C) and add some more charcoal and hickory chips if it is necessary.
7. Once it is done or the internal temperature has reached 170°F (77°C), take the smoked beef ribs out from the smoker and transfer to a serving dish.
8. Serve and enjoy warm.

Nutrition: Calories: 415 Carbs: 0g Fat: 35g Protein: 25g

- ## **Smoked and Pulled Beef**

Preparation Time: 10 minutes

Cooking Time: 6 hours

Servings: 6

Ingredients:

- 4 lb. beef sirloin tip roast
- 1/2 cup BBQ rubs
- 2 bottles of amber beer
- 1 bottle barbecues sauce

Directions:

1. Turn your wood pellet grill onto smoke setting then trim excess fat from the steak.
2. Coat the steak with BBQ rub and let it smoke on the grill for 1 hour.
3. Continue cooking and flipping the steak for the next 3 hours. Transfer the steak to a braising vessel that adds the beers.
4. Braise the beef until tender, then transfer to a platter reserving 2 cups of cooking liquid.
5. Use a pair of forks to shred the beef and return it to the pan. Add the reserved liquid and barbecue sauce. Stir well and keep warm before serving. Enjoy.

Nutrition: Calories 829, Total fat 46g, Saturated fat 18g, Total carbs 4g, Net carbs 4g, Protein 86g, Sugar 0g, Fiber 0g, Sodium: 181mg

• Smoked Midnight Brisket

Preparation Time: 15 minutes

Cooking Time: 12 hours

Servings: 6

Ingredients:

- 1 tbsp. Worcestershire sauce
- 1 tbsp. Pellet beef Rub
- 1 tbsp. Pellet Chicken rubs
- 1 tbsp. Pellet Blackened Saskatchewan rub
- 5 lb. flat cut brisket
- 1 cup beef broth

Directions:

1. Rub the sauce and rubs in a mixing bowl then rub the mixture on the meat.
2. Preheat your grill to 180°F with the lid closed for 15 minutes. You can use super smoke if you desire.
3. Place the meat on the grill and grill for 6 hours or until the internal temperature reaches 160°F.
4. Remove the meat from the grill and double wrap it with foil.
5. Add beef broth and return to grill, with the temperature increased to 225°F. Cook for 4 hours or until the internal temperature reaches 204°F.
6. Remove from grill and let rest for 30 minutes. Serve and enjoy with your favorite BBQ sauce.

Nutrition: Calories 200, Total fat 14g, Saturated fat 6g, Total carbs 3g,

• Grilled Butter Basted Porterhouse Steak

Preparation Time: 15 minutes

Cooking Time: 40 minutes

Servings: 4

Ingredients:

- 4 tbsp. butter, melted
- 2 tbsp. Worcestershire sauce
- 2 tbsp. Dijon mustard
- Pellet Prime rib rub

Directions:

1. Set your wood pellet grill to 225°F with the lid closed for 15 minutes.
2. In a mixing bowl, mix butter, sauce, Dijon mustard until smooth. Brush the mixture on the meat then season with the rub.
3. Arrange the meat on the grill grate and cook for 30 minutes.
4. Use tongs to transfer the meat to a patter then increase the heat to high.
5. Return the meat to the grill grate to grill until your desired doneness is achieved.
6. Baste with the butter mixture again if you desire and let rest for 3 minutes before serving. Enjoy.

Nutrition: Calories 726, Total fat 62g, Saturated fat 37g, Total carbs 5g, Net carbs 4g, Protein 36g, Sugar 1g,

Fiber 1g, Sodium: 97mg, Potassium 608mg

Cocoa Crusted Grilled Flank Steak

Preparation Time: 15 minutes

Cooking Time: 6 minutes

Servings: 7

Ingredients:

- 1 tbsp. cocoa powder.
- 2 tbsp. chili powder
- 1 tbsp. chipotle chili powder
- 1/2 tbsp. garlic powder
- 1/2 tbsp. onion powder
- 1-1/2 tbsp. brown sugar
- 1 tbsp. cumin
- 1 tbsp. smoked paprika
- 1 tbsp. kosher salt
- 1/2 tbsp. black pepper
- Olive oil
- 4 lb. Flank steak

Directions:

1. Whisk together cocoa, chili powder, garlic powder, onion powder, sugar, cumin, paprika, salt, and pepper in a mixing bowl.
2. Drizzle the steak with oil then rub with the cocoa mixture on both sides.
3. Preheat your wood pellet grill for 15 minutes with the lid closed.
4. Cook the meat on the grill grate for 5 minutes or until the internal temperature reaches 135°F.
5. Remove the meat from the grill and let it cool for 15 minutes to allow the juices to redistribute.
6. Slice the meat against the grain and on a sharp diagonal.
7. Serve and enjoy.

Nutrition: Calories 420, Total fat 26g, Saturated fat 8g, Total carbs 21g, Net carbs 13g, Protein 3g, Sugar 7g, Fiber 8g, Sodium: 2410mg

Wood Pellet Grill Prime Rib Roast

Preparation Time: 5 minutes

Cooking Time: 4 hours

Servings: 10

Ingredients:

- 7 lb. bone prime rib roast
- Pellet prime rib rub

Directions:

1. Coat the roast generously with the rub then wrap in a plastic wrap. Let sit in the fridge for 24 hours to marinate.
2. Set the temperatures to 500°F.to to preheat with the lid closed for 15 minutes.
3. Place the rib directly on the grill fat side up and cook for 30 minutes.
4. Reduce the temperature to 300°F and cook for 4 hours or until the internal temperature is 120°F- rare, 130°F-medium rare, 140°F-medium and 150°F-well done.

5. Remove from the grill and let rest for 30 minutes, then serve and enjoy.

Nutrition: Calories 290, Total fat 23g, Saturated fat 9.3g, Total carbs 0g, Net Carbs 0g, Protein 19g,

Sugar 0g, Fiber 0g, Sodium: 54mg, Potassium 275mg

Smoked Longhorn Cowboy Tri-Tip

Preparation Time: 15 minutes

Cooking Time: 4 hours

Servings: 7

Ingredients:

- 3 lb. tri-tip roast
- 1/8 cup coffee, ground
- 1/4 cup Pellet beef rub

Directions:

1. Preheat the grill to 180°F with the lid closed for 15 minutes.
2. Meanwhile, rub the roast with coffee and beef rub. Place the roast on the grill grate and smoke for 3 hours.
3. Remove the roast from the grill and double wrap it with foil. Increase the temperature to 275°F.
4. Return the meat to the grill and let cook for 90 minutes or until the internal temperature reaches 135°F.
5. Remove from the grill, unwrap it and let rest for 10 minutes before serving.
6. Enjoy.

Nutrition: Calories 245, Total fat 14g, Saturated fat 4g, Total Carbs 0g, Net Carbs 0g, Protein 23g, Sugar 0g, Fiber 0g, Sodium: 80mg

Wood Pellet Grill Teriyaki Beef Jerky

Preparation Time: 15 minutes

Cooking Time: 5 hours

Servings: 10

Ingredients:

- 3 cups soy sauce
- 2 cups brown sugar
- 3 garlic cloves
- 2-inch ginger knob, peeled and chopped
- 1 tbsp. sesame oil
- 4 lb. beef, skirt steak

Directions:

1. Place all the ingredients except the meat in a food processor. Pulse until well mixed.
2. Trim any excess fat from the meat and slice into ¼ inch slices. Add the steak with the marinade into a zip lock bag and let marinate for 12-24 hours in a fridge.
3. Set the wood pellet grill to smoke and let preheat for 5 minutes.
4. Arrange the steaks on the grill, leaving a space between each. Let smoke for 5 hours.
5. Remove the steak from grill and serve when warm.

Nutrition: Calories 80, Total fat 1g, Saturated fat 0g, Total Carbs 7g, Net Carbs 0g, Protein 11g, Sugar 6g, Fiber 0g, Sodium: 390mg

• **Grilled Butter Basted Rib-Eye**

Preparation Time: 20 minutes

Cooking Time: 20 minutes

Servings: 4

Ingredients:

- 2 rib-eye steaks, bone-in
- Salt to taste
- Pepper to taste
- 4 tbsp. butter, unsalted

Directions:

1. Mix steak, salt, and pepper in a Ziplock bag. Seal the bag and mix until the beef is well coated. Ensure you get as much air as possible from the Ziplock bag.

2. Set the wood pellet grill temperature to high with closed lid for 15 minutes. Place a cast-iron into the grill.

3. Place the steaks on the hottest spot of the grill and cook for 5 minutes with the lid closed.

4. Open the lid and add butter to the skillet when it's almost melted place the steak on the skillet with the grilled side up.

5. Cook for 5 minutes while busting the meat with butter. Close the lid and cook until the internal temperature is 130°F.

6. Remove the steak from skillet and let rest for 10 minutes before enjoying with the reserved butter.

Nutrition: Calories 745, Total fat 65g, Saturated fat 32g, Total Carbs 5g, Net Carbs 5g, Protein 35g, Sugar 0g, Fiber 0g

BEEF (DINNER)

• <u>Smoked Beef with Smoked Garlic Mayo Dip</u>

Preparation Time: 15 minutes
Cooking Time: 8 hours
Servings: 10
Ingredients:

- 5 pounds beef tenderloin
- ¼ cup minced garlic
- 2 teaspoons black pepper
- 2 teaspoons salt
- 1 ½ teaspoons olive oil
- 5 cloves garlic
- ½ cup mayonnaise
- ¼ cup water
- 2 tablespoons red wine vinegar
- 2 tablespoons chives

Directions:

1. Preheat the smoker to 250°F (121°C). Soak the hickory wood chips for about an hour before using.
2. Combine minced garlic, black pepper, salt, and olive oil then stir until mixed.
3. Rub the beef tenderloin with the spice mixture then place in the smoker.
4. Wrap the garlic cloves with aluminum foil then place next to the beef tenderloin.
5. Smoke the beef tenderloin and garlic for about 8 hours or until the internal temperature of the beef tenderloin reaches 145°F (63°C).
6. Remove the smoked beef tenderloin and garlic from the smoker then cut the smoked beef tenderloin into slices. Set aside.
7. Place mayonnaise and chives in a blender then pour water and red wine vinegar over mayonnaise.
8. Add the smoked garlic to the blender then blend until smooth.
9. Transfer the garlic and mayonnaise dip to a small bowl then place next to the smoked beef tenderloin.
10. Serve and enjoy.

Nutrition: Calories: 205 Carbs: 4g Fat: 12g Protein: 19g

• <u>Simple Smoked Pulled Beef</u>

Preparation Time: 15 minutes
Cooking Time: 9 hours
Servings: 10
Ingredients:

- 1 6-pound chuck roast
- 2 ½ tablespoons salt
- 2 ½ tablespoons black pepper
- 2 ½ tablespoons garlic powder
- ½ cup chopped onion
- 3 cups beef broth

Directions:

1. Preheat the smoker to 225°F (107°C). Let the lid closed and wait for 15 minutes.

2. Mix garlic powder with black pepper and salt until combined.

3. Rub the chuck roast with the spice mixture then using your hand massage the roast until it is thoroughly seasoned.

4. Place the seasoned roast on the grill then cook the roast for 3 hours. Spray the roast with beef broth once every hour.

5. After 3 hours, sprinkle chopped onion on the bottom of a pan then pours the remaining beef broth over the onion—about 2 cups.

6. Transfer the cooked roast to the pan then place the pan on the grill.

7. Increase the smoker's temperature to 250°F (121°C) then cooks for 3 hours more.

8. After 3 hours, cover the pan with aluminum foil then lower the temperature to 165°F (74°C).

9. Cook the roast for another 3 hours until done.

10. Once it is done, transfer the smoked beef to a flat surface and let it cool.

11. Once it is cold, using a fork shred the beef then place on a serving dish.

12. Serve and enjoy!

Nutrition: Calories: 104 Carbs: 6g Fat: 2g Protein: 16g

- ## <u>Smoked Beef Churl Barbecue</u>

Preparation Time: 20 minutes
Cooking Time: 4 hours
Servings: 10
Ingredients:

- 1 5 pound-beef chuck rolls
- 5 tablespoons ground black peppercorns –
- ¼ cup kosher salt

Directions:

1. Combine salt and black peppercorns in a bowl. Mix until combined.

2. Rub the beef chuck with the spice mixture then set aside.

3. Preheat a grill over medium heat for about 10 minutes.

4. Place the charcoal on the grill then waits until the grill reaches 275°F (135°C).

5. Wrap the beef with aluminum foil then place on the grill. Keep the grill's temperature to 275°F (135°C)

6. Cook the beef chuck for 5 hours.

7. When the smoked beef is done, take the smoked beef out of the grill then let it cool for a few minutes.

8. Cut the smoked beef into thin slices then serves with any kind of roasted vegetables, as you desired.

Nutrition: Calories: 230 Carbs: 22g Fat: 9g Protein: 15g

• **Honey Glazed Smoked Beef**

Preparation Time: 10 minutes

Cooking Time: 8 hours

Servings: 10

Ingredients:

- 1 6-pound beef brisket
- 2 ½ tablespoons salt
- 2 ½ tablespoons pepper
- ¾ cup barbecue sauce
- 3 tablespoons red wine
- 3 tablespoons raw honey

Directions:

1. Preheat the smoker to 225°F (107°C). Spread the charcoal on one side.
2. Meanwhile, rub the beef brisket with salt, pepper, and barbecue sauce.
3. When the smoker has reached the desired temperature, place the brisket on the grill with the fat side up. Splash red wine over beef brisket.
4. Smoke the beef brisket for 8 hours. Check the smoker every 2 hours and add more charcoal if it is necessary.
5. Once it is done, take the smoked beef brisket from the smoker then transfers to a serving dish.
6. Drizzle raw honey over the beef and let it sit for about an hour before slicing.
7. Serve with roasted or sautéed vegetables according to your desire.

Nutrition: Calories: 90 Carbs: 8g Fat: 1g Protein: 11g

• **Spiced Smoked Beef with Oregano**

Preparation Time: 10 minutes

Cooking Time: 8 hours

Servings: 10

Ingredients:

- 1 8-pounduntrimmed brisket
- 6 tablespoons paprika
- ¼ cup salt
- 3 tablespoons garlic powder
- 2 tablespoons onion powder
- 1 ½ tablespoons black pepper
- 1 ½ tablespoons dried parsley
- 2 ½ teaspoons cayenne pepper
- 2 ½ teaspoons cumin
- 1 ½ teaspoons coriander
- 2 teaspoons oregano
- ½ teaspoon hot chili powder
- Preheat the smoker prior to smoking.
- Add woodchips during the smoking time.

Directions:

1. Cook the brisket for 6 hours.
2. After 6 hours, usually the smoker temperature decreases to 170°F (77°C).
3. Take the brisket out from the smoker then wrap with aluminum foil.
4. Return the brisket to the smoker then cooks again for 2 hours—this will

increase the tenderness of the smoked beef.

5. Once it is done, remove the smoked beef from the smoker then place in a serving dish.

6. Cut the smoked beef into slices then enjoy!

Nutrition: Calories: 267 Carbs: 0g Fat: 21g Protein: 20g

- ## BBQ Sweet Pepper Meatloaf

Preparation Time: 20 minutes

Cooking Time: 3 hours and 15 minutes

Servings: 8

Ingredients:

- 1 cup chopped red sweet peppers
- 5 pounds ground beef
- 1 cup chopped green onion
- 1 tablespoon salt
- 1 tablespoon ground black pepper
- 1 cup panko breadcrumbs
- 2 tablespoon BBQ rub and more as needed
- 1 cup ketchup
- 2 eggs

Directions:

1. Switch on the Pellet grill, fill the grill hopper with Texas beef blend flavored wood pellets, power the grill on by using the control panel, select 'smoke' on the temperature dial, or set the temperature to 225 degrees F and let it preheat for a minimum of 5 minutes.

2. Meanwhile, take a large bowl, place all the ingredients in it except for ketchup and then stir until well combined.

3. Shape the mixture into meatloaf and then sprinkle with some BBQ rub.

4. When the grill has preheated, open the lid, place meatloaf on the grill grate, shut the grill, and smoke for 2 hours and 15 minutes.

5. Then change the smoking temperature to 375 degrees F, insert a food thermometer into the meatloaf and cook for 45 minutes or more until the internal temperature of meatloaf reaches 155 degrees F.

6. Brush the top of meatloaf with ketchup and then continue cooking for 15 minutes until glazed.

7. When done, transfer food to a dish, let it rest for 10 minutes, then cut it into slices and serve.

Nutrition: Calories: 160.5 Cal Fat: 2.8 g Carbs: 13.2 g Protein: 17.2 g Fiber: 1 g

- ## Blackened Steak

Preparation Time: 10 minutes

Cooking Time: 60 minutes

Servings: 4

Ingredients:

- 2 steaks, each about 40 ounces
- 4 tablespoons blackened rub
- 4 tablespoons butter, unsalted

Directions:

1. Switch on the Pellet grill, fill the grill hopper with hickory flavored wood pellets, power the grill on by using the control panel, select 'smoke' on the temperature dial, or set the temperature to 225 degrees F and let it preheat for a minimum of 15 minutes.

2. Transfer steaks to a dish and then repeat with the remaining steak.

3. Let seared steaks rest for 10 minutes, then slice each steak across the grain and serve.

Nutrition: Calories: 184.4 Cal Fat: 8.8 g Carbs: 0 g Protein: 23.5 g

• Prime Rib Roast

Preparation Time: 24 hours

Cooking Time: 4 hours and 30 minutes

Servings: 8

Ingredients:

- 1 prime rib roast, containing 5 to 7 bones
- Rib rub as needed

Directions:

1. Season rib roast with rib rub until well coated, place it in a large plastic bag, seal it and let it marinate for a minimum of 24 hours in the refrigerator.

2. When ready to cook, switch on the Pellet grill, fill the grill hopper with cherry flavored wood pellets, power the grill on by using the control panel, select 'smoke' on the temperature dial, or set the temperature to 225 degrees F and let it preheat for a minimum of 15 minutes.

3. When the grill has preheated, open the lid, place rib roast on the grill grate fat-side up, change the smoking temperature to 425 degrees F, shut the grill, and smoke for 30 minutes.

4. Then change the smoking temperature to 325 degrees F and continue cooking for 3 to 4 hours until roast has cooked to the desired level, rare at 120 degrees F, medium rare at 130 degrees F, medium at 140 degrees F, and well done at 150 degrees F.

5. When done, transfer roast rib to a cutting board, let it rest for 15 minutes, then cut it into slices and serve.

Nutrition: Calories: 248 Cal Fat: 21.2 g Protein: 28 g

• Thai Beef Skewers

Preparation Time: 15 minutes

Cooking Time: 8 minutes

Servings: 6

Ingredients:

- ½ of medium red bell pepper, destemmed, cored, cut into a ¼-inch piece
- ½ of beef sirloin, fat trimmed

- ½ cup salted peanuts, roasted, chopped
- 1 teaspoon minced garlic
- 1 tablespoon grated ginger
- 1 lime, juiced
- 1 teaspoon ground black pepper
- 1 tablespoon sugar
- 1/4 cup soy sauce
- 1/4 cup olive oil

Directions:

1. Prepare the marinade and for this, take a small bowl, place all of its ingredients in it, whisk until combined, and then pour it into a large plastic bag.
2. Cut into beef sirloin 1-1/4-inch dice, add to the plastic bag containing marinade, seal the bag, turn it upside down to coat beef pieces with the marinade and let it marinate for a minimum of 2 hours in the refrigerator.
3. When ready to cook, switch on the Pellet grill, fill the grill hopper with cherry flavored wood pellets, power the grill on by using the control panel, select 'smoke' on the temperature dial, or set the temperature to 425 degrees F and let it preheat for a minimum of 5 minutes.
4. Meanwhile, remove beef pieces from the marinade and then thread onto skewers.

5. When the grill has preheated, open the lid, place prepared skewers on the grill grate, shut the grill, and smoke for 4 minutes per side until done.
6. When done, transfer skewers to a dish, sprinkle with peanuts and red pepper, and then serve.

Nutrition: Calories: 124 Cal Fat: 5.5 g Carbs: 1.7 g Protein: 15.6 g Fiber: 0 g

- ## **Cowboy Cut Steak**

Preparation Time: 10 minutes
Cooking Time: 1 hour and 15 minutes
Servings: 4
Ingredients:

- 2 cowboy cut steak, each about 2 ½ pounds
- Salt as needed
- Beef rub as needed
- For the Gremolata:
- 2 tablespoons chopped mint
- 1 bunch of parsley, leaves separated
- 1 lemon, juiced
- 1 tablespoon lemon zest
- ½ teaspoon minced garlic
- ¼ teaspoon salt
- 1/8 teaspoon ground black pepper
- 1/4 cup olive oil

Directions:

1. Switch on the Pellet grill, fill the grill hopper with mesquite flavored wood pellets, power the grill on by using the control panel, select 'smoke' on the

temperature dial, or set the temperature to 225 degrees F and let it preheat for a minimum of 5 minutes.

2. When done, transfer steaks to a dish, let rest for 15 minutes, and meanwhile, change the smoking temperature of the grill to 450 degrees F and let it preheat for a minimum of 10 minutes.

3. Then return steaks to the grill grate and cook for 7 minutes per side until the internal temperature reaches 130 degrees F.

Nutrition: Calories: 361 Cal Fat: 31 g Carbs: 1 g Protein: 19 g Fiber: 0.2 g

• Grilled Butter Basted Steak

Preparation Time: 10 minutes

Cooking Time: 40 minutes

Servings: 2

Ingredients:

- 2 steaks, each about 16 ounces, 1 ½-inch thick
- Rib rub as needed
- 2 teaspoon Dijon mustard
- 2 tablespoons Worcestershire sauce
- 4 tablespoons butter, unsalted, melted

Directions:

1. Switch on the Pellet grill, fill the grill hopper with hickory wood pellets, power the grill on by using the control panel, select 'smoke' on the

temperature dial, or set the temperature to 225 degrees F and let it preheat for a minimum of 15 minutes.

2. Then return steaks to the grill grate and cook for 3 minutes per side until the internal temperature reaches 140 degrees F.

3. Transfer steaks to a dish, let rest for 5 minutes and then serve.

Nutrition: Calories: 409.8 Cal Fat: 30.8 g Carbs: 3.1 g Protein: 29.7 g Fiber: 0.4 g

• Chili Rib Eye Steaks

Preparation Time: 10 minutes

Cooking Time: 1 hour

Servings: 4

Ingredients:

- 4 rib-eye steaks, each about 12 ounces
- 1 tablespoon minced garlic
- 1 teaspoon salt
- 1 teaspoon brown sugar
- 2 tablespoons red chili powder
- 1 teaspoon ground cumin
- 2 tablespoons Worcestershire sauce
- 2 tablespoons olive oil

Directions:

1. Prepare the rub and for this, take a small bowl, place all of its ingredients in it and then stir until mixed.

2. Brush the paste on all sides of the steak, rub well, then place steaks into a plastic bag and let it marinate for a minimum of 4 hours.

3. Then return steaks to the grill grate and cook for 3 minutes per side until the internal temperature reaches 140 degrees F.

4. Transfer steaks to a dish, let rest for 5 minutes and then serve.

Nutrition: Calories: 293 Cal Fat: 0 g Protein: 32 g

- ## BBQ Beef Short Ribs

Preparation Time: 15 minutes

Cooking Time: 10 hours

Servings: 8

Ingredients:

- 4 beef short rib racks, membrane removed, containing 4 bones
- 1/2 cup beef rub
- 1 cup apple juice

Directions:

1. Switch on the Pellet grill, fill the grill hopper with apple-flavored wood pellets, power the grill on by using the control panel, select 'smoke' on the temperature dial, or set the temperature to 225 degrees F and let it preheat for a minimum of 15 minutes.

2. Meanwhile, prepare the ribs, and for this, sprinkle beef rub on both sides until well coated.

3. When the grill has preheated, open the lid, place ribs on the grill grate bone-side down, shut the grill, and

smoke for 10 hours until internal temperature reaches 205 degrees F, spritzing with apple juice every hour.

4. When done, transfer ribs to a cutting board, let rest for 10 minutes, then cut into slices and serve.

Nutrition: Calories: 280 Cal Fat: 15 g Carbs: 17 g Protein: 20 g Fiber: 1 g

- ## Thai Beef Salad

Preparation Time: 10 minutes

Cooking Time: 10 minutes

Servings: 4

Ingredients:

- 1 ½ pound skirt steak
- 1 ½ teaspoon salt
- 1 teaspoon ground white pepper
- 4 jalapeño peppers, minced
- ½ teaspoon minced garlic
- 4 tablespoons Thai fish sauce
- 4 tablespoons lime juice
- 1 tablespoon brown sugar
- 1 small red onion, peeled, thinly sliced
- 6 cherry tomatoes, halved
- 2 green onions, ¼-inch diced
- 1 cucumber, deseeded, thinly sliced
- 1 heart of romaine lettuce, chopped
- ½ cup chopped mint
- 2 tablespoons cilantro
- ½ teaspoon red pepper flakes
- 1 tablespoon lime juice
- 2 tablespoons fish sauce

Directions:

1. Switch on the Pellet grill, fill the grill hopper with cherry flavored wood pellets, power the grill on by using the control panel, select 'smoke' on the temperature dial, or set the temperature to 450 degrees F and let it preheat for a minimum of 15 minutes.

2. Take a large salad, place all the ingredients for the salad in it, drizzle with dressing and toss until well coated and mixed.

3. When done, transfer steak to a cutting board, let it rest for 10 minutes and then cut it into slices.

4. Add steak slices into the salad, toss until mixed, and then serve.

Nutrition: Calories: 128 Cal Fat: 6 g Carbs: 6 g Protein: 12 g Fiber: 1 g

• <u>Grilled Almond-Crusted Beef Fillet</u>

Preparation Time: 10 minutes

Cooking Time: 55 minutes

Servings: 4

Ingredients:

- 3 lbs. fillet of beef tenderloin
- Salt and pepper to taste
- 1/4 cup olive oil
- 1/3 cup onion, very finely chopped
- 2 tbsp. curry powder
- 1 cup chicken broth
- 1 tbsp. Dijon mustard
- 1/4 cup sliced almonds, coarsely chopped

Directions:

1. Rub the beef tenderloin with salt and pepper.

2. In a bowl, combine olive oil, onion, curry, chicken broth, mustard, and almonds.

3. Rub your beef meat generously with the curry mixture.

4. Start your pellet grill, set the temperature on High and preheat, lid closed, for 10 to 15 minutes.

5. As a general rule, you should grill steaks on high heat (450-500°F).

6. Grill about 7-10 minutes per side at high temperatures or 15-20 minutes per side at the lower temperatures, or to your preference for doneness.

7. Remove meat from the grill and let cool for 10 minutes.

8. Serve hot.

Nutrition: Calories 479.33 Fiber 1.95g Sugar 0.7g Protein 36.82g

• <u>Grilled Beef Eye Fillet with Herb Rubs</u>

Preparation Time: 1 hour

Cooking Time: 8 hours

Servings: 6

Ingredients:

- 2 lbs. beef eye fillet
- Salt and pepper to taste
- 2 tbsp. Olive oil

- 1/4 cup parsley, fresh and chopped
- 1/4 cup oregano leaves, fresh and chopped
- 2 tbsp. basil, fresh and chopped
- 2 tbsp. rosemary leaves, fresh and chopped
- 3 cloves garlic, crushed

Directions:

1. Season beef roast with salt and pepper and place in a shallow dish.
2. In a medium bowl, combine olive oil, chopped parsley, basil, oregano, rosemary, garlic, and oil. Rub the meat with the herb mixture from both sides
3. Bring the meat to room temperature 30 minutes before you put it on the grill.
4. Start your pellet grill, set the temperature on High and preheat, lid closed, for 10 to 15 minutes.
5. As a general rule, you should grill steaks on high heat (450-500°F).
6. Grill about 7-10 minutes per side at high temperatures or 15-20 minutes per side at the lower temperatures, or to your preference for doneness.
7. When ready, let meat rest for 10 minutes, slice and serve.

Nutrition: Calories 427.93 Fiber 2.17g Sugar 0.2g Protein 30.8g

• <u>Grilled Beef Steak with Molasses and Balsamic Vinegar</u>

Preparation Time: 20 minutes
Cooking Time: 50 minutes
Servings: 5
Ingredients:

- 2 1/2 lbs. beefsteak grass fed
- Salt and ground pepper
- 2 tbsp. molasses
- 1 cup beef broth
- 1 tbsp. red wine vinegar
- 1 tbsp. balsamic vinegar

Directions:

1. Place a beef steak in a large dish.
2. Combine the beef broth, molasses, red wine vinegar and balsamic vinegar in a bowl.
3. Cover, and refrigerate for up to 8 hours.
4. 30 minutes before grilling, remove the steaks from the refrigerator and let sit at room temperature.
5. Start your pellet grill, set the temperature on High and preheat, lid closed, for 10 to 15 minutes.
6. Grill about 7-10 minutes per side at high temperatures or 15-20 minutes per side at the lower temperatures.
7. Transfer meat to a serving dish and let rest about 10 minutes.
8. Serve warm.

Nutrition: Calories 295.3 Sugar 4.92g Protein 52.89g

• Grilled Beef Steak with Peanut Oil and Herbs

Preparation Time: 25 minutes

Cooking Time: 55 minutes

Servings: 6

Ingredients:

- 3 lbs. beef steak, preferably flank
- 1 tsp sea salt
- 2 tbsp. peanut oil
- 1/4 olive oil
- 2 tbsp. fresh mint leaves, finely chopped
- 2 tsp peppercorn black
- 2 tsp peppercorn green
- 1/2 tsp cumin seeds
- 1 pinch of chili flakes

Directions:

1. Rub the beef steaks with coarse salt and place in a large dish.
2. Make a marinade; in a bowl, combine peanut oil, olive oil, fresh mint leave, peppercorn, cumin and chili flakes.
3. Cover and refrigerate for 4 hours.
4. Bring the meat to room temperature 30 minutes before you put it on the grill.
5. Start your pellet grill, set the temperature on High and preheat, lid closed, for 10 to 15 minutes.
6. As a general rule, you should grill steaks on high heat (450-500°F).
7. Grill about 7-10 minutes per side at high temperatures or 15-20 minutes per side at the lower temperatures, or to your preference for doneness.
8. Remove flank steak from the grill and let cool before slicing for 10 -15 minutes.
9. Slice and serve.

Nutrition: Calories 346.3 Fiber 0.07g Protein 32.38g

• Grilled Beef Steaks with Beer-Honey Sauce

Preparation Time: 10 minutes

Cooking Time: 55 minutes

Servings: 4

Ingredients:

- 4 beef steaks
- Salt and pepper to taste
- 1 cup of beer
- 1 tsp thyme
- 1 tbsp. of honey
- 1 lemon juice
- 2 tbsp. olive oil

Directions:

1. Season beef steaks with salt and pepper.
2. In a bowl, combine beer, thyme, honey, lemon juice and olive oil.
3. Rub the beef steaks generously with beer mixture.

4. Start your pellet grill, set the temperature on High and preheat, lid closed, for 10 to 15 minutes.

5. As a general rule, you should grill steaks on high heat (450-500°F).

6. Grill about 7-10 minutes per side at high temperatures or 15 minutes per side at the lower temperatures, or to your preference for doneness.

7. Remove meat from the grill and let cool for 10 minutes.

8. Serve.

Nutrition: Calories 355.77 Fiber 0.18g Sugar 4.69g Protein 49.74g

• <u>Grilled La Rochelle Beef Steak with Curried Pineapple</u>

Preparation Time: 30 minutes

Cooking Time: 55 minutes

Servings: 4

Ingredients:

- 1 1/2 lbs. flank steak
- 1/4 cup olive oil
- 8 oz. pineapple chunks in juice
- 3 tsp curry powder
- 1 tbsp. red currant jelly
- 1/2 tsp salt, or to taste

Directions:

1. Place the flank steak in a shallow dish.

2. In a bowl, combine olive oil, pineapple chunks in juice, curry powder, red currant jelly and salt and pepper.

3. Pour the mixture over flank steak.

4. Cover and refrigerate for 4 hours.

5. Bring the meat to room temperature 30 minutes before you put it on the grill.

6. Start your pellet grill, set the temperature on High and preheat, lid closed, for 10 to 15 minutes.

7. As a general rule, you should grill steaks on high heat (450-500°F).

8. Grill about 7-10 minutes per side at high temperatures or 15-20 minutes per side at the lower temperatures, or to your preference for doneness.

9. Remove flank steak from the grill and let cool for 10 minutes.

10. Serve hot.

Nutrition: Calories 406.26 Fiber 1.85g Sugar 8.23g Protein 32.01g

• <u>Grilled Veal Shoulder Roast with Fennel and Thyme Rub</u>

Preparation Time: 15 minutes

Cooking Time: 55 minutes

Servings: 8

Ingredients:

- 3 1/2 lb. boneless veal shoulder roast
- 2 tbsp. dried thyme leaves
- 1 fresh fennel, thinly sliced
- 2 tbsp. fresh thyme, chopped
- 3/4 tsp kosher salt and ground white pepper

- 4 tbsp. olive oil
- 1/2 cup white wine

Directions:

1. Place a shoulder roast in a large dish and rub with salt and pepper.
2. In a bowl, combine thyme, fennel, salt and pepper, wine and oil.
3. Rub the meat generously.
4. Start your pellet grill, set the temperature on High and preheat, lid closed, for 10 to 15 minutes.
5. Grill about 25 minutes at high temperatures or to your preference for doneness.
6. Remove the veal chops from the grill. Take their temperature with your meat thermometer. The veal chops should have a temperature of 130 degrees Fahrenheit for medium-rare or 140 degrees for medium.
7. Serve hot.

Nutrition: Calories 322.71 Fiber 1.39g Sugar 0.62g Protein 36.23g

• <u>Grilled Veal with Mustard Lemony Crust</u>

Preparation Time: 45 minutes
Cooking Time: 2 hours and 45 minutes
Servings: 8
Ingredients:

- 1 lb. boneless veal leg round roast
- 1 tbsp. Dijon-style mustard
- 1 tbsp. lemon juice
- 1 tsp dried thyme, crushed
- 1 tsp dried basil, crushed
- 2 tbsp. water
- 1/2 tsp coarsely salt and ground pepper
- 1/4 cup breadcrumbs

Directions:

1. Place meat on a rack in a shallow roasting pan.
2. In a small mixing bowl stir together breadcrumbs, water, mustard, lemon juice, basil, thyme, and pepper. Spread the mixture over surface of the meat.
3. Start your pellet grill, set the temperature on High and preheat, lid closed, for 10 to 15 minutes.
4. As a general rule, you should grill steaks on high heat (450-500°F).
5. Grill about 7-10 minutes per side at high temperatures or 15-20 minutes per side at the lower temperatures, or to your preference for doneness.
6. Remove veal meat from the grill and let cool for 10 minutes.

Nutrition: Calories 172 Protein 30g Fat 2g Carbs 16g

• Smoked Cauliflower

Preparation Time: 15 Minutes

Cooking Time: 10 Minutes

Servings: 3-4

Ingredients:

- 1 Head of cauliflower
- 1 Cup of parmesan cheese
- 1 Tablespoon of olive oil
- 2 Crushed garlic cloves
- ¼ Teaspoon of Paprika
- ½ Teaspoon of salt
- ½ Teaspoon of pepper

Directions:

1. Start your Wood Pellet smoker grill with the lid open for about 4 to 5 minutes

2. Set the temperature on about 180°F and preheat with the lid closed for about 10 to 15 minutes

3. Cut the cauliflower into florets of medium-sized; then place the cauliflower right on top of the grate and mix all the ingredients except for the cheese

4. After about 1 hour, remove the cauliflower; then turn the smoker grill on high for about 10 to 15 minutes

5. Brush the cauliflower with the mixture of the ingredients and place it on a sheet tray

6. Place the cauliflower back on the grate for about 10 minutes

7. Sprinkle with the parmesan cheese

8. Serve and enjoy your smoked cauliflower!

Nutrition: Calories: 60 Fat: 3.6g Carbohydrates: 3.1g Dietary Fiber: 1g Protein: 4g

• Grilled Asparagus

Preparation Time: 5 minutes

Cooking Time: 20 minutes

Servings: 4

Ingredients:

- 3 cups of vegetables sliced
- 2 tbsp. of olive oil
- 2 tbsp. of garlic & herb seasoning

Directions:

1. Preheat your Traeger grill to a temperature of about 350°F
2. While your Traeger is heating, slice the vegetables. Cut the spears from the Broccoli and the Zucchini; then wash the outsides and slice into spears; cut the peppers into wide strips. You can also grill carrots, corn, asparagus, and potatoes -grill at a temperature of about 350°F for about 20 minutes. Serve and enjoy!

Nutrition Calories: 47, Fat: 3g, Carbohydrates: 1g, Dietary Fiber: 1g, Protein: 2.2g

• Grill Eggplants

Preparation Time: 5 minutes

Cooking Time: 12 minutes

Servings: 6

Ingredients:

- 1 to 2 large eggplants
- 3 tablespoons of extra virgin olive oil
- 2 tablespoons of balsamic vinegar
- 2 finely minced garlic cloves
- 1 pinch of each thyme, dill; oregano, and basil

Directions:

1. Gather your ingredients.

2. Heat your Traeger grill to a medium-high
3. When the Traeger grill becomes hot; slice the eggplant into slices of about 1/2-inch of thickness
4. In a bowl, whisk the olive oil with the balsamic vinegar, the garlic, the herbs, the salt, and the pepper.
5. Brush both sides of the sliced eggplant with oil and with the vinegar mixture.
6. Place the eggplant over the preheated grill
7. Grill the eggplant for about 12 minutes
8. Serve and enjoy!

Nutrition Calories: 56, Fat: 0.8g, Carbohydrates: 11g, Dietary Fiber: 4.1g, Protein: 4g

• Green Beans with Bacon

Preparation Time: 10 minutes

Cooking Time: 20 minutes

Servings: 6

Ingredients:

- 4 strips of bacon, chopped
- 1 1/2-pound green beans, ends trimmed
- 1 teaspoon minced garlic
- 1 teaspoon salt
- 4 tablespoons olive oil

Directions:

1. Set the temperature to 450 degrees F and let it preheat for a minimum of 15 minutes.
2. Take a sheet tray, place all the ingredients in it, and toss until mixed.
3. When the grill has preheated, open the lid, set the prepared sheet tray on the grill grate, shut the grill, and smoke for 20 minutes until lightly browned and cooked.
4. When done, transfer green beans to a dish and then serve.

Nutrition: Calories: 93 Cal Fat: 4.6 g Carbs: 8.2 g Protein: 5.9 g Fiber: 2.9 g

- ## **Roasted Fall Vegetables**

Preparation Time: 10 minutes

Cooking Time: 35 minutes

Servings: 8

Ingredients:

- Potatoes – ½ pound
- Brussels sprouts, halved – ½ pound
- Butternut squash, dice – ½ pound
- Cremini mushrooms, halved – 1 pint
- Salt – 1 tablespoon
- Ground black pepper – ¾ tablespoon
- Olive oil – 2 tablespoons

Directions:

1. In the meantime, take a large bowl, place potatoes in it, add salt and black pepper, drizzle with oil and then toss until coated.
2. Take a sheet tray and then spread seasoned potatoes on it.
3. When the grill has preheated, place sheet pan containing potatoes on the grilling rack and then grill for 15 minutes.
4. Then add mushrooms and sprouts into the pan, toss to coat and then continue grilling for 20 minutes until all the vegetables have turned nicely browned and thoroughly cooked.
5. Serve immediately.

Nutrition: Calories: 80 Carbs: 7g Fat: 6g Protein: 1g

• Cinnamon Almonds

Preparation Time: 15 minutes

Cooking Time: 1 hour and 30 minutes

Servings: 4

Ingredients:

- Almonds – 1 pound
- Granulated sugar – ½ cup
- Brown sugar – ½ cup
- Cinnamon – 1 tablespoon
- Salt – 1/8 teaspoon
- Egg white – 1

Directions:

1. In the meantime, take a small bowl, place egg white in it, and then whisk until frothy.
2. Add remaining ingredients for the seasoning in it, whisk until blended, then add almonds and toss until well coated.
3. Take a sheet pan and then spread almonds mixture in it.
4. When the grill has preheated, place sheet pan containing almonds mixture on the grilling rack and grill for 90 minutes until almonds have roasted, stirring every 10 minutes.
5. Check the fire after one hour of smoking and add more wood pallets if required.
6. When done, remove sheet pan from grill, let it cool slightly and then serve.

Nutrition: Calories 136.9 Carbs: 15g Fat: 8g Protein: 3g

• Roasted Pumpkin Seeds

Preparation Time: 10 minutes

Cooking Time: 40 minutes

Servings: 8

Ingredients:

- Pumpkin seeds – 1 pound
- Salt – 1 tablespoon
- Olive oil – 1 tablespoon

Directions:

1. In the meantime, take a baking sheet, grease it with oil, spread pumpkin seeds on it and then stir until coated.
2. When the grill has preheated, place baking sheet containing pumpkin sees on the grilling rack and let grill for 20 minutes.
3. Season pumpkin seeds with salt, switch temperature of the grill to 325 degrees F, and continue grilling for 20 minutes until roasted.
4. When done, let pumpkin seeds cool slightly and then serve.

Nutrition: Calories: 130 Carbs: 13g Fat: 5g Protein 8g

• Crispy Garlic Potatoes

Preparation Time: 15 minutes
Cooking Time: 40 minutes
Servings: 4
Ingredients:

- Baby potatoes, scrubbed – 1 pound
- Large white onion, peeled, sliced – 1
- Garlic, peeled, sliced – 3
- Chopped parsley – 1 teaspoon
- Butter, unsalted, sliced – 3 tablespoons

Directions:

1. In the meantime, cut potatoes in slices and then arrange them on a large piece of foil or baking sheet, separating potatoes by onion slices and butter.
2. Sprinkle garlic slices over vegetables, and then season with salt, black pepper, and parsley.
3. When the grill has preheated, place a baking sheet containing potato mixture on the grilling rack and grill for 40 minutes until potato slices have turned tender.
4. Serve immediately.

Nutrition: Calories: 150 Carbs: 15g Fat: 10g Protein: 1g

• Stuffed Avocados

Preparation Time: 5 minutes
Cooking Time: 10 to 15 minutes
Servings: 3 to 4
Ingredients:

- 4 Avocados, Halved, Pit Removed
- 8 Eggs
- 2 Cups Shredded Cheddar Cheese
- 4 Slices Bacon, Cooked and Chopped
- 1/4 Cup Cherry Tomatoes, Halved
- Green Onions, Sliced Thin
- Salt and Pepper, To Taste

Directions:

1. When ready to cook, set the temperature to High and preheat, lid closed for 15 minutes.

2. After removing the pit from the avocado, scoop out a little of the flesh to make enough room to fit 1 egg per half.

3. Fill the bottom of a cast iron pan with kosher salt and nestle the avocado halves into the salt, cut side up. The salt helps to keep them in place while cooking, like ice with oysters.

4. Crack egg into each half, top with a hand full of shredded cheddar cheese, some cherry tomatoes and bacon. Season with salt and pepper to taste.

5. Place the cast iron pan directly on the grill grate and bake the avocados for 12-15 minutes until the cheese is melted and the egg is just set.

6. Remove from the grill and let rest 5-10 minutes. Enjoy!

Nutrition: Carbs: 50g Fat: 103g Protein: 58g

• Bacon-Wrapped Asparagus

Preparation Time: 10 minutes

Cooking Time: 25 to 30 minutes

Servings: 3

Ingredients:

- 1-pound fresh thick asparagus (15 to 20 spears)
- extra-virgin olive oil
- 5 slices thinly sliced bacon
- 1 teaspoon Pete's Western Rub (page 169) or salt and pepper

Directions:

1. Snap off the woody ends of asparagus and trim so they are all about the same length.

2. Divide the asparagus into bundles of 3 spears and spritz with olive oil. Wrap each bundle with 1 piece of bacon and then dust with the seasoning or salt and pepper to taste.

3. Configure your wood pellet smoker-grill for indirect cooking, placing Teflon coated fiberglass mats on top of the grates (to prevent the asparagus from sticking to the grill grates). Preheat to 400°F using any type of pellets. The grill can be preheated while prepping the asparagus.

4. Grill the bacon-wrapped asparagus for 25 to 30 minutes, until the asparagus is tender and the bacon is cooked and crispy.

Nutrition: Calories: 94 Carbs: 5g Fat: 7g Protein: 4g

• Brisket Baked Beans

Preparation Time: 15 minutes

Cooking Time: 1 to 2 hours

Servings: 5

Ingredients:

- 2 tablespoons extra-virgin olive oil 1 large yellow onion, diced
- 1 medium green bell pepper, diced
- 1 medium red bell pepper, diced
- 2 to 6 jalapeño peppers, diced

- 3 cups chopped Texas-Style Brisket Flat (page 91) 1 (28-ounce) can baked beans, like Bush's Country
- Style Baked Beans 1 (28-ounce) can pork and beans
- 1 (14-ounce) can red kidney beans, rinsed and drained 1 cup barbecue sauce, like Sweet Baby Ray's
- Barbecue Sauce ½ cup packed brown sugar
- 3 garlic cloves, chopped
- 2 teaspoons ground mustard
- ½ teaspoon kosher salt
- ½ teaspoon black pepper

Directions:

1. In a skillet over medium heat, warm the olive oil and then add the diced onion, peppers, and jalapeños. Cook until the onions are translucent, about 8 to 10 minutes, stirring occasionally.

2. In a 4-quart casserole dish, mix the chopped brisket, baked beans, pork and beans, kidney beans, cooked onion and peppers, barbecue sauce, brown sugar, garlic, ground mustard, salt, and black pepper.

3. Configure your wood pellet smoker-grill for indirect cooking and preheat to 325°F using your pellets of choice. Cook the brisket baked beans uncovered for 1½ to 2 hours, until the beans are thick and bubbly. Allow to rest for 15 minutes before serving.

Nutrition: Carbs: 35g Fat: 2g Protein: 9g

• Garlic Parmesan Wedges

Preparation Time: 15 minutes

Cooking Time: 45 minutes

Servings: 6

Ingredients:

- 3 large russet potatoes
- ¼ cup extra-virgin olive oil
- 1½ teaspoons salt
- ¾ teaspoon black pepper
- 2 teaspoons garlic powder
- ¾ cup grated Parmesan cheese
- 3 tablespoons chopped fresh cilantro or flat-leaf parsley (optional)
- ½ cup blue cheese or ranch dressing per serving, for dipping (optional)

Directions:

1. Gently scrub the potatoes with cold water using a vegetable brush and allow the potatoes to dry.

2. Cut the potatoes lengthwise in half, then cut those halves into thirds.

3. Use a paper towel to wipe away all the moisture that is released when you cut the potatoes. Moisture prevents the wedges from getting crispy.

4. Place the potato wedges, olive oil, salt, pepper, and garlic powder in a large bowl, and toss lightly with your hands, making sure the oil and spices are distributed evenly.

5. Arrange the wedges in a single layer on a nonstick grilling tray/pan/basket (about 15 × 12 inches).

6. Configure your wood pellet smoker-grill for indirect cooking and preheat to 425°F using any type of wood pellets.

7. Place the grilling tray in your preheated smoker-grill and roast the potato wedges for 15 minutes before turning. Roast the potato wedges for an additional 15 to 20 minutes until potatoes are fork tender on the inside and crispy golden brown on the outside.

8. Sprinkle the potato wedges with Parmesan cheese and garnish with cilantro or parsley, if desired. Serve with blue cheese or ranch dressing for dipping, if desired.

Nutrition: Calories: 324 Fat: 11.6g Cholesterol: 6mg Protein: 8.6g

• __Twice-Baked Spaghetti Squash__

Preparation Time: 20 minutes
Cooking Time: 50 minutes
Servings: 5
Ingredients:

- 1 medium spaghetti squash
- 1 tablespoon extra-virgin olive oil
- 1 teaspoon salt
- ½ teaspoon pepper
- ½ cup shredded mozzarella cheese, divided
- ½ cup grated Parmesan cheese, divided

Directions:

1. Carefully cut the squash in half lengthwise using a large, sharp knife. Remove the seeds and pulp of each half using a spoon.

2. Rub olive oil over the insides of the squash halves and sprinkle with salt and pepper.

3. Configure your wood pellet smoker-grill for indirect cooking and preheat to 375°F using any type of wood pellets.

4. Place the squash halves face-up directly on the hot grill grates.

5. Bake the squash for approximately 45 minutes, until the internal temperature reaches 170°F. When done, the spaghetti squash will be soft and easily pierced with a fork.

6. Transfer the squash to a cutting board and allow to cool for 10 minutes.

7. Increase the wood pellet smoker-grill temperature to 425°F.

8. Being careful to keep the shells intact, use a fork to rake back and forth across the squash to remove the flesh in strands. Note that the stands look like spaghetti.

9. Transfer the strands to a large bowl. Add half the mozzarella and Parmesan cheeses, and stir to combine.

10. Stuff the mixture back in the squash shell halves, and sprinkle the tops with the remaining mozzarella and Parmesan cheeses.

11. Bake the stuffed spaghetti squash halves for another 15 minutes at 425°F, or until the cheese starts to brown.

Nutrition: Calories: 214.3 Total Fat: 3.4g Saturated Fat: 1.7g

• **Smoked Tomatoes**

Preparation Time: 5 minutes
Cooking Time: 45 minutes
Servings: 3
Ingredients:

- Tomatoes, cut in half
- Dried lovage (optional)
- Sea salt
- Black pepper
- Olive oil (enough to coat the tomatoes)

Directions:

1. Set your grill to the Smoke setting.
2. Slice tomatoes in half and coat with olive oil in a bowl large enough to hold them. Add a liberal pinch of sea salt, freshly cracked black pepper, and dried lovage to taste (if using). Use your hands and mix the tomatoes until evenly coated in the mixture.

3. Place tomatoes on a baking sheet and then on the grill.

4. Increase temperature to about 180-200.

5. Tomatoes will be done in approximately 45 minutes. The edges will begin to curl and insides to bubble.

Nutrition: Calories: 50 Carbs: 2g Fat: 5g

• **Smoked Olives**

Preparation Time: 5 minutes
Cooking Time: 30 to 50 minutes
Servings: 4
Ingredients:

- 1 cup black olives such as Greek Kalamata or Atalante, drained lightly
- 1 cup green olives, drained lightly
- 2 tbsp. extra-virgin olive oil
- 2 tbsp. white wine - vermouth works great
- 2 garlic cloves minced
- 3/4 tsp dried rosemary We have also used oregano with some great success but the rosemary has a better all-around taste.
- fresh ground black pepper to taste
- Perfect Mix Pellets

Directions:

1. Set pellet grill at 220 with perfect mix pellets.

2. Arrange the olives in a shallow piece of heavy-duty foil molded into a small tray.

3. Add the remaining **Ingredients:**

4. Place the olives in the smoker and cook until the olives absorb half of the liquid and take on a light but identifiable smoke flavor, 30-50 minutes. Time depends on your grill!! Taste test after about 15-20 minutes.

5. The olives can be served immediately with some asiago grated cheese over them or can sit for several hours to develop the flavor further.

6. Refrigerate any leftovers. Be sure to save the leftover olive oil for bread dipping.

Nutrition: Calories: 40 Carbs: 1g Fat: 4g

• <u>Spaghetti Squash with Brown Butter and Parmesan</u>

Preparation Time: 15 minutes
Cooking Time: 50 to 60 minutes
Servings: 5
Ingredients:

- 1 spaghetti squash, 2 1/2 to 3 lb.
- 4 Tbs. (1/2 stick) unsalted butter
- Pinch of freshly grated nutmeg
- 1/3 cup grated Parmigiano-Reggiano cheese
- Salt and freshly ground pepper, to taste

Directions:

1. Place the whole squash in a large pot and add water to cover. Bring to a boil over high heat, reduce the heat to medium-low and simmer, uncovered, until the squash can be easily pierced with a knife, about 45 minutes.

2. Meanwhile, in a saucepan over medium-high heat, melt the butter and cook it until it turns brown and just begins to smoke, 3 to 4 minutes. Remove immediately from the heat and stir in the nutmeg.

3. When the squash is done, drain and set aside until cool enough to handle. Cut the squash in half lengthwise and, using a fork, scrape out the seeds and discard. Place the squash halves, cut sides up, on a serving platter. Using the fork, scrape the flesh free of the skin, carefully separating it into the spaghetti-like strands that it naturally forms. Leave the strands mounded in the squash halves. If the butter has cooled, place over medium heat until hot.

4. To serve, drizzle the butter evenly over the squash. Sprinkle with the cheese and season with salt and pepper. Serve immediately.

Nutrition: Calories: 214.3 Total Fat: 3.4g Saturated Fat: 1.7g

• **Smoked Jalapeno Poppers**

Preparation Time: 10 minutes

Cooking Time: 20 to 25 minutes

Servings: 4

Ingredients:

- 12 jalapeño peppers
- 8-ounces cream cheese, room temperature
- 10 pieces of bacon

Directions:

1. Preheat your grill or another wood-pellet grill to 350°.
2. Wash and cut the tops off of the peppers, and then slice them in half the long way. Scrape the seeds and the membranes out, and set aside.
3. Spoon softened cream cheese into the popper, and wrap with bacon and secure with a toothpick.
4. Place on wire racks that are non-stick or have been sprayed with non-stick spray, and grill for 20-25 minutes, or until the bacon is cooked.

Nutrition: Calories: 94 Carbs: 5g Fat: 7g

• <u>Baked Heirloom Tomato Tart</u>

Preparation Time: 20 minutes
Cooking Time: 1 hour and 40 minutes
Servings: 6
Ingredients:

- 1 Sheet Puff Pastry
- 2 Lbs. Heirloom Tomatoes, Various Shapes and Sizes
- 1/2 Cup Ricotta
- 5 Eggs
- 1/2 Tbsp. Kosher Salt
- 1/2 Tsp Thyme Leaves
- 1/2 Tsp Red Pepper Flakes
- Pinch of Black Pepper
- 4 Sprigs Thyme
- Salt and Pepper, To Taste

Directions:

1. When ready to cook, set temperature to 350°F and preheat, lid closed for 15 minutes.
2. Place the puff pastry on a parchment lined sheet tray, and make a cut ¾ of the way through the pastry, ½" from the edge.
3. Slice the tomatoes and season with salt. Place on a sheet tray lined with paper towels.
4. In a small bowl combine the ricotta, 4 of the eggs, salt, thyme leaves, red pepper flakes and black pepper. Whisk together until combined. Spread the ricotta mixture over the puff pastry, staying within ½" from the edge.
5. Lay the tomatoes out on top of the ricotta, and sprinkle with salt, pepper and thyme sprigs.
6. In a small bowl whisk the last egg. Brush the egg wash onto the exposed edges of the pastry.
7. Place the sheet tray directly on the grill grate and bake for 45 minutes, rotating half-way through.
8. When the edges are browned and the moisture from the tomatoes has evaporated, remove from the grill and let cool 5-7 minutes before serving. Enjoy!

Nutrition: Calories: 443 Protein: 13.8g Carbs: 36.3g

• <u>Smoked Pickled Green Beans</u>

Preparation Time: 5 minutes
Cooking Time: 15 to 20 minutes
Servings: 2
Ingredients:

- 1 Lb. Green Beans, Blanched
- 1/2 Cup Salt
- 1/2 Cup Sugar
- 1 Tbsp. Red Pepper Flake
- 2 Cups White Wine Vinegar

- 2 Cups Ice Water

Directions:

1. When ready to cook, set temperature to 180°F and preheat, lid closed for 15 minutes.

2. Place the blanched green beans on a mesh grill mat and place mat directly on the grill grate. Smoke the green beans for 30-45 minutes until they've picked up the desired amount of smoke. Remove from grill and set aside until the brine is ready.

3. In a medium sized saucepan, bring all remaining **Ingredients:** except ice water, to a boil over medium high heat on the stove. Simmer for 5-10 minutes then remove from heat and steep 20 minutes more. Pour brine over ice water to cool.

4. Once brine has cooled, pour over the green beans and weigh them down with a few plates to ensure they are completely submerged. Let sit 24 hours before use.

Nutrition: Calories: 99 Fat: 5g Carbs: 19mg

• **Baked Asparagus Pancetta Cheese Tart**

Preparation Time: 10 minutes
Cooking Time: 20 to 30 minutes
Servings: 5
Ingredients:

- 1 Sheet Puff Pastry
- 8 Oz Asparagus, Pencil Spears
- 8 Oz Pancetta, Cooked and Drained
- 1 Cup Cream
- 4 Eggs
- 1/4 Cup Goat Cheese
- 4 Tbsp. Grated Parmesan
- 1 Tbsp. Chopped Chives
- Black Pepper

Directions:

1. When ready to cook, set the temperature to 375°F and preheat, lid closed for 15 minutes.

2. Place the puff pastry on a half sheet tray and score around the perimeter 1-inch in from the edges making sure not to cut all the way through. Prick the center of the puff pastry with a fork.

3. Place the sheet tray directly on the grill grate and bake for 15-20 minutes until the pastry has puffed and browned a little bit.

4. While the pastry bakes combine the cream, 3 eggs, both cheeses and chives in a small bowl. Whisk to mix well.

5. Remove the sheet tray from the grill and pour the egg mixture into the puff pastry. Lay the asparagus spears on top of the egg mixture and sprinkle with cooked pancetta.

6. Whisk remaining egg in a small bowl and brush the top of the pastry with the egg wash.

7. Place back on the grill grate and cook for another 15-20 minutes until the egg mixture is just set.

8. Finish tart with lemon zest, more chopped chives and shaved parmesan.

Nutrition: Calories: 50 Carbs: 4g Fiber: 2g Fat: 2.5g Protein: 2g

• Georgia Sweet Onion Bake

Preparation Time: 10 Minutes

Cooking Time: 30 Minutes

Servings: 4

Ingredients:

- 4 large Vidalia or other sweet onions
- 8 tablespoons (1 stick) unsalted butter, melted
- 4 chicken bouillon cubes
- 1 cup grated Parmesan cheese

Directions:

1. Supply your smoker with wood pellets and follow the manufacturer's specific start-up procedure. Preheat, with the lid closed, to 350°F.

2. Coat a high-sided baking pan with cooking spray or butter.

3. Peel the onions and cut into quarters, separating into individual petals.

4. Spread the onions out in the prepared pan and pour the melted butter over them.

5. Crush the bouillon cubes and sprinkle over the buttery onion pieces, then top with the cheese.

6. Transfer the pan to the grill, close the lid, and smoke for 30 minutes.

7. Remove the pan from the grill, cover tightly with aluminum foil, and poke several holes all over to vent.

8. Place the pan back on the grill, close the lid, and smoke for an additional 30 to 45 minutes.

9. Uncover the onions, stir, and serve hot.

Nutrition: Calories: 50 Carbs: 4g Fiber: 2g Fat: 2.5g Protein: 2g

• Roasted Okra

Preparation Time: 10 Minutes

Cooking Time: 30 Minutes

Servings: 4

Ingredients:

- 1-pound whole okra
- 2 tablespoons extra-virgin olive oil
- 2 teaspoons seasoned salt
- 2 teaspoons freshly ground black pepper

Directions:

1. Supply your smoker with wood pellets and follow the manufacturer's specific start-up procedure. Preheat, with the lid closed, to 400°F. Alternatively, preheat your oven to 400°F.

2. Line a shallow rimmed baking pan with aluminum foil and coat with cooking spray.

3. Arrange the okra on the pan in a single layer. Drizzle with the olive oil,

turning to coat. Season on all sides with the salt and pepper.

4. Place the baking pan on the grill grate, close the lid, and smoke for 30 minutes, or until crisp and slightly charred. Alternatively, roast in the oven for 30 minutes.

5. Serve hot.

6. Smoking Tip: Whether you make this okra in the oven or in your wood pellet grill, be sure to fully preheat the oven or cook chamber for the best results.

Nutrition: Calories: 150 Carbohydrates: 15 g Protein: 79 g Sodium: 45 mg Cholesterol: 49 mg

• <u>**Sweet Potato Chips**</u>

Preparation Time: 10 Minutes

Cooking Time: 12 to 15 Minutes

Servings: 4

Ingredients:

- 2 sweet potatoes
- 1-quart warm water
- 1 tablespoon cornstarch, plus 2 teaspoons
- ¼ cup extra-virgin olive oil
- 1 tablespoon salt
- 1 tablespoon packed brown sugar
- 1 teaspoon ground cinnamon
- 1 teaspoon freshly ground black pepper
- ½ teaspoon cayenne pepper

Directions:

1. Using a mandolin, thinly slice the sweet potatoes.

2. Pour the warm water into a large bowl and add 1 tablespoon of cornstarch and the potato slices. Let soak for 15 to 20 minutes.

3. Supply your smoker with wood pellets and follow the manufacturer's specific start-up procedure. Preheat, with the lid closed, to 375°F.

4. Drain the potato slices, then arrange in a single layer on a perforated pizza pan or a baking sheet lined with aluminum foil. Brush the potato slices on both sides with the olive oil.

5. In a small bowl, whisk together the salt, brown sugar, cinnamon, black pepper, cayenne pepper, and the remaining 2 teaspoons of cornstarch. Sprinkle this seasoning blend on both sides of the potatoes.

6. Place the pan or baking sheet on the grill grate, close the lid, and smoke for 35 to 45 minutes, flipping after 20 minutes, until the chips curl up and become crispy.

7. Store in an airtight container.

Ingredient Tip: Avoid storing your sweet potatoes in the refrigerator's produce bin, which tends to give them a hard center and an unpleasant flavor. What, you don't have a root cellar? Just keep them in a cool, dry area of your kitchen.

Nutrition: Calories: 150 Carbohydrates: 15 g Protein: 79 g Sodium: 45 mgCholesterol: 49 mg

• Southern Slaw

Preparation Time: 10 Minutes

Cooking Time: 12 to 14 Minutes

Servings: 4

Ingredients:

- 1 head cabbage, shredded
- ¼ cup white vinegar
- ¼ cup sugar
- 1 teaspoon paprika
- ½ teaspoon salt
- ½ teaspoon freshly ground black pepper
- 1 cup heavy (whipping) cream

Directions:

1. Place the shredded cabbage in a large bowl.
2. In a small bowl, combine the vinegar, sugar, paprika, salt, and pepper.
3. Pour the vinegar mixture over the cabbage and mix well.
4. Fold in the heavy cream and refrigerate for at least 1 hour before serving.

Nutrition: Calories: 130 Carbohydrates: 5 g Protein: 79 g Sodium: 45 mg Cholesterol: 19 mg

• Wood Pellet Smoked Mushrooms

Preparation Time: 15 minutes,

Cooking Time: 45 minutes.

Servings: 5

Ingredients:

- 4 cup Portobello, whole and cleaned
- 1 tbsp. canola oil
- 1 tbsp. onion powder
- 1 tbsp. granulated garlic
- 1 tbsp. salt
- 1 tbsp. pepper

Directions:

1. Put all the ingredients and mix well.
2. Set the wood pellet temperature to 180°F then place the mushrooms directly on the grill.
3. Smoke the mushrooms for 30 minutes.
4. Increase the temperature to high and cook the mushrooms for a further 15 minutes.
5. Serve and enjoy.

Nutrition: Calories: 1680 Fat: 30g Carbs: 10g Protein: 4g Sodium: 514mg, Potassium: 0mg:

• Wood Pellet Grilled Zucchini Squash Spears

Preparation Time: 5 minutes,

Cooking Time: 10 minutes.

Servings: 5

Ingredients:

- 4 zucchinis, cleaned and ends cut
- 2 tbsp. olive oil
- 1 tbsp. sherry vinegar

- 2 thyme leaves pulled
- Salt and pepper to taste

Directions:

1. Cut the zucchini into halves then cut each half thirds.
2. Add the rest of the ingredients in a zip lock bag with the zucchini pieces. Toss to mix well.
3. Preheat the wood pellet temperature to 350°F with the lid closed for 15 minutes.
4. Remove the zucchini from the bag and place them on the grill grate with the cut side down.
5. Cook for 4 minutes until the zucchini are tender
6. Remove from grill and serve with thyme leaves. Enjoy.

Nutrition: Calories: 74 Fat: 5.4g Carbs: 6.1g Protein: 2.6g Sugar: 3.9g Fiber: 2.3g Sodium: 302mg Potassium: 599mg:

• Whole Roasted Cauliflower with Garlic Parmesan Butter

Preparation Time: 15 minutes
Cooking Time: 45 minutes
Servings: 5
Ingredients:

- 1/4 cup olive oil
- Salt and pepper to taste
- 1 cauliflower, fresh
- 1/2 cup butter, melted
- 1/4 cup parmesan cheese, grated
- 2 garlic cloves, minced
- 1/2 tbsp. parsley, chopped

Directions:

1. Preheat the wood pellet grill with the lid closed for 15 minutes.
2. Meanwhile, brush the cauliflower with oil then season with salt and pepper.
3. Place the cauliflower in a cast Iron: and place it on a grill grate.
4. Cook for 45 minutes or until the cauliflower is golden brown and tender
5. Meanwhile, mix butter, cheese, garlic, and parsley in a mixing bowl.
6. In the last 20 minutes of cooking, add the butter mixture.
7. Remove the cauliflower and top with more cheese and parsley if you desire. Enjoy.

Nutrition: Calories: 156 Fat: 11.1g Carbs: 8.8g Protein: 8.2g Fiber: 3.7g Sodium: 316mg Potassium: 468.2mg

• Wood Pellet Cold Smoked Cheese

Preparation Time: 5 minutes
Cooking Time: 2 minutes
Servings: 10
Ingredients:

- Ice
- 1 aluminum pan, full-size and disposable

- 1 aluminum pan, half-size, and disposable
- Toothpicks
- A block of cheese

Directions:

1. Preheat the wood pellet to 165°F with the lid closed for 15 minutes.
2. Place the small pan in the large pan. Fill the surrounding of the small pan with ice.
3. Place the cheese in the small pan on top of toothpicks then place the pan on the grill and close the lid.
4. Smoke cheese for 1 hour, flip the cheese, and smoke for 1 more hour with the lid closed.
5. Remove the cheese from the grill and wrap it in parchment paper. Store in the fridge for 2 3 days for the smoke flavor to mellow.
6. Remove from the fridge and serve. Enjoy.

Nutrition: Calories: 1910 Total Fat: 7g Saturated Fat: 6g Total Carbs: 2g Net Carbs: 2g Protein: 6g Sugar: 1g Fiber: 0g Sodium: 340mg Potassium: 0mg

• Wood Pellet Grilled Asparagus and Honey Glazed Carrots

Preparation Time: 15 minutes
Cooking Time: 35 minutes
Servings: 5

Ingredients:

- 1 bunch asparagus, trimmed ends
- 1 lb. carrots, peeled
- 2 tbsp. olive oil
- Sea salt to taste
- 2 tbsp. honey
- Lemon zest

Directions:

1. Sprinkle the asparagus with oil and sea salt. Drizzle the carrots with honey and salt.
2. Preheat the wood pellet to 165°F with the lid closed for 15 minutes.
3. Place the carrots in the wood pellet and cook for 15 minutes. Add asparagus and cook for 20 more minutes or until cooked through.
4. Top the carrots and asparagus with lemon zest. Enjoy.

Nutrition: Calories: 1680 Total Fat: 30g Saturated Fat: 2g Total Carbs: 10g Net Carbs: 10g Protein: 4g Sodium: 514mg

• Wood Pellet Grilled Vegetables

Preparation Time: 5 minutes
Cooking Time: 15 minutes
Servings: 8
Ingredients:

- 1 veggie tray
- 1/4 cup vegetable oil
- 2 tbsp. veggie seasoning

Directions:

1. Preheat the wood pellet grill to 375°F
2. Toss the vegetables in oil then place on a sheet pan.
3. Sprinkle with veggie seasoning then place on the hot grill.
4. Grill for 15 minutes or until the veggies are cooked
5. Let rest then serve. Enjoy.

Nutrition: Calories: 44 Total Fat: 5g Saturated Fat: 0g Total Carbs: 1g Net Carbs: 1g Sodium: 36mg Potassium: 10mg

• Wood Pellet Smoked Asparagus

Preparation Time: 5 minutes

Cooking Time: 1 hour

Servings: 4

Ingredients:

- 1 bunch fresh asparagus ends cut
- 2 tbsp. olive oil
- Salt and pepper to taste

Directions:

1. Fire up your wood pellet smoker to 230°F
2. Place the asparagus in a mixing bowl and drizzle with olive oil. Season with salt and pepper.
3. Place the asparagus in a tinfoil sheet and fold the sides such that you create a basket.
4. Smoke the asparagus for 1 hour or until soft turning after half an hour.
5. Remove from the grill and serve. Enjoy.

Nutrition: Calories: 43 Total Fat: 2g Total Carbs: 4g Net Carbs: 2g Protein: 3g Sugar: 2g Fiber: 2g Sodium: 148mg

• Wood Pellet Smoked Acorn Squash

Preparation Time: 10 minutes

Cooking Time: 2 hours

Servings: 6

Ingredients:

- 3 tbsp. olive oil
- 3 acorn squash, halved and seeded
- 1/4 cup unsalted butter
- 1/4 cup brown Sugar:
- 1 tbsp. cinnamon, ground
- 1 tbsp. chili powder
- 1 tbsp. nutmeg, ground

Directions:

1. Brush olive oil on the acorn squash cut sides then covers the halves with foil. Poke holes on the foil to allow steam and smoke through.
2. Fire up the wood pellet to 225°F and smoke the squash for 1 ½-2 hours.
3. Remove the squash from the smoker and allow it to sit.
4. Meanwhile, melt butter, Sugar: and spices in a saucepan. Stir well to combine.
5. Remove the foil from the squash and spoon the butter mixture in each squash half. Enjoy.

Nutrition: Calories: 149 Total Fat: 10g Saturated Fat: 5g Total Carbs: 14g Net Carbs: 12g Protein: 2g

Sugar: 0g Fiber: 2g Sodium: 19mg Potassium: 0mg

• Vegan Smoked Carrot Dogs

Preparation Time: 25 minutes

Cooking Time: 35 minutes

Servings: 4

Ingredients:

- 4 thick carrots
- 2 tbsp. avocado oil
- 1 tbsp. liquid smoke
- 1/2 tbsp. garlic powder
- Salt and pepper to taste

Directions:

1. Preheat the wood pellet grill to 425°F and line a baking sheet with parchment paper.
2. Peel the carrots and round the edges.
3. In a mixing bowl, mix oil, liquid smoke, garlic, salt, and pepper. Place the carrots on the baking dish then pour the mixture over.
4. Roll the carrots to coat evenly with the mixture and use fingertips to massage the mixture into the carrots.
5. Place in the grill and grill for 35 minutes or until the carrots are fork-tender ensuring to turn and brush the carrots every 5 minutes with the marinade.

6. Remove from the grill and place the carrots in hot dog bun. Serve with your favorite toppings and enjoy.

Nutrition: Calories: 149 Total Fat: 1.6g Saturated Fat: 0.3g Total Carbs: 27.9g Net Carbs: 24.3g Protein: 5.4g

Sugar: 5.6g Fiber: 3.6g Sodium: 516mg Potassium: 60mg

• Wood Pellet Smoked Vegetables

Preparation Time: 5 minutes

Cooking Time: 15 minutes

Servings: 6

Ingredients:

- 1 ear corn, fresh, husks and silk strands removed
- 1yellow squash, sliced
- 1 red onion, cut into wedges
- 1 green pepper, cut into strips
- 1 red pepper, cut into strips
- 1 yellow pepper, cut into strips
- 1 cup mushrooms, halved
- 2 tbsp. oil
- 2 tbsp. chicken seasoning

Directions:

1. Soak the pecan wood pellets in water for an hour. Remove the pellets from water and fill the smoker box with the wet pellets.
2. Place the smoker box under the grill and close the lid. Heat the grill on high heat for 10 minutes or until

smoke starts coming out from the wood chips.

3. Meanwhile, toss the veggies in oil and seasonings then transfer them into a grill basket.

4. Grill for 10 minutes while turning occasionally. Serve and enjoy.

Nutrition: Calories: 97 Total Fat: 5g Saturated Fat: 2g Total Carbs: 11g Net Carbs: 8g Protein: 2g Sugar: 1g Fiber: 3g Sodium: 251mg Potassium: 171mg

• **Wood Pellet Grill Spicy Sweet Potatoes**

Preparation Time: 10 minutes
Cooking Time: 35 minutes
Servings: 6
Ingredients:

- 2 lb. sweet potatoes, cut into chunks
- 1 red onion, chopped
- 2 tbsp. oil
- 2 tbsp. orange juice
- 1 tbsp. roasted cinnamon
- 1 tbsp. salt
- 1/4 tbsp. Chipotle chili pepper

Directions:

1. Preheat the wood pellet grill to 425°F with the lid closed.

2. Toss the sweet potatoes with onion, oil, and juice.

3. In a mixing bowl, mix cinnamon, salt, and pepper then sprinkle the mixture over the sweet potatoes.

4. Spread the potatoes on a lined baking dish in a single layer.

5. Place the baking dish in the grill and grill for 30 minutes or until the sweet potatoes are tender.

6. Serve and enjoy.

Nutrition: Calories: 145 Total Fat: 5g Saturated Fat: 0g Total Carbs: 23g Net Carbs: 19g Protein: 2g Sugar: 3g Fiber: 4g Sodium: 428mg Potassium: 230mg

• Wood Pellet Grilled Mexican Street Corn

Preparation Time: 5 minutes

Cooking Time: 25 minutes

Servings: 6

Ingredients:

- 6 ears of corn on the cob
- 1 tbsp. olive oil
- Kosher salt and pepper to taste
- 1/4 cup mayo
- 1/4 cup sour cream
- 1 tbsp. garlic paste
- 1/2 tbsp. chili powder
- Pinch of ground red pepper
- 1/2 cup coria cheese, crumbled
- 1/4 cup cilantro, chopped
- 6 lime wedges

Directions:

1. Brush the corn with oil.
2. Sprinkle with salt.
3. Place the corn on a wood pellet grill set at 350°F. Cook for 25 minutes as you turn it occasionally.
4. Meanwhile mix mayo, cream, garlic, chili, and red pepper until well combined.
5. Let it rest for some minutes then brush with the mayo mixture.
6. Sprinkle cottage cheese, more chili powder, and cilantro. Serve with lime wedges. Enjoy.

Nutrition: Calories: 144 Total Fat: 5g Saturated Fat: 2g Total Carbs: 10g Net Carbs: 10g Protein: 0g Sugar: 0g Fiber: 0g Sodium: 136mg Potassium: 173mg

• Smoked Broccoli

Preparation Time: 10 minutes

Cooking Time: 30 minutes

Servings: 4

Ingredients:

- 2 heads broccoli
- Kosher salt
- 2 tablespoons vegetable oil
- Fresh Pepper (ground)

Directions:

1. Preheat your smoker to 350F.
2. Separate the florets from the heads.
3. Coat the broccoli with vegetable oil by tossing. Thereafter, season with salt and pepper.
4. Using a grilling basket, put the broccoli on the grate of the smoker and smoke for 30 minutes or till crisp.
5. Enjoy!

Nutrition: Calories- 76| Fat- 7g| Saturated fat- 1.3g| Protein- 1.3g| Carbohydrates- 3.1g|

• Smoked Mushrooms 2

Preparation Time: 10 minutes

Cooking Time: 1 hour

Servings: 4

Ingredients:

- 2 lb. mushrooms (Button or Portabella)
- 2 cups Italian dressing
- Pepper
- Salt

Directions:

1. In a gallon zip lock bag, add in the mushrooms.
2. Pour in the Italian dressing in the zip lock bag and some pepper and salt to taste.
3. Refrigerate for 1 hour.
4. Once ready to cook, preheat your smoker to 250F.
5. Smoke mushrooms for an hour or till much soft and a bit smaller in size.
6. Note: mushrooms will smoke well at any temperature so long as they don't burn.

Nutrition: Calories- 392| Fat- 34g| Saturated fat- 5.3g| Carbohydrates- 19.8g| Fiber- 2.3g| Sugar- 13.7g| Protein- 7.6g| Cholesterol- 79mg| Sodium- 196mg|

• **Smoked Potatoes**

Preparation Time: 30 minutes

Cooking Time: 2 hours

Servings: 4

Ingredients:

- 1.5 lb. potatoes (gemstone)
- Fresh parsley (chopped)
- 1/4 cup Parmesan (grated)

Marinade **Ingredients:**

- 6 cloves garlic (minced)
- 2 tablespoons olive oil
- 1/2 teaspoon dried dill
- 1/2 teaspoon basil (dried)
- 1/2 teaspoon oregano (dried)
- 1/2 teaspoon Italian seasoning (dried)
- 1/4 teaspoon fresh pepper (ground)
- 1/2 teaspoon kosher salt

Directions:

1. Initial step is rinsing the potatoes with water. When done, place the potatoes in a large zip lock bag.
2. In a mixing bowl, add and combine the minced garlic cloves, dill, Italian seasoning, basil and ground pepper. Add this mixture in the zip lock bag together with the potatoes.
3. Coat the potatoes by shaking the zip lock bag and refrigerate for 2 hours.
4. Once ready to cook, preheat your smoker to 225F.
5. Use aluminum foil to make a foil packet and place in the potatoes.
6. Pour in two tablespoons of water in the foil and fold it in half on its edges.
7. Put the foil packet on the smoker rack and smoke for 2 hours.
8. Remove from the smoker and top with the grated parmesan and parsley.

Nutrition: Calories- 210| Fat- 8.9g| Saturated fat- 2.1g| Carbohydrates- 28.9g| Fiber-4.3g| Sugars- 2.1g| Protein- 5.5g| Sodium- 368mg| Cholesterol- 5mg|

Smoked Butternut Squash

Preparation Time: 15 minutes

Cooking Time: 1 hour 30 minutes

Servings: 5

Ingredients

- 1 whole butternut squash
- 2 tablespoons olive oil
- 1 tablespoon brown sugar
- 1/2 tablespoon chili powder
- 1 teaspoon black pepper
- 1 teaspoon kosher salt
- 1/2 teaspoon garlic powder

Directions:

1. Preheat your smoker to 325F.
2. Half the squash lengthwise with a knife. Make lines to its flesh as shown above.
3. In a bowl, add the olive oil, garlic pepper, chili powder and brown sugar and combine. Brush this mixture on the expose top part.
4. Put the butternut squash on the smoker and smoke for 1.5 hours or till your preferred tenderness. Brush the squash with the mixture once more on the last 30 minutes of smoking.
5. Remove from the smoker.

Nutrition: Calories- 110| Fat- 5.9g| Saturated fat- 0.8g| Carbohydrates- 15.7g| Protein- 1.3g| Sodium- 478mg| Cholesterol- 0mg|

Smoke-Grilled Eggplant

Preparation Time: 10 minutes

Cooking Time: 10 minutes

Servings: 4

Ingredients:

- 1 eggplant (large in size)
- 4 tablespoons coconut aminos
- 2 tablespoons avocado oil
- 2 teaspoons cumin (ground)
- 2 teaspoons smoked paprika
- 2 teaspoons coriander (ground)
- 2 teaspoons cumin (ground)
- 1/2 teaspoon cayenne pepper
- 1/2 teaspoon garlic powder
- 1/2 teaspoon sea salt

Directions:

1. Cut the eggplant lengthwise to 1/4-inch slices. Drizzle and brush the eggplant slices with the coconut aminos and avocado oil.
2. In a small mixing bowl, combine the spices. Sprinkle the mix on the slices on both sides, ensuring they are full coated.
3. Preheat your grill to medium high heat and place the slices. Grill each side for 3 minutes till they become tender.
4. Remove from the grill and enjoy.

Nutrition: Calories- 62| Fat- 1.5g| Saturated fat- 0.2g| Carbohydrates- 11.6g|

Protein- 1.6g| Calcium- 23mg| Potassium-337mg| Iron- 1mg|

• Smoked Cherry Tomatoes

Preparation Time: 15 minutes

Cooking Time: 1 hour

Servings: 7 tomatoes

Ingredients:

- 25 cherry tomatoes
- 1/8 cup basil (chopped)
- 1/8 cup goat cheese (crumbled)
- 1 tablespoon vinegar (balsamic)
- 2 tablespoons olive oil
- 1 tablespoon water
- Pepper
- Salt

Directions:

1. Initial step is rinsing the tomatoes with water. Put the cherry tomatoes in a zip lock bag.

2. Add the balsamic vinegar, basil, cheese, olive oil, pepper and salt in the same zip lock bag. Shake the bags contents and refrigerate for 2 hours.

3. Once the tomatoes are ready, make a foil pocket with an aluminum foil. Place in the tomatoes and pour in the marinade. Add a tablespoon of water to the pocket and seal it.

4. Preheat your smoker to 225F.

5. Put the foil packet with the tomatoes in the smoker, smoking for an hour.

6. Remove the tomatoes from smoker when done.

7. Top with remaining goat cheese and basil.

Nutrition: Calories- 72| Fat- 4g| Protein-3g| Carbohydrates- 8g| Sugar- 3g| Fiber- 5g| Calcium- 200g| Vitamin C- 21.5mg| Vitamin A- 150IU| Iron- 7.9mg|

• Smoked Acorn Squash

Preparation Time: 15 minutes

Cooking Time: 2 hours

Servings: 6

Ingredients

- 3 halved Acorn squash (seeded)
- 1/4 cup butter
- 1/4 cup brown sugar
- 1 teaspoon cinnamon
- 3 teaspoons olive oil (Extra virgin)
- 1 teaspoon nutmeg
- 1 teaspoon chili powder

Directions:

1. Brush the squash with olive oil.

2. Make a foil pocket using aluminum foil and place in the squash halves. Seal the foil pocket and poke holes on the foil to allow smoke through it.

3. Preheat smoker to 225F.

4. Place the foil on the rack in the smoker and smoke for 1.5 hours to 2 hours. Remove the foil from the smoker when done and let it rest for 10 minutes.

5. In a saucepan, add butter, spices and the sugar. Melt the butter over low

heat and stir to combine. Serve a spoonful of this with each half.

Nutrition: Calories- 149| Fat- 10g| Protein- 2g| Carbohydrates- 14g|

• <u>**Smoked Vegetables**</u>

Preparation Time: 15 minutes

Cooking Time: 45 minutes

Servings: 4

Ingredients:

- Summer squash (sliced)
- Olive oil
- Balsamic vinegar
- Red onion
- Zucchini (sliced)
- Red pepper
- Black pepper
- Garlic (sliced)
- Sea salt

Directions:

1. Add all ingredients in a mixing bowl and combine.
2. Preheat smoker to 350F.
3. Smoked for 30 to 45 minutes or till well cooked through.

Nutrition: Calories- 120| Fat- 7g| Sat fat- 1g| Carbohydrates- 12g| Protein- 2g| Potassium- 514mg| Sodium- 595mg| Fiber- 2g| Sugar- 7g| Vitamin C- 67.3mg| Vitamin A- 1225IU|

• <u>**Smoked Cabbage**</u>

Preparation Time: 15 minutes

Cooking Time: 1 hour

Servings: 4

Ingredients:

- 1 cabbage
- 1/4 cup olive oil
- Garlic powder
- Black pepper
- Kosher salt

Sauce **Ingredients:**

- 1/4 cup cilantro
- 2 cloves garlic (minced)
- 2 green onions (divided in green parts & white parts)
- Lime juice (2 limes)
- 1 jalapeno (chopped)
- 1 green pear (chopped)
- 2 tablespoons olive oil
- 2 tablespoons buttermilk
- 1 tablespoon mayonnaise
- 1 teaspoon black pepper
- 1 teaspoon sea salt

Directions:

1. Preheat your smoker to 250F
2. Peel off the outer cabbage leaves and use a knife to cut 4 quarters.
3. Coat the 4 quarters with olive oil, seasoning with pepper and salt.
4. Place the cabbage quarters on the tray and smoke with the wedge side up for

20 minutes. Flip the cabbage quarters to one wedge side and smoke for 20 minutes and do the same for the other remaining side, smoking for an additional 20 minutes.

5. Remove the cabbage once well-cooked.

6. Put all sauce ingredients in a blender and process. You can adjust its consistency by adding the liquid ingredients to get your preference.

7. Enjoy!

Nutrition: Calories- 303| Protein- 3g| Fat- 23g| Sat fat- 3g|Carbohydrates- 22g| Sugar- 12g| Fiber- 7g| Sodium- 1236mg| Potassium- 457mg| Calcium- 110mg| Vitamin C- 91.1mg| Vitamin A- 390IU|

• **Smoked Vegetables with Vinaigrette**

Preparation Time: 15 minutes

Cooking Time: 4 hours

Servings: 4

Ingredients:

- Zucchini (thickly sliced)
- Red potatoes (small in size & chopped)
- Red onions (chopped)
- Yellow medium squash (thickly sliced)
- Red pepper (chopped)

Vinaigrette **Ingredients:**

- 1/3 cup olive oil
- 1/4 cup vinegar (balsamic)
- 2 teaspoons Dijon mustard
- Pepper
- Salt

Directions:

1. Add and combine balsamic vinegar, olive oil, Mustard, pepper and salt in a bowl.

2. In a casserole dish, add all the vegetables and combine. Coat the vegetables with the balsamic vinaigrette by tossing.

3. Preheat your smoker to 225F.

4. Put the dish with the vegetables in the smoker and smoke for 4 hours.

Nutrition: Calories- 225| Fat- 17.2g| Saturated fat- 2.5g| Carbohydrates- 16.8g| Protein- 2.8g| Sodium- 196mg| Cholesterol- 0mg| Calcium- 35mg| Potassium- 483mg| Iron- 1mg|

• <u>Tandoori Chicken Wings</u>

Preparation Time: 20 minutes

Cooking Time: 1 hour 20 minutes

Servings: 4-6

Ingredients:

- ¼ Cup Yogurt
- 1 Whole Scallions, minced
- 1 Tablespoon minced cilantro leaves
- 2 Teaspoon ginger, minced
- 1 Teaspoon Masala
- 1 Teaspoon salt
- 1 Teaspoon ground black pepper
- 1 ½ pound chicken wings
- ¼ cup yogurt
- 2 tablespoon mayonnaise
- 2 tablespoon Cucumber
- 2 teaspoon lemon juice
- ½ teaspoon cumin
- ½ teaspoon salt
- 1/8 cayenne pepper

Directions:

1. Combine yogurt, scallion, ginger, garam masala, salt, cilantro, and pepper ingredients in the jar of a blender and process until smooth.
2. Put chicken and massage the bag to cat all the wings
3. Refrigerate for 4 to 8 hours. Remove the excess marinade from the wings; discard the marinade

4. Set the temperature to 350F and preheat, lid closed, for 10 to 15 minutes. Brush and oil the grill grate
5. Arrange the wings on the grill. Cook for 45 to 50 minutes, or until the skin is brown and crisp and meat is no longer pink at the bone. Turn once or twice during cooking to prevent the wings from sticking to the grill.
6. Meanwhile combine all sauce ingredients; set aside and refrigerate until ready to serve.
7. When wings are cooked through, transfer to a plate or platter. Serve with yogurt sauce

Nutrition: Calories 241kcal Carbohydrates 11g Protein 12g Fat 16g Saturated Fat 3g

• **Asian BBQ Chicken**

Preparation Time: 12 to 24 hours

Cooking Time: 1 hour

Servings: 4-6

Ingredients:

- 1 whole chicken
- To taste Asian BBQ Rub
- 1 whole ginger ale

Direction:

1. Rinse chicken in cold water and pat dry with paper towels.
2. Cover the chicken all over with Asian BBQ rub; make sure to drop some in the inside too. Place in large bag or

bowl and cover and refrigerate for 12 to 24 hours.

3. When ready to cook, set the Wood pellet grill to 372F and preheat lid closed for 15 minutes.

4. Open can of ginger ale and take a few big gulps. Set the can of soda on a stable surface. Take the chicken out of the fridge and place the bird over top of the soda can. The base of the can and the two legs of the chicken should form a sort of tripod to hold the chicken upright.

5. Stand the chicken in the center of your hot grate and cook the chicken till the skin is golden brown and the internal temperature is about 165F on an instant-read thermometer, approximately 40 minutes to 1 hour.

Nutrition: Calories 140kcal Carbohydrates 18g Protein 4g Fat 4g Sodium 806 mg Potassium 682 mg Fiber 5g

Sugar 8g

• Homemade Turkey Gravy

Preparation Time: 20 minutes

Cooking Time: 3 hours 20 minutes

Servings: 8-12

Ingredients:

- 1 turkey, neck
- 2 large Onion, eight
- 4 celeries, stalks
- 4 large carrots, fresh
- 8 clove garlic, smashed
- 8 thyme sprigs
- 4 cup chicken broth
- 1 teaspoon chicken broth
- 1 teaspoon salt
- 1 teaspoon cracked black pepper
- 1 butter, sticks
- 1 cup all-purpose flour

Directions:

1. When ready to cook, set the temperature to 350F and preheat the wood pellet grill with the lid closed, for 15 minutes.

2. Place turkey neck, celery, carrot (roughly chopped), garlic, onion and thyme on a roasting pan. Add four cups of chicken stock then season with salt and pepper.

3. Move the prepped turkey on the rack into the roasting pan and place in the wood pellet grill.

4. Cook for about 3-4 hours until the breast reaches 160F. The turkey will continue to cook and it will reach a finished internal temperature of 165F.

5. Strain the drippings into a saucepan and simmer on low.

6. In a saucepan, mix butter (cut into 8 pieces) and flour with a whisk stirring until golden tan. This takes about 8 minutes, stirrings constantly.

7. Whisk the drippings into the roux then cook until it comes to a boil. Season with salt and pepper.

Nutrition: Calories 160kcal Carbohydrate 27g Protein 55g Fat 23g Saturated Fat 6.1g

• <u>Bacon Wrapped Turkey Legs</u>

Preparation Time: 10 minutes
Cooking Time: 3 hours
Servings: 4-6
Ingredients:

- Gallon water
- To taste traeger rub
- ½ cup pink curing salt
- ½ cup brown sugar
- 6 whole peppercorns
- 2 whole dried bay leaves
- ½ gallon ice water
- 8 whole turkey legs
- 16 sliced bacon

Directions:

1. In a large stockpot, mix one gallon of water, the rub, curing salt, brown sugar, peppercorns and bay leaves.
2. Boil it to over high heat to dissolve the salt and sugar granules. Take off the heat then add in ½ gallon of ice and water.
3. The brine must be at least to room temperature, if not colder.
4. Place the turkey legs, completely submerged in the brine.
5. After 24 hours, drain the turkey legs then remove the brine.
6. Wash the brine off the legs with cold water, then dry thoroughly with paper towels.
7. When ready to cook, start the wood pellet grill according to grill instructions. Set the heat to 250F and preheat, lid closed for 10 to 15 minutes.
8. Place turkey legs directly on the grill grate.
9. After 2 ½ hours, wrap a piece of bacon around each leg then finish cooking them for 30 to 40 minutes of smoking.
10. The total smoking time for the legs will be 3 hours or until the internal temperature reaches 165F on an instant-read meat thermometer. Serve, Enjoy!

Nutrition: Calories 390kcal Total Fat 14g Saturated Fat 0g Cholesterol 64mg Sodium 738mg Carbohydrates 44g

• <u>Smoke Roasted Chicken</u>

Preparation Time: 20 minutes
Cooking Time: 1 hour 20 minutes
Servings: 4-6
Ingredients:

- 8 tablespoon butter, room temperature
- 1 clove garlic, minced
- 1 scallion, minced
- 2 tablespoon fresh herbs such as thyme, rosemary, sage or parsley

- As needed Chicken rub
- Lemon juice
- As needed vegetable oil

Directions:

1. In a small cooking bowl, mix the scallions, garlic, butter, minced fresh herbs, 1-1/2 teaspoon of the rub, and lemon juice. Mix with a spoon.

2. Remove any giblets from the cavity of the chicken. Wash the chicken inside and out with cold running water. Dry thoroughly with paper towels.

3. Sprinkle a generous amount of Chicken Rub inside the cavity of the chicken.

4. Gently loosen the skin around the chicken breast and slide in a few tablespoons of the herb butter under the skin and cover.

5. Cover the outside with the remaining herb butter.

6. Insert the chicken wings behind the back. Tie both legs together with a butcher's string.

7. Powder the outside of the chicken with more Chicken Rub then insert sprigs of fresh herbs inside the cavity of the chicken.

8. Set temperature to High and preheat, lid closed for 15 minutes.

9. Oil the grill with vegetable oil. Move the chicken on the grill grate, breast-side up then close the lid.

10. After chicken has cooked for 1 hour, lift the lid. If chicken is browning too quickly, cover the breast and legs with aluminum foil.

11. Close the lid then continue to roast the chicken until an instant-read meat thermometer inserted into the thickest part registers a temperature of 165F

12. Take off chicken from grill and let rest for 5 minutes. Serve, Enjoy!

Nutrition: Calories 222kcal Carbohydrates 11g Protein 29g Fat 4g Cholesterol 62mg Sodium 616mg Potassium 620mg

• **Grilled Asian Chicken Burgers**

Preparation Time: 5 minutes
Cooking Time: 50 minutes
Servings: 4-6
Ingredients:

- Pound chicken, ground
- 1 cup panko breadcrumbs
- 1 cup parmesan cheese
- 1 small jalapeno, diced
- 2 whole scallions, minced
- 2 garlic clove
- ¼ cup minced cilantro leaves
- 2 tablespoon mayonnaise
- 2 tablespoon chili sauce
- 1 tablespoon soy sauce
- 1 tablespoon ginger, minced
- 2 teaspoon lemon juice

- 2 teaspoon lemon zest
- 1 teaspoon salt
- 1 teaspoon ground black pepper
- 8 hamburger buns
- 1 tomato, sliced
- Arugula, fresh
- 1 red onion sliced

Directions:

1. Align a rimmed baking sheet with aluminum foil then spray with nonstick cooking spray.
2. In a large bowl, combine the chicken, jalapeno, scallion, garlic, cilantro, panko, Parmesan, chili sauce, soy sauce ginger, mayonnaise, lemon juice and zest, and salt and pepper.
3. Work the mixture with your fingers until the ingredients are well combined. If the mixture looks too wet to form patties and add additional more panko.
4. Wash your hands under cold running water, form the meat into 8 patties, each about an inch larger than the buns and about ¾" thick. Use your thumbs or a tablespoon, make a wide, shallow depression in the top of each
5. Put them on the prepared baking sheet. Spray the tops with nonstick cooking spray. If not cooking right away, cover with plastic wrap and refrigerate.
6. Set the pellet grill to 350F then preheat for 15 minutes, lid closed.
7. Order the burgers, depression-side down, on the grill grate. Remove and discard the foil on the baking sheet so you'll have an uncontaminated surface to transfer the slider when cooked.
8. Grill the burgers for about 25 to 30 minutes, turning once, or until they release easily from the grill grate when a clean metal spatula is slipped under them. The internal temperature when read on an instant-read meat thermometer should be 160F.
9. Spread mayonnaise and arrange a tomato slice, if desired, and a few arugula leaves on one-half of each bun. Top with a grilled burger and red onions, if using, then replace the top half of the bun. Serve immediately. Enjoy

Nutrition: Calories 329kcal Carbohydrates 10g Protein 21g Fat 23g

- ## **Grilled Sweet Cajun Wings**

Preparation Time: 10 minutes

Cooking Time: 45 minutes

Servings: 4-6

Ingredients:

- 2-pound chicken wings
- As needed Pork and Poultry rub
- Cajun shake

Directions:

1. Coat wings in Sweet rub and Cajun shake.

2. When ready to cook, set the pellet grill to 350F and preheat, lid closed for 15 minutes.

3. Cook for 30 minutes until skin is brown and center is juicy and an instant-read thermometer reads at least 165F. Serve, Enjoy!

The Grilled Chicken Challenge

Preparation Time: 15 minutes
Cooking Time: 1 hour and 10 minutes
Servings: 4-6
Ingredients:

- 1 (4-lbs.) whole chicken
- As needed chicken rub

Directions:

1. When ready to cook, set temperature to 375F then preheat, close the lid for 15 minutes.

2. Rinse and dry the whole chicken (remove and discard giblets, if any). Season the entire chicken, including the inside of the chicken using chicken rub.

3. Place the chicken on the grill and cook for 1 hour and 10 minutes.

4. Remove chicken from grill when internal temperature of breast reaches 160F. Check heat periodically throughout as cook times will vary based on the weight of the chicken.

5. Allow chicken to rest until the internal temperature of breast reaches 165F, 15-20 minutes. Enjoy!

Nutrition: Calories 212kcal Carbohydrates 42.6g Protein 6.1g Fat 2.4g Saturated Fat 0.5gFiber 3.4g

Sugar 2.9g

Chicken Breast with Lemon

Preparation Time: 15min
Cooking Time: 15min
Servings: 6
Ingredients:

- 6 Chicken breasts, skinless and boneless
- ½ cup Oil
- 1 - 2 Fresh thyme sprigs
- 1 tsp. ground black pepper
- 2 tsp. Salt
- 2 tsp. of Honey
- 1 Garlic clove, chopped
- 1 Lemon the juice and zest
- For service: Lemon wedges

Directions:

1. In a bowl combine the thyme, black pepper, salt, honey, garlic, and lemon zest and juice. Stir until dissolved and combined. Add the oil and whisk to combine.

2. Clean the breasts and pat dry. Place them in a plastic bag. Pour the pre-made marinade and massage to distribute evenly. Place in the fridge, 4 hours.

3. Preheat the grill to 400F with the lid closed.

4. Drain the chicken and grill until the internal temperature reaches 165F, about 15 minutes.

5. Serve with lemon wedges and a side dish of your choice.

Nutrition: Calories: 230 Proteins: 38g Carbohydrates: 1g Fat: 7g

• **Pellet Smoked Chicken Burgers**

Preparation Time: 20 minutes

Cooking Time: 1 hour and 10 minutes

Servings: 6

Ingredients:

- 2 lb. ground chicken breast
- 2/3 cup of finely chopped onions
- 1 Tbsps. of cilantro, finely chopped
- 2 Tbsp. fresh parsley, finely chopped
- 2 Tbsp. of olive oil
- 1/2 tsp of ground cumin
- 2 Tbsps. of lemon juice freshly squeezed
- 3/4 tsp of salt and red pepper to taste

Directions:

1. In a bowl add all ingredients; mix until combined well.

2. Form the mixture into 6 patties.

3. Start your pellet grill on SMOKE (oak or apple pellets) with the lid open until the fire is established. Set the

heat to 350F and preheat, lid closed, for 10 to 15 minutes.

4. Smoke the chicken burgers for 45 - 50 minutes or until cooked through, turning every 15 minutes.

5. Your burgers are ready when internal temperature reaches 165 F

6. Serve hot.

Nutrition: Calories: 221 Carbohydrates: 2.12g Fat: 8.5g Fiber: 0.4g Protein: 32.5g

• **Perfect Smoked Chicken Patties**

Preparation Time: 20 minutes

Cooking Time: 50 minutes

Servings: 6

Ingredients:

- 2 lb. ground chicken breast
- 2/3 cup minced onion
- 1 Tbsps. cilantro (chopped)
- 2 Tbsp. fresh parsley, finely chopped
- 2 Tbsp. olive oil
- 1/8 tsp crushed red pepper flakes
- 1/2 tsp ground cumin
- 2 Tbsps. fresh lemon juice
- 3/4 tsp kosher salt
- 2 tsp paprika
- Hamburger buns for serving

Directions:

1. In a bowl combine all ingredients from the list.

2. Using your hands, mix well. Form mixture into 6 patties. Refrigerate

until ready to grill (about 30 minutes).

3. Start your pellet grill on SMOKE with the lid open until the fire is established). Set the temperature to 350F and preheat for 10 to 15 minutes.

4. Arrange chicken patties on the grill rack and cook for 35 to 40 minutes turning once.

5. Serve hot with hamburger buns and your favorite condiments.

Nutrition: Calories: 258 Carbohydrates: 2.5g Fat: 9.4g Fiber: 0.6g Protein: 39g

• Smoked Chicken Breasts with Dried Herbs

Preparation Time: 15 minutes
Cooking Time: 40 minutes
Servings: 4
Ingredients:

- 4 chicken breasts boneless
- 1/4 cup garlic-infused olive oil
- 2 clove garlic minced
- 1/4 tsp of dried sage
- 1/4 tsp of dried lavender
- 1/4 tsp of dried thyme
- 1/4 tsp of dried mint
- 1/2 Tbsps. dried crushed red pepper
- Kosher salt to taste

Directions:

1. Place the chicken breasts in a shallow plastic container.

2. In a bowl, combine all remaining ingredients, and pour the mixture over the chicken breast and refrigerate for one hour.

3. Remove the chicken breast from the sauce (reserve sauce) and pat dry on kitchen paper.

4. Start your pellet grill on SMOKE (hickory pellet) with the lid open until the fire is established). Set the temperature to 250F and preheat for 10 to 15 minutes.

5. Place chicken breasts on the smoker. Close pellet grill lid and cook for about 30 to 40 minutes or until chicken breasts reach 165F.

6. Serve hot with reserved marinade.

Nutrition: Calories: 391 Carbohydrates: 0.7g Fat: 3.21g Fiber: 0.12g Protein: 20.25g

• Grilled Chicken with Pineapple

Preparation Time: 1 hour
Cooking Time: 1 hr. 15 mins
Servings: 6
Ingredients:

- 2 lbs. Chicken tenders
- 1 c. sweet chili sauce
- ¼ c. fresh pineapple juice
- ¼ c. honey

Directions:

1. Combine the honey, pineapple juice, and sweet chili sauce in a medium bowl. Whisk together thoroughly.

2. Put ¼ cup of the mixture to one side.

3. Coat the chicken in the sauce.

4. Place a lid over the bowl and leave it in the fridge for 30 minutes to marinate.

5. Heat the grill to high heat.

6. Separate the chicken from the marinade and grill for 5 minutes on each side.

7. Use the reserved sauce to brush over the chicken.

8. Continue to grill for a further 1 minute on each side.

9. Take the chicken off the grill and let it rest for 5 minutes before servings.

Nutrition: Calories: 270 Fat: 2 g, Carbohydrates: 25 g, Protein: 33 g

• **Lemon Chicken Breast**

Preparation Time: 15 minutes

Cooking Time: 30 minutes

Servings: 4

Ingredients:

- 6 chicken breasts, skinless and boneless
- ½ cup oil
- 1-3 fresh thyme sprigs
- 1 teaspoon ground black pepper
- 2 teaspoon salt
- 2 teaspoons honey
- 1 garlic clove, chopped
- 1 lemon, juiced and zested
- Lemon wedges

Directions:

1. Take a bowl and prepare the marinade by mixing thyme, pepper, salt, honey, garlic, lemon zest, and juice. Mix well until dissolved

2. Add oil and whisk

3. Clean breasts and pat them dry, place in a bag alongside marinade and let them sit in the fridge for 4 hours

4. Pre-heat your smoker to 400 degrees F

5. Drain chicken and smoke until the internal temperature reaches 165 degrees, for about 15 minutes

6. Serve and enjoy!

Nutrition: Calories: 230 Fats: 7g Carbohydrates: 1g Fiber: 2g

• **Whole Orange Chicken**

Preparation Time: 15 minutes + marinate time

Cooking Time: 45 minutes

Servings: 4

Ingredients:

- 1 whole chicken, 3-4 pounds' backbone removed
- 2 oranges
- ¼ cup oil
- 2 teaspoons Dijon mustard
- 1 orange, zest
- 2 tablespoons rosemary leaves, chopped
- 2 teaspoons salt

Directions:

1. Clean and pat your chicken dry

2. Take a bowl and mix in orange juice, oil, orange zest, salt, rosemary leaves, Dijon mustard and mix well

3. Marinade chicken for 2 hours or overnight

4. Pre-heat your grill to 350 degrees F

5. Transfer your chicken to the smoker and smoke for 30 minutes' skin down. Flip and smoke until the internal temperature reaches 175 degrees F in the thigh and 165 degrees F in the breast

6. Rest for 10 minutes and carve

7. Enjoy!

Nutrition: Calories: 290 Fats: 15g Carbohydrates: 20g Fiber: 1g

• **Smoked Turkey**

Preparation Time: 8 hours

Cooking Time: 5 hours

Servings: 6 - 8

Ingredients:

- 1 Turkey (12 to 14 lb.) thawed or fresh, excess skin trimmed
- ¾ lb. Butter, unsalted
- Brine:
- 2 Gallons Water and ice
- cups of Sugar
- 2 cups Salt
- Rub:
- ½ cup Black pepper, ground
- ½ cup Salt

Directions:

1. One day before you want to cook the turkey Preparation time is it for brining.

2. In a saucepan combine the sugar and salt. Add water and let it boil until dissolved. Pour the mixture into a big bucket and add water and ice 2 gallons.

3. Put the turkey in the brine and if it starts to float place a large plate on top so that it stays submerged, Cover the bucket and refrigerate until the next day.

4. Preheat the grill 180F with the lid closed.

5. Remove the turkey and make sure the cavity is also empty of brine. Place the turkey on a piece of a cooking sheet.

6. Sprinkle and rub black pepper and salt on the whole turkey but not inside.

7. Cook on the grill for 2 hours. After 2 hours increase the temperature to 225F and cook 1 more hour. Increase again to 325F. When the color of the turkey is according to your taste place it in a pan. Cut the unsalted butter into squares and place it on the meat.

8. Wrap the turkey in a foil and cook on the grill until it reaches 165F (breast) internal temperature and the thigh 180F.

9. Let it rest 30 minutes and serve.

Nutrition: Calories: 380 Proteins: 40g Carbohydrates: 3g Fat: 16g

• Smoked Turkey Patties

Preparation Time: 20 minutes

Cooking Time: 40 minutes

Servings: 6

Ingredients:

- 2 lbs. turkey minced meat
- 1/2 cup of parsley finely chopped
- 2/3 cup of onion finely chopped
- 1 red bell pepper finely chopped
- 1 large egg at room temperature
- Salt and pepper to taste
- 1/2 tsp dry oregano
- 1/2 tsp dry thyme

Directions:

1. In a bowl, combine well all ingredients.
2. Make from the mixture patties.
3. Start pellet grill on (recommended apple or oak pellet) lid open, until the fire is established (4-5 minutes). Increase the temperature to 350F and allow to pre-heat, lid closed, for 10 - 15 minutes.
4. Place patties on the grill racks and cook with lid covered for 30 to 40 minutes.
5. Your turkey patties are ready when you reach a temperature of 130F
6. Serve hot.

Nutrition: Calories: 251 Carbohydrates: 3.4g Fat: 12.5 Fiber: 0.9g Protein: 31.2g

• Apple Smoked Turkey

Preparation Time: 30 Minutes

Cooking Time: 3 Hours

Servings: 5

Ingredients:

- 4 Cups Applewood chips
- 1 Fresh or frozen turkey of about 12 pounds
- 3 Tablespoons of extra-virgin olive oil
- 1 tablespoon of chopped fresh sage
- 2 and ½ teaspoons of kosher salt
- 2 Teaspoons of freshly ground black pepper
- 1 and ½ teaspoons of paprika
- 1 Teaspoon of chopped fresh thyme
- 1 Teaspoon of chopped fresh oregano
- 1 Teaspoon of garlic powder
- 1 Cup of water
- ½ Cup of chopped onion
- ½ Cup of chopped carrot
- ½ Cup of chopped celery

Directions:

1. Soak the wood chips into the water for about 1 hour; then drain very well.
2. Remove the neck and the giblets from the turkey; then reserve and discard the liver. Pat the turkey dry; then trim any excess of fat and start at the neck's cavity
3. Loosen the skin from the breast and the drumstick by inserting your fingers and gently push it between the

meat and skin and lift the wingtips, then over back and tuck under the turkey

4. Combine the oil and the next 7 ingredients in a medium bowl and rub the oil under the skin; then rub it over the breasts and the drumsticks

5. Tie the legs with the kitchen string.

6. Pour 1 cup of water, the onion, the carrot, and the celery into the bottom of an aluminum foil roasting pan

7. Place the roasting rack into a pan; then arrange the turkey with the breast side up over a roasting rack; then let stand at the room temperature for about 1 hour

8. Remove the grill rack; then preheat the charcoal smoker grill to medium-high heat.

9. After preheating the smoker to a temperature of about 225°F

10. Place 2 cups of wood chips on the heating element on the right side.

11. Replace the grill rack; then place the roasting pan with the turkey over the grill rack over the left burner.

12. Cover and smoke for about 3 hours and turn the chicken halfway through the cooking time; then add the remaining 2 cups of wood chips halfway through the cooking time.

13. Place the turkey over a cutting board; then let stand for about 30 minutes

14. Discard the turkey skin; then serve and enjoy your dish!

Nutrition: Calories: 530, Fat: 22g, Carbohydrates: 14g, Protein: 41g, Dietary Fiber 2g

• Special Occasion's Dinner Cornish Hen

Preparation Time: 15 minutes

Cooking Time: 1 hour

Servings: 4

Ingredients:

- 4 Cornish game hens
- 4 fresh rosemary sprigs
- 4 tbsp. butter, melted
- 4 tsp. chicken rub

Directions:

1. Set the temperature of Grill to 375 degrees F and preheat with closed lid for 15 mins.

2. With paper towels, pat dry the hens.

3. Tuck the wings behind the backs and with kitchen strings, tie the legs together.

4. Coat the outside of each hen with melted butter and sprinkle with rub evenly.

5. Stuff each hen with a rosemary sprig.

6. Place the hens onto the grill and cook for about 50-60 mins.

7. Remove the hens from grill and place onto a platter for about 10 mins.

8. Cut each hen into desired-sized pieces and serve.

Nutrition: Calories per serving: 430

Carbohydrates: 2.1g Protein: 25.4g Fat: 33g

Sugar: 0g Sodium: 331mg

Fiber: 0.7g

• Crispy & Juicy Chicken

Preparation Time: 15 minutes

Cooking Time: 5 hours

Servings: 6

Ingredients:

- ¾ C. dark brown sugar
- ½ C. ground espresso beans
- 1 tbsp. ground cumin
- 1 tbsp. ground cinnamon
- 1 tbsp. garlic powder
- 1 tbsp. cayenne pepper
- Salt and ground black pepper, to taste
- 1 (4-lb.) whole chicken, neck and giblets removed

Directions:

1. Set the temperature of Grill to 200-225 degrees F and preheat with closed lid for 15 mins.
2. In a bowl, mix together brown sugar, ground espresso, spices, salt and black pepper.
3. Rub the chicken with spice mixture generously.
4. Put the chicken onto the grill and cook for about 3-5 hours.
5. Remove chicken from grill and place onto a cutting board for about 10 mins before carving.
6. Cut the chicken into desired-sized pieces and serve.

Nutrition: Calories per serving: 540 Carbohydrates: 20.7g Protein: 88.3g Fat: 9.6g Sugar: 18.1g Sodium: 226mg Fiber: 1.2g

• Ultimate Tasty Chicken

Preparation Time: 15 minutes

Cooking Time: 3 hours

Servings: 5

Ingredients:

For Brine:

- 1 C. brown sugar
- ½ C. kosher salt
- 16 C. water

For Chicken:

- 1 (3-lb.) whole chicken
- 1 tbsp. garlic, crushed
- 1 tsp. onion powder
- Salt
- Ground black pepper, to taste
- 1 medium yellow onion, quartered
- 3 whole garlic cloves, peeled
- 1 lemon, quartered
- 4-5 fresh thyme sprigs

Directions:

1. For brine: in a bucket, dissolve brown sugar and kosher salt in water.
2. Place the chicken in brine and refrigerate overnight.
3. Set the temperature of Grill to 225 degrees F and preheat with closed lid for 15 mins.

4. Remove the chicken from brine and with paper towels, pat it dry.

5. In a small bowl, mix together crushed garlic, onion powder, salt and black pepper.

6. Rub the chicken with garlic mixture evenly.

7. Stuff the inside of the chicken with onion, garlic cloves, lemon and thyme.

8. With kitchen strings, tie the legs together.

9. Place the chicken onto grill and cook, covered for about 2½-3 hours.

10. Remove chicken from pallet grill and transfer onto a cutting board for about 10 mins before carving.

11. Cut the chicken in desired sized pieces and serve.

Nutrition: Calories per serving: 641 Carbohydrates: 31.7g Protein: 79.2g Fat: 20.2g Sugar: 29.3g Sodium: 11500mg Fiber: 0.6g

• South-East-Asian Chicken Drumsticks

Preparation Time: 15 minutes

Cooking Time: 2 hours

Servings: 6

Ingredients:

- 1 C. fresh orange juice
- ¼ C. honey
- 2 tbsp. sweet chili sauce
- 2 tbsp. hoisin sauce
- 2 tbsp. fresh ginger, grated finely
- 2 tbsp. garlic, minced
- 1 tsp. Sriracha
- ½ tsp. sesame oil
- 6 chicken drumsticks

Directions:

1. Set the temperature of Grill to 225 degrees F and preheat with closed lid for 15 mins, using charcoal.

2. Mix all the ingredients except for chicken drumsticks and mix until well combined.

3. Set aside half of honey mixture in a small bowl.

4. In the bowl of remaining sauce, add drumsticks and mix well.

5. Arrange the chicken drumsticks onto the grill and cook for about 2 hours, basting with remaining sauce occasionally.

6. Serve hot.

Nutrition: Calories per serving: 385 Carbohydrates: 22.7g Protein: 47.6g Fat: 10.5g Sugar: 18.6g Sodium: 270mg Fiber: 0.6g

• Game Day Chicken Drumsticks

Preparation Time: 15 minutes

Cooking Time: 1 hour

Servings: 8

Ingredients:

For Brine:

- ½ C. brown sugar
- ½ C. kosher salt
- 5 C. water
- 2 (12-oz.) bottles beer
- 8 chicken drumsticks
- For Coating:
- ¼ C. olive oil
- ½ C. BBQ rub
- 1 tbsp. fresh parsley, minced
- 1 tbsp. fresh chives, minced
- ¾ C. BBQ sauce
- ¼ C. beer

Directions:

1. For brine: in a bucket, dissolve brown sugar and kosher salt in water and beer.
2. Place the chicken drumsticks in brine and refrigerate, covered for about 3 hours.
3. Set the temperature of Grill to 275 degrees F and preheat with closed lid for 15 mins.
4. Remove chicken drumsticks from brine and rinse under cold running water.
5. With paper towels, pat dry chicken drumsticks.
6. Coat drumsticks with olive oil and rub with BBQ rub evenly.
7. Sprinkle the drumsticks with parsley and chives.
8. Arrange the chicken drumsticks onto the grill and cook for about 45 mins.
9. Meanwhile, in a bowl, mix together BBQ sauce and beer.
10. Remove from grill and coat the drumsticks with BBQ sauce evenly.
11. Cook for about 15 mins more.
12. Serve immediately.

Nutrition: Calories per serving: 448 Carbohydrates: 20.5g Protein: 47.2g Fat: 16.1g Sugar: 14.9g Sodium: 9700mg Fiber: 0.2g

• Glazed Chicken Thighs

Preparation Time: 15 minutes
Cooking Time: 2 hours and 5 minutes
Servings: 4
Ingredients:

- 2 garlic cloves, minced
- ¼ C. honey
- 2 tbsp. soy sauce
- ¼ tsp. red pepper flakes, crushed
- 4 (5-oz.) skinless, boneless chicken thighs
- 2 tbsp. olive oil
- 2 tsp. sweet rub
- ¼ tsp. red chili powder
- Freshly ground black pepper, to taste

Directions:

1. Set the temperature of Grill to 400 degrees F and preheat with closed lid for 15 mins.
2. In a bowl, add garlic, honey, soy sauce and red pepper flakes and with a wire whisk, beat until well combined.

3. Coat chicken thighs with oil and season with sweet rub, chili powder and black pepper generously.

4. Arrange the chicken drumsticks onto the grill and cook for about 15 mins per side.

5. In the last 4-5 mins of cooking, coat the thighs with garlic mixture.

6. Serve immediately.

Nutrition: Calories per serving: 309 Carbohydrates: 18.7g Protein: 32.3g; Fat: 12.1g Sugar: 17.6g Sodium: 504mg Fiber: 0.2g

• Cajun Chicken Breasts

Preparation Time: 10 minutes

Cooking Time: 6 hours

Servings: 6

Ingredients:

- 2 lb. skinless, boneless chicken breasts
- 2 tbsp. Cajun seasoning
- 1 C. BBQ sauce

Directions:

1. Set the temperature of Grill to 225 degrees F and preheat with closed lid for 15 mins.

2. Rub the chicken breasts with Cajun seasoning generously.

3. Put the chicken breasts onto the grill and cook for about 4-6 hours.

4. During last hour of cooking, coat the breasts with BBQ sauce twice.

5. Serve hot.

Nutrition: Calories per serving: 252 Carbohydrates: 15.1g Protein: 33.8g; Fat: 5.5g Sugar: 10.9g Sodium: 570mg Fiber: 0.3g

• BBQ Sauce Smothered Chicken Breasts

Preparation Time: 15 minutes

Cooking Time: 30 minutes

Servings: 4

Ingredients:

- 1 tsp. garlic, crushed
- ¼ C. olive oil
- 1 tbsp. Worcestershire sauce
- 1 tbsp. sweet mesquite seasoning
- 4 chicken breasts
- 2 tbsp. regular BBQ sauce
- 2 tbsp. spicy BBQ sauce
- 2 tbsp. honey bourbon BBQ sauce

Directions:

1. Set the temperature of Grill to 450 degrees F and preheat with closed lid for 15 mins.

2. In a large bowl, mix together garlic, oil, Worcestershire sauce and mesquite seasoning.

3. Coat chicken breasts with seasoning mixture evenly.

4. Put the chicken breasts onto the grill and cook for about 20-30 mins.

5. Meanwhile, in a bowl, mix together all 3 BBQ sauces.

6. In the last 4-5 mins of cooking, coat breast with BBQ sauce mixture.

7. Serve hot.

Nutrition: Calories per serving: 421 Carbohydrates: 10.1g Protein: 41,2g Fat: 23.3g Sugar: 6.9g Sodium: 763mg Fiber: 0.2g

• Budget Friendly Chicken Legs

Preparation Time: 15 minutes
Cooking Time: 1 hour and 30 minutes
Servings: 6
Ingredients:
For Brine:

- 1 C. kosher salt
- ¾ C. light brown sugar
- 16 C. water
- 6 chicken leg quarters

For Glaze:

- ½ C. mayonnaise
- 2 tbsp. BBQ rub
- 2 tbsp. fresh chives, minced
- 1 tbsp. garlic, minced

Directions

1. For brine: in a bucket, dissolve salt and brown sugar in water.

2. Place the chicken quarters in brine and refrigerate, covered for about 4 hours.

3. Set the temperature of Grill to 275 degrees F and preheat with closed lid for 15 mins.

4. Remove chicken quarters from brine and rinse under cold running water.

5. With paper towels, pat dry chicken quarters.

6. For glaze: in a bowl, add all ingredients and mix till ell combined.

7. Coat chicken quarters with glaze evenly.

8. Place the chicken leg quarters onto grill and cook for about 1-1½ hours.

9. Serve immediately.

Nutrition: Calories per serving: 399 Carbohydrates: 17.2g Protein: 29.1g Fat: 24.7g Sugar: 14.2g Sodium: 15000mg Fiber: 0g

• Thanksgiving Dinner Turkey

Preparation Time: 15 minutes
Cooking Time: 4 hours
Servings: 16
Ingredients:

- ½ lb. butter, softened
- 2 tbsp. fresh thyme, chopped
- 2 tbsp. fresh rosemary, chopped
- 6 garlic cloves, crushed
- 1 (20-lb.) whole turkey, neck and giblets removed
- Salt and ground black pepper

Directions:

1. Set the temperature of Grill to 300 degrees F and preheat with closed lid for 15 mins, using charcoal.

2. In a bowl, place butter, fresh herbs, garlic, salt and black pepper and mix well.

3. Separate the turkey skin from breast to create a pocket.

4. Stuff the breast pocket with ¼-inch thick layer of butter mixture.

5. Season turkey with salt and black pepper.

6. Arrange the turkey onto the grill and cook for 3-4 hours.

7. Remove the turkey from grill and place onto a cutting board for about 15-20 mins before carving.

8. Cut the turkey into desired-sized pieces and serve.

Nutrition: Calories per serving: 965 Carbohydrates: 0.6; Protein: 106.5g Fat: 52g Sugar: 0g Sodium: 1916mg Fiber: 0.2g

• <u>Herb Roasted Turkey</u>

Preparation Time: 15 Minutes

Cooking Time: 3 Hours 30 Minutes

Servings: 12

Ingredients:

- 14 pounds turkey, cleaned
- 2 tablespoons chopped mixed herbs
- Pork and poultry rub as needed
- ¼ teaspoon ground black pepper
- 3 tablespoons butter, unsalted, melted
- 8 tablespoons butter, unsalted, softened

- 2 cups chicken broth

Directions:

1. Clean the turkey by removing the giblets, wash it inside out, pat dry with paper towels, then place it on a roasting pan and tuck the turkey wings by tiring with butcher's string.

2. Switch on the grill, fill the grill hopper with hickory flavored wood pellets, power the grill on by using the control panel, select 'smoke' on the temperature dial, or set the temperature to 325 degrees F and let it preheat for a minimum of 15 minutes.

3. Meanwhile, prepared herb butter and for this, take a small bowl, place the softened butter in it, add black pepper and mixed herbs and beat until fluffy.

4. Place some of the prepared herb butter underneath the skin of turkey by using a handle of a wooden spoon, and massage the skin to distribute butter evenly.

5. Then rub the exterior of the turkey with melted butter, season with pork and poultry rub, and pour the broth in the roasting pan.

6. When the grill has preheated, open the lid, place roasting pan containing turkey on the grill grate, shut the grill and smoke for 3 hours and 30

minutes until the internal temperature reaches 165 degrees F and the top has turned golden brown.

7. When done, transfer turkey to a cutting board, let it rest for 30 minutes, then carve it into slices and serve.

Nutrition: Calories: 154.6 Fat: 3.1 g Carbs: 8.4 g Protein: 28.8 g

• **Turkey Legs**

Preparation Time: 10 Minutes

Cooking Time: 5 Hours

Servings: 4

Ingredients:

- 4 turkey legs
- For the Brine:
- ½ cup curing salt
- 1 tablespoon whole black peppercorns
- 1 cup BBQ rub
- ½ cup brown sugar
- 2 bay leaves
- 2 teaspoons liquid smoke
- 16 cups of warm water
- 4 cups ice
- 8 cups of cold water

Directions:

1. Prepare the brine and for this, take a large stockpot, place it over high heat, pour warm water in it, add peppercorn, bay leaves, and liquid smoke, stir in salt, sugar, and BBQ rub and bring it to a boil.

2. Remove pot from heat, bring it to room temperature, then pour in cold water, add ice cubes and let the brine chill in the refrigerator.

3. Then add turkey legs in it, submerge them completely, and let soak for 24 hours in the refrigerator.

4. After 24 hours, remove turkey legs from the brine, rinse well and pat dry with paper towels.

5. When ready to cook, switch on the grill, fill the grill hopper with hickory flavored wood pellets, power the grill on by using the control panel, select 'smoke' on the temperature dial, or set the temperature to 250 degrees F and let it preheat for a minimum of 15 minutes.

6. When the grill has preheated, open the lid, place turkey legs on the grill grate, shut the grill, and smoke for 5 hours until nicely browned and the internal temperature reaches 165 degrees F. Serve immediately.

Nutrition: Calories: 416 Fat: 13.3 g Carbs: 0 g Protein: 69.8 g

• **Turkey Breast**

Preparation Time: 12 Hours

Cooking Time: 8 Hours

Servings: 6

Ingredients:

For the Brine:

- 2 pounds turkey breast, deboned
- 2 tablespoons ground black pepper
- ¼ cup salt
- 1 cup brown sugar
- 4 cups cold water

For the BBQ Rub:

- 2 tablespoons dried onions
- 2 tablespoons garlic powder
- ¼ cup paprika
- 2 tablespoons ground black pepper
- 1 tablespoon salt
- 2 tablespoons brown sugar
- 2 tablespoons red chili powder
- 1 tablespoon cayenne pepper
- 2 tablespoons sugar
- 2 tablespoons ground cumin

Directions:

1. Prepare the brine and for this, take a large bowl, add salt, black pepper, and sugar in it, pour in water, and stir until sugar has dissolved.
2. Place turkey breast in it, submerge it completely and let it soak for a minimum of 12 hours in the refrigerator.
3. Meanwhile, prepare the BBQ rub and for this, take a small bowl, place all of its ingredients in it and then stir until combined, set aside until required.
4. Then remove turkey breast from the brine and season well with the prepared BBQ rub.
5. When ready to cook, switch on the grill, fill the grill hopper with apple-flavored wood pellets, power the grill on by using the control panel, select 'smoke' on the temperature dial, or set the temperature to 180 degrees F and let it preheat for a minimum of 15 minutes.
6. When the grill has preheated, open the lid, place turkey breast on the grill grate, shut the grill, change the smoking temperature to 225 degrees F, and smoke for 8 hours until the internal temperature reaches 160 degrees F.
7. When done, transfer turkey to a cutting board, let it rest for 10 minutes, then cut it into slices and serve.

Nutrition: Calories: 250 Fat: 5 g Carbs: 31 g Protein: 18 g

• Apple wood-Smoked Whole Turkey

Preparation Time: 10 minutes

Cooking Time: 5 hours

Servings: 6

Ingredients:

- 1 (10- to 12-pound) turkey, giblets removed
- Extra-virgin olive oil, for rubbing

- ¼ cup poultry seasoning
- 8 tablespoons (1 stick) unsalted butter, melted
- ½ cup apple juice
- 2 teaspoons dried sage
- 2 teaspoons dried thyme

Directions:

1. Supply your smoker with wood pellets and follow the manufacturer's specific start-up procedure. Preheat, with the lid closed, to 250°F.
2. Rub the turkey with oil and season with the poultry seasoning inside and out, getting under the skin.
3. In a bowl, combine the melted butter, apple juice, sage, and thyme to use for basting.
4. Put the turkey in a roasting pan, place on the grill, close the lid, and grill for 5 to 6 hours, basting every hour, until the skin is brown and crispy, or until a meat thermometer inserted in the thickest part of the thigh reads 165°F.
5. Let the turkey meat rest for about 15 to 20 minutes before carving.

Nutrition: Calories: 180 Carbs: 3g Fat: 2g Protein: 39g

• <u>Savory-Sweet Turkey Legs</u>

Preparation Time: 10 minutes

Cooking Time: 5 hours

Servings: 4

Ingredients:

- 1 gallon hot water
- 1 cup curing salt (such as Morton Tender Quick)
- ¼ cup packed light brown sugar
- 1 teaspoon freshly ground black pepper
- 1 teaspoon ground cloves
- 1 bay leaf
- 2 teaspoons liquid smoke
- 4 turkey legs
- Mandarin Glaze, for serving

Directions:

1. In a huge container with a lid, stir together the water, curing salt, brown sugar, pepper, cloves, bay leaf, and liquid smoke until the salt and sugar are dissolved; let come to room temperature.
2. Submerge the turkey legs in the seasoned brine, cover, and refrigerate overnight.
3. When ready to smoke, remove the turkey legs from the brine and rinse them; discard the brine.
4. Supply your smoker with wood pellets and follow the manufacturer's specific start-up procedure. Preheat, with the lid closed, to 225°F.
5. Arrange the turkey legs on the grill, close the lid, and smoke for 4 to 5 hours, or until dark brown and a meat thermometer inserted in the thickest part of the meat reads 165°F.

6. Serve with Mandarin Glaze on the side or drizzled over the turkey legs.

Nutrition: Calories: 190 Carbs: 1g Fat: 9g Protein: 24g

• **Marinated Smoked Turkey Breast**

Preparation Time: 15 minutes

Cooking Time: 4 hours

Servings: 6

Ingredients:

- 1 (5 pounds) boneless chicken breast
- 4 cups water
- 2 tablespoons kosher salt
- 1 teaspoon Italian seasoning
- 2 tablespoons honey
- 1 tablespoon cider vinegar
- Rub:
- ½ teaspoon onion powder
- 1 teaspoon paprika
- 1 teaspoon salt
- 1 teaspoon ground black pepper
- 1 tablespoons brown sugar
- ½ teaspoon garlic powder
- 1 teaspoon oregano

Directions:

1. In a huge container, combine the water, honey, cider vinegar, Italian seasoning and salt.
2. Add the chicken breast and toss to combine. Cover the bowl and place it in the refrigerator and chill for 4 hours.

3. Rinse the chicken breast with water and pat dry with paper towels.
4. In another mixing bowl, combine the brown sugar, salt, paprika, onion powder, pepper, oregano and garlic.
5. Generously season the chicken breasts with the rub mix.
6. Preheat the grill to 225°F with lid closed for 15 minutes. Use cherry wood pellets.
7. Arrange the turkey breast into a grill rack. Place the grill rack on the grill.
8. Smoke for about 3 to 4 hours or until the internal temperature of the turkey breast reaches 165°F.
9. Remove the chicken breast from heat and let them rest for a few minutes. Serve.

Nutrition: Calories 903 Fat: 34g Carbs: 9.9g Protein 131.5g

• **Maple Bourbon Turkey**

Preparation Time: 15 minutes

Cooking Time: 3 hours

Servings: 8

Ingredients:

- 1 (12 pounds) turkey
- 8 cup chicken broth
- 1 stick butter (softened)
- 1 teaspoon thyme
- 2 garlic clove (minced)
- 1 teaspoon dried basil
- 1 teaspoon pepper
- 1 teaspoon salt

- 1 tablespoon minced rosemary
- 1 teaspoon paprika
- 1 lemon (wedged)
- 1 onion
- 1 orange (wedged)
- 1 apple (wedged)
- Maple Bourbon Glaze:
- ¾ cup bourbon
- 1/2 cup maple syrup
- 1 stick butter (melted)
- 1 tablespoon lime

Directions:

1. Wash the turkey meat inside and out under cold running water.
2. Insert the onion, lemon, orange and apple into the turkey cavity.
3. In a mixing bowl, combine the butter, paprika, thyme, garlic, basil, pepper, salt, basil and rosemary.
4. Brush the turkey generously with the herb butter mixture.
5. Set a rack into a roasting pan and place the turkey on the rack. Put a 5 cups of chicken broth into the bottom of the roasting pan.
6. Preheat the grill to 350°F with lid closed for 15 minutes, using maple wood pellets.
7. Place the roasting pan in the grill and cook for 1 hour.
8. Meanwhile, combine all the maple bourbon glaze ingredients in a mixing bowl. Mix until well combined.

9. Baste the turkey with glaze mixture. Continue cooking, basting turkey every 30 minutes and adding more broth as needed for 2 hours, or until the internal temperature of the turkey reaches 165°F.
10. Take off the turkey from the grill and let it rest for a few minutes. Cut into slices and serve.

Nutrition: Calories 1536 Fat 58.6g Carbs: 24g Protein 20.1g

• Thanksgiving Turkey

Preparation Time: 15 minutes

Cooking Time: 4 hours

Servings: 6

Ingredients:

- 2 cups butter (softened)
- 1 tablespoon cracked black pepper
- 2 teaspoons kosher salt
- 2 tablespoons freshly chopped rosemary
- 2 tablespoons freshly chopped parsley
- 2 tablespoons freshly chopped sage
- 2 teaspoons dried thyme
- 6 garlic cloves (minced)
- 1 (18 pound) turkey

Directions:

1. In a mixing bowl, combine the butter, sage, rosemary, 1 teaspoon black pepper, 1 teaspoon salt, thyme, parsley and garlic.
2. Use your fingers to loosen the skin from the turkey.

3. Generously, Rub butter mixture under the turkey skin and all over the turkey as well. 4. Season turkey generously with herb mix. 5. Preheat the grill to 300°F with lid closed for 15 minutes.

4. Place the turkey on the grill and roast for about 4 hours, or until the turkey thigh temperature reaches 160°F.

5. Take out the turkey meat from the grill and let it rest for a few minutes. Cut into sizes and serve.

Nutrition: Calories 278 Fat 30.8g Carbs: 1.6g Protein 0.6g

• Spatchcock Smoked Turkey

Preparation Time: 15 minutes
Cooking Time: 4 hours 3 minutes
Servings: 6
Ingredients:

- 1 (18 pounds) turkey
- 2 tablespoons finely chopped fresh parsley
- 1 tablespoon finely chopped fresh rosemary
- 2 tablespoons finely chopped fresh thyme
- ½ cup melted butter
- 1 teaspoon garlic powder
- 1 teaspoon onion powder
- 1 teaspoon ground black pepper
- 2 teaspoons salt or to taste
- 2 tablespoons finely chopped scallions

Directions:

1. Remove the turkey giblets and rinse turkey, in and out, under cold running water.

2. Place the turkey on a working surface, breast side down. Use a poultry shear to cut the turkey along both sides of the backbone to remove the turkey back bone.

3. Flip the turkey over, back side down. Now, press the turkey down to flatten it.

4. In a mixing bowl, combine the parsley, rosemary, scallions, thyme, butter, pepper, salt, and garlic and onion powder.

5. Rub butter mixture over all sides of the turkey.

6. Preheat your grill to HIGH (450°F) with lid closed for 15 minutes.

7. Place the turkey directly on the grill grate and cook for 30 minutes. Reduce the heat to 300°F and cook for an additional 4 hours, or until the internal temperature of the thickest part of the thigh reaches 165°F.

8. Take out the turkey meat from the grill and let it rest for a few minutes. Cut into sizes and serve.

Nutrition: Calories: 780 Fat: 19g Carbs: 29.7g Protein116.4g

• <u>Hoisin Turkey Wings</u>

Preparation Time: 15 minutes

Cooking Time: 1 hour

Servings: 8

Ingredients:

- 2 pounds turkey wings
- ½ cup hoisin sauce
- 1 tablespoon honey
- 2 teaspoons soy sauce
- 2 garlic cloves (minced)
- 1 teaspoons freshly grated ginger
- 2 teaspoons sesame oil
- 1 teaspoons pepper or to taste
- 1 teaspoons salt or to taste
- ¼ cup pineapple juice
- 1 tablespoon chopped green onions
- 1 tablespoon sesame seeds
- 1 lemon (cut into wedges)

Directions:

1. In a huge container, combine the honey, garlic, ginger, soy, hoisin sauce, sesame oil, pepper and salt. Put all the mixture into a zip lock bag and add the wings. Refrigerate for 2 hours.
2. Remove turkey from the marinade and reserve the marinade. Let the turkey rest for a few minutes, until it is at room temperature.
3. Preheat your grill to 300°F with the lid closed for 15 minutes.
4. Arrange the wings into a grilling basket and place the basket on the grill.
5. Grill for 1 hour or until the internal temperature of the wings reaches 165°F.
6. Meanwhile, pour the reserved marinade into a saucepan over medium-high heat. Stir in the pineapple juice.
7. Wait to boil then reduce heat and simmer for until the sauce thickens.
8. Brush the wings with sauce and cook for 6 minutes more. Remove the wings from heat.
9. Serve and garnish it with green onions, sesame seeds and lemon wedges.

Nutrition: Calories: 115 Fat: 4.8g Carbs: 11.9g Protein 6.8g

• <u>Turkey Jerky</u>

Preparation Time: 15 minutes

Cooking Time: 4 hours

Servings: 6

Ingredients:

- Marinade:
- 1 cup pineapple juice
- ½ cup brown sugar
- 2 tablespoons Sirach
- 2 teaspoons onion powder
- 2 tablespoons minced garlic
- 2 tablespoons rice wine vinegar
- 2 tablespoons hoisin

- 1 tablespoon red pepper flakes
- 1 tablespoon coarsely ground black pepper flakes
- 2 cups coconut amino
- 2 jalapenos (thinly sliced)
- Meat:
- 3 pounds turkey boneless skinless breasts (sliced to ¼ inch thick)

Directions:

1. Pour the marinade mixture ingredients in a container and mix until the ingredients are well combined.
2. Put the turkey slices in a gallon sized zip lock bag and pour the marinade into the bag. Massage the marinade into the turkey. Seal the bag and refrigerate for 8 hours.
3. Remove the turkey slices from the marinade.
4. Activate the pellet grill for smoking and leave lip opened for 5 minutes until fire starts.
5. Close the lid and preheat your pellet grill to 180°F, using hickory pellet.
6. Remove the turkey slices from the marinade and pat them dry with a paper towel.
7. Arrange the turkey slices on the grill in a single layer. Smoke the turkey for about 3 to 4 hours, turning often after the first 2 hours of smoking. The jerky should be dark and dry when it is done.
8. Remove the jerky from the grill and let it sit for about 1 hour to cool. Serve immediately or store in refrigerator.

Nutrition: Calories: 109 Carbs: 12g Fat: 1g Protein: 14g

- ## **Smoked Whole Turkey**

Preparation Time: 20 Minutes

Cooking Time: 8 Hours

Servings: 6

Ingredients:

- 1 Whole Turkey of about 12 to 16 lb.
- 1 Cup of your Favorite Rub
- 1 Cup of Sugar
- 1 Tablespoon of minced garlic
- ½ Cup of Worcestershire sauce
- 2 Tablespoons of Canola Oil

Directions:

1. Thaw the Turkey and remove the giblets
2. Pour in 3 gallons of water in a non-metal bucket of about 5 gallons
3. Add the BBQ rub and mix very well
4. Add the garlic, the sugar and the Worcestershire sauce; then submerge the turkey into the bucket.
5. Refrigerate the turkey in the bucket for an overnight.
6. Place the Grill on a High Smoke and smoke the Turkey for about 3 hours
7. Switch the grilling temp to about 350 degrees F; then push a metal meat

thermometer into the thickest part of the turkey breast

8. Cook for about 4 hours; then take off the wood pellet grill and let rest for about 15 minutes

9. Slice the turkey, then serve and enjoy your dish!

Nutrition: Calories: 165 Fat: 14g Carbs: 0.5g Protein: 15.2g

• **Smoked Turkey Breast**

Preparation Time: 10 Minutes

Cooking Time: 1 Hour 30 minutes

Servings: 6

Ingredients:

- For The Brine
- 1 Cup of kosher salt
- 1 Cup of maple syrup
- ¼ Cup of brown sugar
- ¼ Cup of whole black peppercorns
- 4 Cups of cold bourbon
- 1 and ½ gallons of cold water
- 1 Turkey breast of about 7 pounds
- For The Turkey
- 3 Tablespoons of brown sugar
- 1 and ½ tablespoons of smoked paprika
- 1 ½ teaspoons of chipotle chili powder
- 1 ½ teaspoons of garlic powder
- 1 ½ teaspoons of salt
- 1 and ½ teaspoons of black pepper
- 1 Teaspoon of onion powder
- ½ teaspoon of ground cumin
- 6 Tablespoons of melted unsalted butter

Directions:

1. Before beginning; make sure that the bourbon; the water and the chicken stock are all cold

2. Now to make the brine, combine altogether the salt, the syrup, the sugar, the peppercorns, the bourbon, and the water in a large bucket.

3. Remove any pieces that are left on the turkey, like the neck or the giblets

4. Refrigerate the turkey meat in the brine for about 8 to 12 hours in a reseal able bag

5. Remove the turkey breast from the brine and pat dry with clean paper towels; then place it over a baking sheet and refrigerate for about 1 hour

6. Preheat your pellet smoker to about 300°F; making sure to add the wood chips to the burner

7. In a bowl, mix the paprika with the sugar, the chili powder, the garlic powder, the salt, the pepper, the onion powder and the cumin, mixing very well to combine.

8. Carefully lift the skin of the turkey; then rub the melted butter over the meat

9. Rub the spice over the meat very well and over the skin

10. Smoke the turkey breast for about 1 ½ hours at a temperature of about 375°

Nutrition: Calories: 94 Fat: 2g Carbs: 1g Protein: 18g

• **Whole Turkey**

Preparation Time: 10 Minutes

Cooking Time: 7 Hours And 30 Minutes

Servings: 10

Ingredients:

- 1 frozen whole turkey, giblets removed, thawed
- 2 tablespoons orange zest
- 2 tablespoons chopped fresh parsley
- 1 teaspoon salt
- 2 tablespoons chopped fresh rosemary
- 1 teaspoon ground black pepper
- 2 tablespoons chopped fresh sage
- 1 cup butter, unsalted, softened, divided
- 2 tablespoons chopped fresh thyme
- ½ cup water
- 14.5-ounce chicken broth

Directions:

1. Open hopper of the smoker, add dry pallets, make sure ash-can is in place, then open the ash damper, power on the smoker and close the ash damper.

2. Set the temperature of the smoker to 180 degrees F, let preheat for 30 minutes or until the green light on the dial blinks that indicate smoker has reached to set temperature.

3. Meanwhile, prepare the turkey and for this, tuck its wings under it by using kitchen twine.

4. Place ½ cup butter in a bowl, add thyme, parsley, and sage, orange zest, and rosemary, stir well until combined and then brush this mixture generously on the inside and outside of the turkey and season the external of turkey with salt and black pepper.

5. Place turkey on a roasting pan, breast side up, pour in broth and water, add the remaining butter in the pan, then place the pan on the smoker grill and shut with lid.

6. Smoke the turkey for 3 hours, then increase the temperature to 350 degrees F and continue smoking the turkey for 4 hours or until thoroughly cooked and the internal temperature of the turkey reaches to 165 degrees F, basting turkey with the dripping every 30 minutes, but not in the last hour.

7. When you are done, take off the roasting pan from the smoker and let the turkey rest for 20 minutes.

8. Carve turkey into pieces and serve.

Nutrition: Calories: 146 Fat: 8 g Protein: 18   g Carbs: 1 g

• **Herbed Turkey Breast**

Preparation Time: 8 Hours And 10 Minutes

Cooking Time: 3 Hours

Servings: 12

Ingredients:

- 7 pounds turkey breast, bone-in, skin-on, fat trimmed
- 3/4 cup salt
- 1/3 cup brown sugar
- 4 quarts water, cold
- For Herbed Butter:
- 1 tablespoon chopped parsley
- ½ teaspoon ground black pepper
- 8 tablespoons butter, unsalted, softened
- 1 tablespoon chopped sage
- ½ tablespoon minced garlic
- 1 tablespoon chopped rosemary
- 1 teaspoon lemon zest
- 1 tablespoon chopped oregano
- 1 tablespoon lemon juice

Directions:

1. Prepare the brine and for this, pour water in a large container, add salt and sugar and stir well until salt and sugar has completely dissolved.
2. Add turkey breast in the brine, cover with the lid and let soak in the refrigerator for a minimum of 8 hours.
3. Then remove turkey breast from the brine, rinse well and pat dry with paper towels.
4. Open hopper of the smoker, add dry pallets, make sure ash-can is in place, then open the ash damper, power on the smoker and close the ash damper.
5. Set the temperature of the smoker to 350 degrees F, let preheat for 30 minutes or until the green light on the dial blinks that indicate smoker has reached to set temperature.
6. Meanwhile, take a roasting pan, pour in 1 cup water, then place a wire rack in it and place turkey breast on it.
7. Prepare the herb butter and for this, place butter in a heatproof bowl, add remaining ingredients for the butter and stir until just mix.
8. Loosen the skin of the turkey from its breast by using your fingers, then insert 2 tablespoons of prepared herb butter on each side of the skin of the breastbone and spread it evenly, pushing out all the air pockets.
9. Place the remaining herb butter in the bowl into the microwave wave and heat for 1 minute or more at high heat setting or until melted.
10. hen brush melted herb butter on the outside of the turkey breast and place

roasting pan containing turkey on the smoker grill.

11. Shut the smoker with lid and smoke for 2 hours and 30 minutes or until the turkey breast is nicely golden brown and the internal temperature of turkey reach to 165 degrees F, flipping the turkey and basting with melted herb butter after 1 hour and 30 minutes smoking.

12. When done, transfer the turkey breast to a cutting board, let it rest for 15 minutes, then carve it into pieces and serve.

Nutrition: Calories: 97 Fat: 4 g Protein: 13 g Carbs: 1 g

• **Jalapeno Injection Turkey**

Preparation Time: 15 Minutes

Cooking Time: 4 Hours And 10 Minutes

Servings: 4

Ingredients:

- 15 pounds whole turkey, giblet removed
- ½ of medium red onion, peeled and minced
- 8 jalapeño peppers
- 2 tablespoons minced garlic
- 4 tablespoons garlic powder
- 6 tablespoons Italian seasoning
- 1 cup butter, softened, unsalted
- ¼ cup olive oil
- 1 cup chicken broth

Directions:

1. Open hopper of the smoker, add dry pallets, make sure ash-can is in place, then open the ash damper, power on the smoker and close the ash damper.

2. Make the temperature of the smoker up to 200 degrees F, let preheat for 30 minutes or until the green light on the dial blinks that indicate smoker has reached to set temperature.

3. Meanwhile, place a large saucepan over medium-high heat, add oil and butter and when the butter melts, add onion, garlic, and peppers and cook for 3 to 5 minutes or until nicely golden brown.

4. Pour in broth, stir well, let the mixture boil for 5 minutes, then remove pan from the heat and strain the mixture to get just liquid.

5. Inject turkey generously with prepared liquid, then spray the outside of turkey with butter spray and season well with garlic and Italian seasoning.

6. Place turkey on the smoker grill, shut with lid, and smoke for 30 minutes, then increase the temperature to 325 degrees F and continue smoking the turkey for 3 hours or until the internal temperature of turkey reach to 165 degrees F.

7. When done, transfer turkey to a cutting board, let rest for 5 minutes, then carve into slices and serve.

Nutrition: Calories: 131 Fat: 7 g Protein: 13 g Carbs: 3 g

• <u>Smoked Turkey Mayo with Green Apple</u>

Preparation Time: 20 minutes
Cooking Time: 4 hours 10 minutes
Servings: 10
Ingredients:

- Whole turkey (4-lbs., 1.8-kg.)
- The Rub
- Mayonnaise – ½ cup
- Salt – ¾ teaspoon
- Brown sugar – ¼ cup
- Ground mustard – 2 tablespoons
- Black pepper – 1 teaspoon
- Onion powder – 1 ½ tablespoons
- Ground cumin – 1 ½ tablespoons
- Chili powder – 2 tablespoons
- Cayenne pepper – ½ tablespoon
- Old Bay Seasoning – ½ teaspoon
- The Filling
- Sliced green apples – 3 cups

Directions:

1. Place salt, brown sugar, brown mustard, black pepper, onion powder, ground cumin, chili powder, cayenne pepper, and old bay seasoning in a bowl then mix well. Set aside.

2. Next, fill the turkey cavity with sliced green apples then baste mayonnaise over the turkey skin.

3. Sprinkle the dry spice mixture over the turkey then wrap with aluminum foil.

4. Marinate the turkey for at least 4 hours or overnight and store in the fridge to keep it fresh.

5. On the next day, remove the turkey from the fridge and thaw at room temperature.

6. Meanwhile, plug the wood pellet smoker then fill the hopper with the wood pellet. Turn the switch on.

7. Set the wood pellet smoker for indirect heat then adjust the temperature to 275°F (135°C).

8. Unwrap the turkey and place in the wood pellet smoker.

9. Smoke the turkey for 4 hours or until the internal temperature has reached 170°F (77°C).

10. Remove the smoked turkey from the wood pellet smoker and serve.

Nutrition: Calories: 340 Carbs: 40g Fat: 10g Protein: 21g

• <u>Buttery Smoked Turkey Beer</u>

Preparation Time: 15 minutes
Cooking Time: 4 hours
Servings: 6
Ingredients:

- Whole turkey (4-lbs., 1.8-kg.)
- The Brine
- Beer – 2 cans
- Salt – 1 tablespoon
- White sugar – 2 tablespoons
- Soy sauce – ¼ cup
- Cold water – 1 quart
- The Rub
- Unsalted butter – 3 tablespoons
- Smoked paprika – 1 teaspoon
- Garlic powder – 1 ½ teaspoons
- Pepper – 1 teaspoon
- Cayenne pepper – ¼ teaspoon

Directions:

1. Pour beer into a container then add salt, white sugar, and soy sauce then stir well.
2. Put the turkey into the brine mixture cold water over the turkey. Make sure that the turkey is completely soaked.
3. Soak the turkey in the brine for at least 6 hours or overnight and store in the fridge to keep it fresh.
4. On the next day, remove the turkey from the fridge and take it out of the brine mixture.
5. Wash and rinse the turkey then pat it dry.
6. Next, plug the wood pellet smoker then fill the hopper with the wood pellet. Turn the switch on.
7. Set the wood pellet smoker for indirect heat then adjust the temperature to 275°F (135°C).
8. Open the beer can then push it in the turkey cavity.
9. Place the seasoned turkey in the wood pellet smoker and make a tripod using the beer can and the two turkey-legs.
10. Smoke the turkey for 4 hours or until the internal temperature has reached 170°F (77°C).
11. Once it is done, remove the smoked turkey from the wood pellet smoker and transfer it to a serving dish.

Nutrition: Calories: 229 Carbs: 34g Fat: 8g Protein: 3g

• **Barbecue Chili Smoked Turkey Breast**

Preparation Time: 15 minutes
Cooking Time: 4 hours 20 minutes
Servings: 8
Ingredients:

- Turkey breast (3-lb., 1.4-kg.)
- The Rub
- Salt – ¾ teaspoon
- Pepper – ½ teaspoon
- The Glaze
- Olive oil – 1 tablespoon
- Ketchup – ¾ cup
- White vinegar – 3 tablespoons
- Brown sugar – 3 tablespoons

- Smoked paprika – 1 tablespoons
- Chili powder – ¾ teaspoon
- Cayenne powder – ¼ teaspoon

Directions:

1. Score the turkey breast at several places then sprinkle salt and pepper over it.
2. Let the seasoned turkey breast rest for approximately 10 minutes.
3. In the meantime, plug the wood pellet smoker then fill the hopper with the wood pellet. Turn the switch on.
4. Set the wood pellet smoker for indirect heat then adjust the temperature to 275°F (135°C).
5. Place the seasoned turkey breast in the wood pellet smoker and smoke for 2 hours.
6. In the meantime, combine olive oil, ketchup, white vinegar, brown sugar, smoked paprika; chili powder, garlic powder, and cayenne pepper in a saucepan then stir until incorporated. Wait to simmer then remove from heat.
7. After 2 hours of smoking, baste the sauce over the turkey breast and continue smoking for another 2 hours.
8. Once the internal temperature of the smoked turkey breast has reached 170°F (77°C) remove from the wood pellet smoker and wrap with aluminum foil.
9. Let the smoked turkey breast rest for approximately 15 minutes to 30 minutes then unwrap it.
10. Cut the smoked turkey breast into thick slices then serve.

Nutrition: Calories: 290 Carbs: 2g Fat: 3g Protein: 63g

- ## **Hot Sauce Smoked Turkey Tabasco**

Preparation Time: 20 minutes
Cooking Time: 4 hours 15 minutes
Servings: 8
Ingredients:

- Whole turkey (4-lbs., 1.8-kg.)
- The Rub
- Brown sugar – ¼ cup
- Smoked paprika – 2 teaspoons
- Salt – 1 teaspoon
- Onion powder – 1 ½ teaspoons
- Oregano – 2 teaspoons
- Garlic powder – 2 teaspoons
- Dried thyme – ½ teaspoon
- White pepper – ½ teaspoon
- Cayenne pepper – ½ teaspoon
- The Glaze
- Ketchup – ½ cup
- Hot sauce – ½ cup
- Cider vinegar – 1 tablespoon
- Tabasco – 2 teaspoons
- Cajun spices – ½ teaspoon

- Unsalted butter – 3 tablespoons

Directions:

1. Rub the turkey with 2 tablespoons of brown sugar, smoked paprika, salt, onion powder, garlic powder, dried thyme, white pepper, and cayenne pepper. Let the turkey rest for an hour.
2. Plug the wood pellet smoker then fill the hopper with the wood pellet. Turn the switch on.
3. Set the wood pellet smoker for indirect heat then adjust the temperature to 275°F (135°C).
4. Place the seasoned turkey in the wood pellet smoker and smoke for 4 hours.
5. In the meantime, place ketchup, hot sauce, cider vinegar, Tabasco, and Cajun spices in a saucepan then bring to a simmer.
6. Remove the sauce from heat and quickly add unsalted butter to the saucepan. Stir until melted.
7. After 4 hours of smoking, baste the Tabasco sauce over the turkey then continue smoking for 15 minutes.
8. Once the internal temperature of the smoked turkey has reached 170°F (77°C), remove from the wood pellet smoker and place it on a serving dish.

Nutrition: Calories: 160 Carbs: 2g Fat: 14g Protein: 7g

- ## Cured Turkey Drumstick

Preparation Time: 20 minutes

Cooking Time: 2.5 hours to 3 hours

Servings: 3

Ingredients:

- 3 fresh or thawed frozen turkey drumsticks
- 3 tablespoons extra virgin olive oil
- Brine component
- 4 cups of filtered water
- ¼ Cup kosher salt
- ¼ cup brown sugar
- 1 teaspoon garlic powder
- Poultry seasoning 1 teaspoon
- 1/2 teaspoon red pepper flakes
- 1 teaspoon pink hardened salt

Directions:

1. Put the salt water ingredients in a 1 gallon sealable bag. Add the turkey drumstick to the salt water and refrigerate for 12 hours.
2. After 12 hours, remove the drumstick from the saline, rinse with cold water, and pat dry with a paper towel.
3. Air dry the drumstick in the refrigerator without a cover for 2 hours.
4. Remove the drumsticks from the refrigerator and rub a tablespoon of extra virgin olive oil under and over each drumstick.

5. Set the wood pellet or grill for indirect cooking and preheat to 250 degrees Fahrenheit using hickory or maple pellets.

6. Place the drumstick on the grill and smoke at 250 ° F for 2 hours.

7. After 2 hours, increase grill temperature to 325 ° F.

8. Cook the turkey drumstick at 325 ° F until the internal temperature of the thickest part of each drumstick is 180 ° F with an instant reading digital thermometer.

9. Place a smoked turkey drumstick under a loose foil tent for 15 minutes before eating.

Nutrition: Calories: 278 Carbs: 0g Fat: 13g Protein: 37g

• **Tailgate Smoked Young Turkey**

Preparation Time: 20 Minutes
Cooking Time: 4 To 4 Hours 30 Minutes
Servings: 6
Ingredients:

- 1 fresh or thawed frozen young turkey
- 6 glasses of extra virgin olive oil with roasted garlic flavor
- 6 original Yang dry lab or poultry seasonings

Directions:

1. Remove excess fat and skin from turkey breasts and cavities.

2. Slowly separate the skin of the turkey to its breast and a quarter of the leg, leaving the skin intact.

3. Apply olive oil to the chest, under the skin and on the skin.

4. Gently rub or season to the chest cavity, under the skin and on the skin.

5. Set up tailgate wood pellet smoker grill for indirect cooking and smoking. Preheat to 225 ° F using apple or cherry pellets.

6. Put the turkey meat on the grill with the chest up.

7. Suck the turkey for 4-4 hours at 225 ° F until the thickest part of the turkey's chest reaches an internal temperature of 170 ° F and the juice is clear.

8. Before engraving, place the turkey under a loose foil tent for 20 minutes

Nutrition: Calories: 240 Carbs: 27g Fat: 9g Protein: 15g

• **Roast Turkey Orange**

Preparation Time: 30 Minutes
Cooking Time: 2 hours 30 minutes
Servings:
Ingredients:

- 1 Frozen Long Island turkey
- 3 tablespoons west
- 1 large orange, cut into wedges
- Three celery stems chopped into large chunks
- Half a small red onion, a quarter
- Orange sauce:

- 2 orange cups
- 2 tablespoons soy sauce
- 2 tablespoons orange marmalade
- 2 tablespoons honey
- 3 teaspoons grated raw

Directions:

1. Remove the nibble from the turkey's cavity and neck and retain or discard for another use. Wash the duck and pat some dry paper towel.

2. Remove excess fat from tail, neck and cavity. Use a sharp scalpel knife tip to pierce the turkey's skin entirely, so that it does not penetrate the duck's meat, to help dissolve the fat layer beneath the skin.

3. Add the seasoning inside the cavity with one cup of rub or seasoning.

4. Season the outside of the turkey with the remaining friction or seasoning.

5. Fill the cavity with orange wedges, celery and onion. Duck legs are tied with butcher twine to make filling easier. Place the turkey's breast up on a small rack of shallow roast bread.

6. To make the sauce, mix the ingredients in the saucepan over low heat and cook until the sauce is thick and syrupy. Set aside and let cool.

7. Set the wood pellet smoker grill for indirect cooking and use the pellets to preheat to 350 ° F.

8. Roast the turkey at 350 ° F for 2 hours.

9. After 2 hours, brush the turkey freely with orange sauce.

10. Roast the orange glass turkey for another 30 minutes, making sure that the inside temperature of the thickest part of the leg reaches 165 ° F.

11. Place turkey under loose foil tent for 20 minutes before serving.

12. Discard the orange wedge, celery and onion. Serve with a quarter of turkey with poultry scissors.

Nutrition: Calories: 216 Carbs: 2g Fat: 11g Protein: 34g

- ## **Smoked Chicken in Maple Flavor**

Preparation Time: 30 minutes

Cooking Time: 6 Hours

Servings: 1

Ingredients:

- Boneless chicken breast (5-lbs., 2.3-kgs)
- The Spice
- Chipotle powder – 1 tablespoon
- Salt – 1 ½ teaspoons
- Garlic powder – 2 teaspoons
- Onion powder – 2 teaspoons
- Pepper – 1 teaspoon
- The Glaze
- Maple syrup – ½ cup
- The Fire

- Preheat the smoker an hour prior to smoking.
- Use charcoal and maple wood chips for smoking.

Directions:

1. Preheat a smoker to 225°F (107°C) with charcoal and maple wood chips.
2. Place chipotle, salt, garlic powder, onion powder, and pepper in a bowl then mix to combine.
3. Rub the chicken with the spice mixture then place on the smoker's rack.
4. Smoke the chicken for 4 hours and brush with maple syrup once every hour.
5. When the internal temperature has reached 160°F (71°C), remove the smoked chicken breast from the smoker and transfer to a serving dish.
6. Serve and enjoy right away.

Nutrition: Carbohydrates: 27 g Protein: 19 g Sodium: 65 mg Cholesterol: 49 mg

- ## Hot and Spicy Smoked Chicken Wings

Preparation Time: 30 minutes

Cooking Time: 3 Hours

Servings: 1

Ingredients:

- Chicken wings (6-lbs., 2.7-kgs)
- The Rub
- Olive oil – 3 tablespoons
- Chili powder – 2 ½ tablespoons
- Smoked paprika – 3 tablespoons
- Cumin – ½ teaspoon
- Garlic powder – 2 teaspoons
- Salt – 1 ¾ teaspoons
- Pepper – 1 tablespoon
- Cayenne – 2 teaspoons
- The Fire
- Preheat the smoker an hour prior to smoking.
- Add soaked hickory wood chips during the smoking time.

Directions:

1. Divide each chicken wing into two then place in a bowl. Set aside.
2. Combine olive oil with chili powder, smoked paprika, cumin, garlic powder, salt, pepper, and cayenne then mix well.
3. Rub the chicken wings with the spice mixture then let them sit for about an hour.
4. Meanwhile, preheat a smoker to 225°F (107°C) with charcoal and hickory wood chips. Prepare indirect heat.
5. When the smoker is ready, arrange the spiced chicken wings on the smoker's rack.
6. Smoke the chicken wings for 2 hours or until the internal temperature of the chicken wings has reached 160°F (71°C).

7. Take the smoked chicken wings from the smoker and transfer to a serving dish.

8. Serve and enjoy immediately.

Nutrition: Carbohydrates: 17 g Protein: 29 g Sodium: 55 mg Cholesterol: 48 mg

• Sweet Smoked Chicken in Black Tea Aroma

Preparation Time: 30 minutes

Cooking Time: 10 Hours

Servings: 1

Ingredients:

- Chicken breast (6-lbs., 2.7-kgs)
- The Rub
- Salt – ¼ cup
- Chili powder – 2 tablespoons
- Chinese five-spice – 2 tablespoons
- Brown sugar – 1 ½ cups
- The Smoke
- Preheat the smoker an hour prior to smoking.
- Add soaked hickory wood chips during the smoking time.
- Black tea – 2 cups

Directions:

1. Place salt, chili powder, Chinese five-spice, and brown sugar in a bowl then stir to combine.

2. Rub the chicken breast with the spice mixture then marinate overnight. Store in the refrigerator to keep it fresh.

3. In the morning, preheat a smoker to 225°F (107°C) with charcoal and hickory wood chips. Prepare indirect heat.

4. Pour black tea into a disposable aluminum pan then place in the smoker.

5. Remove the chicken from the refrigerator then thaw while waiting for the smoker.

6. Once the smoker has reached the desired temperature, place the chicken on the smoker's rack.

7. Smoke the chicken breast for 2 hours then check whether the internal temperature has reached 160°F (71°C).

8. Take the smoked chicken breast out from the smoker and transfer to a serving dish.

9. Serve and enjoy immediately.

Nutrition: Carbohydrates: 27 g Protein: 19 g Sodium: 65 mg Cholesterol: 49 mg

Sweet Smoked Gingery Lemon Chicken

Preparation Time: 30 minutes

Cooking Time: 6 Hours

Servings: 1

Ingredients:

- Whole chicken 2 (4-lbs., 1.8-kgs)
- Olive oil – ¼ cup
- The Rub
- Salt – ¼ cup
- Pepper – 2 tablespoons
- Garlic powder – ¼ cup
- The Filling
- Fresh Ginger – 8, 1-inch each
- Cinnamon sticks – 8
- Sliced lemon – ½ cup
- Cloves - 6
- The Smoke
- Preheat the smoker an hour prior to smoking.
- Add soaked hickory wood chips during the smoking time.

Directions:

1. Preheat a smoker to 225°F (107°C). Use soaked hickory wood chips to make indirect heat.
2. Rub the chicken with salt, pepper, and garlic powder then set aside.
3. Fill the chicken cavities with ginger, cinnamon sticks, cloves, and sliced lemon then brush olive oil all over the chicken.
4. When the smoker is ready, place the whole chicken on the smoker's rack.
5. Smoke the whole chicken for 4 hours then check whether the internal temperature has reached 160°F (71°C).
6. When the chicken is done, remove the smoked chicken from the smoker then let it warm for a few minutes.
7. Serve and enjoy right away or cut into slices.

Nutrition: Carbohydrates: 27 g Protein: 19 g Sodium: 65 mg Cholesterol: 49 mg

Hellfire Chicken Wings

Preparation Time: 30 minutes

Cooking Time: 6 Hours

Servings: 1

Ingredients:

- For Hellfire chicken wings
- 3 lbs. of chicken wings
- 2 tablespoon of vegetable oil
- For the rub
- 1 teaspoon of onion powder
- 1 tablespoon of paprika
- 1 teaspoon of celery seed
- 1 teaspoon of salt
- 1 teaspoon of cayenne pepper
- 1 teaspoon of freshly ground black pepper
- 1 teaspoon of granulated garlic
- 2 teaspoons of brown sugar
- For the sauce
- 2 -4 thinly sliced crosswise jalapeno poppers
- 2 tablespoons of butter; unsalted
- ½ cup of hot sauce
- ½ cup of cilantro leaves

Directions:

1. Take the chicken wings and cut off the tips and discard them
2. Now cut each of the wings into two separate pieces through the joint
3. Move this in a large mixing bowl and pour oil right over it
4. For the rub: Take a small-sized bowl and add sugar, black pepper, paprika, onion powder, salt, celery seed, cayenne, and granulated garlic in it
5. Now sprinkle this mixture over the chicken and toss it gently to coat the wings thoroughly
6. Put the smoker to preheat by putting the temperature to 350 degrees F
7. Grill the wings for approximately 40 minutes or till the time the skin turns golden brown and you feel that it has cooked through. Make sure to turn it once when you are halfway.
8. For the sauce: Take a small saucepan and melt the butter by keeping the flame on medium-low heat. Now add jalapenos to it and cook for 3 minutes, stir cilantro along with a hot sauce
9. Now, pour this freshly made sauce over the wings and toss it to coat well
10. Serve and enjoy

Nutrition: Carbohydrates: 27 g Protein: 19 g Sodium: 65 mg Cholesterol: 49 mg

Buffalo Chicken Thighs

Preparation Time: 30 minutes

Cooking Time: 6 Hours

Servings: 1

Ingredients:

- 4-6 skinless, boneless chicken thighs
- Pork and poultry rub

- 4 tablespoons of butter
- 1 cup of sauce; buffalo wing
- Bleu cheese crumbles
- Ranch dressing

Directions:

1. Set the grill to preheat by keeping the temperature to 450 degrees F and keeping the lid closed
2. Now season the chicken thighs with the poultry rub and then place it on the grill grate
3. Cook it for 8 to 10 minutes while making sure to flip it once midway
4. Now take a small saucepan and cook the wing sauce along with butter by keeping the flame on medium heat. Make sure to stir in between to avoid lumps
5. Now take the cooked chicken and dip it into the wing sauce and the butter mix. Make sure to coat both the sides in an even manner
6. Take the chicken thighs that have been sauced to the grill and then cook for further 15 minutes. Do so until the internal temperature reads 175 degrees
7. Sprinkle bleu cheese and drizzle the ranch dressing
8. Serve and enjoy

Nutrition: Carbohydrates: 29 g Protein: 19 g Sodium: 25 mg Cholesterol: 19 mg

- ## Sweet and Sour Chicken Drumsticks

Preparation Time: 30 minutes

Cooking Time: 2 Hours

Servings: 1

Ingredients:

- 8 pieces of chicken drumsticks
- 2 tablespoon of rice wine vinegar
- 3 tablespoon brown sugar
- 1 cup of ketchup
- ¼ cup of soy sauce
- Minced garlic
- 2 tablespoons of honey
- 1 tablespoon of sweet heat rub
- Minced ginger
- ½ lemon; juice
- 1/2 juiced lime

Directions:

1. Take a mixing bowl and add soy sauce along with brown sugar, ketchup, lemon, rice wine vinegar, sweet heat rub, honey, ginger, and garlic.
2. Now keep half of the mixture for dipping sauce and therefore set it aside
3. Take the leftover half and pour it in a plastic bag that can be re-sealed
4. Now add drumsticks to it and then seal the bag again
5. Refrigerate it for 4 to 12 hours
6. Take out the chicken from the bag and discard the marinade

7. Fire the grill and set the temperature to 225 degrees F

8. Now smoke the chicken over indirect heat for 2 to 3 hours a make sure to turn it once or twice

9. Add more glaze if needed

10. Remove it from the grill and let it stand aside for 10 minutes

11. Add more sauce or keep it as a dipping sauce

12. Serve and enjoy

Nutrition: Carbohydrates: 29 g Protein: 19 g Sodium: 25 mg Cholesterol: 19 mg

• <u>**Smoked Whole Chicken with Honey Glaze**</u>

Preparation Time: 30 minutes

Cooking Time: 3 Hours

Servings: 1

Ingredients:

- 1 4 pounds of chicken with the giblets thoroughly removed and patted dry
- 1 ½ lemon
- 1 tablespoon of honey
- 4 tablespoons of unsalted butter
- 4 tablespoon of chicken seasoning

Directions:

1. Fire up your smoker and set the temperature to 225 degrees F

2. Take a small saucepan and melt the butter along with honey over a low flame

3. Now squeeze ½ lemon in this mixture and then move it from the heat source

4. Take the chicken and smoke by keeping the skin side down. Do so until the chicken turns light brown and the skin starts to release from the grate.

5. Turn the chicken over and apply the honey butter mixture to it

6. Continue to smoke it making sure to taste it every 45 minutes until the thickest core reaches a temperature of 160 degrees F

7. Now remove the chicken from the grill and let it rest for 5 minutes

8. Serve with the leftover sliced lemon and enjoy

Nutrition: Carbohydrates: 29 g Protein: 19 g Sodium: 25 mg Cholesterol: 19 mg

• <u>**Beer-Braised Chicken Tacos with Jalapenos Relish**</u>

Preparation Time: 30 minutes

Cooking Time: 3 Hours

Servings: 1

Ingredients:

- For the braised chicken
- 2 lbs. of chicken thighs; boneless, skinless
- ½ small-sized diced onion
- 1 de-seeded and chopped jalapeno
- 1 (12 oz.) can of Modulo beer

- 1 tablespoon of olive oil
- 1 EA chipotle Chile in adobo
- 1 clove of minced garlic
- 4 tablespoon of adobo sauce
- 1 teaspoon of chili powder
- 1 teaspoon of garlic powder
- 1 teaspoon of salt
- 1 teaspoon of black pepper
- Juice of 2 limes
- For the tacos
- 8-12 tortillas; small flour
- Hot sauce
- Cilantro
- Cotija cheese
- For the jalapeno relish
- ¼ cup of finely diced red onion
- 3 seeded and diced jalapenos
- 1 clove of minced garlic
- 1/3cup of water
- 1 tablespoon of sugar
- 2/3 cup of white wine vinegar
- 1 tablespoon of salt
- For pickled cabbage
- 2 cups of red cabbage; shredded
- ½ cup of white wine vinegar
- 1 tablespoon of sugar
- 1 tablespoon of salt

Directions:

1. For the jalapeño relish: take all the ingredients and mix then in a non-reactive dish and then keep it aside to be used.

2. For the pickled cabbage: take another non-reactive dish and mix all its respective ingredients and keep it aside

3. Now, transfer both the relish along with the pickled cabbage to your refrigerator and allow it to see for a couple of hours or even overnight if you so desire

4. Take the chicken thighs and season it with an adequate amount of salt and pepper

5. Take a Dutch oven and keep the flame over medium-high heat. Heat 1 tablespoon of olive oil in it

6. Now place the chicken thighs skin side down and brown

7. Remove them from the heat and then set it aside

8. Now, add 1 tablespoon of butter and keep the flame to medium-high

9. When the butter has melted, add jalapeno along with onion and sauté it for 3 to 5 minutes until they turn translucent

10. Add minced garlic to it and sauté it for 30 more seconds

11. Now add adobo sauce along with lime juice, chili powder, and chipotle chile.

12. Add the chicken thighs in the oven and pour in the beer

13. Now set the grill to pre-heat by keeping the temperature to 350 degrees F
14. Place the oven on the grill and let it braise for 30 minutes
15. Remove the chicken from the braising liquid and slowly shred it
16. For the tacos: place the shredded part of chicken on the tortillas. Top it with jalapeno relish along with cotija, cabbage, and cilantro and pour the hot sauce
17. Serve and enjoy

Nutrition: Carbohydrates: 29 g Protein: 19 g Sodium: 25 mg Cholesterol: 19 mg

• **Smoked Teriyaki Chicken Wings with Sesame Dressing**

Preparation Time: 30 minutes

Cooking Time: 4 Hours

Servings: 1

Ingredients:

- Chicken wings
- For the homemade Teriyaki Glaze:
- 2/3 cup mirin
- 2 tablespoons of minced ginger
- 3 tablespoons of cornstarch
- 2 tablespoon of rice vinegar
- 1 cup of soy sauce
- 1/3 cup of brown sugar
- 8 minced garlic cloves
- 2 teaspoon of sesame oil
- 3 tablespoons of water
- For creamy sesame dressing:
- 1 green onion, chopped
- 1/2 cup of mayonnaise
- 1/4 cup rice wine vinegar
- 1 teaspoon of ground garlic
- 1 tablespoon of soy sauce
- 2 tablespoon of sesame oil
- 1/2 teaspoon of ground ginger
- 1 teaspoon siracha
- 2 tablespoon of maple syrup
- Salt and pepper to taste

Directions:

1. Use the light pellets for the sake of getting the smokey flavor
2. Set the grill to smoke mode by keeping the temperature to 225 degrees F
3. Now trim the wings and make them into drumettes and season with sea salt and black pepper
4. Smoke them for nearly 45 minutes
5. For the teriyaki glaze
6. Mince both garlic and ginger by using a teaspoon of sesame oil
7. Then mix all the ingredients except for cornstarch and water
8. Take a pan and boil cornstarch and water on low heat
9. Simmer for 15 minutes and then when done, mix it with an immersion blender

10. Now add cornstarch and water and stir it until it has mixed well
11. Add this mix to the teriyaki glaze and mix it well until it thickens. Set it aside
12. For the creamy dressing
13. Take a blender and blend all the ingredients thoroughly until you get a smooth mixture
14. Now set the grill for direct flame grilling and put the temperature to medium
15. Grill the wings for approx. 10 minutes
16. The internal temperature should reach 165 degrees F when you remove the wings from the grill
17. Toss them in the glaze when done
18. Sprinkle some sesame seeds along with green onion
19. Serve hot and spicy

Nutrition: Carbohydrates: 39 g Protein: 29 g Sodium: 15 mg Cholesterol: 19 mg

• Smoked Turkey Legs

Preparation Time: 30 minutes

Cooking Time: 6 Hours

Servings: 1

Ingredients:

- 4 turkey legs
- 2 bay leaves
- 1 cup of BBQ rubs
- 1 tablespoon of crushed allspice berries
- 2 teaspoons of liquid smoke
- ½ gal of cold water
- 4 cups of ice
- 1 gal of warm water
- ½ cup of brown sugar
- ½ cup of curing salt
- 1 tablespoon of peppercorns; whole black

Directions:

1. Take a large stockpot and mix a gallon of warm water to curing salt, rub, peppercorns, brown sugar, liquid smoke, allspice and bay leaves
2. Bring this mix to boil by keeping the flame on high heat and let all salt granules dissolve thoroughly
3. Now let it cool to room temperature
4. Now add ice and cold water and let the whole thing chill in the refrigerator
5. Add turkey legs and make sure they are submerged in the brine
6. Let it stay for a day
7. Now drain the turkey legs and get rid of the brine
8. Wash off the brine from the legs with the help of cold water and then pat it dry
9. Set the grill to preheat by keeping the temperature to 250 degrees F
10. Lay the legs directly on the grate of the grill

11. Smoke it for 4 to 5 hours till the internal temperature reaches 165 degrees F

12. Serve and enjoy

Nutrition: Carbohydrates: 39 g Protein: 29 g Sodium: 15 mg Cholesterol: 19 mg

• <u>Spiced Lemon Chicken</u>

Preparation Time: 30 minutes

Cooking Time: 5 Hours

Servings: 1

Ingredients:

- 1 whole chicken
- 4 cloves of minced garlic
- Zest of 2 fresh lemons
- 1 tablespoon of olive oil
- 1 tablespoon of smoked paprika
- 1 ½ teaspoon of salt
- ½ teaspoon of black pepper
- ½ teaspoon of dried oregano
- 1 tablespoon of ground cumin

Directions:

1. Preheat the grill by pushing the temperature to 375 degrees F

2. Now take the chicken and spatchcock it by cutting it on both the sides right from the backbone to the tail via the neck

3. Lay it flat and push it down on the breastbone. This would break the ribs

4. Take all the leftover ingredients in a bowl except ½ teaspoon of salt and crush them to make a smooth rub

5. Spread this rub evenly over the chicken making sure that it seeps right under the skin

6. Now place the chicken on the grill grates and let it cook for an hour until the internal temperature reads 165 degrees F

7. Let it rest for 10 minutes

8. Serve and enjoy

Nutrition: Carbohydrates: 39 g Protein: 29 g Sodium: 15 mg Cholesterol: 19 mg

• <u>Slow Roasted Shawarma</u>

Preparation Time: 30 minutes

Cooking Time: 4 Hours

Servings: 1

Ingredients:

- 5 ½ lbs. of chicken thighs; boneless, skinless
- 4 ½ lbs. of lamb fat
- Pita bread
- 5 ½ lbs. of top sirloin
- 2 yellow onions; large
- 4 tablespoons of rub
- Desired toppings like pickles, tomatoes, fries, salad and more

Directions:

1. Slice the meat and fat into ½" slices and place then in 3 separate bowls

2. Season each of the bowls with the rub and massage the rub into the meat to make sure it seeps well

3. Now place half of the onion at the base of each half skewer. This will make for a firm base

4. Add 2 layers from each of the bowls at a time

5. Make the track as symmetrical as you can

6. Now, put the other 2 half onions at the top of this

7. Wrap it in a plastic wrap and let it refrigerate overnight

8. Set the grill to preheat keeping the temperature to 275 degrees F

9. Lay the shawarma on the grill grate and let it cook for approx. 4 hours. Make sure to turn it at least once

10. Remove from the grill and shoot the temperature to 445 degrees F

11. Now place a cast iron griddle on the grill grate and pour it with olive oil

12. When the griddle has turned hot, place the whole shawarma on the cast iron and smoke it for 5 to 10 minutes per side

13. Remove from the grill and slice off the edges

14. Repeat the same with the leftover shawarma

15. Serve in pita bread and add the chosen toppings

16. Enjoy

Nutrition: Carbohydrates: 39 g Protein: 29 g Sodium: 15 mg Cholesterol: 19 mg

• __Duck Poppers__

Preparation Time: 30 minutes

Cooking Time: 4 Hours

Servings: 1

Ingredients:

- 8 – 10 pieces of bacon, cut event into same-sized pieces measuring 4 inches each

- 3 duck breasts; boneless and with skin removed and sliced into strips measuring ½ inches

- Sriracha sauce

- 6 de-seeded jalapenos, with the top cut off and sliced into strips

Directions:

1. Wrap the bacon around one trip of pepper and one slice of duck

2. Secure it firmly with the help of a toothpick

3. Fire the grill on low flame and keep this wrap and grill it for half an hour until the bacon turns crisp

4. Rotate often to ensure even cooking

5. Serve with sriracha sauce

Nutrition: Carbohydrates: 39 g Protein: 29 g Sodium: 15 mg Cholesterol: 19 mg

• __BBQ Pulled Turkey Sandwiches__

Preparation Time: 30 minutes

Cooking Time: 4 Hours

Servings: 1

Ingredients:

- 6 skin-on turkey thighs
- 6 split and buttered buns
- 1 ½ cups of chicken broth
- 1 cup of BBQ sauce
- Poultry rub

Directions:

1. Season the turkey thighs on both the sides with poultry rub
2. Set the grill to preheat by pushing the temperature to 180 degrees F
3. Arrange the turkey thighs on the grate of the grill and smoke it for 30 minutes
4. Now transfer the thighs to an aluminum foil which is disposable and then pour the brine right around the thighs
5. Cover it with a lid
6. Now increase the grill, temperature to 325 degrees F and roast the thigh till the internal temperature reaches 180 degrees F
7. Remove the foil from the grill but do not turn off the grill
8. Let the turkey thighs cool down a little
9. Now pour the dripping and serve
10. Remove the skin and discard it
11. Pull the meat into shreds and return it to the foil
12. Add 1 more cup of BBQ sauce and some more dripping
13. Now cover the foil with lid and re-heat the turkey on the smoker for half an hour
14. Serve and enjoy

Nutrition: Carbohydrates: 39 g Protein: 29 g Sodium: 15 mg Cholesterol: 19 mg

- ## **Smoked Deviled Eggs**

Preparation Time: 30 minutes

Cooking Time: 4 Hours

Servings: 1

Ingredients:

- 7 cooked and peeled eggs; hard-boiled
- 3 teaspoons of diced chives
- 2 teaspoons of crumbled bacon
- 3 tablespoons of mayonnaise
- 1 teaspoon of apple cider vinegar
- 1 teaspoon of brown mustard
- Dash of hot sauce
- Salt and pepper as per taste
- Paprika for dusting

Directions:

1. Set the grill to preheat with the temperature close to 180 degrees F
2. Now place the eggs that are cooked and peeled on the grill grate and then smoke them for 30 minutes

3. Remove from the grill and let it cool

4. Slice the eggs across their length and then scoop the yolk into a zip-top bag

5. Add chives along with the hot sauce, mayonnaise, vinegar, mustard, and salt and pepper to the zip-top bag.

6. Again, zip it closed and then knead all the ingredients in a way that they are mixed evenly and make a smooth paste

7. Now squeeze the mixture on to one corner of the bag and cut a very small part of the corner.

8. Drain off this mixture into hardboiled egg whites

9. Top these eggs with crumbled bacon and paprika

10. Chill it

11. Serve and enjoy

Nutrition: Carbohydrates: 19 g Protein: 29 g Sodium: 15 mg Cholesterol: 59 mg

• **Baked Garlic Parmesan Wings**

Preparation Time: 30 minutes

Cooking Time: 3 Hours

Servings: 1

Ingredients:

- For the chicken wings
- 5lbs. of chicken wings
- ½ cup of chicken rub
- For the garnish
- 1 cup of shredded parmesan cheese
- 3 tablespoons of chopped parsley
- For the sauce
- 10 cloves of finely diced garlic
- 1 cup of butter
- 2 tablespoon of chicken rub

Directions:

1. Set the grill on preheat by keeping the temperature to high

2. Take a large bowl and toss the wings in it along with the chicken rub

3. Now place the wings directly on the grill grate and cook it for 10 minutes

4. Flip it and cook for the ten minutes

5. Check the internal temperature and it needs to reach in the range of 165 to 180 degrees F

6. For the garlic sauce

7. Take a midsized saucepan and mix garlic, butter, and the leftover rub.

8. Cook it over medium heat on a stovetop

9. Cook for 10 minutes while stirring in between to avoid the making of lumps

10. Now when the wings have been cooked, remove them from the grill and place in a large bowl

11. Toss the wings with garlic sauce along with parsley and parmesan cheese

12. Serve and enjoy

Nutrition: Carbohydrates: 19 g Protein: 29 g Sodium: 15 mg Cholesterol: 59 mg

Grilled Chicken in Wood Pellets

Preparation Time: 10 minutes

Cooking Time: 30 minutes

Servings: 8

Ingredients:

- Whole chicken - 4-5 lbs.
- Grilled chicken mix

Directions:

1. Preheat the wood pellet grill with the 'smoke' option for 5 minutes.
2. Preheat another 10 minutes and keep the temperature on high until it reaches 450 degrees.
3. Use baker's twine to tie the chicken's legs together.
4. Keep the breast side up when you place the chicken in the grill.
5. Grill for 70 minutes. Do not open the grill during this process.
6. Check the temperature of your grilled chicken. Make sure it is 165 degrees. If not, leave the chicken in for longer.
7. Carefully take the chicken out of the grill.
8. Set aside for 15 minutes.
9. Cut and serve.

Nutrition: Carbohydrates: 0 g Protein: 107 g Fat: 0 g Sodium: 320 mg Cholesterol: 346 mg

Smoked Chicken Leg Quarter in a Pellet Grill

Preparation Time: 10 minutes

Cooking Time: 30 minutes

Servings: 8

Ingredients:

- Chicken leg quarters - 4
- Dry rub spice mix for chicken - 3 tablespoon
- Olive oil - 1 tablespoon
- Salt

Directions:

1. Wash and dry the chicken legs.
2. Add some olive oil. Sprinkle the dry rub spice mix all over the chicken.
3. Set aside for 20 minutes.
4. Preheat the grill on 'smoke' for 10-15 minutes.
5. Place the chicken on the grill with skin side up to smoke for 1 hour.
6. Increase the heat to 350 degrees and cook for another 30 to 60 minutes, depending on the size of the pieces and the number of chicken legs.
7. Poke into the thickest part of the thighs.
8. When done, serve one leg quarter with a side sauce of your choice.

Nutrition: Carbohydrates: 1.5 g Protein: 16 gFat:21g

Grilled Chicken Kebabs

Preparation Time: 10 minutes

Cooking Time: 40 minutes

Servings: 8

Ingredients:

For Marinade

- Olive oil - ½ cup
- Lemon juice - 1 tablespoon
- White vinegar - 2 tablespoon
- Salt - 1 ½ tablespoon
- Minced garlic - 1 tablespoon
- Fresh thyme - 1 ½ tablespoon
- Fresh Italian parsley - 2 tablespoon
- Fresh chives - 2 tablespoon
- Ground pepper - ½ tablespoon
- For Kebabs
- Orange, yellow, and red bell peppers
- Chicken breasts - 1 ½, boneless and skinless
- Mushrooms of your choice - 10-12 medium size

Directions:

1. Mix all the ingredients for the marinade.
2. Add the chicken and mushrooms to the marinade and put it in the refrigerator.
3. Preheat your wood pellet grill to 450 degrees.
4. Remove the marinated chicken from the refrigerator and place it on the grill.
5. Grill the kebabs on one side for 6 minutes. Flip to grill on the other side.
6. Serve with a side dish of your choice.

Nutrition: Carbohydrates: 1 g Fat: 2 g Sodium: 582 mg

Chicken Fajitas on a Wood Pellet Grill

Preparation Time: 10 minutes

Cooking Time: 40 minutes

Servings: 1

Ingredients:

- Chicken breast - 2 lbs., thin sliced
- Red bell pepper - 1 large
- Onion - 1 large
- Orange bell pepper - 1 large
- Seasoning mix
- Oil - 2 tablespoon
- Onion powder - ½ tablespoon
- Granulated garlic - ½ tablespoon
- Salt - 1 tablespoon

Directions:

1. Preheat the grill to 450 degrees.
2. Mix the seasonings and oil.
3. Add the chicken slices to the mix.
4. Line a large pan with a non-stick baking sheet.
5. Let the pan heat for 10 minutes.

6. Place the chicken, peppers, and other vegetables in the grill.

7. Grill for 10 minutes or until the chicken is cooked.

8. Remove it from the grill and serve with warm tortillas and vegetables.

Nutrition: Carbohydrates: 5 g Protein: 29 g Fat: 6 g Sodium: 360 mg Cholesterol: 77 mg

Chicken Wings in Wood Pellets

Preparation Time: 10 minutes

Cooking Time: 50 minutes

Servings: 1

Ingredients:

- Chicken wings - 6-8 lbs.
- Canola oil – 1/3 cup
- Barbeque seasoning mix - 1 tablespoon

Directions:

1. Combine the seasonings and oil in one large bowl.

2. Put the chicken wings in the bowl and mix well.

3. Turn your wood pellet to the 'smoke' setting and leave it on for 4-5 minutes.

4. Set the heat to 350 degrees and leave it to preheat for 15 minutes with the lid closed.

5. Place the wings on the grill with enough space between the pieces.

6. Let it cook for 45 minutes or until the skin looks crispy.

7. Remove from the grill and serve with your choice of sides.

Nutrition: Protein: 33 g Fat: 8 g Sodium: 134 mg Cholesterol: 141 mg

Smoked Cornish Chicken in Wood Pellets

Preparation Time: 10 minutes

Cooking Time: 50 minutes

Servings: 1

Ingredients:

- Cornish hens - 6
- Canola or avocado oil - 2-3 tablespoon
- Spice mix - 6 tablespoon

Directions:

1. Preheat your wood pellet grill to 275 degrees.

2. Rub the whole hen with oil and the spice mix. Use both of these ingredients liberally.

3. Place the breast area of the hen on the grill and smoke for 30 minutes.

4. Flip the hen so the breast side is facing up. Increase the temperature to 400 degrees.

5. Cook until the temperature goes down to 165 degrees.

6. Pull it out and leave it for 10 minutes.

7. Serve warm with a side dish of your choice.

Nutrition: Carbohydrates: 1 g Protein: 57 g Fat: 50 g Sodium: 165 mg Cholesterol: 337 mg

Wild Turkey Egg Rolls

Preparation Time: 10 minutes

Cooking Time: 55 minutes

Servings: 1

Ingredients:

- Corn - ½ cup
- Leftover wild turkey meat - 2 cups
- Black beans - ½ cup
- Taco seasoning - 3 tablespoon
- Water ½ cup
- Rotel chilies and tomatoes - 1 can
- Egg roll wrappers- 12
- Cloves of minced garlic- 4
- 1 chopped Poblano pepper or 2 jalapeno peppers
- Chopped white onion - ½ cup

Directions:

1. Add some olive oil to a fairly large skillet. Heat it over medium heat on a stove.
2. Add peppers and onions. Sauté the mixture for 2-3 minutes until it turns soft.
3. Add some garlic and sauté for another 30 seconds. Add the Rotel chilies and beans to the mixture. Keeping mixing the content gently. Reduce the heat and then simmer.
4. After about 4-5 minutes, pour in the taco seasoning and 1/3 cup of water over the meat. Mix everything and coat the meat well. If you feel that it is a bit dry, you can add 2 tablespoons of water. Keep cooking until everything is heated all the way through.
5. Remove the content from the heat and box it to store in a refrigerator. Before you stuff the mixture into the egg wrappers, it should be completely cool to avoid breaking the rolls.
6. Place a spoonful of the cooked mixture in each wrapper and then wrap it securely and tightly. Do the same with all the wrappers.
7. Preheat the pellet grill and brush it with some oil. Cook the egg rolls for 15 minutes on both sides, until the exterior is nice and crispy.
8. Remove them from the grill and enjoy with your favorite salsa!

Nutrition: Carbohydrates: 26.1 g Protein: 9.2 g Fat: 4.2 g Sodium: 373.4 mg Cholesterol: 19.8 mg

Grilled Filet Mignon

Preparation Time: 10 minutes

Cooking Time: 20 minutes

Servings: 1

Ingredients:

- Salt
- Pepper
- Filet mignon - 3

Directions:

1. Preheat your grill to 450 degrees.

2. Season the steak with a good amount of salt and pepper to enhance its flavor.

3. Place on the grill and flip after 5 minutes.

4. Grill both sides for 5 minutes each.

5. Take it out when it looks cooked and serve with your favorite side dish.

Nutrition: Carbohydrates: 0 g Protein: 23 g Fat: 15 g Sodium: 240 mg Cholesterol: 82 mg

• **Fish Stew**

Preparation Time: 20min

Cooking Time: 25min

Servings: 8

Ingredients:

- 1 jar (28oz.) Crushed Tomatoes
- 2 oz. of Tomato paste
- ¼ cup of White wine
- ¼ cup of Chicken Stock
- 2 tbsp. Butter
- 2 Garlic cloves, minced
- ¼ Onion, diced
- ½ lb. Shrimp divined and cleaned
- ½ lb. of Clams
- ½ lb. of Halibut
- Parsley
- Bread

Directions:

1. Preheat the grill to 300F with a closed lid.
2. Place a Dutch oven over medium heat and melt the butter.
3. Sauté the onion for 4 - 7 minutes. Add the garlic -cook 1 more minute.
4. Add the tomato paste. Cook until the color becomes rust red. Pour the stock and wine. Cook 10 minutes. Add the tomatoes, simmer.
5. Chop the halibut, and together with the other seafood, add in the Dutch oven. Place it on the grill and cover with a lid.
6. Let it cook for 20 minutes.
7. Season with black pepper and salt and set aside.
8. Top with chopped parsley and serve with bread.
9. Enjoy!

Nutrition: Calories: 188 Protein: 25g Carbohydrates: 7g Fat: 12g

• **Grilled Tilapia "Ceviche"**

Preparation Time: 30 minutes

Cooking Time: 10 minutes

Servings: 4

Ingredients:

- 1 lb. tilapia filets
- ¼ c. chopped parsley
- ¼ c. chopped fresh cilantro
- ¼ c. freshly squeezed lime juice
- 2 tbsps. olive oil
- ½ tsp. red chili flakes
- 5 minced green onions
- 2 diced tomatoes
- 2 sliced celery stalks
- ½ minced green bell pepper
- Salt
- Pepper

Directions:

1. In a large bowl, mix lime juice, olive oil, vegetables, and herbs.
2. Grilling:
3. Preheat the grill to 400F.
4. Sprinkle pepper and salt on both sides of the tilapia and place on the grid.
5. Close the dome and cook for 3 minutes.
6. Gently flip the fish and cook for another 2-3 minutes or until the fish is opaque. Set aside.
7. Flake apart the tilapia filets and gently stir into the vegetable mixture to combine.
8. Serve room temperature or chilled.

Nutrition: Calories: 220, Fat: 4 g, Carbohydrates: 17 g, Protein: 33 g

- ## Sweet Honey Soy Smoked Salmon

Preparation Time: 10 minutes

Cooking Time: 2 Hours

Servings: 10

Ingredients:

- Salmon fillet (4-lbs., 1.8-kg.)

The Brine

- Brown sugar - ¾ cup
- Soy sauce - 3 tablespoons
- Kosher salt - 3 teaspoons
- Coldwater - 3 cups

The Glaze

- Butter - 2 tablespoons
- Brown sugar - 2 tablespoons
- Olive oil - 2 tablespoons
- Honey - 2 tablespoons
- Soy sauce - 1 tablespoon

Directions:

1. Add brown sugar, soy sauce, and kosher salt to the cold water, then stir until dissolved.
2. Put the salmon fillet into the brine mixture and soak it for at least 2 hours.
3. After 2 hours, take the salmon fillet out of the brine, then wash and rinse it.
4. Plug the wood pellet smoker and place the wood pellet inside the hopper. Turn the switch on.
5. Set the temperature to 225°F (107°C) and prepare the wood pellet smoker for indirect heat. Wait until the wood pellet smoker is ready.

6. Place the salmon fillet in the wood pellet smoker and smoke it for 2 hours.

7. In the meantime, melt the butter over low heat, then mix it with brown sugar, olive oil, honey, and soy sauce. Mix well.

8. After an hour of smoking, baste the glaze mixture over the salmon fillet and repeat it once every 10 minutes.

9. Smoke until the salmon is flaky and remove it from the wood pellet smoker.

10. Transfer the smoked salmon fillet to a serving dish and baste the remaining glaze mixture over it.

11. Serve and enjoy.

Nutrition: Calories: 188 Fat: 12g Protein: 25g Carbohydrates: 7g

• **Cranberry Lemon Smoked Mackerel**

Preparation Time: 10 Minutes

Cooking Time: 2 Hours

Servings: 10

Ingredients:

- Mackerel fillet (3,5-lb., 2.3-kg.)

The Brine

- Cranberry juice - 3 cans
- Pineapple juice - ½ cup
- Coldwater - 3 cups
- Brown sugar - ¼ cup
- Cinnamon stick - 2
- Fresh lemons - 2
- Bay leaves - 2
- Fresh thyme leaves - 3

The Rub

- Kosher salt - ¾ teaspoon
- Pepper - ¾ teaspoon

Directions:

1. Mix the cranberry juice and pineapple juice with water, then stir well.

2. Stir in brown sugar to the liquid mixture, then mix until dissolved.

3. Cut the lemons into slices, then add them to the liquid mixture and cinnamon sticks, bay leaves, and fresh thyme leaves.

4. Put the mackerel fillet into the brine and soak it for at least 2 hours. Store it in the refrigerator to keep the mackerel fillet fresh.

5. After 2 hours, remove the mackerel fillet from the refrigerator and take it out of the brine mixture.

6. Plug the wood pellet smoker and place the wood pellet inside the hopper. Turn the switch on.

7. Set the temperature to 225°F (107°C) and prepare the wood pellet smoker

for indirect heat. Wait until the wood pellet smoker is ready.

8. Sprinkle salt and pepper over the mackerel fillet, then place it in the wood pellet smoker.

9. Smoke the mackerel fillet for 2 hours or until it flakes and remove it from the wood pellet smoker.

10. Transfer the smoked mackerel fillet to a serving dish and serve.

11. Enjoy!

Nutrition: Calories: 188 Fat: 12g Protein: 25g Carbohydrates: 7g

• **Citrusy Smoked Tuna Belly with Sesame Aroma**

Preparation Time: 10 Minutes

Cooking Time: 2 Hours

Servings: 10

Ingredients:

- Tuna belly (4-lbs., 1.8-kg.)

The Marinade

- Sesame oil - 3 tablespoons
- Soy sauce - ½ cup
- Lemon juice - 2 tablespoons
- Orange juice - ½ cup
- Chopped fresh parsley - 2 tablespoons

- Oregano - ½ teaspoon
- Minced garlic - 1 tablespoon
- Brown sugar - 2 tablespoons
- Kosher salt - 1 teaspoon
- Pepper - ½ teaspoon

The Glaze

- Maple syrup - 2 tablespoons
- Balsamic vinegar - 1 tablespoon

Directions:

1. Combine sesame oil with soy sauce, lemon juice, and orange juice, then mix well.

2. Add oregano, minced garlic, brown sugar, kosher salt, pepper, and chopped parsley to the wet mixture, then stir until incorporated.

3. Carefully apply the wet mixture over the tuna fillet and marinate it for 2 hours. Store it in the refrigerator to keep the tuna fresh.

4. After 2 hours, remove the marinated tuna from the wood pellet smoker and thaw it at room temperature.

5. Plug the wood pellet smoker and place the wood pellet inside the hopper. Turn the switch on.

6. Set the temperature to 225°F (107°C) and prepare the wood pellet smoker for indirect heat. Wait until the wood pellet smoker is ready.

7. Place the marinated tuna fillet in the wood pellet smoker and smoke it until flaky.

8. Once it is done, remove the smoked tuna fillet from the wood pellet smoker and transfer it to a serving dish.

9. Mix the maple syrup with balsamic vinegar then baste the mixture over the smoked tuna fillet.

10. Serve and enjoy.

Nutrition: Calories: 220, Protein: 33 g Fat: 4 g, Carbohydrates: 17 g,

• <u>Savory Smoked Trout with Fennel and Black Pepper Rub</u>

Preparation Time: 10 Minutes

Cooking Time: 2 Hours

Servings: 10

Ingredients:

- Trout fillet (4,5-lb., 2.3-kg.)

The Rub

- Lemon juice - 2 tablespoons
- Fennel seeds - 3 tablespoons
- Ground coriander - 1 ½ tablespoon
- Black pepper - 1 tablespoon
- Chili powder - ½ teaspoon
- Kosher salt - 1 teaspoon
- Garlic powder - 1 teaspoon

The Glaze

- Olive oil - 3 tablespoons

Directions:

1. Drizzle lemon juice over the trout fillet and let it rest for approximately 10 minutes.

2. In the meantime, combine the fennel seeds with coriander, black pepper, chili powder, salt, and garlic powder then mix well.

3. Rub the trout fillet with the spice mixture then set aside.

4. Plug the wood pellet smoker and place the wood pellet inside the hopper. Turn the switch on.

5. Set the temperature to 225°F (107°C) and prepare the wood pellet smoker for indirect heat. Wait until the wood pellet smoker is ready.

6. Place the seasoned trout fillet in the wood pellet smoker and smoke it for 2 hours.

7. Baste olive oil over the trout fillet and repeat it once every 20 minutes.

8. Once the smoked trout flakes, remove it from the wood pellet smoker and transfer it to a serving dish.

9. Serve and enjoy.

Nutrition: Calories: 220, Carbohydrates: 17 g, Fat: 4 g, Protein: 33 g

Garlic Salmon

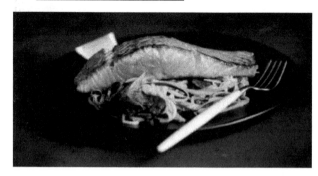

Preparation Time: 10 Minutes

Cooking Time: 16 Minutes

Servings: 6 - 8

Ingredients:

- 1 skin on Salmon Filet
- 2 tbsp. Garlic, minced
- 1 bottle BBQ Sauce
- 4 Green onions sprigs, chopped
- Salmon Seasoning

Directions:

1. Season the fish with Salmon seasoning.
2. In a bowl, add the BBQ sauce, 2 springs green onion (chopped), and garlic. Stir well to combine and set aside.
3. Preheat the grill to 450F with closed lid.
4. Brush the fish with the sauce mixture. Grill with the skin down for 8 min per side.
5. Serve sprinkled with green onion. Enjoy!

Nutrition: Calories: 240;Proteins: 23g;Carbs: 3g;Fat: 16g

Seared Tuna Steaks

Preparation time: 5 Minutes

Cooking Time: 5 Minutes

Servings: 2 - 4

Ingredients:

- 3 -inch Tuna
- Black pepper
- Sea Salt
- Olive oil
- Sriracha
- Soy Sauce

Directions:

1. Baste the tuna steaks with oil and sprinkle with black pepper and salt.
2. Preheat the grill to high with closed lid.
3. Grill the tuna for 2 ½ minutes per side.
4. Remove from the grill. Let it rest for 5 minutes.
5. Cut into thin pieces and serve with Sriracha and Soy Sauce. Enjoy.

Nutrition: Calories: 120;Proteins: 34g;Carbs: 0;Fat: 1.5g

Classic Smoked Trout

Preparation Time: 15 minutes

Cooking Time: 1 Hour

Servings: 3

Ingredients:

- 4 cups of water
- 1-2 cups dark-brown sugar
- 1 cup of sea salt
- 3 pounds of trout, backbone and pin bones removed
- 4 tablespoons of olive oil

Directions:

1. Preheat the electrical smoker grill, by setting the temperature to 250 degrees F, for 15 minutes by closing the lid.
2. Take a cooking pot, and combine all the brine ingredients, including water, sugar, and salt.
3. Submerged the fish in the brine mixture for a few hours.
4. Afterward, take out the fish, and pat dry with the paper towel.
5. Drizzle olive oil over the fish, and then place it over the grill grate for cooking.
6. Smoke the fish, until the internal temperature reaches 140 degrees Fahrenheit, for 1 hour.
7. Then serve.

Nutrition: Calories: 220, Carbohydrates: 17 g, Fat: 4 g, Protein: 33 g

• Blackened Mahi-Mahi Tacos

Preparation Time: 15 minutes

Cooking Time: 45 minutes

Servings: 6

Ingredients:

- 4 mahi-mahi fillets, each about 4 ounces
- 4 teaspoons habanero spice
- 2 tablespoons olive oil
- 12 small tortillas, toasted
- 1/3 cup diced red onion
- 2 tablespoons lime juice
- 2 cups shredded red cabbage
- 1 cup mango salsa
- 1 cup sour cream

Directions:

1. Open hopper of the smoker, add dry pallets, make sure ash-can is in place, then open the ash damper, power on the smoker and close the ash damper.
2. Set the temperature of the smoker to 400 degrees F, switch smoker to open flame cooking mode, press the open flame 3, remove the grill grates and the batch, replace batch with direct flame insert, then return grates on the grill in the lower position and let preheat for 30 minutes or until the green light on the dial blinks that indicate smoker has reached to set temperature.
3. Meanwhile, rinse the fillets with water, pat dry with paper towels, then rub with oil and season with habanero

seasoning on both sides, set aside until required.

4. Place fillets on the smoker grill, shut with lid and smoke for 7 minutes per side or until cooked.

5. When done, transfer fillets to a cutting board, let rest for 5 minutes and then cut into bite-size pieces.

6. Assemble the tacos and for this, stack the tortillas in two, then evenly place fillet pieces in them, top with onion, cabbage, salsa and cream and drizzle with lime juice.

7. Serve straight away.

Nutrition: Calories: 230;Total Fat: 8 g;Saturated Fat: 1.5 g;Protein: 13 g;Carbs: 26 g;Fiber: 4 g;Sugar: 2 g

• **Salmon Cakes**

Preparation Time: 45 minutes

Cooking Time: 7 minutes

Servings: 4

Ingredients:

- 1 cup cooked salmon, flaked
- 1/2 of red pepper, diced
- 1 tablespoon mustard
- 1/2 tablespoon rib rub
- 1 1/2 cups breadcrumb
- 2 eggs
- 1/2 tablespoon olive oil
- 1/4 cup mayonnaise
- For the Sauce:
- 1 cup mayonnaise, divided

- 1/2 tablespoon capers, diced
- 1/4 cup dill pickle relish

Directions:

1. Place all the ingredients for the salmon cakes in a bowl, except for oil, stir until well mixed and then let rest for 15 minutes.

2. Open hopper of the smoker, add dry pallets, make sure ash-can is in place, then open the ash damper, power on the smoker and close the ash damper.

3. Set the temperature of the smoker to 350 degrees F, switch smoker to open flame cooking mode, press the open flame 3, remove the grill grates and the batch, replace batch with direct flame insert, then return grates on the grill in the lower position, place the sheet pan and let preheat for 30 minutes or until the green light on the dial blinks that indicate smoker has reached to set temperature.

4. Meanwhile, prepare the sauce and for this, place all the ingredients for the sauce in a bowl and whisk until combined, set aside until required.

5. Then place the salmon mixture on the heated sheet pan, about 2 tablespoons per patty, press with a spatula to form a patty, grill for 5 minutes, then flip the patties, continue smoking for 2 minutes.

6. When done, transfer salmon cakes to a dish and serve with prepared sauce.

Nutrition: Calories: 229.7; Total Fat: 9 g; Saturated Fat: 2 g; Protein: 22.4 g;Carbs: 13 g;Fiber: 1.1 g; Sugar: 2.8 g

• Grilled Red Snapper

Preparation Time: 10 minutes

Cooking Time: 1 hour and 15 minutes

Servings: 4

Ingredients:

- 4 fillets of red snapper, large
- 1 lime, juiced, zested, sliced
- 2 medium onions, thinly sliced
- 1 teaspoon minced garlic
- 3 teaspoon chopped cilantro
- 1 teaspoon ground black pepper
- 1 teaspoon ancho chili powder
- ½ teaspoon lime zest
- 1 teaspoon salt
- ½ teaspoon cumin
- 1/3 cup olive oil
- ¼ cup ponzu sauce

Directions:

1. Open hopper of the smoker, add dry pallets, make sure ash-can is in place, then open the ash damper, power on the smoker and close the ash damper.

2. Set the temperature of the smoker to 350 degrees F, switch smoker to open flame cooking mode, press the open flame 3, remove the grill grates and the batch, replace batch with direct flame insert, then return grates on the grill in the lower position and let preheat for 30 minutes or until the green light on the dial blinks that indicate smoker has reached to set temperature.

3. Meanwhile, prepare the baste and for this, place all its ingredients in a bowl and stir until mixed.

4. Take a heatproof cooking basket, then breakfast onion slices and line them on the bottom of the basket along with lime slices.

5. Brush both sides of fillets with the baste mixture, place them in the basket, then the basket on the smoker grill, shut with lid and smoke for 30 to 45 minutes or more until cooked, brushing with the baste every 15 minutes.

6. Serve straight away.

Nutrition: Calories: 311; Total Fat: 8.8 g; Saturated Fat: 1.2 g; Protein: 45 g; Carbs: 11 g; Fiber: 3 g; Sugar: 1.3 g

• Sugar Cured Salmon

Preparation Time: 6 hours and 10 minutes

Cooking Time: 1 hour

Servings: 4

Ingredients:

- 3 pounds' salmon, skinned
- 2 tablespoons seafood Rub

- 3 cups brown sugar
- 1 ½ cup sea salt
- 1/3 cup BBQ Sauce

Directions:

1. Prepare the cure and for this, place salt, sugar, and rub in a medium bowl and stir until mixed.
2. Take a large baking dish, spread ¼-inch of the cure in its bottom, top with salmon, then top evenly with the remaining cure, cover the dish and let it rest in the refrigerator for 6 hours.
3. When ready to cook, open hopper of the smoker, add dry pallets, make sure ash-can is in place, then open the ash damper, power on the smoker and close the ash damper.
4. Set the temperature of the smoker to 300 degrees F, let preheat for 30 minutes or until the green light on the dial blinks that indicate smoker has reached to set temperature.
5. Meanwhile, remove the baking dish from the refrigerator, uncover it, remove the salmon from the cure, rinse well and pat dry with paper towels.
6. Place salmon on the smoker grill, shut with lid, smoke it for 20 minutes, then brush salmons with BBQ sauce and continue smoking for 10 minutes or until glazed.
7. Serve straight away.

Nutrition: Calories: 70; Total Fat: 1 g; Saturated Fat: 0 g; Protein: 14 g; Carbs: 2 g; Fiber: 0 g; Sugar: 2 g

• **Cured Cold-Smoked Lox**

Preparation Time: 20 minutes
Cooking Time: 6 hours
Servings: 4 to 6
Ingredients:

- ¼ cup salt
- ¼ cup sugar
- 1 tablespoon freshly ground black pepper
- 1 bunch dill, chopped
- 1-pound sashimi-grade salmon, skin removed
- 1 avocado, sliced
- 8 bagels
- 4 ounces' cream cheese
- 1 bunch alfalfa sprouts
- 1 (3.5-ounce) jar capers

Directions:

1. In a small bowl, combine the salt, sugar, pepper, and fresh dill to make the curing mixture. Set aside.
2. On a smooth surface, lay out a large piece of plastic wrap and spread half of the curing salt mixture in the middle, spreading it out to about the salmon's size.
3. Place the salmon on top of the curing salt.
4. Top the fish with the remaining curing salt, covering it completely.

Wrap the salmon, leaving the ends open to drain.

5. Place the wrapped fish in a rimmed baking pan or dish lined with paper towels to soak up the liquid.

6. Place a weight on the salmon evenly, like a pan with a couple of heavy jars of pickles on top.

7. Put the salmon pan with weights in the refrigerator. Place something (a dishtowel, for example) under the back of the pan to slightly tip it down, so the liquid drains away from the fish.

8. Leave the salmon to cure in the refrigerator for 24 hours.

9. Place the wood pellets in the smoker, but do not follow the start-up procedure and do not preheat.

10. Remove the salmon from the refrigerator, unwrap it, rinse it off, and pat dry.

11. Put the salmon in the smoker while still cold from the refrigerator to slow down the cooking process. You'll need to use a cold-smoker attachment or enlist a smoker tube's help to hold the temperature at 80°F and maintain that for 6 hours to absorb smoke and complete the cold-smoking process.

12. Remove the salmon from the smoker, place it in a sealed plastic bag, and refrigerate for 24 hours. The salmon will be translucent all the way through.

13. Thinly slice the lox and serve with sliced avocado, bagels, cream cheese, alfalfa sprouts, and capers.

Nutrition: Calories: 70; Total Fat: 1 g; Saturated Fat: 0 g; Protein: 14 g; Carbs: 2 g; Fiber: 0 g; Sugar: 2 g

• Grilled Salmon

Preparation Time: 20 minutes

Cooking Time: 4 hours

Servings: 8

Ingredients:

- Salmon, large, deboned – 1, about 3 pounds
- Salt – 1 cup
- Brown sugar – 1 cup
- Ground black pepper – ½ cup

Directions:

1. Before preheating the grill, cure the salmon and for this, take a small bowl and stir all of its ingredients in it.
2. Take a large piece of plastic wrap, about 6-inches longer than salmon fillet, and then spread half of the cure mixture on it.
3. Top it with salmon, cover evenly with remaining cure mixture and then wrap by folding the edges of plastic wrap.
4. Transfer wrapped salmon in a rectangle baking dish, top with a heavy pan or couple of can and let it rest in the refrigerator for a minimum of 8 hours.
5. Then remove salmon from the baking dish, uncover it, rinse well and pat dry.
6. Take a sheet tray, place a wire rack on it, then place salmon on it skin-side down and let it cool in the refrigerator for a minimum of 8 hours until completely dry.
7. When the grill has preheated, place salmon on the grilling rack and let smoke for 4 hours or until the control panel shows the internal temperature of 150 degrees F.
8. Check the fire after one hour of smoking and add more wood pallets if required.
9. When done, cut salmon into slices and then serve immediately.

Nutrition: Calories: 311; Total Fat: 8.8 g; Saturated Fat: 1.2 g; Protein: 45 g; Carbs: 11 g; Fiber: 3 g; Sugar: 1.3 g

• Pacific Northwest Salmon

Preparation Time: 15 minutes

Cooking Time: 1 hour and 15 minutes

Servings: 4

Ingredients:

- 1 (2-pound) half salmon fillet
- 1 batch Dill Seafood Rub

- 2 tablespoons butter, cut into 3 or 4 slices

Directions:

1. Supply your smoker with wood pellets and follow the manufacturer's specific start-up procedure. Preheat the grill, with the lid closed, to 180°F.
2. Season the salmon all over with the rub. Using your hands, work the rub into the flesh.
3. Place the salmon directly on the grill grate, skin-side down, and smoke for 1 hour.
4. Place the butter slices on the salmon, equally spaced. Increase the grill's temperature to 300°F and continue to cook until the salmon's internal temperature reaches 145°F. Remove the salmon from the grill and serve immediately.

Nutrition: Calories: 117Total Fat: 4.3gCholesterol: 23gPotassium: 175mg

• Hot-Smoked Salmon

Preparation Time: 15 minutes

Cooking Time: 4 to 6 hours

Servings: 4

Ingredients:

- 1 (2-pound) half salmon fillet
- 1 batch Dill Seafood Rub

Directions:

1. Supply your smoker with wood pellets and follow the manufacturer's specific start-up procedure. Preheat the grill, with the lid closed, to 180°F
2. Season the salmon all over with the rub. Using your hands, work the rub into the flesh.
3. Place the salmon directly on the grill grate, skin-side down, and smoke until its internal temperature reaches 145°F. Remove the salmon from the grill and serve immediately.

Nutrition: Calories: 117Total Fat: 4.3gCholesterol: 23gPotassium: 175mg

• Cajun Catfish

Preparation Time: 15 minutes

Cooking Time: 15 minutes

Servings: 2

Ingredients:

- 2½ pounds catfish fillets
- 2 tablespoons olive oil
- 1 batch Cajun Rub

Directions:

1. 2½ pounds catfish fillets
2. 2 tablespoons olive oil
3. 1 batch Cajun Rub
4. Supply your smoker with wood pellets and follow the manufacturer's specific start-up procedure. Preheat the grill, with the lid closed, to 300°F.
5. Coat the catfish fillets all over with olive oil and season with the rub. Using your hands, work the rub into the flesh

6. Place the fillets directly on the grill grate and smoke until their internal temperature reaches 145°F. Remove the catfish from the grill and serve immediately.

Nutrition: Calories: 301Carbs: 0gFat: 18gProtein: 36g

• **Rogue Salmon Sandwich**

Preparation Time: 5 minutes

Cooking Time: 5 minutes

Servings: 1

Ingredients:

- 1 English muffin, split
- 2 tablespoons cream cheese
- 4 ounces smoked salmon (I suggest using Hot-Smoked Salmon, but any store brand will work)
- 2 (1-ounce) slices Swiss cheese

Directions:

1. Supply your smoker with wood pellets and follow the manufacturer's specific start-up procedure. Preheat the grill, with the lid closed, to 375°F.
2. Place the muffin halves, cut-side down, directly on the grill grate and warm for 2 minutes.
3. Remove the warmed muffin halves and spread 1 tablespoon of cream cheese on each half. Top each with smoked salmon and then Swiss cheese.
4. Place the topped muffin halves on a baking sheet and put the sheet on the grill. Cook for about 3 minutes, until the cheese melts. Remove them from the grill and serve immediately.

Nutrition: Calories: 229.7; Total Fat: 9 g; Saturated Fat: 2 g; Protein: 22.4 g;Carbs: 13 g;Fiber: 1.1 g; Sugar: 2.8 g

• **Spring Lining Cod**

Preparation Time: 20 minutes

Cooking Time: 30 minutes

Servings: 4 to 5

Ingredients:

- 5-10 mini sweet bell peppers
- 2 lbs. fresh lingcod fillets
- 8 oz. of cherry tomatoes
- 1 whole leek
- 1/2 cup of olive oil
- 4 oz. of Kalamata olives
- 1 lemon
- 3 fresh cloves of minced garlic
- 1 tsp of fresh thyme
- 5-10 leaves fresh basil for garnish
- 2 small yellow squash
- 1 tsp of fresh dill
- 1 tsp of sea salt

- 1 tsp of fresh ground black pepper

Directions:

1. Take the cod fillets and slather the whole fish in olive oil, along with salt and pepper, garlic, herbs, and juice of ½ lemon plus zest

2. Keep this in an oven-safe baking dish

3. Take the remaining ½ lemon and slice it into three rounds and arrange it on top of the fish fillet

4. Slice the vegetable into thin strips and then toss it together and pour it over the fillet

5. Smoke at 350 degrees F for half an hour

6. Garnish with fresh basil

7. Serve

Nutrition: Calories: 229.7; Total Fat: 9 g; Saturated Fat: 2 g; Protein: 22.4 g;Carbs: 13 g;Fiber: 1.1 g;

• **Baja-Style Fish Tacos**

Preparation Time: 15 minutes

Cooking Time: 15 minutes

Servings: 4

Ingredients:

- 1 Lb. White Fish Such as Cod, Monkfish, Or Halibut (Skinless)
- 2 Limes
- 2 Tsp. Dijon-Style Mustard
- 1/2 Tsp. Salt
- 1/2 Tsp. Black Pepper, Freshly Ground
- 1/2 Cup Vegetable Oil, Or Olive Oil
- 2 Cloves Garlic, Minced
- As Needed Traeger Cajun Rub
- 8 Corn Tortillas
- For Serving Shredded Cabbage, Diced Red Onions, Cilantro Leaves, Pickled Jalapeno Slices, Diced Avocado, Pico De Gallo or Salsa, Sour Cream

Directions:

1. Juice one lime. Cut the other lime in wedges; set aside until serving time.

2. Make the marinade: In a small mixing bowl, combine the lime juice, mustard, and salt and pepper. Slowly whisk in the oil, then stir in the garlic.

3. Place the fish in a resalable plastic bag, pour the marinade over it, and refrigerate for no more than 1 hour.

4. When ready to cook, start the Traeger grill on Smoke with the lid open until the fire is established (4 to 5 minutes). Set the temperature to 400F (High on a 3-position controller) and preheat, lid closed, for 10 to 15 minutes.

5. Remove the fish from the marinade and pat off any excess marinade with paper towels. Season generously on both sides with Traeger Cajun Rub.

6. Arrange the fish on the grill grate and grill until the fish is opaque and flakes easily when pressed with a fork. (There is no need to turn it.) Remove to a cutting board and cut into bite-

size chunks. Meanwhile, warm the tortillas on the Traeger until pliant and hot.

7. Arrange the fish, tortillas, and suggested accompaniments on a large platter. Garnish with the reserved lime wedges. Serve immediately.

Nutrition: Carbs: 27g Fat: 10g Protein: 13g

• **Grilled Penang Curry Salmon**

Preparation Time: 10 minutes

Cooking Time: 10 to 15 minutes

Servings: 5

Ingredients:

- Penang Curry Salmon
- 1 (12 Oz) Jar Thai fusions Penang Curry
- 1 (4-7 Lb.) Salmon Fillet
- 2 Sprigs Thai Basil, Roughly Chopped
- 1/2 Red Bell Pepper Sliced Thinly, Lengthwise
- 1 Lime, Sliced into Thin Crosscut Pieces
- Mussels with Prawns (Optional)
- 1/2 Lb. Prawns, Shelled and Deveined
- 1/2 Lb. Mussels de bearded and Washed
- Handful Thai Basil, Chopped

Directions:

1. Season both sides of the salmon with salt and pepper.

2. Brush a little canola oil on the salmon fillet and marinate with a 1/2 cup of Thai fusions Penang Curry in a shallow pan. Cover and marinate at room temperature for about 30 minutes.

3. When ready to cook, set temperature to High and preheat, lid closed for 15 minutes.

4. Brush some canola oil onto the grill so the salmon won't stick. Place salmon fillet directly on the grill grate and brush on about another 1/4 cup of Thai fusions Penang Curry and top with sliced red bell pepper and lime slices.

5. Grill salmon until an internal temperature of 145°F, about 10-15 minutes.

6. For the Mussels and Prawns: Pour last 1/4 cup of Penang Curry into a sauce pan, add prawns, mussels, Thai basil and cover sauce pan and finish on the Traeger. When the mussels have opened, take off the grill and set aside.

7. Take salmon off the grill as gently as possible and top salmon with mussels and prawns if desired. Garnish with Thai basil. Enjoy!

Nutrition: Calories: 336.7 Sodium: 109.9mg Total Fat: 13.1g Saturated Fat: 2g

• <u>Lemon Garlic Smoked Salmon</u>

Preparation Time: 5 minutes

Cooking Time: 10 minutes

Servings: 3

Ingredients:

- 6 5 oz. Prime Waters Seafood Salmon Filets
- 4 tbsp. softened butter
- 2 tsp lemon juice
- 1 tsp lemon zest
- 1 tsp salt
- 1 tsp pepper
- 1 clove garlic minced

Directions:

1. Preheat wood pellet smoker to 350 degrees F
2. Combine all of the ingredients (except the salmon) in a bowl and mix well.
3. Add a generous amount of the butter mixture on top of each filet of salmon, and top with lemon slices if desired
4. Add each filet to the wood pellet grill and cook until an internal temperature of 125 degrees is reached.
5. Remove the filets from the grill and tent with aluminum foil. Let rest for 10 minutes before serving.
6. Garnish with lemon slices and additional spices for presentation

Nutrition: Calories: 117 Total Fat: 4.3g Cholesterol: 23mg

• <u>Smoked Tilapia</u>

Preparation Time: 10 minutes

Cooking Time: 2 hours

Servings: 4

Ingredients:

- 6 tilapia fillets
- 3 tbsp./45 ml vegetable oil
- 2 tbsp./30 ml fresh lemon juice
- 1/2 tsp./2.5 ml garlic powder
- 1 tsp./5 ml kosher salt
- 1/2 tsp./2.5 ml lemon pepper

Directions:

1. Prepare smoker for a 2-hour smoke.
2. Wash fish and remove all bones. Combine oil, lemon juice, garlic powder, salt, and lemon pepper in a small bowl. Brush liquid mixture onto both sides of the tilapia fillets.
3. Place in the smoker for 1 1/2 to 2 hours.
4. When finished, remove from heat and serve.

Nutrition: Calories: 280 Fat: 11g Carbs: 1g Protein: 45g

• <u>Maple Glazed Salmon</u>

Preparation Time: 15 minutes

Cooking Time: 40 to 60 minutes

Servings: 5

Ingredients:

- 1/2 C + 3 Tbsp. soy sauce

- 1 C maple syrup (the real stuff)
- Really fresh thick salmon, skin on (I prefer Sockeye, however, that is the strongest of the selection. If you're working with some people you hope to convert, the farm-raised stuff is a little lighter.)

Directions:

1. Mix a 1/2 C of soy with a 1/2 C of maple syrup in a dish big enough that the salmon fits flat but not so deep that the skin is covered.
2. Put in the fridge. This isn't a "longer is better" type of meat to marinate, so 15 minutes per inch should suffice with at least 30 minutes' total, regardless of size. (For 2 inches, 45-60 minutes is a safe window.)
3. Set grill to 400 degrees F and lightly oil just enough of the grate to accommodate the fish flesh side down.
4. Heat 1/2 C of maple syrup and 3 Tbsp. of soy sauce in a skillet pan (not cast iron and not non-stick) until the glaze thickens a bit. Note: You can also have some fun here. Brown sugar, honey, mustard and cherry juice can all be mixed around for good flavors. Even adding some spice to the party can change this dish around.
5. Brush the salmon with the glaze and put it flesh side down on the hot grill and shut the lid.
6. Flip fish after a few minutes. If it is ready to be turned over (and you've oiled your grill grates), it shouldn't stick.
7. Cook the salmon until the internal temperature reaches 140 degrees F. Less is fine, more is okay, but understand that a little rare for fresh salmon will never hurt you, but a little too much will destroy the meal.

Nutrition: Calories: 280 Fat: 11g Carbs: 1g Protein: 45g

Charcoal-Grilled Striped Bass

Preparation Time: 10 Minutes
Cooking Time: 30 Minutes
Servings: 4
Ingredients:

- 1 (3-to 4-pound) striped bass, gutted
- Salt and freshly ground black pepper
- 1 clove garlic, peeled
- 1 large sprig fresh rosemary
- 1 bay leaf
- Oil
- ¼ pound (1 stick) butter, melted and kept hot
- ¼ cup chopped fresh parsley
- Lemon wedges

Directions:

1. Prepare a charcoal fire. When white ash forms on top of coals, they are ready.
2. Meanwhile, prepare fish. Rub it inside and out with salt and pepper.
3. Cut garlic clove into slivers.
4. Using a sharp paring knife, make a few small incisions along backbone of fish.
5. Insert slivers of garlic.
6. Place rosemary sprig and bay leaf in cavity of fish. Tie fish in two or three places with string to secure cavity. Rub fish generously all over with oil. Place fish on hot grill and cook 10 to 15 minutes on one side, brushing occasionally with butter.
7. Using a pancake turner or spatula or both, loosen fish from grill and turn it to other side.
8. Cook 10 to 15 minutes on that side, or until fish is done and flesh flakes easily when tested with a fork. Cooking time will depend on size of fish, intensity of heat and how close fish is to coals.
9. Transfer fish to a hot platter and pour remaining butter over it. Sprinkle with parsley and garnish with lemon wedges.

Nutrition: Calories: 130 Carbohydrates: 5 g Protein: 79 g Sodium: 45 mg Cholesterol: 19 mg

Greek-Style Fish with Marinated Tomatoes

Preparation Time: 10 Minutes
Cooking Time: 45 Minutes
Servings: 4
Ingredients:

- 2 cups of your favorite Sun Gold cherry tomatoes, cut in half
- 4 tablespoons olive oil, or more as needed
- 2 tablespoons white wine vinegar
- 1 tablespoon chopped fresh hot peppers, such as jalapeño, or more to taste
- 1 fresh oregano cooker or 1 coffee stove
- 4 garlic cloves, sliced or more to taste
- Salt and freshly ground black pepper
- 1 large whole fish or 2 small fish (2 to 3 pounds in total), such as striped sea bass, redfish or trout; preferably butter and boneless, or simply emptied lemon sliced into noodles
- 4 to 6 sprigs of fresh thyme

Directions:

1. Prepare the grill; the heat should be medium to high and about 4 inches from the fire.
2. Join in tomatoes, 2 tablespoons olive oil, vinegar, mashed beans, oregano, steam garlic slices and a pinch of salt

and pepper in a bowl; let them sit in the room temperature for 30 minutes.

3. Then make a sharp blade of three or four parallel bars on each side of the fish, approximately at the bottom. Sprinkle the inside of the fish with salt.

4. Also, pepper, at the time, stuffed with garlic residue, a layer of lemon slices, and thyme twigs. On the outside, coat the fish with the remaining 2 tablespoons of oil and sprinkle salt and pepper.

5. Bake until firm enough to rotate, 5 to 8 minutes. Turn and cook the other side 5 to 8 minutes. The fish is cooked when it is cold outside and the paddle is easy to pass through the meat.

6. Try the tomato mixture and change the spice, including more oil if needed. Serve fish garnished with tomatoes and their liquid.

Nutrition: Calories: 130 Carbohydrates: 5 g Protein: 79 g Sodium: 45 mg Cholesterol: 19 mg

• **Grilled Fish with Aromatics**

Preparation Time: 10 Minutes
Cooking Time: 50 Minutes
Servings: 4
Ingredients:

- 4 (1 kilogram) salty guide, cod or snack or 1 (4 to 5 kilograms) salmon,
- cleaned upside down
- Vegetable oil for baking, scoops and baking.
- 6 tablespoons extra virgin olive oil
- 20 peeled garlic cloves
- 12 twigs of fresh thyme
- 12 sprigs of fresh rosemary
- 2 bay leaves
- Kosher or coarse sea salt and freshly ground black pepper to taste

Directions:

1. Rinse and dry the fish. Make 3 or 4 shallow cuts through the skin of the fish,

2. It may expand during cooking. Refrigerate in cool until ready.

3. Kindle and light a fire on the outdoor grill.

4. Preheat the oven to 300 degrees.

5. When the coals are bright red and evenly dusted with ash, grill and allow to warm for 2 to 3 minutes. Grill well, using vegetable oil and paper toweling, being careful not to use so much oil that it will drip on coals and cause them to flame up.

6. Place the fish on the grill so that the steps below are perpendicular. Cook until fish has golden grill marks, about 3 minutes on each side. Using a metal spatula, lightly brush the vegetable oil into one or two greased baking dishes, depending on the amount of fish you are preparing.

7. Put them in the oven and bake until they are opaque; it will be about 12 minutes for small fish, 20 to 25 minutes for large fish.

8. About 10 minutes before the end, pour the fish 6 tablespoons of olive oil into a baking pan or mold and place in the oven to warm slightly.

9. On a high heat, boil 2 cups of water at the bottom of the steam. Put the garlic cloves in the garlic, cover and simmer until they are almost soft, about 8 minutes.

10. Add the remaining herbs to the steamer in an even layer, cover and continue cooking for 3 minutes.

11. To serve, pour equal amounts of olive oil into the middle of hot dishes. If small fish are used, put them whole over the oil. If you are using large fish, such as salmon, remove the fillets and place the fillets of the same size in the oil.

12. Season to taste with thick salt and pepper.

13. Put the cooked herbs and garlic on one side of the plate and serve immediately.

Nutrition: Calories: 130 Carbohydrates: 5 g Protein: 79 g Sodium: 45 mg Cholesterol: 19 mg

• **Baked Fresh Wild Sockeye Salmon**

Preparation Time: 10 Minutes

Cooking Time: 40 Minutes

Servings: 4

Ingredients:

- 2 fresh wild sockeye salmon filets, skin on
- 2 teaspoons Seafood Seasoning
- ¾ teaspoon Old Bay seasoning

Directions:

1. Flush the salmon filets with cold water and pat them dry with a paper towel.

2. Delicately dust the filets with the seasonings.

3. On the wood pellet smoker-grill

4. Arrange the wood pellet smoker-grill for a non-direct cooking and preheat to 400°F utilizing any pellets.

5. Lay the salmon skin-side down on a Teflon-covered fiberglass tangle or directly on the grill grates.

6. Bake the salmon for 15/20 minutes, until the internal temperature arrives at 140°F and additionally the substance chips effectively with a fork.

7. Rest the salmon for 5-6 minutes before serving.

Notes: This recipe works similarly well with Chinook (ruler), Coho (silver), pink (humpback), or cultivated Atlantic salmon. Salmon will in general dry effectively when baking, so bake it skin-side down to help hold moisture.

Nutrition: Calories: 322 Carbs: 2g Fat: 24g Protein: 24g

• **Creole Wild Pacific Rockfish**

Preparation Time: 10 Minutes

Cooking Time: 1 hours

Servings: 4

Ingredients:

- 4 to 8 (4 to 7-ounce) fresh, wild Pacific rockfish filets
- 3 teaspoons roasted garlic–seasoned extra-virgin olive oil
- 2 tablespoons Creole Seafood Seasoning or any Creole seasoning

Directions:

1. Rub the two sides of the filets with the olive oil.
2. Residue the two sides with the seasoning.
3. On the wood pellet smoker-grill
4. Design the wood pellet smoker-grill for a non-direct cooking and preheat to 225°F utilizing birch pellets.
5. Place the filets on a Teflon-coated fiberglass mat to keep them from adhering to the grill grates.
6. Smoke the filets for approximately an hour and a half, until they arrive at an internal temperature of 140°F or

potentially the flesh flakes easily with a fork.

Nutrition: Calories: 322 Carbs: 2g Fat: 24g Protein: 24g

• **Wood-Smoked Boned Trout**

Preparation Time: 10 Minutes

Cooking Time: 2 hours

Servings: 4

Ingredients:

- 4 fresh boned entire trout, skin on and pin bones removed
- 5 cups Salmon and Trout Brine

Directions:

1. Put the trout in a 2-liter plastic bag or on a brine rack. Place the bag on a shallow plate in case it spills and refrigerate for 2 hours, turning the trout on wheels to make sure it remains submerged. In case of spillage, place the bag on a shallow plate
2. Air-dry the brined trout in the refrigerator, revealed, for 2 hours to enable the pellicle to frame.
3. On the wood pellet smoker-grill
4. Configure the wood pellet smoker-grill for a non-direct cooking. On the off chance that your grill has cold-smoking capabilities, at that point configure your pellet smoker-grill for cold-smoking.
5. Preheat the grill to 190°F utilizing alder pellets. A pit temperature of

190°F should result in a cold-smoke temperature of 70°F to 100°F in your smoker box, contingent upon the encompassing temperature.

6. Cold-smoke the trout for 90 minutes.

7. Following 90 minutes, move the cold-smoked boned trout to the wood pellet smoker-grill pit territory and increase the wood pellet smoker-grill temperature to 230°F.

8. Keep cooking the trout until the internal temperature of the trout at the thickest part arrives at 145°F.

9. Remove the trout from the grill and wait 5 minutes before serving.

10. Search for boned trout in the fish department of your nearby supermarket, fish market, or even better, get your very own and remove every one of the bones yourself.

11. Boned trout ought to be liberated from bones, yet consistently take care when eating fish.

12. Cold-smoking happens at temperatures somewhere in the range of 70°F and 100°F.

Nutrition: Calories: 322 Carbs: 2g Fat: 24g Protein: 24g

- ## Spiced Salmon Kebabs

Preparation Time: 20 minutes

Cooking Time: 25 minutes

Servings: 4

Ingredients:

- 2 tbsp. of chopped fresh oregano
- 2 tsp of sesame seeds
- 1 tsp ground cumin
- 1 tsp Kosher salt
- 1/4 tsp crushed red pepper flakes
- 1 1/2 pounds of skinless salmon fillets, cut into 1" pieces
- 2 lemons, thinly sliced into rounds
- 2 tbsp. of olive oil
- 16 bamboo skewers soaked in water for one hour

Directions:

1. Set up the grill for medium heat. Mix the oregano, sesame seeds, and cumin, salt, and red pepper flakes in a little bowl. Put the spice blend aside.

2. String the salmon and the lemon slices onto 8 sets of parallel skewers in order to make 8 kebabs.

3. Spoon with oil and season with the spice blend.

4. Grill and turn at times until the fish is cooked.

Nutrition: Calories: 230 Fat: 10g Carbs: 1g Protein: 30g

- ## **Grilled Onion Butter Cod**

Preparation Time: 10 minutes

Cooking Time: 15 minutes

Servings: 4

Ingredients:

- 1/4 cup butter
- 1 finely chopped small onion
- 1/4 cup white wine
- 4 (6ounce) cod fillets
- 1 tbsp. of extra virgin olive oil
- 1/2 tsp salt (or to taste)
- 1/2 tsp black pepper
- Lemon wedges

Directions:

1. Set up the grill for medium-high heat.

2. In a little skillet liquefy the butter. Add the onion and cook for 1or 2 minutes.

3. Add the white wine and let stew for an extra 3 minutes. Take away and let it cool for 5 minutes.

4. Spoon the fillets with extra virgin olive oil and sprinkle with salt and pepper. Put the fish on a well-oiled rack and cook for 8 minutes.

5. Season it with sauce and cautiously flip it over. Cook for 6 to 7 minutes more, turning more times or until the fish arrives at an inside temperature of 145°F.

6. Take away from the grill, top with lemon wedges, and serve.

Nutrition: Calories: 140 Fat: 5g Cholesterol: 46mg Carbs: 4g Protein: 20g

- ## **Grilled Cuttlefish with Spinach and Pine Nuts Salad**

Preparation Time: 15 minutes

Cooking Time: 30 minutes

Servings: 6

Ingredients:

- 1/2 cup of olive oil
- 1 tbsp. of lemon juice
- 1 tsp oregano
- Pinch of salt
- 8 large cuttlefish, cleaned
- Spinach, pine nuts, olive oil and vinegar for serving

Directions:

1. Prepare marinade with olive oil, lemon juice, oregano and a pinch of salt pepper (be careful, cuttlefish do not need too much salt).
2. Place the cuttlefish in the marinade, tossing to cover evenly. Cover and marinate for about 1 hour.
3. Remove the cuttlefish from marinade and pat dry them on paper towel.
4. Start the pellet grill, and set the temperature to high and preheat, lid closed, for 10 to 15 minutes.
5. Grill the cuttlefish just 3 - 4 minutes on each side.
6. Serve hot with spinach, pine nuts, olive oil, and vinegar.

Nutrition: Calories: 299 Fat: 19g Cholesterol: 186mg Carbs: 3g Protein: 28g

• Grilled Trout in White Wine and Parsley Marinade

Preparation Time: 20 minutes

Cooking Time: 45 minutes

Servings: 4

Ingredients:

- 1/4 cup olive oil
- 1 lemon juice
- 1/2 cup of white wine
- 2 cloves garlic minced
- 2 tbsp. fresh parsley, finely chopped
- 1 tsp fresh basil, finely chopped
- Salt and freshly ground black pepper to taste
- 4 trout fish, cleaned
- Lemon slices for garnish

Directions:

1. In a large container, stir olive oil, lemon juice, wine, garlic, parsley, basil and salt and freshly ground black pepper to taste.
2. Submerge fish in sauce and toss to combine well.

3. Cover and marinate in refrigerate overnight.

4. When ready to cook, start the pellet grill on Smoke with the lid open for 4 to 5 minutes. Set the temperature to 400°F and preheat, lid closed, for 10 to 15 minutes.

5. Remove the fish from marinade and pat dry on paper towel; reserve marinade.

6. Grill trout for 5 minutes from both sides (be careful not to overcook the fish).

7. Pour fish with marinade and serve hot with lemon slices.

Nutrition: Calories: 267 Fat: 18g Carbs: 3g Protein: 16g

• **Grilled Salmon Steaks with Cilantro Yogurt Sauce**

Preparation Time: 10 minutes

Cooking Time: 10 minutes

Servings: 4

Ingredients:

- Vegetable oil (for the grill)
- 2 serrano chilies
- 2 garlic cloves
- 1 cup cilantro leaves
- ½ cup plain whole-milk Greek yogurt
- 1 tbsp. of extra virgin olive oil
- 1 tsp honey
- Kosher salt
- 2 12oz bone-in salmon steaks

Directions:

1. Set up the grill for medium-high heat, then oil the grate.

2. Expel and dispose of seeds from one chili. Mix the two chilies, garlic, cilantro, the yogurt, oil, the nectar, and ¼ cup water in a blender until it becomes smooth, then season well with salt.

3. Move half of the sauce to a little bowl and put it aside. Season the salmon steaks with salt.

4. Grill it, turning more than once, until it's beginning to turn dark, about 4 minutes.

5. Keep on grilling, turning frequently, and seasoning with residual sauce for at least 4 minutes longer.

Nutrition: Calories: 290 Fat: 14g Cholesterol: 80g Carbs: 1g Protein: 38g

• **Southwestern Whitefish**

Preparation Time: 10-15 minutes

Cooking Time: 2 hour

Serving: 4

Ingredients:

- 2 pounds' whitefish, raw
- 1 tablespoon paprika

- 1 tablespoon garlic powder
- 1 tablespoon onion powder
- ½ teaspoon cumin
- Salt and pepper to taste
- Fresh lemon, juiced
- Fresh cilantro, chopped

Directions:

1. Take your drip pan and add water, cover with aluminum foil. Pre-heat your smoker to 200 degrees F on low heat settings
2. Use water fill water pan halfway through and place it over drip pan. Add wood chips to the side tray.
3. Brush fillets with olive oil
4. Take a bowl and add paprika, cumin, onion powder, garlic powder, salt, pepper, mix well
5. Rub the mixture all over fish
6. Spray fillets with more olive oil, transfer seasoned fillets to smoker rack and smoke for 2 hours
7. Garnish with fresh lemon juice, chopped cilantro
8. Enjoy!

Nutrition: Calories: 142 Fat: 2g Carbohydrates: 0g Protein: 30g

• **Full-On Trout**

Preparation Time: 10-15 minutes + 6 hours

Cooking Time: 3 hours

Serving: 4

Ingredients

- 4 trout fillets
- 1 cup white cooking wine
- ¼ cup of soy sauce
- ¼ cup lemon juice

Directions:

1. Take your drip pan and add water, cover with aluminum foil. Pre-heat your smoker to 150 degrees F
2. Take a small bowl and add listed ingredients (except trout) and mix well
3. Transfer trout fillets on a plate and pour marinade all over, mix well to ensure that the fillets are covered in marinade
4. Let it sit for 6 hours
5. Transfer marinated trout fillets to your smoking tray and let it rest for 30 minutes
6. Use water fill water pan halfway through and place it over drip pan. Add wood chips to the side tray.
7. Place fish inside your smoker and smoke for 3 hours, take the trout out and serve
8. Enjoy!

Nutrition: Calories: 382 Fat: 16g Carbohydrates: 24g Protein: 63g

• **Lemon Pepper Tuna**

Preparation Time: 10-15 minutes + 4 hours

Cooking Time: 1 hour

Serving: 4

Ingredients:

- 6 ounces' tuna steaks, 1 inch thick
- 3 tablespoons salt
- 3 tablespoons brown sugar
- ¼ cup extra virgin olive oil
- Lemon pepper seasoning
- 1 teaspoon ground garlic
- 12 thin slices, fresh lemon
- Water

Directions:

1. Take your drip pan and add water, cover with aluminum foil. Pre-heat your smoker to 145 degrees F
2. Place tuna steaks on plate and season with salt and sugar, add seasoned steaks in a sealed pack, and let it chill for 4 hours.
3. Use water fill water pan halfway through and place it over drip pan. Add wood chips to the side tray.
4. Add tuna steaks on a plate and dry the brine off it, season both sides with olive oil, garlic powder, lemon pepper seasoning
5. Transfer steaks to smoker rack and add 2 lemon slices on top, put rack inside your smoker and smoke for 1 hour
6. Check whether the steaks have an internal temperature of 154 degrees F
7. Transfer smoked steak to a cutting board and let it rest, slice and season with lime wedges and avocado slices
8. Enjoy!

Nutrition: Calories: 235 Fat: 28g Carbohydrates: 34g Protein: 32g

• Pineapple Maple Glaze Fish

Preparation Time: 10 minutes

Cooking Time: 15 Minutes

Servings: 6 Servings

Ingredients:

- 3 pounds of fresh salmon
- 1/4 cup maple syrup
- 1/2 cup pineapple juice
- Brine Ingredients
- 3 cups of water
- Sea salt, to taste
- 2 cups of pineapple juice
- ½ cup of brown sugar
- 5 tablespoons of Worcestershire sauce
- 1 tablespoon of garlic salt

Directions:

1. Combine all the brine ingredients in a large cooking pan.
2. Place the fish into the brine and let it sit for 2 hours for marinating.
3. After 2 hours, take out the fish and pat dry with a paper towel and set aside.
4. Preheat the smoker grill to 250 degrees Fahrenheit, until the smoke started to appear.
5. Put salmon on the grill and cook for 15 minutes.
6. Meanwhile, mix pineapple and maple syrup in a bowl and baste fish every 5 minutes.
7. Once the salmon is done, serve and enjoy.

Nutrition: Calories 123 Total Fat 4.9g6 % Saturated Fat 1.5g8 % Cholesterol 60mg20 % Sodium 29mg1 %

Total Carbohydrate 0g0 % Dietary Fiber 0g0 % Sugar 0g

• Smoked Catfish Recipe

Preparation Time: 10 minutes

Cooking Time: 5 Minutes

Servings: 3 Servings

Ingredients:

Ingredients for the Rub

- 2 tablespoons paprika
- 1/4 teaspoon salt
- 1 tablespoon garlic powder
- 1 tablespoon onion powder
- 1/2 tablespoon dried thyme
- 1/2 tablespoon cayenne

Other ingredients

- 2 pounds fresh catfish fillets
- 4 tablespoons butter, soften

Directions:

1. Take a mixing bowl, and combine all the rub ingredients in it, including the paprika, salt, garlic powder, onion powder, and thyme and cayenne paper.
2. Rub the fillet with the butter, and then sprinkle a generous amount of rub on top

3. Coat fish well with the rub.

4. Preheat the smoker grill at 200 degrees Fahrenheit for 15 minutes.

5. Cook fish on the grill for 10 minutes, 5minutes per side.

6. Once done, serve and enjoy.

Nutrition: Calories 146 - Total Fat 4.2g - Saturated Fat 2.5g - Cholesterol 61mg Sodium 28mg

• Cajun Smoked Shrimp

Preparation Time: 10 minutes

Cooking Time: 10 Minutes

Servings: 2 Servings

Ingredients:

- 2 tablespoons of virgin olive oil
- 1/2 lemon, juiced
- 3 cloves garlic, finely minced
- 2 tablespoons of Cajun spice
- Salt, to taste
- 1.5 pounds of shrimp, raw, peeled, deveined

Directions:

1. Take a zip lock bag and combine olive oil, lemon juice, garlic cloves, Cajun spice, salt, and shrimp.

2. Toss the ingredients well for fine coating.

3. Preheat the smoker grill for 10 minutes until the smoke starts to establish.

4. Put the fish on the grill grate and close lid.

5. Turn the temperature to high and allow the fish to cook the shrimp for 10 minutes, 5 minutes per side.

6. Once done, serve.

Nutrition: Calories 446 Total Fat 4.8g Saturated Fat 6.5g Cholesterol 53mg Sodium 48mg

• Candied Smoked Salmon with Orange Ginger Rub

Preparation Time: 10 minutes

Cooking Time: 2 Hours 10 Minutes

Servings: 10 servings

Ingredients:

The Marinade

- Brown sugar – ¼ cup
- Salt – ½ teaspoon

The Rub

- Minced garlic – 2 tablespoons
- Grated fresh ginger – 1 teaspoon
- Grated orange zest – ½ teaspoon
- Chili powder – ½ teaspoon
- Cayenne pepper – ½ teaspoon

The Glaze

- Red wine – 2 tablespoons
- Dark rum – 2 tablespoons
- Brown sugar – 1 ½ cups
- Honey – 1 cup

Directions:

1. Mix salt with brown sugar then apply over the salmon fillet. Let it rest for approximately an hour or until the sugar is melted.

2. In the meantime, combine minced garlic with grated fresh ginger, orange zest, chili powder, and cayenne pepper. Mix well.

3. Rub the salmon fillet with the spice mixture then set aside.

4. Plug the wood pellet smoker then fill the hopper with the wood pellet. Turn the switch on.

5. Set the wood pellet smoker for indirect heat then adjust the temperature to 225°F (107°C).

6. Place the seasoned salmon in wood pellet smoker and smoke for 2 hours.

7. Mix red wine with dark rum, brown sugar, and honey then stir until dissolved.

8. During the smoking process, baste the honey mixture over the salmon fillet for several times.

9. Once the smoked salmon flakes, remove it from the wood pellet smoker and transfer it to a serving dish.

10. Serve and enjoy.

Nutrition: Calories: 433 Fats: 39g Carbs: 4g Fiber: 0g

• Juicy Lime Smoked Tuna Belly

Preparation Time: 10 minutes
Cooking Time: 2 Hours 10 Minutes
Servings: 10 servings
Ingredients:

- Tuna belly (3-lb., 1.4-kg.)

The Marinade

- Fresh limes – 2
- White sugar – 2 tablespoons
- Brown sugar – 3 tablespoons
- Pepper – ½ teaspoon
- Soy sauce – 1 tablespoon
- Sriracha sauce – 2 tablespoons

Directions:

1. Cut the limes into halves then squeeze the juice over the tuna belly. Marinate the tuna belly with the juice for 10 minutes. Meanwhile, combine white sugar with brown sugar, pepper, soy sauce, and Sriracha sauce then mix well. Wash and rinse the tuna belly then pat it dry. Then, plug the wood pellet smoker then fill the hopper with the wood pellet. Turn the switch on.

2. Set the wood pellet smoker for indirect heat then adjust the temperature to 225°F (107°C).

3. Wait until the wood pellet smoker reaches the desired temperature then place the seasoned tuna belly in it. Smoke the tuna belly for 2 hours or until it flakes and once it is done, remove it from the wood pellet smoker.

4. Serve and enjoy.

Nutrition: Calories: 392 Fats: 27g Carbs: 2g Fiber: 0g

Lemon Butter Smoked Mackerel with Juniper Berries Brine

Preparation Time: 10 minutes

Cooking Time: 2 Hours 10 Minutes

Servings: 10 servings

Ingredients:

- Mackerel fillet (4-lbs., 1.8-kg.)

The Brine

- Cold water – 4 cups
- Mustard seeds – 1 tablespoon
- Dried juniper berries – 1 tablespoon
- Bay leaves – 3
- Salt – 1 tablespoon

The Glaze

- Butter – 2 tablespoons
- Lemon juice – 2 tablespoons

Directions:

1. Pour cold water into a container, then season with salt, bay leaves, dried juniper berries, and mustard seeds, then stir well.

2. Add the mackerel fillet to the brine mixture, then soak for approximately 20 minutes, then wash and rinse it. Pat the mackerel dry.

3. Then, plug the wood pellet smoker then fill the hopper with the wood pellet. Turn the switch on.

4. Set the wood pellet smoker for indirect heat then adjust the temperature to 225°F (107°C).

5. Place the seasoned mackerel on a sheet of aluminum foil then baste butter over it.

6. Drizzle lemon juice then wraps the mackerel fillet with the aluminum foil.

7. Smoke the wrapped mackerel for 2 hours or until it flakes and once it is done, remove from the wood pellet smoker. Unwrap the smoked mackerel and serve. Enjoy!

Nutrition: Calories: 467 Fats: 55g Carbs: 4g Fiber: 0g

Smoked Crab Paprika Garlic with Lemon Butter Flavor

Preparation Time: 5 minutes

Cooking Time: 30 Minutes

Servings: 10 servings

Ingredients:

- Fresh Crabs (7-lb., 3.2-kg.)

The Sauce

- Salt – 1 tablespoon
- Cayenne pepper – 1 ½ teaspoon
- Salted butter – 2 cups
- Lemon juice – ½ cup
- Worcestershire sauce – 1 tablespoon
- Garlic powder – 2 teaspoons
- Smoked paprika – 2 teaspoons

Directions:

1. Preheat a saucepan over low heat then melt the butter. Let it cool.

2. Season the melted butter with salt, cayenne pepper, Worcestershire sauce, garlic powder, and smoked paprika, then pour lemon juice into the melted butter. Stir until incorporated and set aside.

3. Then, plug the wood pellet smoker then fill the hopper with the wood pellet. Turn the switch on.

4. Set the wood pellet smoker for indirect heat then adjust the temperature to 350°F (177°C).

5. Arrange the crabs in a disposable aluminum pan then drizzle the sauce over the crabs.

6. Smoke the crabs for 30 minutes then remove from the wood pellet smoker.

7. Transfer the smoked crabs to a serving dish then serve.

8. Enjoy!

Nutrition: Calories: 455 Fats: 53g Carbs: 3g Fiber: 0g

• **Cayenne Garlic Smoked Shrimp**

Preparation Time: 5 minutes

Cooking Time: 15 Minutes

Servings: 10 servings

Ingredients:

- Fresh Shrimps (3-lb., 1.4-kg.)

The Spices

- Olive oil – 2 tablespoons
- Lemon juice – 2 tablespoons
- Salt – ¾ teaspoon
- Smoked paprika – 2 teaspoons
- Pepper – ½ teaspoon
- Garlic powder – 2 tablespoons
- Onion powder – 2 tablespoons
- Dried thyme – 1 teaspoon
- Cayenne pepper – 2 teaspoons

Directions:

1. Combine salt, smoked paprika, pepper, garlic powder, onion powder, dried thyme, and cayenne pepper then mix well. Set aside. Then, peel the shrimps and discard the head. Place in a disposable aluminum pan. Drizzle olive oil and lemon juice over the shrimps and shake to coat. Let the shrimps rest for approximately 5 minutes. Then, plug the wood pellet smoker then fill the hopper with the wood pellet. Turn the switch on.

2. Set the wood pellet smoker for indirect heat then adjust the temperature to 350°F (177°C).

3. Sprinkle the spice mixture over the shrimps then stir until the shrimps are completely seasoned.

4. Place the disposable aluminum pan with shrimps in the wood pellet smoker and smoke the shrimps for 15 minutes. The shrimps will be opaque and pink. Remove the smoked shrimps from the wood pellet smoker and transfer to a serving dish.

5. Serve and enjoy.

Nutrition: Calories: 233 - Fats: 25g - Carbs: 7g - Fiber: 0g

• Cinnamon Ginger Juicy Smoked Crab

Preparation Time: 10 minutes

Cooking Time: 30 Minutes

Servings: 10 servings

Ingredients:

- Fresh Crabs (7-lb., 3.2-kg.)

The Spices

- Salt – 1 tablespoon
- Ground celery seeds – 3 tablespoons
- Ground mustard – 2 teaspoons
- Cayenne pepper – ½ teaspoon
- Black pepper – ½ teaspoon
- Smoked paprika – 1 ½ teaspoon
- Ground clove – A pinch
- Ground allspice – ¾ teaspoon
- Ground ginger – 1 teaspoon
- Ground cardamom – ½ teaspoon
- Ground cinnamon – ½ teaspoon
- Bay leaves - 2

Directions:

1. Combine the entire spices—salt, ground celery seeds, mustard, cayenne pepper, black pepper, smoked paprika, clove, allspice, ginger, cardamom, and cinnamon in a bowl then mix well. Sprinkle the spice mixture over the crabs then wrap the crabs with aluminum foil. Then, plug the wood pellet smoker then fill the hopper with the wood pellet. Turn the switch on. Set the wood pellet smoker for indirect heat then adjust the temperature to 350°F (177°C). Place the wrapped crabs in the wood pellet smoker and smoke for 30 minutes. Once it is done, remove the wrapped smoked carbs from the wood pellet smoker and let it rest for approximately 10 minutes.

2. Unwrap the smoked crabs and transfer it to a serving dish.

3. Serve and enjoy!

Nutrition: Calories: 355 - Fats: 22g - Carbs: 8g - Fiber: 0g

• Pellet Grilled Salmon Fillet

Preparation Time: 10 minutes

Cooking Time: 15 Minutes

Pellets: Gold Blend

Servings: 4

Hardwood: Gold Blend

Directions:

1. Go to your local boat store, buy a boat, a truck to pull it, a salmon rod, a license, and tow the whole rig to the west coast in late summer or early fall to hopefully catch one of these. Or, go to the local market, and pay a few bucks per pound.

2. Lightly dust both sides of the fish that has been skinned with salt and pepper. If not skinned, dust with seasonings, as well. Melt a few

tablespoons of butter (olive oil is an acceptable substitute), and brush both sides of the fish with it.

3. Place the fish on the grill at 400-450°F (204-232°C), skin side down (it will not matter which side, if it's skinless).

4. Turn the fish after about 8 minutes (assuming 1" filet). Peel the skin off. If it does not come off easily, flip the fish over for a couple of minutes and then try again. Put some salt and pepper lightly after you remove the skin. Baste with butter. Cook for another 5-6 minutes, and then turn it over for about 2 more minutes. Check the doneness by separating the center with a fork. The fish should just be slightly pink, with only a small amount of juice. Remove from the grill, cover, and let stand for 5 minutes as it will continue to cook.

5. Remember that salmon, like all fish, cooks quickly. Make sure you are ready when you start to grill. I always make sure to have my aluminum foil out and ready and any supplies I might need while grilling. You do not want to be stranded looking for tongs, while your fish overcooks in the meantime. Be prepared for quick cook time, and all will turn out well. Perfect!

- ## Roasted Cod with Lemon Herb Butter

Preparation Time: 10 minutes
Cooking Time: 12 minutes
Hardwood: Alder

Ingredients

- 1 ½ to 2 lbs. cod fillets
- 4 tbsp. salted butter at room temperature
- ½ lemon, zested and juiced
- 1 clove garlic, peeled and finely minced
- 1 tbsp. chopped fresh herbs: tarragon, parsley, basil, or chives
- 2 tsp. salmon shake seasoning

Directions

1. Start your grill on smoke with the lid open until the fire is established (about 5 minutes).

2. Preheat the grill to 400 degrees F or High, lid closed, for 10 to 15 minutes.

3. Compound the butter by combining the butter, lemon zest and juice, garlic, herbs, and the Traeger Salmon Shake. Refrigerate the mixture if you will not use it right away.

4. Use a tablespoon of butter to grease a heat-proof baking dish.

5. Arrange the cod fillets in a single layer in the baking dish. Dot evenly with bits of the compound butter.

6. Bake for 12 to 15 minutes or until the fish is cooked through.

7. Spoon the sauce over each serving. Enjoy!

• Smoked Trout

Preparation Time: 1 Hour

Cooking Time: 2 Hours

Hardwood: Oak

Ingredients

- 6 to 8 rainbow trout
- 1-gallon water
- ¼ cup brown sugar
- 1 tbsp. ground black pepper
- 2 tbsp. soy sauce

Directions

1. Clean the fresh fish and butterfly it.

2. For the brine: Combine the water, brown sugar, soy sauce, salt, and pepper. Brine the trout in the refrigerator for 60 minutes.

3. When ready to cook, set the temperature to 225°F and preheat, lid closed, for 15 minutes. For the optimal flavor, use Super Smoke if available.

4. Remove the fish from the brine and pat dry.

5. Place fish directly on the grill grate for 1 1/2 to 2 hours, depending on the thickness of the trout.

6. Fish is done when it turns opaque and starts to flake. Serve hot or cold. Enjoy!

• Finnan Had die Recipe

Preparation Time: 5 minutes

Cooking Time: 35 minutes

Ingredients

- 2 pounds smoked haddock fillets
- 2 tablespoons all-purpose flour
- 1/4 cup melted butter
- 2 cups warm milk
- Add all ingredients to list

Directions

1. Preheat the oven to 325 degrees F (165 degrees C).

2. Place smoked haddock into a glass baking dish. Whisk the flour into the melted butter until smooth, then whisk in milk, and pour over the haddock.

3. Bake in the preheated oven until the sauce has thickened and the fish flakes easily with a fork, about 35 minutes.

• Home Grilled Salmon

Ingredients

- 1 ½ lb. of salmon fillets
- Lemon pepper to taste
- Garlic powder to taste
- Salt to taste
- 1/3 cup soy sauce
- 1/3 cup brown sugar
- 1/3 cup water
- ¼ cup of vegetable oil

Directions

1. Mix all the ingredients in a large bowl.
2. Season the salmon fillets with lemon pepper, garlic powder, and salt.
3. In a small bowl, stir together the soy sauce, brown sugar, water, and vegetable oil until sugar is dissolved. Place the fish in a large resealable plastic bag with the soy sauce mixture, seal, and turn to coat. Refrigerate for at least 2 hours.
4. Preheat the grill to low and slow heat.
5. Lightly oil the grill grate. Place the salmon on the preheated grill and discard the marinade. Cook the salmon for 6 to 8 minutes per side or until the fish is flaking easily with a fork.

• Smoked Fish Pie

Preparation Time: 20 minutes

Cooking Time: 45 minutes

Servings: 8 individuals

Ingredients

For the Crust:

- 1/2 cup (1 stick) butter (cold)
- 1 1/4 cup all-purpose flour
- 1/2 teaspoon salt
- 3 tablespoons Emmental cheese, grated
- 3 tablespoons water

For the Filling:

- 1 cup smoked salmon, chopped
- 1/2 cup leeks white part only, chopped
- 3 eggs
- 1/2 cup whole milk
- 3/4 cup heavy whipping cream
- 1/3 cup dill chopped, fresh
- 1 teaspoon lemon pepper
- 1/2 teaspoon salt
- 3/4 cup cheese Emmental cheese, grated

Directions:

Prepare the Crust

- Gather the ingredients.
- Preheat the oven to 400°F.
- In a medium bowl, cut the butter into the flour and salt until it resembles coarse crumbs.
- Add the grated cheese and water and combine until the crust comes together.
- Roll out the crust on a lightly floured surface.
- Press the crust into a 9-inch pie pan, folding and crimping the top edge.
- Prick the crust all over with a fork.
- Then bake at 400°F for 15 minutes.

Prepare the Pie

- Gather the ingredients.
- Place the chopped salmon and leek into the prepared pie crust.

- In a large bowl, whisk together the eggs, milk, cream, dill, lemon pepper, and salt.
- Pour the egg mixture over the salmon and leek in the crust.
- Sprinkle with grated Emmental cheese.
- Return the pie to the oven and bake for 27 to 30 minutes.
- Cool at least 15 minutes before cutting and serving.
- Enjoy!

Tip: If you are creating the pastry by hand, make sure to be quick in blending the pastry when mixing the butter and flour. Do not handle the butter too much because the heat from your hand may overly warm it up. Remember, it needs to be as cool as possible.

• Grilled Lobster Tail

Preparation Time: 10 minutes
Cooking Time: 15 minutes
Servings: 4
Smoke Temperature: 450°F and 140°F
Ingredients:

- 2 (8 ounces each) lobster tails
- 1/4 tsp. old bay seasoning
- ½ tsp. oregano
- 1 tsp. paprika
- Juice from one lemon
- 1/4 tsp. Himalayan salt
- 1/4 tsp. freshly ground black pepper
- 1/4 tsp. onion powder
- 2 tbsp. freshly chopped parsley
- ¼ cup melted butter

Directions:

1. Slice the tail in the middle with a kitchen shear. Pull the shell apart slightly and run your hand through the meat to separate the meat partially, keeping it attached to the base of the tail partially.
2. Combine the old bay seasoning, paprika, oregano, salt, pepper and onion powder in a mixing bowl.
3. Drizzle lobster tail with lemon juice and season generously with the seasoning mixture.
4. Preheat your wood pellet smoker to 450°F, using apple wood pellets.
5. Place the lobster tail directly on the grill grate, meat side down. Cook for about 15 minutes or until the internal temperature of the tails reaches 140°F.
6. Take the tails off the grill and let them rest for a few minutes to cool.
7. Drizzle melted butter over the tails.
8. Serve and garnish with fresh chopped parsley.

Nutrition: Calories 146 Total Fat 11.7g Saturated Fat 7.3g Cholesterol 56mg Sodium 295mg Total Carbohydrate 2.1g Dietary Fiber 0.8g Total Sugars 0.5g Protein 9.3g Vitamin D 8mcg Calcium 15mg Iron 0mg Potassium 53mg

• Halibut

Preparation Time: 10 minutes

Cooking Time: 30 minutes

Servings: 4

Smoke Temperature: 275°F and 135°F

Ingredients:

- 1-pound fresh halibut filet (cut into 4 equal sizes)
- 1 tbsp. fresh lemon juice
- 2 garlic cloves (minced)
- 2 tsp. soy sauce
- ½ tsp. ground black pepper
- ½ tsp. onion powder
- 2 tbsp. honey
- ½ tsp. oregano
- 1 tsp. dried basil
- 2 tbsp. butter (melted)
- Maple syrup for serving

Directions:

1. In a mixing bowl, combine the lemon juice, honey, soy sauce, onion powder, oregano, dried basil, pepper and garlic.
2. Brush the halibut filets generously with the filet the mixture. Wrap the filets with aluminum foil and refrigerate for 4 hours.
3. Remove the filets from the refrigerator and let them sit for about 2 hours, or until they are at room temperature.
4. Activate your wood pellet grill on smoke, leaving the lid opened for 5 minutes or until fire starts.
5. Heat your grill to 275°F for 15 minutes after closing the lid, using fruit wood pellets.
6. Place the halibut filets directly on the grill grate and smoke for 30 minutes or until the internal temperature of the fish reaches 135°F.
7. Remove the filets from the grill and let them rest for 10 minutes.
8. Serve and top with maple syrup to taste

Nutrition: Calories 180 Total Fat 6.3g Saturated Fat 3.7g Cholesterol 35mg Sodium 247mg Total Carbohydrate 10g Dietary Fiber 0.3g Total Sugars 8.9g Protein 20.6g Vitamin D 4mcg Calcium 11mg Iron 0mg Potassium 34mg

• BBQ Shrimp

Preparation Time: 20 minutes

Cooking Time: 8 minutes

Servings: 6

Smoke Temperature: 450°F

Ingredients:

- 2-pound raw shrimp (peeled and deveined)
- ¼ cup extra virgin olive oil
- ½ tsp. paprika
- ½ tsp. red pepper flakes
- 2 garlic cloves (minced)
- 1 tsp. cumin

- 1 lemon (juiced)
- 1 tsp. kosher salt
- 1 tbsp. chili paste
- Bamboo or wooden skewers (soaked for 30 minutes, at least)

Directions:

1. In a large mixing bowl, combine the pepper flakes, cumin, lemon, salt, chili, paprika, garlic and olive oil. Add the shrimp and toss to combine.
2. Transfer the shrimp and marinade into a zip-lock bag and refrigerate for 4 hours.
3. Take the shrimp off the marinade and allow it to rest until it is a room temperature.
4. Start your grill on smoke, leaving the lid opened for 5 minutes, or until fire starts. Use hickory wood pellet.
5. Cover the lid and l allow the grill to heat to high for 15 minutes.
6. Thread shrimps onto skewers and arrange the skewers on the grill grate.
7. Smoke shrimps for 8 minutes, 4 minutes per side.
8. Serve and enjoy.

Nutrition: Calories 267 Total Fat 11.6g Saturated Fat 2g Cholesterol 319mg Sodium 788mg Total Carbohydrate 4.9g Dietary Fiber 0.4g Total Sugars 1g Protein 34.9g Calcium 149mg Iron 1mg Potassium 287mg

- ## **Oyster in Shell**

Preparation Time: 25 minutes
Cooking Time: 8 minutes
Servings: 4
Smoke Temperature: 450°F
Ingredients:

- 12 medium oysters
- 1 tsp. oregano
- 1 lemon (juiced)
- 1 tsp. freshly ground black pepper
- 6 tbsp. unsalted butter (melted)
- 1 tsp. salt or more to taste
- 2 garlic cloves (minced)

Garnish:

- 2 ½ tbsp. grated parmesan cheese
- 2 tbsp. freshly chopped parsley

Directions:

1. Start by scrubbing the outside of the shell with a scrub brush under cold running water to remove dirt.
2. Hold an oyster in a towel, flat side up. Insert an oyster knife in the hinge of the oyster.
3. Twist the knife with pressure to pop open the oyster. Run the knife along the oyster hinge to open the shell completely. Discard the top shell.
4. Gently run the knife under the oyster to loosen the oyster foot from the bottom shell.
5. Repeat step 2 and 3 for the remaining oysters.

6. Combine melted butter, lemon, pepper, salt, garlic and oregano in a mixing bowl.

7. Pour ½ to 1 tsp. of the butter mixture on each oyster.

8. Start your wood pellet grill on smoke, leaving the lid opened for 5 minutes, or until fire starts.

9. Close the lid and let the grill heat to high with lid closed for 15 minutes.

10. Gently arrange the oysters onto the grill grate.

11. Grill oyster for 6 to 8 minutes or until the oyster juice is bubbling and the oyster is plump.

12. Remove oysters from heat. Serve and top with grated parmesan and chopped parsley.

Nutrition: Calories 200 Total Fat 19.2g Saturated Fat 11.9g Cholesterol 66mg Sodium 788mg Total Carbohydrate 3.9g Dietary Fiber 0.8g Total Sugars 0.7g Protein 4.6g Vitamin D 12mcg Calcium 93mg Iron 2mg Potassium 120mg

• Grilled King Crab Legs

Preparation Time: 10 minutes

Cooking Time: 25 minutes

Servings: 4

Smoke Temperature: 225°F

Ingredients:

- 4 pounds king crab legs (split)
- 4 tbsp. lemon juice
- 2 tbsp. garlic powder
- 1 cup butter (melted)
- 2 tsp. brown sugar
- 2 tsp. paprika
- 2 tsp. ground black pepper or more to taste

Directions:

1. In a mixing bowl, combine the lemon juice, butter, sugar, garlic, paprika and pepper.

2. Arrange the split crab on a baking sheet, split side up.

3. Drizzle ¾ of the butter mixture over the crab legs.

4. Configure your pellet grill for indirect cooking and preheat it to 225°F, using mesquite wood pellets.

5. Arrange the crab legs onto the grill grate, shell side down.

6. Cover the grill and cook 25 minutes.

7. Remove the crab legs from the grill.

8. Serve and top with the remaining butter mixture.

Nutrition: Calories 894 Total Fat 53.2g 68% Saturated Fat 29.3g 147% Cholesterol 374mg 125% Sodium 5189mg 226% Total Carbohydrate 6.1g Dietary Fiber 1.2g Total Sugars 3g Protein 88.6g Vitamin D 32mcg Calcium 301mg Iron 4mg Potassium 119mg

• Cajun Smoked Catfish

Preparation Time: 15 minutes

Cooking Time: 2 hours

Servings: 4

Smoke Temperature: 200°F

Ingredients:

- 4 catfish fillets (5 ounces each)
- ½ cup Cajun seasoning
- 1 tsp. ground black pepper
- 1 tbsp. smoked paprika
- 1 /4 tsp. cayenne pepper
- 1 tsp. hot sauce
- 1 tsp. granulated garlic
- 1 tsp. onion powder
- 1 tsp. thyme
- 1 tsp. salt or more to taste
- 2 tbsp. chopped fresh parsley

Directions:

1. Pour water into the bottom of a square or rectangular dish. Add 4 tbsp. salt. Arrange the catfish fillets into the dish. Cover the dish and refrigerate for 3 to 4 hours.

2. Meanwhile, combine the paprika, cayenne, hot sauce, onion, salt, thyme, garlic, pepper and Cajun seasoning in a mixing bowl.

3. Remove the fish from the dish and let it sit for a few minutes, or until it is at room temperature. Pat the fish fillets dry with a paper towel.

4. Rub the seasoning mixture over each fillet generously.

5. Start your grill on smoke, leaving the lid opened for 5 minutes, or until fire starts.

6. Cover the lid and allow the grill to heat to 200°F, using mesquite hardwood pellets.

7. Arrange the fish fillets onto the grill grate and close the grill. Cook for about 2 hours, or until the fish is flaky.

8. Remove the fillets from the grill and let the fillets rest for a few minutes to cool.

9. Serve and garnish with chopped fresh parsley.

Nutrition: Calories 204 Total Fat 11.1g Saturated Fat 2g Cholesterol 67mg Sodium 991mg Total Carbohydrate 2.7g Dietary Fiber 1.1g Total Sugars 0.6g Protein 22.9g Calcium 29mg Iron 3mg Potassium 532mg

• Rosemary-Smoked Lamb Chops

Preparation Time: 15 minutes

Cooking Time: 2 hours and 5 minutes

Servings: 4

Ingredients:

- Wood Pellet Flavor: Mesquite
- 4½ pounds bone-in lamb chops
- 2 tablespoons olive oil
- Salt
- Freshly ground black pepper
- 1 bunch fresh rosemary

Directions:

1. Supply your smoker with wood pellets and follow the manufacturer's specific start-up procedure. Preheat the grill to 180°F.
2. Rub the lamb generously with olive oil and season on both sides with salt and pepper.
3. Spread the rosemary directly on the grill grate, creating a surface area large enough for all the chops to rest on. Place the chops on the rosemary and smoke until they reach an internal temperature of 135°F.
4. Increase the grill's temperature to 450°F, remove the rosemary, and continue to cook the chops until their internal temperature reaches 145°F.
5. Take off the chops from the grill and let them rest for 5 minutes before serving.

Nutrition: Calories: 50 Carbs: 4g Fiber: 2g Fat: 2.5g Protein: 2g

• Greek-Style Roast Leg of Lamb

Preparation Time: 25 minutes

Cooking Time: 1 hour and 30 minutes

Servings: 12

Ingredients:

- 7 pounds leg of lamb, bone-in, fat trimmed
- 2 lemons, juiced
- 8 cloves of garlic, peeled, minced
- Salt as needed
- Ground black pepper as needed
- 1 teaspoon dried oregano
- 1 teaspoon dried rosemary
- 6 tablespoons olive oil

Directions:

1. Make a small cut into the meat of lamb by using a paring knife, then stir together garlic, oregano, and rosemary and stuff this paste into the slits of the lamb meat.
2. Take a roasting pan, place lamb in it, then rub with lemon juice and olive oil, cover with a plastic wrap and let marinate for a minimum of 8 hours in the refrigerator.

3. When ready to cook, switch on the Pellet grill, fill the grill hopper with oak flavored wood pellets, power the grill on by using the control panel, select 'smoke' on the temperature dial, or set the temperature to 400 degrees F and let it preheat for a minimum of 15 minutes.

4. Meanwhile, remove the lamb from the refrigerator, bring it to room temperature, uncover it and then season well with salt and black pepper.

5. When the grill has preheated, open the lid, place food on the grill grate, shut the grill, and smoke for 30 minutes.

6. Change the smoking temperature to 350 degrees F and then continue smoking for 1 hour until the internal temperature reaches 140 degrees F.

7. When done, transfer lamb to a cutting board, let it rest for 15 minutes, then cut it into slices and serve.

Nutrition: Calories: 168 Cal Fat: 10 g Carbs: 2 g Protein: 17 g Fiber: 0.7 g

• Lamb Chops

Preparation Time: 10 minutes
Cooking Time: 10 minutes
Servings: 8
Ingredients:
For the Lamb:

- 16 lamb chops, fat trimmed

- 2 tablespoons Greek Freak seasoning

For the Mint Sauce:

- 1 tablespoon chopped parsley
- 12 cloves of garlic, peeled
- 1 tablespoon chopped mint
- 1/4 teaspoon dried oregano
- 1 teaspoon salt
- 1/4 teaspoon ground black pepper
- 3/4 cup lemon juice
- 1 cup olive oil

Directions:

1. Prepare the mint sauce and for this, place all of its ingredients in a food processor and then pulse for 1 minute until smooth.

2. Pour 1/3 cup of the mint sauce into a plastic bag, add lamb chops in it, seal the bag, turn it upside to coat lamb chops with the sauce and then let them marinate for a minimum of 30 minutes in the refrigerator.

3. When ready to cook, switch on the Pellet grill, fill the grill hopper with apple-flavored wood pellets, power the grill on by using the control panel, select 'smoke' on the temperature dial, or set the temperature to 450 degrees F and let it preheat for a minimum of 15 minutes.

4. Meanwhile, remove lamb chops from the marinade and then season with Greek seasoning.

5. When the grill has preheated, open the lid, place lamb chops on the grill grate, shut the grill and smoke for 4 to 5 minutes per side until cooked to the desired level.

6. When done, transfer lamb chops to a dish and then serve.

Nutrition: Calories: 362 Cal Fat: 26 g Carbs: 0 g Protein: 31 g Fiber: 0 g

• Classic Lamb Chops

Preparation Time: 10 minutes

Cooking Time: 30 minutes

Servings: 4

Ingredients

- Wood Pellet Flavor: Alder
- 4 (8-ounce) bone-in lamb chops
- 2 tablespoons olive oil
- 1 batch Rosemary-Garlic Lamb Seasoning

Directions:

1. Supply your smoker with wood pellets and follow the manufacturer's specific start-up procedure. Preheat the grill to 350°F. Close the lid

2. Rub the lamb generously with olive oil and coat them on both sides with the seasoning.

3. Put the chops directly on the grill grate and grill until their internal temperature reaches 145°F. Remove the lamb from the grill and serve immediately.

Nutrition: Calories: 50 Carbs: 4g Fiber: 2g Fat: 2.5g Protein: 2g

• Seared lamb chops

Preparation Time: 10 minutes

Cooking Time: 20 minutes

Servings: 4

Ingredients:

- Wood Pellet Flavor: Alder
- 4 (8-ounce) bone-in lamb chops
- 2 tablespoons olive oil
- 1 batch Rosemary-Garlic Lamb Seasoning

Directions:

1. Supply your smoker with wood pellets and follow the manufacturer's specific start-up procedure. Preheat the grill to 500F. Close the lid

2. Rub the lamb chops all over with olive oil and coat them on both sides with the seasoning.

3. Put the chops directly on the grill grate and grill until they reach an internal temperature of 120°F for rare, 130°F for medium, and 145F for well-done. Remove the lamb from the grill then serve immediately.

Nutrition: Calories: 50 Carbs: 4g Fiber: 2g Fat: 2.5g Protein: 2g

• **Roasted Leg of Lamb**

Preparation Time: 15 minutes

Cooking Time: 1-2 hours

Servings: 4

Ingredients:

- Wood Pellet Flavor: Hickory
- 1 (6- to 8-pound) boneless leg of lamb
- 2 batches Rosemary-Garlic Lamb Seasoning

Directions:

1. Supply your smoker with wood pellets and follow the manufacturer's specific start-up procedure. Preheat the grill to 350°F. Close the lid
2. Using your hands, rub the lamb leg with the seasoning, rubbing it under and around any netting.
3. Put the lamb directly on the grill grate and smoke until its internal temperature reaches 145°F.
4. Take off the lamb from the grill and let it rest for 20 to 30 minutes, before removing the netting, slicing, and serving.

Nutrition: Calories: 50 Carbs: 4g Fiber: 2g Fat: 2.5g Protein: 2g

- ## Hickory-Smoked Leg of Lamb

Preparation Time: 15 minutes

Cooking Time: 5-7 hours

Servings: 4

Ingredients:

- WOOD PELLET FLAVOR: Hickory
- 1 (6- to 8-pound) boneless leg of lamb
- 2 batches Rosemary-Garlic Lamb Seasoning

Directions:

1. Supply your smoker with wood pellets and follow the manufacturer's specific start-up procedure. Preheat the grill to 225F. Close the lid

2. Using your hands, rub the lamb leg with the seasoning, rubbing it under and around any netting.

3. Move the lamb directly on the grill grate and smoke until its internal temperature reaches 145F.

4. Take off the lamb from the grill and let it rest for 20 to 30 minutes, before removing the netting, slicing, and serving.

- ## Smoked Rack of Lamb

Preparation Time: 25 minutes

Cooking Time: 4-6 hours

Servings: 4

Ingredients:

- Wood Pellet Flavor: Hickory

- 1 (2-pound) rack of lamb
- 1 batch Rosemary-Garlic Lamb Seasoning

Directions:

1. Supply your smoker with wood pellets and follow the manufacturer's specific start-up procedure. Preheat the grill to 225°F.Close the lid

2. Using a boning knife, score the bottom fat portion of the rib meat.

3. Using your hands, rub the rack of lamb all over with the seasoning, making sure it penetrates into the scored fat.

4. Place the rack directly on the grill grate, fat-side up, and smoke until its internal temperature reaches 145°F.

5. Take off the rack from the grill and let it rest for 20 to 30 minutes, before slicing it into individual ribs to serve.

Nutrition: Calories: 50 Carbs: 4g Fiber: 2g Fat: 2.5g Protein: 2g

- ## Smoked Lamb Sausage

Preparation Time: 2 hours

Cooking Time: 6 hours

Servings: 6

Ingredients:

Pellets: Cherry

- 1 teaspoon cumin
- 1/2 teaspoon cayenne pepper
- 1 tablespoon parsley

- 1 teaspoon black pepper
- 1 Hog Casing
- 1 tablespoon garlic
- 1 teaspoon paprika
- 2 tablespoons salt
- 2 tablespoons fennel, diced
- 1 tablespoon cilantro
- 2 lbs. lamb shoulders

Yogurt sauce:

- 3 cup yogurt
- Lemon juice to taste
- 1 clove garlic, minced
- Salt and pepper
- 1 cucumber, diced
- 1 onion, minced

Directions:

1. Chop the lamb into pieces before grinding the meat in a meat grinder.
2. Mix the lamb with all of the spices and refrigerate.
3. Then use a sausage horn to attach the hog casing and begin pushing the sausage through the grinder and into the casing, twisting into links. Make holes in the casing before refrigerating.
4. Mix all ingredients for the yogurt sauce and set aside.
5. When ready to cook, set your smoker to 225F and preheat.
6. Lay the sausage on the grill and smoke it for one hour.

7. Then, take the links off the grill and increase the grill's temperature to 500°F.
8. Put the links back on the grill for 5 minutes on each side, then serve with the yogurt sauce.

Nutrition: Calories: 50 Carbs: 4g Fiber: 2g Fat: 2.5g Protein: 2g

• **Pistachio Roasted Lamb**

Preparation Time: 20 minutes

Cooking Time: 40 minutes

Servings: 6

Ingredients:

Pellets: Cherry

- 1 tablespoon vegetable oil
- 2 lamb racks
- 3 carrots, peeled and chopped
- 1 lb. potatoes
- 1 tablespoon olive oil
- 1/2 teaspoon salt
- 1/2 teaspoon pepper
- 1 clove garlic, minced
- 2 teaspoons thyme
- 3 cups pistachios
- 2 tablespoons breadcrumbs
- 1 tablespoon butter
- 1 teaspoon olive oil
- 3 tablespoons Dijon mustard

Instructions

1. When ready to cook, set your smoker to 450F and preheat.

2. Place a large pan on the grill and add vegetable oil.

3. Pat the lamb dry and then season each rack of lamb with salt and black pepper.

4. Add the carrots to a mixing bowl with the salt, potatoes, garlic, olive oil, pepper, and thyme. Set aside.

5. Place lamb in the pan and cook for eight minutes. Transfer lamb from the grill to rest before mixing the pistachios, butter, salt, bread crumbs, and olive oil

6. Spread mustard on the fat-side of each rack of lamb. Pat pistachio mixture on top of the mustard.

7. Place the carrots and lamb onto the pan and then cook them alongside the lamb for 15 minutes.

8. Open the lid and cook for ten more minutes before serving.

Nutrition: Calories: 50 Carbs: 4g Fiber: 2g Fat: 2.5g Protein: 2g

- ## Lamb Wraps

Preparation Time: 1 hour

Cooking Time: 2 hours

Servings: 4

Ingredients:

Pellets: Apple

- 1 leg of lamb
- 3 lemons, juiced
- Olive oil
- Big game rub
- 2 cups yogurt
- 2 cucumbers, diced
- 2 cloves garlic, minced
- 4 tablespoons dill, finely diced
- 2 tablespoons mint leaves, finely diced
- Salt and pepper
- 12 pitas
- 3 tomatoes, diced
- 1 red onion, thinly sliced
- 8 oz. feta cheese

Directions:

1. Rub your lamb with the lemon juice, olive oil, and the rub.

2. When ready to cook, set your smoker temperature to 500°F and preheat. Put the leg of lamb on the smoker and cook for 30 minutes.

3. Lower the heat to 350F and keep cooking for another hour.

4. While the lamb is roasting, create the tzatziki sauce by mixing the yogurt, cucumbers, garlic, dill, mint leaves, in a bowl and mix to combine. Place in the refrigerator to chill.

5. Get the pittas and wrap in foil, then place on the grill to warm.

6. Put the lamb at a cutting board and leave to rest for 15 minutes before slicing.

7. Fill the warm pita with red onion, lamb, diced tomato, tzatziki sauce, and feta.

Nutrition: Calories: 50 Carbs: 4g Fiber: 2g Fat: 2.5g Protein: 2g

• Moroccan Kebabs

Preparation Time: 20 minutes

Cooking Time: 30 minutes

Servings: 2

Ingredients:

Pellets: Cherry

- 1 cup onions, finely diced
- 1 tablespoon fresh mint, finely diced
- 1 teaspoon paprika
- 1 teaspoon salt
- 1/2 teaspoon ground coriander
- 1/4 teaspoon ground cinnamon
- Pita Bread
- 2 cloves garlic, minced
- 3 tablespoons cilantro leaves, finely diced
- 1 tablespoon ground cumin
- 1 1/2 lbs. ground lamb

Directions:

1. In a bowl, mix the ingredients except for the pita bread. Mix into meatballs, and skewer each meatball.
2. Next, wet your hands with water and shape the meat into a sausage shape about as large as your thumb. Cover and refrigerate for 30 minutes.
3. When ready to cook, set your smoker temperature to 350°F and preheat.

Put the kebabs on the smoker and cook for 30 minutes.

4. Serve with the pita bread.

• Braised Lamb Shank

Preparation Time: 15 minutes

Cooking Time: 4 hours

Servings: 4

Ingredients:

Pellets: Mesquite

- 4 lamb shanks
- Prime rib rub
- 1 cup beef broth
- 1 cup red wine
- 4 sprigs rosemary and thyme

Directions:

1. Season the lamb with the prime rib rub.
2. Turn your smoker to 500F and preheat.
3. Place the lamb straight on the grill and smoke for 20 minutes.
4. Transfer the lamb to a pan and pour in the wine, beef broth, and herbs. Cover and put back on the grill, lowering the temperature to 325F.
5. Braise the lamb for 4 hours before serving.

Nutrition: Calories: 50 Carbs: 4g Fiber: 2g Fat: 2.5g Protein: 2g

• **Braised Lamb Tacos**

Preparation Time: 2 hours

Cooking Time: 5 hours

Servings: 4

Ingredients:

Pellets: Mesquite

- 1/4 tablespoon cumin seeds
- 1/4 tablespoon coriander seeds
- 1/4 tablespoon pumpkin seeds
- 2 oz. guajillo peppers
- 1 tablespoon paprika
- 1 tablespoon lime juice
- 1 tablespoon fresh oregano, diced
- 3 cloves garlic, minced
- 2 tablespoons olive oil
- 1 tablespoon salt
- 3 lbs. lamb shoulders

Directions:

1. Grind all of the seeds together before microwaving the chili with water for two minutes on high.
2. Mix the seeds, lime juice, paprika, garlic cloves, salt, oil, and oregano with the chili.
3. Put the meat in a pan, then rub the seasoning mixture over it. Leave for two hours in the fridge.
4. When ready to cook, turn your smoker to 325F and preheat.
5. Pour 1/2 cup of water to the pan and cover with foil. Cook the lamb for two hours, adding water when needed.
6. Discard the foil and cook for 2 hours more, then leave for 20 minutes before shredding.
7. Serve on corn tortillas.

• **Smoked Rack of Lamb**

Preparation Time: 10 minutes

Cooking Time: 1 hour and 15 minutes

Servings: 4

Ingredients:

- 1 rack of lamb rib, membrane removed

For the Marinade:

- 1 lemon, juiced
- 2 teaspoons minced garlic
- 1 teaspoon salt
- 1 teaspoon ground black pepper
- 1 teaspoon dried thyme
- ¼ cup balsamic vinegar
- 1 teaspoon dried basil

For the Glaze:

- 2 tablespoons soy sauce
- ¼ cup Dijon mustard
- 2 tablespoons Worcestershire sauce
- ¼ cup red wine

Directions:

1. Prepare the marinade and for this, take a small bowl, place all the

ingredients in it and whisk until combined.

2. Place the rack of lamb into a large plastic bag, pour in marinade, seal the bag, turn it upside down to coat lamb with the marinade and let it marinate for a minimum of 8 hours in the refrigerator.

3. When ready to cook, switch on the Pellet grill, fill the grill hopper with flavored wood pellets, power the grill on by using the control panel, select 'smoke' on the temperature dial, or set the temperature to 300 degrees F and let it preheat for a minimum of 5 minutes.

4. Meanwhile, prepare the glaze and for this, take a small bowl, place all of its ingredients in it and whisk until combined.

5. When the grill has preheated, open the lid, place lamb rack on the grill grate, shut the grill and smoke for 15 minutes.

6. Brush with glaze, flip the lamb and then continue smoking for 1 hour and 15 minutes until the internal temperature reaches 145 degrees F, basting with the glaze every 30 minutes.

7. When done, transfer lamb rack to a cutting board, let it rest for 15 minutes, cut it into slices, and then serve.

Nutrition: Calories: 323 Cal Fat: 18 g Carbs: 13 g Protein: 25 g Fiber: 1 g

• **Rosemary Lamb**

Preparation Time: 10 minutes

Cooking Time: 3 hours

Servings: 2

Ingredients:

- 1 rack of lamb rib, membrane removed
- 12 baby potatoes
- 1 bunch of asparagus, ends trimmed
- Ground black pepper, as needed
- Salt, as needed
- 1 teaspoon dried rosemary
- 2 tablespoons olive oil
- 1/2 cup butter, unsalted

Directions:

1. Switch on the Pellet grill, fill the grill hopper with flavored wood pellets, power the grill on by using the control panel, select 'smoke' on the temperature dial, or set the temperature to 225 degrees F and let it preheat for a minimum of 5 minutes.

2. Meanwhile, drizzle oil on both sides of lamb ribs and then sprinkle with rosemary.

3. Take a deep baking dish, place potatoes in it, add butter and mix until coated.

4. When the grill has preheated, open the lid, place lamb ribs on the grill grate along with potatoes in the baking dish, shut the grill and smoke for 3 hours until the internal temperature reaches 145 degrees F.

5. Add asparagus into the baking dish in the last 20 minutes and, when done, remove baking dish from the grill and transfer lamb to a cutting board.

6. Let lamb rest for 15 minutes, cut it into slices, and then serve with potatoes and asparagus.

Nutrition: Calories: 355 Cal Fat: 12.5 g Carbs: 25 g Protein: 35 g Fiber: 6 g

• <u>Lamb Chops with Rosemary and Olive oil</u>

Preparation Time: 10 minutes

Cooking Time: 50 minutes

Servings: 4

Ingredients:

- 12 Lamb loin chops, fat trimmed
- 1 tablespoon chopped rosemary leaves
- Salt as needed for dry brining
- Jeff's original rub as needed
- ¼ cup olive oil

Directions:

1. Take a cookie sheet, place lamb chops on it, sprinkle with salt, and then refrigerate for 2 hours.

2. Meanwhile, take a small bowl, place rosemary leaves in it, stir in oil and let the mixture stand for 1 hour.

3. When ready to cook, switch on the Pellet grill, fill the grill hopper with apple-flavored wood pellets, power the grill on by using the control panel, select 'smoke' on the temperature dial, or set the temperature to 225 degrees F and let it preheat for a minimum of 5 minutes.

4. Meanwhile, brush rosemary-oil mixture on all sides of lamb chops and then sprinkle with Jeff's original rub.

5. When the grill has preheated, open the lid, place lamb chops on the grill grate, shut the grill and smoke for 50 minutes until the internal temperature of lamb chops reach to 138 degrees F.

6. When done, wrap lamb chops in foil, let them rest for 7 minutes and then serve.

Nutrition: Calories: 171.5 Cal Fat: 7.8 g Carbs: 0.4 g Protein: 23.2 g Fiber: 0.1 g

• <u>Boneless Leg of Lamb</u>

Preparation Time: 10 minutes

Cooking Time: 4 hours

Servings: 4

Ingredients:

- 2 1/2 pounds leg of lamb, boneless, fat trimmed

For the Marinade:

- 2 teaspoons minced garlic
- 1 tablespoon ground black pepper

- 2 tablespoons salt
- 1 teaspoon thyme
- 2 tablespoons oregano
- 2 tablespoons olive oil

Directions:

1. Take a small bowl, place all the ingredients for the marinade in it and then stir until combined.
2. Rub the marinade on all sides of lamb, then place it in a large sheet, cover with a plastic wrap and marinate for a minimum of 1 hour in the refrigerator.
3. When ready to cook, switch on the Pellet grill, fill the grill hopper with apple-flavored wood pellets, power the grill on by using the control panel, select 'smoke' on the temperature dial, or set the temperature to 250 degrees F and let it preheat for a minimum of 5 minutes.
4. Meanwhile,
5. When the grill has preheated, open the lid, place the lamb on the grill grate, and shut the grill and smoke for 4 hours until the internal temperature reaches 145 degrees F.
6. When done, transfer lamb to a cutting board, let it stand for 10 minutes, then carve it into slices and serve.

Nutrition: Calories: 213 Cal Fat: 9 g Carbs: 1 g Protein: 29 g Fiber: 0 g

- ## Smoked Lamb Shoulder

Preparation Time: 10 minutes

Cooking Time: 4 hours

Servings: 6

Ingredients:

- 8 pounds lamb shoulder, fat trimmed
- 2 tablespoons olive oil
- Salt as needed

For the Rub:

- 1 tablespoon dried oregano
- 2 tablespoons salt
- 1 tablespoon crushed dried bay leaf
- 1 tablespoon sugar
- 2 tablespoons dried crushed sage
- 1 tablespoon dried thyme
- 1 tablespoon ground black pepper
- 1 tablespoon dried basil
- 1 tablespoon dried rosemary
- 1 tablespoon dried parsley

Directions:

1. Switch on the Pellet grill, fill the grill hopper with cherry flavored wood pellets, power the grill on by using the control panel, select 'smoke' on the temperature dial, or set the temperature to 250 degrees F and let it preheat for a minimum of 5 minutes.
2. Meanwhile, prepare the rub and for this, take a small bowl, place all of its ingredients in it and stir until mixed.

3. Brush lamb with oil and then sprinkle with prepared rub until evenly coated.

4. When the grill has preheated, open the lid, place lamb should on the grill grate fat-side up, shut the grill and smoke for 3 hours.

5. Then change the smoking temperature to 325 degrees F and continue smoking to 1 hour until fat renders, and the internal temperature reaches 195 degrees F.

6. When done, wrap lamb should in aluminum foil and let it rest for 20 minutes.

7. Pull lamb shoulder by using two forks and then serve.

Nutrition: Calories: 300 Cal Fat: 24 g Carbs: 0 g Protein: 19 g Fiber: 0 g

• <u>**Herby Lamb Chops**</u>

Preparation Time: 10 minutes

Cooking Time: 2 hours

Servings: 4

Ingredients:

- 8 lamb chops, each about ¾-inch thick, fat trimmed

For the Marinade:

- 1 teaspoon minced garlic
- Salt as needed
- 1 tablespoon dried rosemary
- Ground black pepper as needed
- ½ tablespoon dried thyme
- 3 tablespoons balsamic vinegar
- 1 tablespoon Dijon mustard

- ½ cup olive oil

Directions:

1. Prepare the marinade and for this, take a small bowl, place all of its ingredients in it and stir until well combined.

2. Place lamb chops in a large plastic bag, pour in marinade, seal the bag, turn it upside down to coat lamb chops with the marinade and let it marinate for a minimum of 4 hours in the refrigerator.

3. When ready to cook, switch on the Pellet grill, fill the grill hopper with flavored wood pellets, power the grill on by using the control panel, select 'smoke' on the temperature dial, or set the temperature to 450 degrees F and let it preheat for a minimum of 5 minutes.

4. Meanwhile, remove lamb chops from the refrigerator and bring them to room temperature.

5. When the grill has preheated, open the lid, place lamb chops on the grill grate, shut the grill and smoke for 5 minutes per side until seared.

6. When done, transfer lamb chops to a dish, let them rest for 5 minutes and then serve.

Nutrition: Calories: 280 Cal Fat: 12.3 g Carbs: 8.3 g Protein: 32.7 g Fiber: 1.2 g

Garlic Rack of Lamb

Preparation Time: 10 minutes

Cooking Time: 3 hours

Servings: 4

Ingredients:

- 1 rack of lamb, membrane removed

For the Marinade:

- 2 teaspoons minced garlic
- 1 teaspoon dried basil
- 1/3 cup cream sherry
- 1 teaspoon dried oregano
- 1/3 cup Marsala wine
- 1 teaspoon dried rosemary
- ½ teaspoon ground black pepper
- 1/3 cup balsamic vinegar
- 2 tablespoons olive oil

Directions:

1. Prepare the marinade and for this, take a small bowl, place all of its ingredients in it and stir until well combined.
2. Place lamb rack in a large plastic bag, pour in marinade, seal the bag, turn it upside down to coat lamb with the marinade and let it marinate for a minimum of 45 minutes in the refrigerator.
3. When ready to cook, switch on the Pellet grill, fill the grill hopper with flavored wood pellets, power the grill on by using the control panel, select 'smoke' on the temperature dial, or set the temperature to 250 degrees F and let it preheat for a minimum of 5 minutes.
4. Meanwhile,
5. When the grill has preheated, open the lid, place lamb rack on the grill grate, shut the grill, and smoke for 3 hours until the internal temperature reaches 165 degrees F.
6. When done, transfer lamb rack to a cutting board, let it rest for 10 minutes, then cut into slices and serve.

Nutrition: Calories: 210 Cal Fat: 11 g Carbs: 3 g Protein: 25 g Fiber: 1 g

• Sweet & Spicy Chicken Thighs

Preparation Time: 15 minutes

Cooking Time: 15 minutes

Servings: 4

Ingredients:

- 2 garlic cloves, minced
- ¼ cup honey
- 2 tablespoons soy sauce
- ¼ teaspoon red pepper flakes, crushed
- 4 (5-ounce) skinless, boneless chicken thighs
- 2 tablespoons olive oil
- 2 teaspoons sweet rub
- ¼ teaspoon red chili powder
- Ground black pepper, as required

Directions

1. Preheat the Z Grills Wood Pellet Grill & Smoker on grill setting to 400 degrees F.
2. In a small bowl, add garlic, honey, soy sauce and red pepper flakes and with a wire whisk, beat until well combined.
3. Coat chicken thighs with oil and season with sweet rub, chili powder and black pepper generously.
4. Arrange the chicken drumsticks onto the grill and cook for about 15 minutes per

5. In the last 4-5 minutes of cooking, coat drumsticks with garlic mixture.
6. Serve immediately.

Nutrition: Calories 309 Total Fat 12.1 g Saturated Fat 2.9 g Cholesterol 82 mg Sodium 504 mg Total Carbs 18.7 g Fiber 0.2 g Sugar 17.6 g Protein 32.3 g

• Bacon Wrapped Chicken Breasts

Preparation Time: 0 minute

Cooking Time: 3 hours

Servings: 6

Ingredients:

For Brine:

- ¼ cup brown sugar
- ¼ cup kosher salt
- 4 cups water

For Chicken:

- 6 skinless, boneless chicken breasts
- ¼ cup chicken rub
- 18 bacon slices
- 1½ cups BBQ sauce

Directions:

1. For brine: in a large pitcher, dissolve sugar and salt in water.
2. Place the chicken breasts in brine and refrigerate for about 2 hours, flipping once in the middle way.
3. Preheat the Z Grills Wood Pellet Grill & Smoker on grill setting to 230 degrees F.

4. Remove chicken breasts from brine and rinse under cold running water.

5. Season chicken breasts with rub generously.

6. Arrange 3 bacon strips of bacon onto a cutting board, against each other.

7. Place 1 chicken breast across the bacon, leaving enough bacon on the left side to wrap it over just a little.

8. Wrap the bacon strips around chicken breast and secure with toothpicks.

9. Repeat with remaining breasts and bacon slices.

10. Arrange the chicken breasts into pellet grill and cook for about 2½ hours.

11. Coat the breasts with BBQ sauce and cook for about 30 minutes more.

12. Serve immediately.

Nutrition: Calories 481 Total Fat 12.3 g Saturated Fat 4.2 g Cholesterol 41 mg Sodium 3000 mg Total Carbs 32 g Fiber 0.4g Sugar 22.2 g Protein 55.9 g

• **Glazed Chicken Wings**

Preparation Time: 15 minutes

Cooking Time: 2 hours

Servings: 6

Ingredients:

- 2 pounds' chicken wings
- 2 garlic cloves, crushed
- 3 tablespoons hoisin sauce
- 2 tablespoons soy sauce
- 1 teaspoon dark sesame oil
- 1 tablespoon honey
- ½ teaspoon ginger powder
- 1 tablespoon sesame seeds, toasted lightly

Directions:

1. Preheat the Wood Pellet Grill & Smoker on grill setting to 225 degrees F.

2. Arrange the wings onto the lower rack of grill and cook for about 1½ hours.

3. Meanwhile, in a large bowl, mix together remaining all ingredients.

4. Remove wings from grill and place in the bowl of garlic mixture.

5. Coat wings with garlic mixture generously.

6. Now, set the grill to 375 degrees F.

7. Arrange the coated wings onto a foil-lined baking sheet and sprinkle with sesame seeds.

8. Place the pan onto the lower rack of pellet grill and cook for about 25-30 minutes.

9. Serve immediately.

Nutrition: Calories 336 Total Fat 13 g Saturated Fat 3.3 g Cholesterol 135 mg Sodium 560 mg Total Carbs 7.6 g Fiber 0.5 g Sugar 5.2 g Protein 44.7 g

Chicken Casserole

Preparation Time: 15 minutes

Cooking Time: 55 minutes

Servings: 8

Ingredients:

- 2 (15-ounce) cans cream of chicken soup
- 2 cups milk
- 2 tablespoons unsalted butter
- ¼ cup all-purpose flour
- 1 pound skinless, boneless chicken thighs, chopped
- ½ cup hatch chiles, chopped
- 2 medium onions, chopped
- 1 tablespoon fresh thyme, chopped
- Salt and ground black pepper, as required
- 1 cup cooked bacon, chopped
- 1 cup tater tots

Directions:

1. Preheat the Wood Pellet Grill & Smoker on grill setting to 400 degrees F.
2. In a large bowl, mix together chicken soup and milk.
3. In a skillet, melt butter over medium heat.
4. Slowly, add flour and cook for about 1-2 minutes or until smooth, stirring continuously.
5. Slowly, add soup mixture, beating continuously until smooth.
6. Cook until mixture starts to thicken, stirring continuously.
7. Stir in remaining ingredients except bacon and simmer for about 10-15 minutes.
8. Stir in bacon and transfer mixture into a 2½-quart casserole dish.
9. Place tater tots on top of casserole evenly.
10. Arrange the pan onto the grill and cook for about 30-35 minutes.
11. Serve hot.

Nutrition: Calories 440 Total Fat 25.8 g Saturated Fat 9.3 g Cholesterol 86 mg Sodium 1565 mg Total Carbs 22.2 g Fiber 1.5 g Sugar 4.6 g Protein 28.9 g

Buttered Turkey

Preparation Time: 15 minutes

Cooking Time: 4 hours

Servings: 16

Ingredients:

- ½ pound butter, softened
- 2 tablespoons fresh thyme, chopped
- 2 fresh rosemary, chopped
- 6 garlic cloves, crushed
- 1 (20-pound) whole turkey, neck and giblets removed
- Salt and ground black pepper, as required

Directions:

1. Preheat the Z Grills Wood Pellet Grill & Smoker on smoke setting to 300 degrees F, using charcoal.

2. In a bowl, place butter, fresh herbs, garlic, salt and black pepper and mix well.

3. With your fingers, separate the turkey skin from breast to create a pocket.

4. Stuff the breast pocket with ¼-inch thick layer of butter mixture.

5. Season the turkey with salt and black pepper evenly.

6. Arrange the turkey onto the grill and cook for 3-4 hours.

7. Remove turkey from pallet grill and place onto a cutting board for about 15-20 minutes before carving.

8. With a sharp knife, cut the turkey into desired-sized pieces and serve.

Nutrition: Calories 965 Total Fat 52 g Saturated Fat 19.9 g Cholesterol 385 mg Sodium 1916 mg Total Carbs 0.6 g Fiber 0.2 g Sugar 0 g Protein 106.5 g

• **Glazed Turkey Breast**

Preparation Time: 15 minutes

Cooking Time: 4 hours

Servings: 6

Ingredients:

- ½ cup honey
- ¼ cup dry sherry
- 1 tablespoon butter
- 2 tablespoons fresh lemon juice
- Salt, as required
- 1 (3-3½-pound) skinless, boneless turkey breast

Directions:

1. In a small pan, place honey, sherry and butter over low heat and cook until the mixture becomes smooth, stirring continuously.

2. Remove from heat and stir in lemon juice and salt. Set aside to cool.

3. Transfer the honey mixture and turkey breast in a sealable bag.

4. Seal the bag and shake to coat well.

5. Refrigerate for about 6-10 hours.

6. Preheat the Wood Pellet Grill & Smoker on grill setting to 225-250 degrees F.

7. Place the turkey breast onto the grill and cook for about 2½-4 hours or until desired doneness.

8. Remove turkey breast from pallet grill and place onto a cutting board for about 15-20 minutes before slicing.

9. With a sharp knife, cut the turkey breast into desired-sized slices and serve.

Nutrition: Calories 443 Total Fat 11.4 g Saturated Fat 4.8 g Cholesterol 159 mg Sodium 138 mg Total Carbs 23.7 g Fiber 0.1 g Sugar 23.4 g Protein 59.2 g

• Crispy Duck

Preparation Time: 15 minutes

Cooking Time: 4 hours 5 minutes

Servings: 6

Ingredients:

- ¾ cup honey
- ¾ cup soy sauce
- ¾ cup red wine
- 1 teaspoon paprika
- 1½ tablespoons garlic salt
- Ground black pepper, as required
- 1 (5-pound) whole duck, giblets removed and trimmed

Directions:

1. Preheat the Wood Pellet Grill & Smoker on grill setting to 225-250 degrees F.
2. In a bowl, add all ingredients except for duck and mix until well combined.
3. With a fork, poke holes in the skin of the duck.
4. Coat the duck with honey mixture generously.
5. Arrange duck in pellet gill, breast side down and cook for about 4 hours, coating with honey mixture one after 2 hours.
6. Remove the duck from grill and place onto a cutting board for about 15 minutes before carving.
7. With a sharp knife, cut the duck into desired-sized pieces and serve.

Nutrition: Calories 878 Total Fat 52.1 g Saturated Fat 13.9 g Cholesterol 3341 mg Sodium 2300 mg
Total Carbs 45.4 g Fiber 0.7 g Sugar 39.6 g Protein 51 g

• Jerked Up Tilapia

Preparation Time: 20 minutes

Cooking Time: 45 minutes

Serving: 8

Ingredients:

- 5 cloves of garlic
- 1 small sized onion
- 3 Jalapeno Chiles
- 3 teaspoon of ground ginger
- 3 tablespoon of light brown sugar
- 3 teaspoon of dried thyme
- 2 teaspoons of salt
- 2 teaspoons of ground cinnamon
- 1 teaspoon of black pepper
- 1 teaspoon of ground allspice
- ¼ teaspoon of cayenne pepper
- 4 -6 ounce of tilapia fillets
- ¼ cup of olive oil
- 1 cup of sliced up carrots
- 1 bunch of whole green onions
- 2 tablespoon of whole allspice

Directions:

1. Take a blending bowl and combine the first 11 of the listed ingredients and puree them nicely using your blender or food processor

2. Add the fish pieces in a large-sized zip bag and toss in the pureed mixture alongside olive oil

3. Seal it up and press to make sure that the fish is coated well

4. Let it marinate in your fridge for at least 30 minutes to 1 hour

5. Take your drip pan and add water, cover with aluminum foil. Pre-heat your smoker to 225 degrees F

6. Use water fill water pan halfway through and place it over drip pan. Add wood chips to the side tray

7. Take a medium-sized bowl and toss in some pecan wood chips and soak them underwater alongside whole allspice

8. Prepare an excellent 9x 13-inch foil pan by poking a dozen holes and spraying it with non-stick cooking spray

9. Spread out the carrots, green onions across the bottom of the pan

10. Arrange the fishes on top of them

11. Place the container in your smoker

12. Smoke for about 45 minutes making sure to add more chips after every 15 minutes until the internal temperature of the fish rises to 145 degrees Fahrenheit

13. Serve hot

Nutrition: Calories: 347 Fats: 19g Carbs: 18g Fiber: 1g

• **Premium Salmon Nuggets**

Preparation Time: 20 minutes +marinate time

Cooking Time: 1-2 hours

Servings: 8

Ingredients:

- 3 cups of packed brown sugar
- 1 cup of salt
- 1 tablespoon of onion, minced
- 2 teaspoons of chipotle seasoning
- 2 teaspoons of fresh ground black pepper
- 1 garlic clove, minced
- 1-2 pound of salmon fillets, cut up into bite-sized portions

Directions:

1. Take a large-sized bowl and stir in brown sugar, salt, chipotle seasoning, onion, garlic and pepper

2. Transfer salmon to a large shallow marinating dish

3. Pour dry marinade over fish and cover, refrigerate overnight

4. Take your drip pan and add water, cover with aluminum foil. Pre-heat your smoker to 180 degrees F

5. Use water fill water pan halfway through and place it over drip pan. Add wood chips to the side tray

6. Rinse the salmon chunks thoroughly and remove salt

7. Transfer them to grill rack and smoke for 1-2 hours

8. Remove the heat and enjoy it!

Nutrition: Calories: 120 Fats: 18g Carbs: 3g Fiber: 2g

• <u>Creative Sablefish</u>

Preparation Time: 15 minutes

Cooking Time: 3 hours

Servings: 8

Ingredients:

- 2-3 pounds of sablefish fillets
- 1 cup of kosher salts
- ¼ cup of sugar
- 2 tablespoon of garlic powder
- Honey for glazing
- Sweet paprika for dusting

Directions:

1. Take a bowl and mix salt, garlic powder, and sugar
2. Pour on a healthy layer of your mix into a lidded plastic tub, large enough to hold the fish
3. Cut up the fillet into pieces
4. Gently massage the salt mix into your fish meat and place them with the skin side down on to the salt mix in the plastic tub
5. Cover up the container and keep it in your fridge for as many hours as the fish weighs
6. Remove the sablefish from the tub and place it under cold water for a while
7. Pat, it dries using a kitchen towel and puts it back to the fridge, keep it uncovered overnight
8. Take your drip pan and add water, cover with aluminum foil. Pre-heat your smoker to 225 degrees F
9. Use water fill water pan halfway through and place it over drip pan. Add wood chips to the side tray
10. Smoke for 2-3 hours
11. After the first hour of smoking, make sure to baste the fish with honey and keep repeating this after every hour
12. One done, move the fish to a cooling rack and baste it with honey one last time
13. Let it cool for about an hour
14. Use tweezers to pull out the bone pins
15. Dust the top with some paprika and wait for 30 minutes to let the paprika sink in
16. Put the fish in your fridge
17. Serve hot or chilled!

Nutrition: Calories: 171 Fats: 10g Carbs: 13g Fiber: 1g

• <u>Halibut Delight</u>

Preparation Time: 4-6 hours

Cooking Time: 15 minutes

Servings: 4-6

Ingredients:

- ½ a cup of salt
- ½ a cup of brown sugar
- 1 teaspoon of smoked paprika

- 1 teaspoon of ground cumin
- 2 pound of halibut
- 1/3 cup of mayonnaise

Directions:

1. Take a small bowl and add salt, brown sugar, cumin, and paprika
2. Coat the halibut well and cover, refrigerate for 4-6 hours
3. Take your drip pan and add water, cover with aluminum foil. Pre-heat your smoker to 200 degrees F
4. Use water fill water pan halfway through and place it over drip pan. Add wood chips to the side tray
5. Remove the fish from refrigerator and rinse it well, pat it dry
6. Rub the mayonnaise on the fish
7. Transfer the halibut to smoker and smoke for 2 hours until the internal temperature reaches 120 degrees Fahrenheit

Nutrition: Calories: 375 Fats: 21g Carbs: 10g Fiber: 2g

• Roast Rack of Lamb

Preparation Time: 10 minutes

Cooking Time: 1 hour

Servings: 6-8

Ingredients:

- Wood Pellet Flavor: Alder
- 1 (2-pound) rack of lamb
- 1 batch Rosemary-Garlic Lamb Seasoning

Directions:

1. Supply your smoker with wood pellets and follow the manufacturer's specific start-up procedure. Preheat the grill to 450°F.
2. Using a boning knife, score the bottom fat portion of the rib meat.
3. Using your hands, rub the rack of lamb with the lamb seasoning, making sure it penetrates into the scored fat.
4. Place the rack directly on the grill grate and smoke until its internal temperature reaches 145F.
5. Take off the rack from the grill and let it rest for 20 to 30 minutes, before slicing into individual ribs to serve.

Nutrition: Calories: 50 Carbs: 4g Fiber: 2g Fat: 2.5g Protein: 2g

• Ultimate Lamb Burgers

Preparation Time: 20 minutes

Cooking Time: 30 minutes

Servings: 4

Ingredients:

Pellets: Apple

Burger:

- 2 lbs. ground lamb
- 1 jalapeño
- 6 scallions, diced
- 2 tablespoons mint
- 2 tablespoons dill, minced
- 3 cloves garlic, minced
- Salt and pepper
- 4 brioche buns

- 4 slices manchego cheese

Sauce:

- 1 cup mayonnaise
- 2 teaspoons lemon juice
- 2 cloves garlic
- 1 bell pepper, diced
- salt and pepper

Directions

1. When ready to cook, turn your smoker to 400F and preheat.
2. Add the mint, scallions, salt, garlic, dill, jalapeño, lamb, and pepper to the mixing bowl.
3. Form the lamb mixture into eight patties.
4. Lay the pepper on the grill and cook for 20 minutes.
5. Take the pepper from the grill and place it in a bag, and seal. After ten minutes, remove pepper from the bag, remove seeds and peel the skin.
6. Add the garlic, lemon juice, mayo, roasted red pepper, salt, and pepper and process until smooth. Serve alongside the burger.
7. Lay the lamb burgers on the grill, and cook for five minutes per side, then place in the buns with a slice of cheese, and serve with the homemade sauce.

Nutrition: Calories: 50 Carbs: 4g Fiber: 2g Fat: 2.5g Protein: 2g

• **Citrus- Smoked Trout**

Preparation Time: 10 minutes

Cooking Time: 1 to 2 hours

Servings: 6 to 8

Ingredients:

- 6 to 8 skin-on rainbow trout, cleaned and scaled
- 1-gallon orange juice
- ½ cup packed light brown sugar
- ¼ cup salt
- 1 tablespoon freshly ground black pepper
- Nonstick spray, oil, or butter, for greasing
- 1 tablespoon chopped fresh parsley
- 1 lemon, sliced

Directions:

1. Fillet the fish and pat dry with paper towels
2. Pour the orange juice into a large container with a lid and stir in the brown sugar, salt, and pepper
3. Place the trout in the brine, cover, and refrigerate for 1 hour
4. Cover the grill grate with heavy-duty aluminum foil. Poke holes in the foil and spray with cooking spray
5. Supply your smoker with wood pellets and follow the manufacturer's specific start-up procedure. Preheat, with the lid closed, to 225°F
6. Remove the trout from the brine and pat dry. Arrange the fish on the foil-

covered grill grate, close the lid, and smoke for 1 hour 30 minutes to 2 hours, or until flaky

7. Remove the fish from the heat. Serve garnished with the fresh parsley and lemon slices.

Nutrition: Calories: 220, Protein: 33 g Fat: 4 g, Carbohydrates: 17 g,

• Sunday Supper Salmon with Olive Tapenade

Preparation Time: 1 hour and 20 minutes

Cooking Time: 1 to 2 hours

Servings: 10 to 12

Ingredients:

- 2 cups packed light brown sugar
- ½ cup salt
- ¼ cup maple syrup
- ⅓ cup crab boil seasoning
- 1 (3- to 5-pound) whole salmon fillet, skin removed
- ¼ cup extra-virgin olive oil
- 1 (15-ounce) can pitted green olives, drained
- 1 (15-ounce) can pitted black olives, drained
- 3 tablespoons jarred sun-dried tomatoes, drained
- 3 tablespoons chopped fresh basil
- 1 tablespoon dried oregano
- 2 tablespoons freshly squeezed lemon juice
- 2 tablespoons jarred capers, drained
- 2 tablespoons chopped fresh parsley, plus more for sprinkling

Directions:

1. In a medium bowl, combine the brown sugar, salt, maple syrup, and crab boil seasoning.

2. Rub the paste all over the salmon and place the fish in a shallow dish. Cover and marinate in the refrigerator for at least 8 hours or overnight.

3. Remove the salmon from dish, rinse, and pat dry, and let stand for 1 hour to take off the chill.

4. Meanwhile, in a food processor, pulse the olive oil, green olives, black olives, sun-dried tomatoes, basil, oregano, lemon juice, capers, and parsley to a chunky consistency. Refrigerate the tapenade until ready to serve.

5. Supply your smoker with wood pellets and follow the manufacturer's specific start-up procedure. Preheat, with the lid closed, to 250°F.

6. Place the salmon on the grill grate (or on a cedar plank on the grill grate), close the lid, and smoke for 1 to 2 hours, or until the internal temperature reaches 140°F to 145°F. When the fish flakes easily with a fork, it's done.

7. Remove the salmon from the heat and sprinkle with parsley. Serve with the olive tapenade.

Nutrition: Calories: 240; Proteins: 23g; Carbs: 3g; Fat: 16g

• <u>Grilled Tuna</u>

Preparation Time: 20 minutes

Cooking Time: 4 hours

Servings: 6

Ingredients:

- Albacore tuna fillets – 6, each about 8 ounces
- Salt – 1 cup
- Brown sugar – 1 cup
- Orange, zested – 1
- Lemon, zested – 1

Directions:

1. Before preheating the grill, brine the tuna, and for this, prepare brine stirring together all of its ingredients until mixed.
2. Take a large container, layer tuna fillets in it, covering each fillet with it, and then let them sit in the refrigerator for 6 hours.
3. Then remove tuna fillets from the brine, rinse well, pat dry and cool in the refrigerator for 30 minutes.
4. When the grill has preheated, place tuna fillets on the grilling rack and let smoke for 3 hours, turning halfway.
5. Check the fire after one hour of smoking and add more wood pallets if required.
6. Then switch temperature of the grill to 225 degrees F and continue grilling for another 1 hour until tuna has turned nicely golden and fork-tender.
7. Serve immediately.

Nutrition: Calories: 311; Fiber: 3 g; Saturated Fat: 1.2 g; Protein: 45 g; Carbs: 11 g; Total Fat: 8.8 g; Sugar: 1.3 g

• <u>Grilled Swordfish</u>

Preparation Time: 10 minutes

Cooking Time: 18 minutes

Servings: 4

Ingredients:

- Swordfish fillets – 4
- Salt – 1 tablespoon
- Ground black pepper – ¾ tablespoon
- Olive oil – 2 tablespoons
- Ears of corn – 4
- Cherry tomatoes – 1 pint
- Cilantro, chopped – 1/3 cup
- Medium red onion, peeled, diced – 1
- Serrano pepper, minced – 1
- Lime, juiced – 1
- Salt – ½ teaspoon
- Ground black pepper – ¼ teaspoon

Directions:

1. In the meantime, prepare fillets and for this, brush them with oil and then season with salt and black pepper.
2. Prepare the corn, and for this, brush with olive oil and season with ¼ teaspoon each of salt and black pepper.
3. When the grill has preheated, place fillets on the grilling rack along with corns and grill corn for 15 minutes until light brown and fillets for 18 minutes until fork tender.
4. When corn has grilled, cut kernels from it, place them into a medium bowl, add remaining ingredients for the salsa and stir until mixed.
5. When fillets have grilled, divide them evenly among plates, top with corn salsa and then serve.

Nutrition: Calories: 311; Total Fat: 8.8 g; Saturated Fat: 1.2 g; Fiber: 3 g; Protein: 45 g; Sugar: 1.3 g Carbs: 11 g;

- ## **Lamb Kebabs**

Preparation Time: 15 minutes

Cooking Time: 10 minutes

Servings: 4

Ingredients:

Pellets: Mesquite

- 1/2 tablespoon salt
- 2 tablespoons fresh mint
- 3 lbs. leg of lamb
- 1/2 cup lemon juice
- 1 tablespoon lemon zest
- 15 apricots, pitted
- 1/2 tablespoon cilantro
- 2 teaspoons black pepper
- 1/2 cup olive oil
- 1 teaspoon cumin
- 2 red onion

Directions:

1. Combine the olive oil, pepper, lemon juice, mint, salt, lemon zest, cumin, and cilantro. Add lamb leg, then place in the refrigerator overnight.
2. Remove the lamb from the marinade, cube them, and then thread onto the skewer with the apricots and onions.
3. When ready to cook, turn your smoker to 400F and preheat.
4. Lay the skewers on the grill and cook for ten minutes.
5. Remove from the grill and serve.

Nutrition: Calories: 50 Carbs: 4g Fiber: 2g Fat: 2.5g Protein: 2g

• Grilled Carrots

Preparation Time: 5 Minutes

Cooking Time: 20 Minutes

Servings: 6

Ingredients

- 1 lb. carrots, large
- 1/2 tbsp. salt
- 6 oz. butter
- 1/2 tbsp. black pepper
- Fresh thyme

Direction

1. Thoroughly wash the carrots and do not peel. Pat them dry and coat with olive oil.
2. Add salt to your carrots.
3. Meanwhile, preheat a pellet grill to 350°F.
4. Now place your carrots directly on the grill or on a raised rack.
5. Close and cook for about 20 minutes.
6. While carrots cook, cook butter in a saucepan, small, over medium heat until browned. Stir constantly to avoid it from burning. Remove from heat.
7. Remove carrots from the grill onto a plate then drizzle with browned butter.
8. Add pepper and splash with thyme.
9. Serve and enjoy.

Nutrition: Calories 250, Total fat 25g, Saturated fat 15g, Total Carbs 6g, Net Carbs 4g, Protein 1g, Sugars 3g, Fiber 2g, Sodium 402mg, Potassium 369mg

• Grilled Brussels Sprouts

Preparation Time: 15 Minutes

Cooking Time: 20 Minutes

Servings: 8

Ingredients

- 1/2 lb. bacon, grease reserved
- 1 lb. Brussels Sprouts
- 1/2 tbsp. pepper
- 1/2 tbsp. salt

Directions:

1. Cook bacon until crispy on a stovetop, reserve its grease then chop into small pieces.
2. Meanwhile, wash the Brussels sprouts, trim off the dry end, and remove dried leaves if any. Half them and set aside.
3. Place 1/4 cup reserved grease in a pan, cast-iron, over medium-high heat.
4. Season the Brussels sprouts with pepper and salt.
5. Brown the sprouts on the pan with the cut side down for about 3-4 minutes.
6. In the meantime, preheat your pellet grill to 350-375°F.

7. Place bacon pieces and browned sprouts into your grill-safe pan.
8. Cook for about 20 minutes.
9. Serve immediately.

Nutrition: Calories 153, Total fat 10g, Saturated fat 3g, Total Carbs 5g, Net Carbs 3g, Protein 11g, Sugars 1g, Fiber 2g, Sodium 622mg, Potassium 497mg

• Wood Pellet Spicy Brisket

Preparation Time: 20 Minutes

Cooking Time: 9 Hours

Servings: 10

Ingredients

- 2 tbsp. garlic powder
- 2 tbsp. onion powder
- 2 tbsp. paprika
- 2 tbsp. chili powder
- 1/3 cup salt
- 1/3 cup black pepper
- 12 lb. whole packer brisket, trimmed
- 1-1/2 cup beef broth

Directions:

1. Set your wood pellet temperature to 225°F. Let preheat for 15 minutes with the lid closed.
2. Meanwhile, mix garlic, onion, paprika, chili, salt, and pepper in a mixing bowl.
3. The brisket generously on all sides.
4. Place the meat on the grill with the fat side down and let it cool until the internal temperature reaches 160°F.

5. Remove the meat from the grill and double wrap it with foil. Return it to the grill and cook until the internal temperature reaches 204°F.
6. Remove from grill, unwrap the brisket and let rest for 15 minutes.
7. Slice and serve.

Nutrition: Calories 270, Total fat 20g, Saturated fat 8g, Total Carbs 3g, Net Carbs 3g, Protein 20g, Sugar 1g, Fiber 0g, Sodium: 1220mg

• Pellet Grill Funeral Potatoes

Preparation Time: 10 Minutes

Cooking Time: 60 Minutes

Servings: 8

Ingredients

- 1, 32 oz., package frozen hash browns
- 1/2 cup cheddar cheese, grated
- 1 can cream of chicken soup
- 1 cup sour cream
- 1 cup Mayonnaise
- 3 cups corn flakes, whole or crushed
- 1/4 cup melted butter

Directions:

1. Preheat your pellet grill to 350°F.
2. Spray a 13 x 9 baking pan, aluminum, using a cooking spray, non-stick.
3. Mix hash browns, cheddar cheese, chicken soup cream, sour cream, and mayonnaise in a bowl, large.

4. Spoon the mixture into a baking pan gently.

5. Mix corn flakes and melted butter then sprinkle over the casserole.

6. Grill for about 1-1/2 hours until potatoes become tender. If the top browns too much, cover using a foil until potatoes are done.

7. Remove from the grill and serve hot.

Nutrition: Calories 403, Total fat 37g, Saturated fat 12g, Total Carbs 14g, Net Carbs 14g, Protein 4g, Sugars 2g, Fiber 0g, Sodium 620mg, Potassium 501mg

• <u>Smoky Caramelized Onions on the Pellet Grill</u>

Preparation Time: 5 Minutes
Cooking Time: 60 Minutes
Servings: 4
Ingredients

- 5 large, sliced onions
- 1/2 cup fat of your choice
- Pinch of Sea salt

Directions:

1. Place all the ingredients into a pan. For a deep rich brown caramelized onion, cook them off for about 1hour on a stovetop.

2. Keep the grill temperatures not higher than 250 - 275ºF.

3. Now transfer the pan into the grill.

4. Cook for about 1-1½ hours until brown in color. Check and stir with a spoon, wooden, after every 15

minutes. Make sure not to run out of pellets.

5. Now remove from the grill and season with more salt if necessary.

6. Serve immediately or place in a refrigerator for up to 1 week.

Nutrition: Calories 286, Total fat 25.8g, Saturated fat 10.3g, Total Carbs 12.8g, Net Carbs 9.8g, Protein 1.5g, Sugars 5.8g, Fiber 3g Sodium 6mg, Potassium 201mg

• <u>Hickory Smoked Green Beans</u>

Preparation Time: 15 Minutes
Cooking Time: 3 Hours
Servings: 10
Ingredients

- 6 cups fresh green beans, halved and ends cut off
- 2 cups chicken broth
- 1 tbsp. pepper, ground
- 1/4 tbsp. salt
- 2 tbsp. apple cider vinegar
- 1/4 cup diced onion
- 6-8 bite-size bacon slices
- **Optional:** sliced almonds

Directions:

1. Add green beans to a colander then rinse well. Set aside.

2. Place chicken broth, pepper, salt, and apple cider in a pan, large. Add green beans.

3. Blanch over medium heat for about 3-4 minutes then remove from heat.

4. Transfer the mixture into an aluminum pan, disposable. Make sure all mixture goes into the pan so do not drain them.

5. Place bacon slices over the beans and place the pan into the wood pellet smoker,

6. Smoke for about 3 hours uncovered.

7. Remove from the smoker and top with almonds slices.

8. Serve immediately.

Nutrition: Calories 57, Total fat 3g, Saturated fat 1g, Total Carbs 6g, Net Carbs 4g, Protein 4g, Sugars 2g, Fiber 2g, Sodium 484mg, Potassium 216mg

• **Smoked Corn on the Cob**

Preparation Time: 5 Minutes

Cooking Time: 60 Minutes

Servings: 4

Ingredients

- 4 corn ears, husk removed
- 4 tbsp. olive oil
- Pepper and salt to taste

Directions:

1. Preheat your smoker to 225ºF.
2. Meanwhile, brush your corn with olive oil. Season with pepper and salt.
3. Place the corn on a smoker and smoke for about 1 hour 15 minutes.
4. Remove from the smoker and serve.
5. Enjoy!

Nutrition: Calories 180, Total fat 7g, Saturated fat 4g, Total Carbs 31g, Net Carbs 27g, protein 5g, Sugars 5g, Fiber 4g, Sodium 23mg, Potassium 416mg

• **Easy Grilled Corn**

Preparation Time: 5 Minutes

Cooking Time: 40 Minutes

Servings: 6

Ingredients

- 6 fresh corn ears, still in the husk
- Pepper, salt, and butter

Directions:

1. Preheat your wood pellet grill to 375-400ºF.
2. Cut off the large silk ball from the corn top and any hanging or loose husk pieces.
3. Place the corn on your grill grate directly and do not peel off the husk.
4. Grill for about 30-40 minutes. Flip a few times to grill evenly all round.
5. Transfer the corn on a platter, serve, and let guests peel their own.
6. Now top with pepper, salt, and butter.
7. Enjoy!

Nutrition: Calories 77, Total fat 1g, Saturated fat 1g, Total carbs 17g, Net carbs 15g, Protein 3g, Sugars 6g, Fiber 2g, Sodium 14mg, Potassium 243mg

• Seasoned Potatoes on Smoker

Preparation Time: 10 Minutes
Cooking Time: 45 Minutes
Servings: 6
Ingredients

- 1-1/2 lb. creamer potatoes
- 2 tbsp. olive oil
- 1 tbsp. garlic powder
- 1/4 tbsp. oregano
- 1/2 tbsp. thyme, dried
- 1/2 tbsp. parsley, dried

Directions:

1. Preheat your pellet grill to 350ºF.
2. Spray an 8x8 inch foil pan using non-stick spray.
3. Mix all ingredients in the pan and place it into the grill.
4. Cook for about 45 minutes until potatoes are done. Stir after every 15 minutes.
5. Serve and enjoy!

Nutrition: Calories 130, Total fat 4g, Saturated fat 2g, Total Carbs 20g, Net Carbs 18g, Protein 2g, Sugars 2g, Fiber 2g, Sodium 7mg, Potassium 483mg

• Atomic Buffalo Turds

Preparation Time: 30-45 minutes
Cooking Time: 1.5 hours to 2 hours
Servings: 6-10
Recommended pellets: Hickory, blend

Ingredients:

- 10 Medium Jalapeno Pepper
- 8 oz. regular cream cheese at room temperature
- ¾Cup Monterey Jack and Cheddar Cheese Blend Shred (optional)
- 1 teaspoon smoked paprika
- 1 tsp garlic powder
- 1/2 teaspoon cayenne pepper
- Teaspoon red pepper flakes (optional)
- 20 smoky sausages
- 10 sliced bacon, cut in half

Directions:

1. Wear food service gloves when using. Jalapeno peppers are washed vertically and sliced. Carefully remove seeds and veins using a spoon or paring knife and discard. Place Jalapeno on a grilled vegetable tray and set aside.
2. In a small bowl, mix cream cheese, shredded cheese, paprika, garlic powder, cayenne pepper if used, and red pepper flakes if used, until thoroughly mixed.
3. Mix cream cheese with half of the jalapeno pepper.
4. Place the Little Smokies sausage on half of the filled jalapeno pepper.
5. Wrap half of the thin bacon around half of each jalapeno pepper.
6. Fix the bacon to the sausage with a toothpick so that the pepper does not

pierce. Place the ABT on the grill tray or pan.

7. Set the wood pellet smoker grill for indirect cooking and preheat to 250 degrees Fahrenheit using hickory pellets or blends.

8. Suck jalapeno peppers at 250 ° F for about 1.5 to 2 hours until the bacon is cooked and crisp.

9. Remove the ABT from the grill and let it rest for 5 minutes before hors d'oeuvres.

• **Smashed Potato Casserole**

Preparation Time: 30-45 minutes

Cooking Time: 45-60 minutes

Servings: 8

Recommended pellet: Optional

Ingredients:

- 8-10 bacon slices
- ¼ cup (½ stick) salt butter or bacon grease
- 1 sliced red onion
- 1 sliced small pepper
- 1 sliced small red pepper
- 1 sliced small pepper
- 3 cups mashed potatoes
- ¾ cup sour cream
- 1.5 teaspoon Texas BBQ Love
- 3 cups of sharp cheddar cheese
- 4 cups hashed brown potato

Directions:

1. Cook the bacon in a large skillet over medium heat until both sides are crispy for about 5 minutes. Set the bacon aside.

2. Transfer the rendered bacon grease to a glass container.

3. In the same large frying pan, heat the butter or bacon grease over medium heat and fry the red onions and peppers until they become al dente. Set aside.

4. Spray a 9 x 11-inch casserole dish with a non-stick cooking spray and spread the mashed potatoes to the bottom of the dish.

5. Layer sour cream on mashed potatoes and season with Texas BBQ Love.

6. Layer the stir-fried vegetables on the potatoes and pour butter or bacon grease into a pan.

7. Sprinkle 1.5 cups of sharp cheddar cheese followed by frozen hash brown potatoes.

8. Spoon the remaining butter or bacon grease from the stir-fried vegetables over the hash browns and place the crushed bacon.

9. Place the remaining 1.5 cups of sharp cheddar cheese and cover the casserole dish with a lid or aluminum foil.

10. Using the selected pellets, set up a wood pellet smoking grill for indirect cooking and preheat to 350 ° F.

11. Bake the crushed potato casserole for 45-60 minutes until the cheese foams.

12. Rest for 10 minutes before eating.

• <u>Mushrooms Stuffed with Crab Meat</u>

Preparation Time: 20 minutes

Cooking Time: 30-45 minutes

Servings: 4-6

Recommended pellet: Optional

Ingredients:

- 6 medium-sized portobello mushrooms
- Extra virgin olive oil
- 1/3 Grated parmesan cheese cup
- Club Beat Staffing:
- 8 oz. fresh crab meat or canned or imitation crab meat
- 2 tablespoons extra virgin olive oil
- 1/3 Chopped celery
- Chopped red peppers
- ½ cup chopped green onion
- ½ cup Italian breadcrumbs
- ½Cup mayonnaise
- 8 oz. cream cheese at room temperature
- 1/2 teaspoon of garlic
- 1 tablespoon dried parsley
- Grated parmesan cheese cup
- 1 1 teaspoon of Old Bay seasoning
- ¼ teaspoon of kosher salt
- ¼ teaspoon black pepper

Directions:

1. Clean the mushroom cap with a damp paper towel. Cut off the stem and save it.

2. Remove the brown gills from the bottom of the mushroom cap with a spoon and discard.

3. Prepare crab meat stuffing. If you are using canned crab meat, drain, rinse, and remove shellfish.

4. Heat the olive oil in a frying pan over medium high heat. Add celery, peppers and green onions and fry for 5 minutes. Set aside for cooling.

5. Gently pour the chilled sauteed vegetables and the remaining ingredients into a large bowl.

6. Cover and refrigerate crab meat stuffing until ready to use.

7. Put the crab mixture in each mushroom cap and make a mound in the center.

8. Sprinkle extra virgin olive oil and sprinkle parmesan cheese on each stuffed mushroom cap. Put the mushrooms in a 10 x 15-inch baking dish.

9. Use the pellets to set the wood pellet smoker grill to indirect heating and preheat to 375 ° F.

10. Bake for 30-45 minutes until the filling becomes hot (165 degrees Fahrenheit as measured by an instant-read digital thermometer)

and the mushrooms begin to release juice.

• **Bacon Wrapped with Asparagus**

Preparation Time: 15 minutes

Cooking Time: 25-30 minutes

Servings: 4-6

Recommended pellet: Optional

- 1-pound fresh thick asparagus (15-20 spears)
- Extra virgin olive oil
- 5 sliced bacon
- 1 teaspoon of Western Love or salted pepper

Directions:

1. Cut off the wooden ends of the asparagus and make them all the same length.
2. Divide the asparagus into a bundle of three spears and split with olive oil. Wrap each bundle with a piece of bacon, then dust with seasonings or salt pepper for seasoning.
3. Set the wood pellet smoker grill for indirect cooking and place a Teflon coated fiberglass mat on the grate (to prevent asparagus from sticking to the grate grate). Preheat to 400 degrees Fahrenheit using all types of pellets. The grill can be preheated during asparagus Preparation Guide.
4. Bake the asparagus wrapped in bacon for 25-30 minutes until the asparagus

is soft and the bacon is cooked and crispy.

• **Bacon Cheddar Slider**

Preparation Time: 30 minutes

Cooking Time: 15 minutes

Servings: 6-10 (1-2 sliders each as an appetizer)

Recommended pellet: Optional

Ingredients:

- 1-pound ground beef (80% lean)
- 1/2 teaspoon of garlic salt
- 1/2 teaspoon salt
- 1/2 teaspoon of garlic
- 1/2 teaspoon onion
- 1/2 teaspoon black pepper
- 6 bacon slices, cut in half
- ½Cup mayonnaise
- 2 teaspoons of creamy wasabi (optional)
- 6 (1 oz.) sliced sharp cheddar cheese, cut in half (optional)
- Sliced red onion
- ½Cup sliced kosher dill pickles
- 12 mini breads sliced horizontally
- Ketchup

Directions:

1. Place ground beef, garlic salt, seasoned salt, garlic powder, onion powder and black hupe pepper in a medium bowl.
2. Divide the meat mixture into 12 equal parts, shape into small thin round

patties (about 2 ounces each) and save.

3. Cook the bacon on medium heat over medium heat for 5-8 minutes until crunchy. Set aside.

4. To make the sauce, mix the mayonnaise and horseradish in a small bowl, if used.

5. Set up a wood pellet smoker grill for direct cooking to use griddle accessories. Contact the manufacturer to see if there is a griddle accessory that works with the wooden pellet smoker grill.

6. Spray a cooking spray on the griddle cooking surface for best non-stick results.

7. Preheat wood pellet smoker grill to 350 ° F using selected pellets. Griddle surface should be approximately 400 ° F.

8. Grill the putty for 3-4 minutes each until the internal temperature reaches 160 ° F.

9. If necessary, place a sharp cheddar cheese slice on each patty while the patty is on the griddle or after the patty is removed from the griddle. Place a small amount of mayonnaise mixture, a slice of red onion, and a hamburger pate in the lower half of each roll. Pickled slices, bacon, and ketchup.

• <u>**Garlic Parmesan Wedge**</u>

Preparation Time: 15 minutes

Cooking Time: 30-35 minutes

Servings: 3

Recommended pellet: Optional

- 3 large russet potatoes
- ¼ cup of extra virgin olive oil
- 1 tsp salt
- ¾ teaspoon black hu pepper
- 2 tsp garlic powder
- ¾ cup grated parmesan cheese
- 3 tablespoons of fresh coriander or flat leaf parsley (optional)
- ½ cup blue cheese or ranch dressing per serving, for soaking (optional)

Directions:

1. Gently rub the potatoes with cold water using a vegetable brush to dry the potatoes.

2. Cut the potatoes in half vertically and cut them in half.

3. Wipe off any water released when cutting potatoes with a paper towel. Moisture prevents wedges from becoming crunchy.

4. Put the potato wedge, olive oil, salt, pepper, and garlic powder in a large bowl and shake lightly by hand to distribute the oil and spices evenly.

5. Place the wedges on a single layer of non-stick grill tray / pan / basket (about 15 x 12 inches).

6. Set the wood pellet r grill for indirect cooking and use all types of wood pellets to preheat to 425 degrees Fahrenheit.

7. Put the grill tray in the preheated smoker grill, roast the potato wedge for 15 minutes, and turn. Roast the potato wedge for an additional 15-20 minutes until the potatoes are soft inside and crispy golden on the outside.

8. Sprinkle potato wedge with parmesan cheese and add coriander or parsley as needed. If necessary, add blue cheese or ranch dressing for the dip.

• Grilled Mushroom Skewers

Preparation Time: 5 Minutes

Cooking Time: 60 Minutes

Servings: 6

Ingredients:

- 16 - oz. 1 lb. Baby Portobello Mushrooms

For the marinade:

- ¼ - cup olive oil
- ¼ - cup lemon juice
- Small handful of parsley
- 1 - tsp sugar
- 1 - tsp salt
- ¼ - tsp pepper
- ¼ - tsp cayenne pepper
- 1 to 2 - garlic cloves
- 1 - Tbsp. balsamic vinegar

What you will need:

- 10 - inch bamboo/wood skewers

Directions:

1. Add the beans to the plate of a lipped container, in an even layer. Shower the softened spread uniformly out ludicrous, and utilizing a couple of tongs tenderly hurl the beans with the margarine until all around covered.

2. Season the beans uniformly, and generously, with salt and pepper.

3. Preheat the smoker to 275 degrees. Include the beans, and smoke 3-4 hours, hurling them like clockwork or until delicate wilted, and marginally seared in spots.

4. Spot 10 medium sticks into a heating dish and spread with water. It's critical to douse the sticks for in any event 15 minutes (more is better) or they will consume too rapidly on the flame broil.

5. Spot the majority of the marinade fixings in a nourishment processor and heartbeat a few times until marinade is almost smooth.

6. Flush your mushrooms and pat dry. Cut each mushroom down the middle, so each piece has half of the mushroom stem.

7. Spot the mushroom parts into an enormous gallon-size Ziploc sack, or a medium bowl and pour in the marinade. Shake the pack until the

majority of the mushrooms are equally covered in marinade. Refrigerate and marinate for 30mins to 45mins.

8. Preheat your barbecue about 300F

9. Stick the mushrooms cozily onto the bamboo/wooden sticks that have been dousing (no compelling reason to dry the sticks). Piercing the mushrooms was a bit of irritating from the outset until I got the hang of things.

10. I've discovered that it's least demanding to stick them by bending them onto the stick. In the event that you simply drive the stick through, it might make the mushroom break.

11. Spot the pierced mushrooms on the hot barbecue for around 3mins for every side, causing sure the mushrooms don't consume to the flame broil. The mushrooms are done when they are delicate; as mushrooms ought to be Remove from the barbecue. Spread with foil to keep them warm until prepared to serve

Nutrition: Calories: 230 Carbs: 10g Fat: 20g Protein: 5g

• Caprese Tomato Salad

Preparation Time: 5 Minutes
Cooking Time: 60 Minutes
Servings: 4
Ingredients:

- 3 - cups halved multicolored cherry tomatoes
- 1/8 - teaspoon kosher salt
- ½ - cup fresh basil leaves
- 1 - tablespoon extra-virgin olive oil
- 1 - tablespoon balsamic vinegar
- ½ - teaspoon black pepper
- ¼ - teaspoon kosher salt
- 1 - ounce diced fresh mozzarella cheese (about 1/3 cup)

Directions:

1. Join tomatoes and 1/8 tsp. legitimate salt in an enormous bowl. Let represent 5mins. Include basil leaves, olive oil, balsamic vinegar, pepper, 1/4 tsp. fit salt, and mozzarella; toss.

Nutrition: Calories 80 Fat 5.8g Protein 2g Carb 5g Sugars 4g

• Watermelon-Cucumber Salad

Preparation Time: 12 Minutes
Cooking Time: 0 Minutes
Servings: 4
Ingredients:

- 1 - tablespoon olive oil
- 2 - teaspoons fresh lemon juice
- ¼ - teaspoon salt
- 2 - cups cubed seedless watermelon
- 1 - cup thinly sliced English cucumber
- ¼ - cup thinly vertically sliced red onion
- 1 - tablespoon thinly sliced fresh basil

Directions:

1. Consolidate oil, squeeze, and salt in a huge bowl, mixing great. Include watermelon, cucumber, and onion; toss well to coat. Sprinkle plate of mixed greens equally with basil.

Nutrition: Calories 60 Fat 3.5g Protein 0.8g Carb 7.6g

• **Fresh Creamed Corn**

Preparation Time: 5 Minutes

Cooking Time: 30 Minutes

Servings: 4

Ingredients:

- 2 - teaspoons unsalted butter
- 2 - cups fresh corn kernels
- 2 - tablespoons minced shallots
- ¾ - cup 1% low-fat milk
- 2 - teaspoons all-purpose flour
- ¼ - teaspoon salt

Directions:

1. Melt butter in a huge nonstick skillet over medium-excessive warmness.
2. Add corn and minced shallots to pan; prepare dinner 1 minute, stirring constantly.
3. Add milk, flour, and salt to pan; bring to a boil.
4. Reduce warmness to low; cover and cook dinner 4 minutes.

Nutrition: Calories 107 Fat 3.4g Protein 4g Carb 18g

• Spinach Salad with Avocado and Orange

Preparation Time: 5 Minutes

Cooking Time: 20 Minutes

Servings: 4

Ingredients:

- 1 ½ - tablespoons fresh lime juice
- 4 - teaspoons extra-virgin olive oil
- 1 - tablespoon chopped fresh cilantro
- 1/8 - teaspoon kosher salt
- ½ - cup diced peeled ripe avocado
- ½ - cup fresh orange segments
- 1 - (5-ounce) package baby spinach
- 1/8 - teaspoon freshly ground black pepper

Directions:

1. Combine first 4 substances in a bowl, stirring with a whisk.
2. Combine avocado, orange segments, and spinach in a bowl. Add oil combination; toss. Sprinkle salad with black pepper.

Nutrition: Calories 103 Fat 7.3g Sodium 118mg

• Raspberry and Blue Cheese Salad

Preparation Time: 5 Minutes

Cooking Time: 20 Minutes

Servings: 4

Ingredients:

- 1 ½ - tablespoons olive oil
- 1 ½ - teaspoons red wine vinegar
- ¼ - teaspoon Dijon mustard
- 1/8 - teaspoon salt
- 1/8 - teaspoon pepper
- 5 - cups mixed baby greens
- ½ - cup raspberries
- ¼ - cup chopped toasted pecans
- 1 - ounce blue cheese

Directions:

1. Join olive oil, vinegar, Dijon mustard, salt, and pepper.
2. Include blended infant greens; too.
3. Top with raspberries, walnuts, and blue cheddar.

Nutrition: Calories 133 Fat 12.2g Sodium 193mg

• Crunchy Zucchini Chips

Preparation Time: 15 Minutes

Cooking Time: 25 Minutes

Servings: 4

Ingredients:

- 1/3 - cup whole-wheat panko
- 3 - tablespoons uncooked amaranth
- ½ - teaspoon garlic powder
- ¼ - teaspoon kosher salt
- ¼ - teaspoon freshly ground black pepper
- 1 - ounce Parmesan cheese, finely grated
- 12 - ounces zucchini, cut into

- ¼ - inch-thick slices
- 1 - tablespoon olive oil Cooking spray

Directions:

1. Preheat stove to 425°. Join the initial 6 ingre-dients in a shallow dish. Join zucchini and oil in an enormous bowl; toss well to coat. Dig zucchini in panko blend, squeezing tenderly to follow. Spot covered cuts on an ovenproof wire rack covered with cooking shower; place the rack on a preparing sheet or jam move dish.

2. Heat at 425° for 26 minutes or until cooked and fresh. Serve chips right away.

Nutrition: Calories 132 Fat 6.5g Protein 6g Carb 14g Sugars 2g

Grilled Green Onions and Orzo and Sweet Peas

Preparation Time: 5 Minutes
Cooking Time: 15 Minutes
Servings: 4
Ingredients:

- ¾ - cup whole-wheat orzo
- 1 - cup frozen peas
- 1 - bunch green onions, trimmed
- 1 - teaspoon olive oil
- ½ - teaspoon grated lemon rind
- 1 - tablespoon lemon juice
- 1 - teaspoon olive oil
- ¼ - teaspoon salt
- 1 - ounce shaved Montego cheese

Directions:

1. Plan orzo as indicated by way of headings, discarding salt and fat. Include peas throughout most recent 2mins of cooking; channel.

2. Warm a fish fry skillet over high warmness. Toss inexperienced onions with 1 teaspoon olive oil. Cook 2 minutes on each facet. Cleave onions; upload to orzo. Include lemon skin, lemon juice, 1 teaspoon olive oil, and salt; toss. Sprinkle with shaved Manchego cheddar.

Nutrition: Calories 197 Fat 5.6g Sodium 204mg

Tequila Slaw with Lime and Cilantro

Preparation Time: 5 Minutes
Cooking Time: 5 Minutes
Servings: 6
Ingredients:

- ¼ - cup canola mayonnaise (such as Hellmann's)
- 3 - tablespoons fresh lime juice
- 1 - tablespoon silver tequila
- 2 - teaspoons sugar
- ¼ - teaspoon kosher salt
- 1/3 - cup thinly sliced green onions
- ¼- cup chopped fresh cilantro
- 1 - (14-ounce) package coleslaw

Directions:

1. Add the first 5 ingredients in a big bowl. Add remaining ingredients; toss.

Nutrition: Calories 64 Fat 3g Protein 0.8g Carb 6.4g

• <u>Cranberry-Almond Broccoli Salad</u>

Preparation Time: 10 Minutes

Cooking Time: 60 Minutes

Servings: 8

Ingredients:

- ¼ - cup finely chopped red onion
- 1/3 - cup canola mayonnaise
- 3 - tablespoons 2% reduced-fat Greek yogurt
- 1 - tablespoon cider vinegar
- 1 - tablespoon honey
- ¼ - teaspoon salt
- ¼ - teaspoon freshly ground black pepper
- 4 - cups coarsely chopped broccoli florets
- 1/3 - cup slivered almonds, toasted
- 1/3 - cup reduced-sugar dried cranberries
- 4 - center-cut bacon slices, cooked and crumbled

Directions:

1. Absorb red onion cold water for 5 minutes; channel.
2. Consolidate mayonnaise and then 5 fixings (through pepper), blending

admirably with a whisk. Mix in red onion, broccoli, and remaining fixings. Spread and chill 1 hour before serving.

Nutrition: Calories 104 Fat 5.9g Carb 11g Sugars 5g

• <u>Grilled French Dip</u>

Preparation Time: 15 Minutes

Cooking Time: 35 Minutes

Servings: 8 to 12

Ingredients:

- 3 lbs. onions, thinly sliced (yellow)
- 2 tbsp. oil
- 2 tbsp. of Butter
- Salt to taste
- Black pepper to taste
- 1 tsp. Thyme, chopped
- 2 tsp. of Lemon juice
- 1 cup Mayo
- 1 cup of Sour cream

Directions:

1. Preheat the grill to high with closed lid.
2. In a pan combine the oil and butter. Place on the grill to melt. Add 2 tsp. salt and add the onions.
3. Stir well and close the lid of the grill. Cook 30 minutes stirring often.
4. Add the thyme. Cook for an additional 3 minutes. Set aside and add black pepper.

5. Once cooled add lemon juice, mayo, and sour cream. Stir to combine.

6. Serve with veggies or chips. Enjoy!

Nutrition: Calories: 60 Protein: 4g Carbs: 5g Fat: 6g

- ## **Roasted Cashews**

Preparation Time: 15 Minutes

Cooking Time: 12 Minutes

Servings: 6

Ingredients:

- ¼ cup Rosemary, chopped
- 2 ½ tbsp. Butter, melted
- 2 cups Cashews, raw
- ½ tsp. of Cayenne pepper
- 1 tsp. of salt

Directions:

1. Preheat the grill to 350F with closed lid.

2. In a baking dish layer, the nuts. Combine the cayenne, salt rosemary, and butter. Add on top.

3. Grill for 12 minutes.

4. Serve and enjoy!

Nutrition: Calories: 150 Proteins: 5g Carbs: 7g Fat: 15g

- ## **Smoked Jerky**

Preparation Time: 20 Minutes

Cooking Time: 6 Hours

Servings: 6 to 8

Ingredients:

- 1 Flank Steak (3lb.)
- ½ cup of Brown Sugar

- 1 cup of Bourbon
- ¼ cup Jerky rub
- 2 tbsp. of Worcestershire sauce
- 1 can of Chipotle
- ½ cup Cider Vinegar

Directions:

1. Slice the steak into ¼ inch slices.

2. Combine the remaining ingredients in a bowl. Stir well.

3. Place the steak in a plastic bag and add the marinade sauce. Marinade in the fridge overnight.

4. Preheat the grill to 180F with closed lid.

5. Remove the flank from marinade. Place directly on a rack and on the grill.

6. Smoke for 6 hours.

7. Cover them lightly for 1 hour before serving. Store leftovers in the fridge.

Nutrition: Calories: 105 Protein: 14g Carbs 4g: Fat: 3g

- ## **Bacon BBQ Bites**

Preparation Time: 10 Minutes

Cooking Time: 25 Minutes

Servings: 2 to 4

Ingredients:

- 1 tbsp. Fennel, ground
- ½ cup of Brown Sugar
- 1 lb. Slab Bacon, cut into cubes (1 inch)
- 1 tsp. Black pepper
- Salt

Directions:

1. Take an aluminum foil and then fold in half.
2. Preheat the grill to 350F with closed lid.
3. In a bowl combine the black pepper, salt, fennel, and sugar. Stir.
4. Place the pork in the seasoning mixture. Toss to coat. Transfer on the foil.
5. Place the foil on the grill. Bake for 25 minutes, or until crispy and bubbly.
6. Serve and enjoy!

Nutrition: Calories: 300 Protein: 27g Carbs: 4g Fat: 36g

• Smoked Guacamole

Preparation Time: 25 Minutes

Cooking Time: 30 Minutes

Servings: 6 to 8

Ingredients:

- ¼ cup chopped Cilantro
- 7 Avocados, peeled and seeded
- ¼ cup chopped Onion, red
- ¼ cup chopped tomato
- 3 ears corn
- 1 tsp. of Chile Powder
- 1 tsp. of Cumin
- 2 tbsp. of Lime juice
- 1 tbsp. minced Garlic
- 1 Chile, poblano
- Black pepper and salt to taste

Directions:

1. Preheat the grill to 180F with closed lid.
2. Smoke the avocado for 10 min.
3. Set the avocados aside and increase the temperature of the girl to high.
4. Once heated grill the corn and chili. Roast for 20 minutes.
5. Cut the corn. Set aside. Place the chili in a bowl.
6. In a bowl mash the avocados, leave few chunks. Add the remaining ingredients and mix.
7. Serve right away because it is best eaten fresh. Enjoy!

Nutrition: Calories: 51 Protein: 1g Carbs: 3g Fat: 4.5g

• Jalapeno Poppers

Preparation Time: 15 Minutes

Cooking Time: 60 Minutes

Servings: 4 to 6

Ingredients:

- 6 Bacon slices halved
- 12 Jalapenos, medium
- 1 cup grated Cheese
- 8 oz. softened Cream cheese
- 2 tbsp. Poultry seasoning

Directions:

1. Preheat the grill to 180F with closed lid.
2. Cut the jalapenos lengthwise. Clean them from the ribs and seeds.
3. Mix the poultry seasoning, grated cheese, and cream cheese.

4. Fill each jalapeno with the mixture and wrap with 1 half bacon. Place a toothpick to secure it.

5. Increase the temperature of the grill to 375F. Cook for 30 minutes more.

6. Serve and enjoy!

Nutrition: Calories: 60 Protein: 4g Carbs: 2g Fat: 8g

• **Shrimp Cocktail**

Preparation Time: 10 Minutes

Cooking Time: 10 Minutes

Servings: 2 to 4

Ingredients:

- 2 lbs. of Shrimp with tails, deveined
- Black pepper and salt
- 1 tsp. of Old Bay
- 2 tbsp. Oil
- ½ cup of Ketchup
- 1 tbsp. of Lemon Juice
- 2 tbsp. Horseradish, Prepared
- 1 tbsp. of Lemon juice
- For garnish: chopped parsley
- Optional: Hot sauce

Directions:

1. Preheat the grill to 350F with closed lid.

2. Clean the shrimp. Pat dry using paper towels.

3. In a bowl add the shrimp, Old Bay, and oil. Toss to coat. Spread on a baking tray.

4. In the meantime, make the sauce: Combine the lemon juice, horseradish, and ketchup.

5. Serve the shrimp with the sauce and enjoy!

Nutrition: Calories: 80 Protein: 8g Carbs: 5g Fat: 1g

• **Deviled Eggs**

Preparation Time: 15 Minutes

Cooking Time: 30 Minutes

Servings: 4 to 6

Ingredients:

- 3 tsp. diced chives
- 3 tbsp. Mayo
- 7 Eggs, hard - boiled, peeled
- 1 tsp. Cider vinegar
- 1 tsp. Mustard, brown
- 1/8 tsp. Hot sauce
- 2 tbsp. crumbled Bacon
- Black pepper and salt to taste
- For dusting: Paprika

Directions:

1. Preheat the grill to 180F with closed lid.

2. Place the cooked eggs on the grate. Smoke 30 minutes. Set aside and let them cool.

3. Slice the eggs in half lengthwise. Scoop the yolks and transfer into a Ziplock bag.

4. Cut one corner and squeeze the mixture into the egg whites.

5. Top with bacon and dust with paprika.

6. Serve and enjoy! Or chill in the fridge until serving.

Nutrition: Calories: 140 Protein: 6g Carbs: 2g Fat: 6g

• Smoked Summer Sausage

Preparation Time: 15 Minutes

Cooking Time: 4 Hours

Servings: 4 to 6

Ingredients:

- 1 ½ tsp. of Morton Salt
- ½ lb. Ground venison
- ½ lb. of ground Boar
- 1 tbsp. Salt
- ½ tsp. of mustard seeds
- ½ tsp. of Garlic powder
- ½ tsp. of Black pepper

Directions:

1. Add all ingredients into a bowl and mix until combined. Cover the bowl with a plastic bag and let it rest in the fridge overnight

2. Form a log from the mixture and wrap with a plastic wrap. Twist the log's end tightly.

3. Preheat the grill to 225F with closed lit.

4. Grill the meat for 4 hours. Set aside and let it cool for 1 hour.

5. Once cooled wrap and store in the fridge.

6. Serve and enjoy!

Nutrition: Calories: 170 Protein: 8g Carbs 0 Fat: 14g

• Roasted Tomatoes

Preparation Time: 10 Minutes

Cooking Time: 3 Hours

Servings: 2 to 4

Ingredients:

- 3 ripe Tomatoes, large
- 1 tbsp. black pepper
- 2 tbsp. Salt
- 2 tsp. Basil
- 2 tsp. of Sugar
- Oil

Directions:

1. Place a parchment paper on a baking sheet. Preheat the grill to 225F with closed lid.

2. Remove the stems from the tomatoes. Cut them into slices (1/2 inch).

3. In a bowl combine the basil, sugar, pepper, and salt. Mix well.

4. Pour oil on a plate. Dip the tomatoes (just one side) in the oil.

5. Dust each slice with the mixture.

6. Grill the tomatoes for 3 hours.

7. Serve and enjoy! (You can serve it with mozzarella pieces).

Nutrition: Calories: 40 Protein: 1g Carbs: 2g Fat: 3g

Onion Bacon Ring

Preparation Time: 10 Minutes

Cooking Time: 1 Hour and 30 Minutes

Servings: 6 to 8

Ingredients:

- 2 large Onions, cut into ½ inch slices
- 1 Package of Bacon
- 1 tsp. of Honey
- 1 tbsp. Mustard, yellow
- 1 tbsp. Garlic chili sauce

Direction:

1. Wrap Bacon around onion rings. Wrap until you out of bacon. Place on skewers.
2. Preheat the grill to 400F with closed lid.
3. In the meantime, on a bowl combine the mustard and garlic chili sauce. Add honey and stir well.
4. Grill the onion bacon rings for 1 h and 30 minutes. Flip once.
5. Serve with the sauce and enjoy!

Nutrition: Calories: 90 Protein: 2g Carbs: 9g Fat: 7g

• Grilled Watermelon

Preparation Time: 10 Minutes

Cooking Time: 15 Minutes

Servings: 4

Ingredients:

- 2 Limes
- 2 tbsp. oil
- ½ Watermelon, sliced into wedges
- ¼ Tsp. Pepper flakes
- 2 tbsp. Salt

Directions:

1. Preheat the grill to high with closed lid.
2. Brush the watermelon with oil. Grill for 15 minutes. Flip once.
3. In a blender mix the salt and pepper flakes until combined.
4. Transfer the watermelon on a plate.
5. Serve and enjoy!

Nutrition: Calories: 40 Protein: 1g Carbs: 10g Fat: 0

• Smoked Popcorn with Parmesan Herb

Preparation Time: 10 Minutes

Cooking Time: 10 Minutes

Servings: 2 to 4

Ingredients:

- ¼ cup of Popcorn Kernels
- 1 tsp. of salt
- 1 tsp. of Garlic powder
- ½ cup grated Parmesan
- 2 tsp. of Italian seasoning
- 2 tbsp. oil
- 4 tbsp. of Butter

Directions:

1. Preheat the grill to 250F with closed lid.

2. In a saucepan add the butter and oil. Melt and add the salt, garlic powder, and Italian seasoning.
3. Add the kernels in a paper bag. Fold it two times to close.
4. Place in the microwave. Turn on high heat and set 2 minutes.
5. Open and transfer into a bowl.
6. Pour the butter. Toss. Transfer on a baking tray and grill for about 10 minutes.
7. Serve and enjoy!

Nutrition: Calories: 60 Protein: 1g Carbs: 5g Fat: 3g

CONCLUSION

You have obtained every secret to cooking with a Wood Pellet Smoker and Grill Cookbook, and you have tons of great recipes to try again and again. All you need to do is follow the ingredients and instructions accurately. You have many kinds of recipes, so you can try a new dish every day and test your cooking skills. Practicing will improve your ability to obtain great flavors from this smoker-grill.

After building the smoker from a Wood Pellet Smoker and Grill Cookbook, you have had time to play and master your new smoker grill. You know how exactly to season the grill and the smoker. You have had time to learn the recipes and techniques for cooking on a smoker grill. You have completed your smoker grill cookbook. You love to try the great new recipes you have collected. You love you smoker grill more than any other piece of equipment in your great kitchen. You love all the great flavors you can achieve with your smoker grill. You love to eat, and you love to cook, and you love to improve the quality of your food with your smoker grill.

Every day, your experience with the Wood Pellet Smoker and Grill Cookbook gives you the opportunity to get better at smoking and grilling. You can have the most amazing tasting food in your memory, every time you put on your smoker grill. As you begin to advance in the skill of knowing how to operate a smoker grill, you remember different methods for smoking food at different temperatures. You sometimes remember how to achieve different flavors in your smoked foods. You discover new ways to improve the quality of your smoked food. There are many ways to achieve great tasting meat. There are many ways to achieve great tasting vegetables from your smoker grill. You can get awesome tasting fish, poultry, and game from your smoker grill. You find all these tasty flavors in your food every time you cook.

You have become a cooking genius with your quality smoker grill. You can use your amazing smoker grill to get all of the delicious flavors in the wonderful smoked food you like so much. You can get all the best tasting food recipes and cook methods for a quality smoker grill. You love finding new in your smoker grill. You can achieve the greatest, most quality dishes with your amazing smoker grill. You are an incredible person for having built and mastering your awesome smoker grill. You can have the most amazing food flavors when you use your smoker grill.

You have smoked and grilled many things on your exclusive Wood Pellet Smoker and Grill Cookbook. You have had many fine meals on your amazing smoker grill. You have experimented with many flavors in your awesome smoker grill. You have had more amazing, unforgettable, and rare dishes on your amazing smoker grill than you could ever process or remember. Every time, you can achieve the absolute best taste for your favorite food with your smoker grill.

You have learned to cook with your quality smoker grill, and you have given your family many wonderful gifts , Labor Day Weekend at your house. You have cooked for your family with BBQ Ribs. It was a great Labor Day Weekend. You had great ribs on your smoker grill. You had the best barbecue ribs that you have ever had in your entire life. You have had many occasions to cook BBQ Ribs in the delicious flavors you have achieved on your quality smoker grill. You love your smoker grill, and that is why you have made the best BBQ ribs on it every time you cook there for your family. You have made enough BBQ ribs in your life to have stopped the world and made those ribs a record..

CPSIA information can be obtained
at www.ICGtesting.com
Printed in the USA
LVHW052243130121
676357LV00008B/459